D1519920

WORK ON TRIAL
Canadian Labour Law Struggles

WORK ON TRIAL

Canadian Labour Law Struggles

edited by

JUDY FUDGE AND ERIC TUCKER

Published for The Osgoode Society for Canadian Legal History
by Irwin Law

Toronto

Printed and bound in Canada by Irwin Law Inc.

ISBN 978-1-55221-167-0

Cataloguing in Publication data available from Library and Archives Canada

The publisher acknowledges the financial support of the Government of Canada through the Book Publishing Industry Development Program (BPIDP) for its publishing activities.

We acknowledge the assistance of the OMDC Book Fund, an initiative of Ontario Media Development Corporation.

1 2 3 4 5   14 13 12 11 10

CONTENTS

Foreword

THE WORLD OF WORK, so important to individuals' economic well-being and to their sense of self, has been fundamentally shaped by law, both collective bargaining law and individual employment law. We are grateful to Professors Fudge and Tucker for putting together this volume, which looks behind significant Canadian court battles over many aspects of labour law to unearth the historical context of the cases and analyze the individuals involved. Authors from across the country each take on a famous labour case in a series of case studies, from early cases about constitutional jurisdiction (*Snider*; *John East*), though picketing classics (*Hersees*; *Harrison v. Carswell*), to more recent employment law and human rights milestones (*Wallace*; *Meioren*). Each chapter tells an interesting story of how and why the case got to court and how the issues were resolved. This volume will interest not just those in the labour and employment law field; anybody concerned with the litigation process will enjoy reading the details of what lies behind the law reports.

The purpose of the Osgoode Society for Canadian Legal History is to encourage research and writing in the history of Canadian law. The Society, which was incorporated in 1979 and is registered as a charity, was founded at the initiative of the Honourable R. Roy McMurtry — formerly the Attorney General for Ontario and a Chief Justice of the province — and officials of the Law Society of Upper Canada. The Society seeks to stimulate the study of legal history in Canada by supporting researchers, collecting oral histories, and publishing volumes that contribute to legal-historical scholarship in Canada. It has published seventy-eight books on topics such as the courts, the judiciary, and the legal profession, as well as on the history of crime and punishment, women and law, law and economy, the legal treatment of ethnic minorities, and famous cases and significant trials in all areas of the law.

The current directors of the Osgoode Society for Canadian Legal History are Robert Armstrong, Christopher Bentley, Kenneth Binks, Patrick Brode, Brian Bucknall, David Chernos, Kirby Chown, J. Douglas Ewart, Martin Friedland, John Honsberger, Horace Krever, C. Ian Kyer, Virginia MacLean, Patricia McMahon, Roy McMurtry, Lawrie H. Pawlitz, Jim Phillips, Paul Reinhardt, Joel Richler, William Ross, Paul Schabas, Robert Sharpe, James Spence, Richard Tinsley, and Michael Tulloch.

The annual report and information about membership may be obtained by writing to the Osgoode Society for Canadian Legal History, Osgoode Hall, 130 Queen Street West, Toronto, Ontario, M5H 2N6. Telephone: 416-947-3321. E-mail: mmacfarl@lsuc.on.ca. Website: osgoodesociety.ca

R. Roy McMurtry
PRESIDENT

Jim Phillips
EDITOR-IN-CHIEF

Preface

Harry Arthurs

IN THEIR PREVIOUS GROUNDBREAKING work — *Labour Before the Law*[1] — Judy
Fudge and Eric Tucker depict in broad brushstrokes the role played by law
in the emergence of "industrial pluralism" as the dominant paradigm of
post-war Canadian industrial relations. In their present volume — *Work on
Trial* — their technique is very different. While they and their co-contributors
are mindful of the social, political, and legal contexts and consequences of
the landmark judgments they reconstruct, the brushstrokes in this volume
are less broad, the details etched in more painstakingly and precisely.

Yet the results are no less subversive of conventional understandings of
law — if anything, more so. While the previous broad-brush approach imposes meaning on individual cases by locating them within a comprehensive narrative (or within competing narratives), the present focus on what
Daphne Taras calls the "micropolitics" of decision-making[2] reminds us how
accidental and ambiguous are the canonical cases of Canadian labour law.

The historical circumstance or social context in which a case arises; the
background of the judges who happen to sit on a given trial or appeal; the
presence of charismatic, obsessive, or hapless litigants; their deep pockets or
shallow motives and the way they frame their real or imagined grievances;
the symbolic significance with which all of these are invested by commentators and jurists; small evidentiary and procedural quibbles that permit litigants to deflect or engage great principles of law; the impulses of ideology,
empathy, and craft that are so often at war within the bosom of a single judge

or court; the choice of discursive strategies that produce alchemical transformations of meaning: all of these seem to influence litigation outcomes to a significant extent. Indeed, the very notion of "litigation outcomes" is problematic. As these case studies remind us, things seldom turn out in real life the way one might expect. Some "winners" never taste the full fruits of their victories; some "losers" somehow manage to survive relatively unscathed, except for their legal bills. And most importantly, the principles supposedly settled by authoritative judicial pronouncements do not necessarily become part of the living law: they may be ignored or circumvented by public officials or private actors; they may be reinterpreted or "disappeared" (in the Latin American sense) by later judges; or they may acquire a vigorous afterlife of their own, quite different from what their judicial authors actually said or intended.

Adjudication is not supposed to happen this way. Legal judgments are supposed to rest on a foundation of proven or probable facts. They are supposed to emerge from the reasoned application of rules to those facts — rules grounded in principle and applied in a way that is respectful of precedent. They are supposed to be articulated in a language that knits them into the fabric of the law without gaps or discontinuities, so that the law is left clear and coherent for the guidance of future disputants and decision makers. And judgments — especially those of the highest courts — are supposed to be binding on the litigants and on posterity. Law's legitimacy, its power to convince if not coerce, rests on the conformity of legal judgments to these ideal-type characteristics. But labour law judgments, it seems, do not conform.

In this regard, broad-brush and "micropolitical" approaches reinforce each other. Critical scholars (including many contributors to this volume) have already demonstrated the ideological content and hegemonic functions of contemporary labour law in the "industrial pluralist" paradigm, and documented its failure to accurately reflect workers' values or effectively advance their interests. For readers familiar with this body of scholarship, the legitimacy of labour law has already been placed in question. For other readers, however, law is more than the sum of previous decisions; law retains the potential to correct itself, to transform itself, to improve the lot of workers, and to advance the cause of social justice and equality. For readers of this latter persuasion, the current volume will be especially disconcerting. The careful scrutiny accorded the "micropolitics" of adjudication by most contributors to this volume reveals law's indeterminacy and its instrumentalist character.

Here is how they sum up their findings: "there was no possible 'pro-labour' result";[3] "the moment [engendered by the decision] . . . soon elapsed and left little behind";[4] "far from settling the issues . . . [the case] complicates them";[5] the "eventual undoing of [the case] was partly contingent on a shift in the judicial imagery of organized labour . . . to that of a senior citizen who no longer poses a threat";[6] "[trade unionists] opted for the courts . . . . [h]istorians will continue to debate whether they made the right choices";[7] "the legislature has now occupied the field";[8] "incremental gains are not the final antidote to women workers' subordination";[9] "[subsequent] developments suggest a more sceptical assessment of the Court's commitment to [the] larger project [of human rights jurisprudence];[10] and, plaintively, "is this a sensible way to craft employment law?"[11]

What are we to make of these conclusions? That adjudication in labour matters falls below the standards that prevail in other areas of law? That the fault lies not with the legal system *per se*, but with processes, personnel, and norms unique to labour law? That the legal system in general suffers not only from inherent weaknesses of design and execution, but also from its incurable tendency to align itself with the dominant forces of society? That labour law epitomizes this tendency and that workers should therefore abandon all hope of advancing their interest "before the law"? Or that — contrary to E.P. Thompson's assertion — the rule of law is not, after all, "an unqualified human good"?[12]

These are the disturbing questions raised in this volume. They are not just questions for labour lawyers. They are questions for everyone who cares about law and ponders its place in just and democratic societies.

Notes

1   Judy Fudge & Eric Tucker, *Labour Before the Law: The Regulation of Workers' Collective Action in Canada, 1900–1948* (Toronto: University of Toronto Press, 2004).

2   Daphne Taras, "The Micropolitics of *Wallace v. United Grain Growers Ltd.*," in this volume at 357.

3   R. Blake Brown & Jennifer J. Llewellyn, in this volume at 36.

4   Beth Bilson, in this volume at 64.

5   Mark Leier, in this volume at 111.

6   Eric Tucker, in this volume at 217.

7   Malcolm Davidson, in this volume at 175.

8   Philip Girard & Jim Phillips, in this volume at 249.

9   Joan Sangster, in this volume at 283.

10 Judy Fudge & Hester Lessard, in this volume at 315.

11 Daphne Taras, in this volume at 357.

12 E.P. Thompson, *Whigs and Hunters: The Origin of the Black Act* (New York: Pantheon Books, 1975).

Acknowledgements

All academic work is collaborative, and this book in no exception. The idea for the project was drawn from the American Law Stories series published by Foundation Press, which, as of the date of writing, contains collections of law stories in thirty-two subject areas. We were fortunate to find two Canadian publishers who were enthusiastic about the project and who have actively supported it through all its stages. In particular, we would like to thank Jeff Miller and William Kaplan from Irwin Law, and Jim Phillips, editor-in-chief of the Osgoode Society. The engaged participation and strong scholarly skills of the contributors of the chapters made the book a reality. They reached across disciplinary boundaries, respected deadlines, and patiently responded to multiple requests for revision.

We also had the good fortune of the support of many individuals and institutions in helping us to develop an integrated collection. Crucial, in this respect, was the workshop we held at the University of Victoria in June 2008, where each of the chapters was presented and discussed. We received financial support from the Social Sciences and Humanities Research Council through a workshop grant and financial contributions from the Faculty of Law and the Vice-President of Research at the University of Victoria, Osgoode Hall Law School, York University, and Professor Daphne Taras. We were lucky to attract a very talented group of graduate students who made an invaluable contribution to the workshop by presenting critical readings of the draft chapters and participating more generally in the discussions that followed. We would like to thank Cameron Bean, Lisa Helps, David Huxtable, Frank Luce, Eryck Martin, Nicole O'Byrne, Kerry Sloan, and Ania Zbyszewski for their many insights and helpful suggestions. We would also like to thank Professors Harry Arthurs and Harry Glasbeek for providing the foreword and afterword to the collection, and Professor Harry Glasbeek and Professor Heather Raven for participating in the workshop, sharing their knowledge, and contributing incisive observations throughout.

After a round of revisions following the workshop, two anonymous reviewers, along with the editor-in-chief of the Osgoode Society, Professor Jim Phillips, provided detailed and constructive feedback for which we are grateful. Kay Nguyen, an Osgoode Hall Law School student, provided outstanding assistance with the preparation of the manuscript, including tracking down photographs and photo credits. Rosemary Garton provided assistance with a myriad of tasks at the University of Victoria. We would also like to thank Jeff Miller, Heather Raven, and Lesley Steeve from Irwin Law for transforming the manuscript into a book.

Eric Tucker would like to thank Lisa Brand for her cockeyed optimism.

Judy Fudge would like to thank Tawney Meiorin for her indefatigable determination to right a wrong, and Ken Massicotte for his patience with the travails of research.

Introduction

Judy Fudge and Eric Tucker

THE LEGAL REPORTS OF cases often beg as many questions as they answer. The law of evidence functions as a sieve that filters out much of the messy reality of what may have catalyzed a legal dispute, and in this way the facts that are recited in legal decisions can obscure what actually happened as much as they can reveal it. The personal histories of the judges, lawyers, and litigants involved in a particular case are absent from the legal report, although these histories may be crucial to understanding why, for example, an aggrieved individual might devote years of her life to pursuing legal redress, or why a judge would decide a case in a particular way. A reported case is similar to a snapshot, freezing what may be an ongoing process that is unfolding in complex ways, into a fixed tableau. Reports of cases isolate legal disputes from the other social processes in which they may be embedded. The personal, social, and political context of a case helps us to answer questions that remain at the end of the report and provides us with a deeper understanding of the case. For a historian or political scientist, a legal case "is a burlesque interpretation, one that titillates rather than satisfies."[1]

Paid work is central to every aspect of our society. It is our source of livelihood and a primary source of our personal identity. Work is deeply related to our sense of human dignity, but it can also involve exploitation. Work is both an individual experience and the basis for collective solidarity. Both the centrality of work to our lives and these contradictions make stories about work compelling.

1

Stories about the law of work are similarly compelling. As Cooper and Fisk note, "The law of work shapes the life stories of real people."[2] It also influences the relative power resources of employees and employers. It encapsulates the central contradiction in the slogan "labour is not only a commodity" because it infuses the civil law of property and contract with such liberal values as freedom from discrimination and freedom of association.

The goal of this collection is to tell the stories behind a selection of cases about the law of work. In doing so we have used the "case study" method, which as Constance Backhouse has so eloquently argued, "permits the pinpointing of the concrete impact of legal rules upon real people at specific times. The thick description of a microscopic event allows a fuller dissection of how the law interacts with the wider social, political, economic, and cultural surroundings."[3]

We use the term "law of work" rather than the more familiar terms — employment and labour law — because the stories told in this book disrupt traditional legal categories. While most of the stories recounted in this collection have to do with aspects of collective bargaining law (traditionally known as labour law), some deal with human rights, referred to as anti-discrimination law, and at least one focuses on the contract of employment. But while we use the law of work expansively to cover many dimensions of the legal regulation of paid employment, we have excluded from our stories cases involving unpaid, but socially necessary work.

Collections, like the reports of legal cases, are necessarily selective, and this one is no different. While it covers some of the major cases that everyone familiar with the law of work knows, it also includes more obscure ones. The less well-known cases have been selected because they tell compelling stories about issues (for example, the right of pregnant women to work) and places (for example, the oil rights of the coast of Newfoundland and Labrador) that have yet to be told.

In telling these stories about specific cases the authors have emphasized some common features. Each case is situated in its broader social, economic, political, and legal context. Most of the studies also tell us about the people involved, including the parties and their legal representatives, and the strategic and legal choices they made. Characters matter in these stories. Several of the case studies focus on a crusading plaintiff who drove the litigation forward; Myron Kuzych, Tawney Meiorin, and Jack Wallace are the clearest examples of individuals without whom there would have been no case. Other studies focus on the law's princes — the judges. In some instances, they left an indelible mark upon the law of work through a judgment in a particular case: Lord Haldane in *Snider*, Justice Aylseworth in *Hersees*, Chief Justice Laskin and Justice Dickson in *Harrison*, and, of course, Justice Rand in his eponymous arbitration award in the Ford strike. Others, like Justice McRuer in the Royal York case and *Hersees*, made their influence felt through the volume of decisions they issued, despite sometimes being overruled on appeal. Litigators also played an important role in some of these cases: for example, Andrew Brewin in *John East Iron Works*, David Lewis in the *Royal York* case, and Horace Krever in *Hersees*. Finally, in some stories, such as Sean Cadigan's tale of the struggle to unionize Newfoundland's offshore oil workers, an individual such as Morgan C. Cooper, who was appointed by the provincial government to investigate and make recommendations about labour relations in that sector, and then later, as chair of the Newfoundland and Labrador Labour Relations Board, was able exert a significant influence on legal developments. In contrast, in Joan Sangster's discussion of how pregnancy was treated in grievance arbitration, the grievors, their union representatives, and the arbitrators are largely unknown.

Legal process also matters in these stories because it squeezes the complex totality of a messy social dispute into particular paths and categories. It often involves the use of experts, especially medical and scientific witnesses. For example, experts played an important role in the litigation by Tawney Meiorin to challenge the validity of the fitness test that discriminated against women firefighters, and in the Canadian Airline Flight Attendants Association's (CALFAA) challenge to Pacific Western Airlines' (PWA) prohibition on flight attendants flying while pregnant. Similarly, legal process is almost always expensive, especially when it involves experts or is drawn out by appeals. The involvement of unions, which have resources to pursue legal claims, as in the above examples, can be crucial in such situations. Where individual litigants are involved, as in *Kuzych* or *Wallace*, the question of who paid can itself become a crucial question for the case study.

Attention is also directed at the processes by which cases are established as legal precedents. The purpose of placing these cases in their social context is, as A.W. Brian Simpson explains, to provide "[a] fuller understanding not simply of the particular decision discussed, but of more general issues about the nature of judicial decision in the common law system, the extent to which the evolution of legal doctrine and its persistence over time require separate explanations, the degree to which decisions can be shown to be politically motivated, or the products of accidental circumstances."[4] Beth Bilson's study of *John*

East Iron Works, along with Philip Girard and Jim Phillips' study of *Harrison v. Carswell*, and Tucker's look at *Hersees* explore the reception of these decisions and the conditions that helped sustain them as longstanding precedents.

The case in context methodology not only provides a way of illuminating cases, but it also provides us with a lens through which we can better understand the context, moving between an overview of the broad sweep of history and a more fine-grained focus on significant detail that might otherwise escape our attention. The cases in this collection provide us with such a lens, beginning with Blake Brown and Jennifer Llewellyn's study of the *Snider* case, which authoritatively determined that, as a matter of constitutional law, Canadian labour law must be built primarily at the provincial level. Their essay articulates how — along with long-term government strategy — short-term political concerns about the federal government's capacity to simultaneously suppress large-scale strikes by Canadian miners in Nova Scotia and deal with the consequences of a strike by Toronto Hydro-employed electricians affected the timing of the legal confrontation over federal jurisdiction and inadvertently decreased the likelihood of it being upheld.

Three of the chapters — Bilson's on *John East*, William Kaplan's on the Rand Formula, and Mark Leier's on the *Kuzych* cases — focus our attention on the establishment of the post–World War II collective bargaining regime, which was built on the principles that (1) employers would be obliged to recognize and bargain with unions that won majority support among a state-determined bargaining unit, and (2) unions would only be allowed to strike and employers to lock out when no collective bargaining agreement was in force and after collective bargaining and conciliation had failed. Additionally, these three chapters illuminate the development of some of the post-World War II collective bargaining regime's specific features that are taken for granted today but were contested at the time. For example, Bilson's study of the *John East* case reveals that the question of whether administrative tribunals had the constitutional authority to adjudicate disputes arising out of collective bargaining statutes was far from clear in the late 1940s, and that the legal resolution depended on the Law Lords' understanding of the collective bargaining regime as an instrument of policy to secure industrial peace, a matter outside the courts' historic jurisdiction.

The importance of that policy to the post-war industrial relations system is also emphasized in Kaplan's study of Rand's arbitration award that settled a ninety-nine day strike by Windsor auto workers in 1945, conducted largely over the issue of union security. The Rand Formula, which provides for the employer to deduct and remit union dues for each bargaining unit member regardless of whether the employee is a union member, provided institutional security for trade unions, but was made contingent on the unions' enforcement of the collective agreement which stated that they must do everything in their power to avoid illegal work stoppages. As Kaplan's study shows, concern about labour radicalism and militancy was a very much a part of the context that shaped the specific form of the post-war regime.

Finally in this group of "founding" stories, Leier's study of Myron Kuzych, a dissident worker who was forced to become a union member as a condition of his employment and was then expelled for disloyal activity, provides another insight into the politics of union security, this time focusing on the complex and sometimes troubled relationship between unions as institutions and rank and file democracy. Leier's chapter reveals that the judiciary was reluctant to become involved in regulating internal trade-union affairs, despite their general propensity to favour individual rights over collective interests. Whether intentional or not, their insistence that dissident workers exhaust their internal remedies before coming to court was both consistent with, and reinforced, the Rand Formula policy that required trade unions to be in a position to discipline their members.

Another group of chapters — Malcolm Davidson's study of the Royal York case, Tucker's examination of *Hersees*, and Girard and Phillips' discussion of *Harrison* — focus on the operation of the post-war regime which, notwithstanding the appearance of stability, was regularly beset by conflict not just within its legal parameters, but also over what those parameters should be. One issue over which there was recurring controversy was the scope for workers' collective action. Davidson's study of the Royal York case, involving the issue of whether workers on a legal strike could be lawfully terminated simply because they were on strike, reveals that the meaning of the "right" to strike in the post-war statutory collective bargaining schemes was not very well defined. While the new legislation carefully limited when workers could strike, much less was said about their rights while on strike, and it took a decision made by the Supreme Court of Canada to establish that workers did indeed have a right not to be fired for striking.

If little was said in post-war collective bargaining legislation about the right to strike, even less was said about the scope for strike-related activity (such as picketing). This left ample room for legal disputes over this issue in subsequent years as the Tucker and Girard and Phillips chapters demonstrate. Tucker's study of the *Hersees* case shows that not only did the courts continue to play an important role in regulating picketing, but that their historic role as defenders of private property and freedom of contract, in conjunction with growing concern over trade union militancy at a time when the level and intensity of strike activity was increasing, took precedence over the otherwise legitimate claim that lawfully-striking workers enjoyed a legal privilege to engage in peaceful picketing of retail shops to advance their common interests. This led the Ontario Court of Appeal to hold that secondary picketing — that is, picketing at a site other than the employer's place of business — was unlawful. Similarly, Girard and Phillips' chapter on *Harrison* demonstrates that property rights, which protected the right of property owners to exclude, trumped the claim that striking workers should be able to picket in front of their employers' places of business when those businesses were located on privately-owned mall property.

Cadigan's study of organizing offshore oil workers in Newfoundland draws our attention to further dimensions of the context that shaped the operation of the post-war collective bargaining regime — regionalism and the resource economy. While the decentralized constitutional infrastructure created by *Snider* made the Canadian industrial relations regime particularly amenable to these influences, relatively little attention has been paid to them.[5] As Cadigan's chapter shows, while the priority given by governments to resource extraction in Newfoundland has exerted a profound influence over the development of labour policy, it did not preclude a role for unions and collective bargaining. It did, however, make their participation conditional on their willingness to participate in arrangements that minimized the potential for disruptive industrial strife. The decision by the Newfoundland and Labrador Labour Relations Board to certify a bargaining unit of offshore oil workers was the culmination of such a process of adjustment.

The last set of cases shifts our attention to aspects of human rights and the individual contract of employment within the law of work. Sangster's study of the legal struggle of women flight attendants to gain the right to fly pregnant, along with Judy Fudge and Hester Lessard's chapter on the *Meiorin* case, illuminate the difficulties faced by workers challenging the continuing employment practices based on hegemonic gender-based assumptions. (Assumptions that, it should be noted, left employers free to require flight attendants to conform to the image of young, attractive, sexually available women, and to impose a male fitness standard for firefighting that ignored differences between men's and women's aerobic and physical capacities.) Yet these chapters also show that with a strong union commitment to equality rights, in conjunction with feminist mobilization, those assumptions and the discriminatory practices that they justified could be successfully challenged. In *Meiorin*, the Supreme Court of Canada reformed the law of employment discrimination by creating a more rigorous test that must be satisfied by employers in order to defend job standards that are *prima facie* discriminatory, while women flight attendants, despite the unsuccessful cases covered by Sangster's study, did eventually achieve the right to fly pregnant.

Although nearly all the cases in this collection arise out of the unionized work force, collective bargaining never came close to achieving universal coverage. Indeed, at its peak, only about half of all workers were covered by a collective agreement, and the percentage has been dropping since. In 2007, less than 35 percent of workers were covered by a collective agreement.[6] In the first six months of 2008, the unionization rate in Canada was 29.3 percent.[7] Therefore, the individual employment contract and the law regulating it are vital to the majority of workers. The human rights regime discussed in Sangster and in Fudge and Lessard's case studies applies to both union and non-union workers, thus their stories partially illuminate this individual employment context.

Daphne Taras's study of *Wallace* is unique in this collection in its exclusive focus on the common law of the individual contract of employment. Wallace's fight to get damages that compensated him not only for being fired without notice, but also for the bad-faith behaviour of his employer in the process, provides a window into the changing judicial attitudes toward the importance of work to individual well-being and social worth — while also raising questions about the capacity and commitment of common law courts to regulate employment contracts. Reflecting that tension, the Court's decision in *Wallace* held that although employers have a duty to act in good faith at the point of discharge, damages would be limited to increased notice of termination.

Thus far we have emphasized how the case in context method provides a window on the substantive development of the labour and employment regime. Additionally, the cases illuminate the law of work's institutional pluralism. Bilson's study of the *John East* case provides insight into the constitutional foundations of that pluralism, based on the courts' acceptance that the role played by labour boards under statutory collective bargaining schemes was not analogous to the historic role of courts applying the common law to individual contracts of employment. As a result, labour boards were not considered to be section 96 courts and thus within provincial jurisdiction to create and to staff. This acceptance made it possible to give labour boards substantial powers to interpret and apply collective bargaining statutes, as is demonstrated by Cadigan's examination of the role of the Newfoundland and Labrador Labour Relations Board in the unionization of offshore oil workers. The Board's underlying commitment to the promotion of collective bargaining as a matter of public policy led it to adopt a broad definition of the appropriate bargaining unit and a liberal approach to membership evidence. Cadigan's study also demonstrates, however, that there are limits to the courts' toleration of pluralism; the Board's holding that the termination of twenty-five workers violated the statutory freeze on changing conditions of work while negotiations were taking place was overturned twice by Newfoundland courts.

The institutional pluralism of the post-war regime encompassed other players in addition to labour boards. As a number of the case studies demonstrate, arbitrators also exercised significant powers, sometimes in settling contracts (interest arbitration) and, more frequently, in resolving disputes over the interpretation and application of collective agreements (grievance arbitration). Kaplan's study of the Rand Formula is a classic case of the former, in this instance involving the consent of both parties to submit unresolved differences to a third-party for resolution. The importance of this precedent, not just to the immediate parties but also to the post-war labour regime, cannot be understated.

Compulsory arbitration of grievances, which became a standard feature of the collective bargaining regime, played an important role in both Sangster's and Fudge and Lessard's case studies. These chapters demonstrate that an arbitrator's scope for independent action is constrained by the express terms of the collective agreement, the conventional understandings of the time, and judicial oversight. In Sangster's case study, arbitrators accepted prevailing gender stereotypes and upheld the employer's right to terminate women flight attendants once they married, while in Fudge and Lessard's case study, one arbitrator upheld the employer's unilateral right to impose a fitness test, while another found that the employer had failed to accommodate a woman forest firefighter who could not pass its aerobic capacity component. The BC Court of Appeal overturned the latter award, but it was reversed by the Supreme Court of Canada.

Not only did the courts retain a supervisory jurisdiction over labour boards and arbitrators, they also kept primary jurisdiction in a number of areas, including constitutional interpretation, the enforcement of statutory schemes where prosecution remained an option, and the application of the common law where it had not been displaced by statute. Both Brown and

Llewellyn's and Bilson's chapters illustrate the power of the courts over matters of constitutional law, including the question of which level of government has primary jurisdiction over labour and employment (*Snider*) and whether the provinces have the power to confer quasi-judicial powers on provincially appointed labour boards (*John East*).

The second situation is raised by Davidson's study of the Royal York case, where the union obtained the labour board's consent to prosecute the employer for committing an unfair labour practice (firing workers for going on strike). This meant that the court, not the labour board, exercised the power to interpret and apply the *Labour Relations Act* in the first instance. Sangster's study also looks at a prosecution for a violation of the *Canada Labour Code*'s prohibition of dismissing a pregnant employee. As these cases demonstrate, the results were mixed: the courts in the Royal York case found that striking employees had the right not be fired, while in the PWA prosecution, the court found for the employer, taking a narrow view of the statutory protection given to pregnant workers.

The continuing application of the common law in the collective bargaining regime is a theme that runs through many of the chapters in this book. Tucker's study of *Hersees* demonstrates the vital role played by the common law in regulating picketing and the judiciary's reflexive preference for the rights of business over the freedom of workers. The chapter on *Harrison* makes a similar point with respect to private property and also provides evidence of the judiciary's reluctance to modify the common law to accommodate actions like picketing that were a normal part of a statutory collective bargaining scheme even if not directly addressed in the legislation. The common law also continued to play a role in trade union affairs, a point made by Leier's study of *Kuzych*. This was possible because trade unions were still legally conceptualized as private clubs, constituted and governed by the contract among its members, notwithstanding their role in the statutory collective bargaining scheme.

Finally, there is the individual contract of employment, which, apart from statutory minimum standards, is quintessentially an area governed by the common law, as Taras's study of *Wallace* makes evident. Whether a terminated employee is entitled to notice, the basis for calculating the length of such notice, and the availability of other heads of damages are questions that are entirely in the hands of the judiciary in the absence of legislation.

These cases also illuminate the normative pluralism of the law at work, by which we mean the continuing salience of diverse values that are asserted by workers and employers, and that, to different degrees, gain support from legal decision makers. For example, the chapters about picketing illustrate the continuing role of classical liberalism in elevating rights of property and contract over workers' privilege to engage in collective action to improve their terms and conditions of employment. Yet in other chapters, such as Cadigan's discussion of offshore oil workers, we can see a more collectivist ethos at play in the decision making of the labour board as it sought to foster the development of collective bargaining as a matter of policy. There are also sharp differences over the norm of gender equality, a point well-illustrated in Fudge and Lessard's chapter which reveals that the British Columbia Court of Appeal adopted an extremely hostile attitude toward equality rights, only to have its judgment overturned by the Supreme Court of Canada. The Court's decision required employers to not just accommodate individual women, but to build conceptions of equality into the workplace standards themselves.

This normative pluralism does not always track institutional pluralism in the ways one might expect. For example, although the majority of the Supreme Court of Canada in *Harrison* behaved very much as we might expect, it did not in the *Kuzych* and *Royal York* cases. It is precisely because the law of work has never been simply a reflection of the balance of class forces at a given moment in time — nor has it been the product of unswerving institutional commitments — that makes its history such an interesting field of study, and its future a contested arena.

In conclusion, this is a collection of case studies, not a comprehensive study of Canadian law at work. As a result, there are some obvious and important gaps in coverage. The cases recounted focus on the second half of the twentieth century and they disproportionately emphasize the collective bargaining scheme at the expense of cases on the individual contract of employment and the statutory regimes that impose standards at work (for example, occupational health and safety law, workers' compensation, and employment standards). There are no cases from Quebec and an absence of cases that consider race, ethnicity, and aboriginality. We regard this collection of stories about the law of work as only beginning the bigger task of recounting a wide range of important narratives that need to be told. Nevertheless, within these limitations, we hope that readers will find that presenting these cases in context methodology offers a reward that enriches their understanding both of the cases themselves and of the socio-legal context in which they arose.

Notes

1   Alan Grove & Ross Lambertson, "Pawns of the Powerful: The Politics of Litigation in the Union Colliery Case," (1994) 103 BC Studies 3 at 3.

2   Laura J. Cooper & Catherine L. Fisk, eds., *Labor Law Stories* (New York: Foundation Law Press, 2005) at 9.

3   Constance Backhouse, *Colour-Coded: A Legal History of Racism in Canada, 1900–1950* (Toronto: Osgoode Society of Canadian Legal History and University of Toronto, 1999) at 15–16.

4   A.W. Brian Simpson, *Leading Cases in Common Law* (Oxford: Oxford University Press, 1995) at 12.

5   For a notable exception, see Mark Thompson, Joseph B. Rose, & Anthony E. Smith, eds., *Beyond the National Divide: Regional Dimensions of Industrial Relations* (Montreal: McGill-Queen's University Press, 2003).

6   For union membership, see Human Resources and Social Development Canada, Strategic Policy, Analysis, and Workplace Information Directorate Labour Program, *Union Membership in Canada*, online: www.hrsdc.gc.ca/en/lp/wid/union_membership.shtml. For coverage, see Ernest B. Akyeampong, "Non-unionized but covered by a collective agreement" (Autumn 2000) 12:3 Perspectives on Labour and Income 33.

7   Human Resources and Skills Development Canada, Union Membership in Canada — 2008, online: www.hrsdc.gc.ca/eng/labour/labour_relations/info_analysis/union_membership/index.shtml.

PART ONE

Constitutions and Institutions

"Capitalist 'Justice' as Peddled by the 'Noble Lords'": *Toronto Electric Commissioners v. Snider et al.*

R. Blake Brown and Jennifer J. Llewellyn

TORONTO ELECTRIC COMMISSIONERS V. *Snider et al.* is one of the most famous cases in Canadian labour and constitutional history. It began as a rather uneventful dispute between electrical workers and Toronto's publicly-owned power utility. It culminated in an appeal to the Judicial Committee of the Privy Council (referred to as the JCPC or the Privy Council), which in 1925 found the federal government's *Industrial Disputes Investigation Act* (IDIA) unconstitutional, despite being an Act that had operated with considerable success since its creation in 1907. After more than eighty years, *Snider* remains the "leading case"[1] for the rule that the regulation of labour relations is largely a provincial responsibility.

The Privy Council's decision is required reading for Canadian law students, but, surprisingly, scholars have not delved into the background of the case. They have not explored the political circumstances that led to *Snider*, the identities of the litigants, or the legal strategies employed. Rather, constitutional scholars have cited *Snider* as an example of the process whereby the meaning of the *British North America Act* (*BNA Act*) was reinterpreted in the late-nineteenth and early-twentieth centuries to strengthen provincial areas of legislative jurisdiction.[2] Labour historians, for the most part, focus on the practical results of the decision, in particular, the ensuing difficulty of developing a national system of industrial relations.[3]

We use a contextual case study approach from which five new insights into *Snider* emerge. First, the federal government had long avoided using the

IDIA to intervene in employment disputes between municipally-owned corporations and their workers because of Ottawa's concern that the courts might find the Act unconstitutional. A confluence of events, however, including a desire to ensure that the electrical workers did not interrupt the Canadian National Exhibition and a belief that the Canadian army lacked enough soldiers to concurrently suppress an ongoing labour revolt in Cape Breton and a large work stoppage in Toronto, forced the Department of Labour to employ the *IDIA*. Second, Ottawa's attempt to avoid litigation, while preserving the *IDIA* in the short term, only ensured its inevitable demise in the long term. Through the late 1910s and early 1920s, constitutional caselaw grew increasingly antagonistic to the Dominion's claim that it should legislate for labour relations. By delaying litigation, the federal government increased the chance that courts would find the legislation unconstitutional. Third, the Toronto Electric Commissioners were intent on pursuing a constitutional challenge. In the past, they had employed the machinery of the *IDIA* to their advantage, but by the early 1920s they believed that the appointment process for the *IDIA*'s conciliation boards meant, in effect, that the federal government was forcing employers to grant wage increases. Fourth, the Canadian lower court and appellate judges' support for the constitutionality of the *IDIA* was not rooted in their support for the labour movement, but, rather, in the belief that industrial unions posed a substantial threat to Canadian society and thus had to be regulated. Finally, the reasoning of several of the judges who heard the *Snider* case reveals that tensions inherent in the liberal state could undermine government policies. *Snider* demonstrates that the desire to protect freedom of property and contract has not always been compatible with the desire to ensure public safety.

These conclusions are demonstrated in a three-part analysis. Part one explores the background to *Snider*, including the lengthy period of acrimony before litigation began. Part two examines the strategies of the litigants and the judicial treatment of the case. Part three considers the reaction to the Privy Council's decision and the response of Canadian legislators.

Background to the Dispute

IN THE EARLY DECADES of the twentieth century, privately-owned and publicly-owned electric utilities competed with one another to supply electricity to Ontario's homes and businesses. To regulate the sector, Ontario created the Hydro-Electric Power Commission in 1906. This body supervised the electricity sector and set power rates. In January 1908, the citizens of Toronto voted to establish a public utility to compete with a private, for-profit, company, Toronto Electric Light Company. The new Toronto Hydro-Electric System (Toronto Hydro) commenced operation in 1911. A three-member board, the Toronto Electric Commissioners, supervised the new utility. The Hydro-Electric Power Commission, however, set power rates, often at very low levels.[4] These rates ensured that Toronto Hydro had to watch its costs carefully, including its labour costs, to ensure that Toronto's citizens did not have to underwrite the utility.

Despite this concern with expenses, the employees of Toronto Hydro asked for, and usually received, increases in their wages throughout the 1910s. There was an increase in 1914, and in 1917 Toronto Hydro granted a permanent 5 percent raise in wages and a special 5 percent increase to help deal with wartime inflation. The next year, Toronto Hydro increased wages to match those offered at the private power utility. In 1919, workers asked that the special wartime raise be made permanent, and in 1920 workers demanded, and received, a 15 percent increase in light of continued inflation.[5]

The *IDIA* played a considerable role in these settlements. Drafted by William Lyon Mackenzie King, who was then the deputy minister of labour and would later become prime minister, the 1907 legislation revolutionized labour relations in Canada through its mechanisms designed to limit the number of strikes and lock outs in key industries.[6] The Act provided that an industrial dispute between an employer and ten or more employees that could not be amicably settled could be referred to a tripartite "board of conciliation and investigation." Boards of conciliation could be established if the employer operated "any mining property, agency of transportation or communication, or public service utility, including . . . railways, whether operated by steam, electricity, or other motive power, steamships, telegraph and telephone lines, gas, electric light, water, and power works."[7] Conciliation boards had the power to investigate disputes and to make recommendations, but could not impose results. A strike or lock out in any of the enumerated industries, however, was unlawful until the board reported on the dispute. These boards consisted of one representative appointed by the employees, one selected by the employer, and a chair nominated by the first two board members chosen. If the two members could not agree on a chair, then the minister of labour could choose one. Labour problems in industries other than those enumerated could be settled through the machinery of the Act by the agreement of both parties. Amendments in 1918 and 1920 also authorized the minister of labour to establish a board on his own initiative, upon the request of a municipality where, in any industry, a strike or lock out had occurred, or seemed imminent.[8] In the period immediately preceding the *Snider* case, the *IDIA* was put to good use. From 1920 to 1924, 246 applications were made for boards of conciliation. Over ninety percent of the applications came from employees.[9]

Several disputes between Toronto Hydro and its employees prior to *Snider* had been settled through the *IDIA*, but in 1921 the utility decided to oppose the appointment of new conciliation boards. Edward Montague Ashworth, acting general manager, reported in 1921 that three *IDIA* conciliation boards had been established in the previous ten years. Combined with wage increases voluntarily granted by Toronto Hydro, these conciliations almost tripled the wages of linemen from about twenty-eight cents to seventy-eight cents per hour. Toronto Hydro was unwilling to budge when employees demanded that the hourly wage of linemen increase to eighty-five cents per hour. When the electrical workers requested a conciliation board in 1921, Toronto Hydro opposed it. Ashworth offered several reasons for Toronto Hydro's opposition: the cost of living had declined since the end of the Great War, wages had been generously increased, and the process of conciliation boards was too time-consuming for Toronto Hydro's executives. Ashworth did not mention another factor. Toronto Hydro had recently arranged for the purchase of its private sector competitor, and was determined to keep wages down now that the competition for labour had been eliminated.[10]

The federal government refused to establish a board because of growing concerns about Ottawa's jurisdiction over labour relations.[11] Before World War I, the courts seemed to support the *IDIA*'s constitutionality. In 1911, the employees of the Montreal Street Railway Company requested a board of conciliation under the *IDIA*. The company attempted to prevent this by arguing, among other things, that the *IDIA* was *ultra vires*. The railway received a temporary injunction, but in 1912 a justice of the Superior Court of Quebec refused the application for a permanent injunction and held the *IDIA* constitutional. On appeal, in 1913, the Superior Court of the Montreal District allowed a permanent injunction on the ground that the dispute in question was outside of the scope of the Act, although the court also held the *IDIA* constitutional.[12]

Despite the *Montreal Street Railway* decision, the federal government became reluctant to use the *IDIA* to settle disputes concerning provincial or municipal utilities. Municipal utilities were creatures of provincial govern-

Toronto Transit Co. car 2438 at Queen Street and Connaught Avenue, August 1923
Library and Archives Canada, PA-171205

ment legislation, which had legislative jurisdiction under the *BNA Act* for "municipal institutions" (s. 91(8)). Constitutional arguments based on excessive federal intervention into provincial jurisdiction were therefore seen as especially likely in relation to the regulation of municipal employees. Reluctance also stemmed from the broad trends in Canadian constitutional law, by which the courts increasingly emphasized the importance of several areas of provincial jurisdiction, while downgrading the Dominion government's responsibilities.[13] Federal concerns crystallized following a 1917 fight between the Edmonton street railway system and its employees. The federal minister of labour set up a conciliation board following a request by the employees, but the city of Edmonton asked for an injunction to restrain the conciliation board from taking any action. The labour dispute soon fizzled and the city dropped the case,[14] but Edmonton's actions unnerved the federal government, which responded by henceforth only establishing boards in disputes concerning public utilities under provincial or municipal control with the agreement of the employer and the employees.[15] As a result, from 1918 to March 1921, twenty-one disputes involving municipal employees were referred to federal boards of conciliation and investigation, but in nine

James Murdock, c. 1942–48
Library and Archives Canada, PA-047528

other such cases the federal government refused to create a board because the employer refused to consent.[16] It would be the "failure to adhere to this policy," Fudge and Tucker note correctly, that "led to the *Snider* case."[17]

In January 1923, the Canadian Electrical Trades Union (Toronto branch), which represented the electrical workers of both the Toronto Transit Commission and Toronto Hydro, requested a wage increase that, if granted, would have added approximately $100,000 per year to the wage bills of both companies.[18] When an agreement could not be reached, the union asked the federal Department of Labour in June to establish a conciliation board.[19]

According to Minister of Labour James Murdock, several factors played a role in the federal government's decision to acquiesce to the workers' request, despite the concerns about the applicability of the Act to the employees of municipal utilities. Prior to becoming labour minister, Murdock had served for fifteen years as vice-president of the Canadian branch of the Brotherhood of Railway Trainmen, a conservative union that tended to favour conciliation over strike action.[20] His rationale for using the *IDIA* reflected his conservative union background. He said that the government appointed a conciliation board because an electrical workers' strike could have become a city-wide strike, and the federal government did not possess enough soldiers to suppress a Toronto work stoppage *and* the labour revolt occurring at that time in Nova Scotia.[21] Large scale strikes by miners and steelworkers in Nova Scotia in 1922 and 1923 had resulted in the use of the militia to suppress the unrest.[22]

The timing of the dispute and electoral politics were also significant. Murdock was adamant that the labour fight should not interfere with the Canadian National Exhibition; a strike would have prevented many people from attending the exhibition because the city's electric street railways would not be running.[23] Murdock explained that the Department of Labour was "confronted with the fact that some few years previously a somewhat similar dispute in Toronto had developed to the extent of tying up the transportation facilities of Toronto for a short time during the exhibition."[24] The Liberals' precarious position in Parliament meant that pleasing the Ontario electorate by preventing an interruption in the exhibition was especially important. The Liberals had won the 1921 election by capturing a bare majority of seats — 118 of 235. Their tenuous hold on power meant that close attention was given to Ontario, which offered ample opportunity for future electoral success, as the Liberals had won just twenty-one of eighty-two Ontario ridings in 1921.[25] Murdock was thus especially concerned about Ontario's voters, noting later that if a serious strike had occurred during the exhibition he knew "who would have been blamed."[26]

The Department of Labour asked the Toronto Electric Commissioners to consent to a conciliation board to avoid jurisdiction questions, but the Commissioners again refused because they believed a board would recommend wage increases.[27] The three commissioners at the time were members of Toronto's industrial and political elite. P.W. Ellis, a former president of the Canadian Manufacturers' Association, was chair. George Wright, a prominent hotel proprietor, had served as a commissioner since 1918, and the third member was Charles A. Maguire, who sat as a commissioner during his short tenure as mayor of Toronto from 1922 to 1923.[28] Before entering politics, Maguire had been vice-president of the Hydro-Electric Railway Association. Ashworth, the acting general manager, offered a new factor in the decision to fight the appointment of a board: the process for selecting conciliation boards gave the federal government too much say in the ultimate result. The "great objection" to the Act, he said, "is that if two representatives don't agree on a chairman within five days[,] the [D]epartment of [L]abour proceeds to appoint one, which simply makes the arbitration board the commission of the department."[29] Ashworth's complaint about the appointment process of conciliation boards had some merit. Of the 142 conciliation boards constituted under the *IDIA* between 1919 and 1924, only a minority were appointed without government intervention. In eighty-eight cases, or 62 percent of the boards, the first two members failed to agree on a chair, and the minister of labour had to select the third member.[30]

The utility believed that boards so constituted would increase wages at a time when Toronto Hydro was intent on holding down labour costs. Ashworth claimed that in 1920 the wages were adjusted up at the peak of the cost of living, and that wages had not since been decreased, as they had been for employees in many other industries.[31] In Ashworth's view, "the cost of current to the citizen of Toronto is radically affected by anything of this nature, and the commissioners have to bear that in mind."[32] The commissioners said they had received legal advice to the effect that the *IDIA* did not apply to municipal public servants. As a result, they decided to test the constitutionality of the Act.[33]

The lawyer advising the commissioners was Thomas Langton Church, a long-serving director of the Canadian National Exhibition who had served as mayor of Toronto from 1915 to 1921. As mayor, Church had been an Electric Commissioner, and was thus well acquainted with the electrical workers' demands, demands which he consistently opposed. Elected as a Conservative member of the House of Commons in 1921, Church aggressively argued for Toronto Hydro's interests throughout the conflict.[34] In early August 1923, Church sent a telegram to Prime Minister King to suggest to him that the dispute was near an amicable settlement, and argued with Murdock about whether the *IDIA* applied to municipally-owned corporations. He told Murdock that the "[g]overnment might better be employed getting its own employees better working conditions," rather than "meddle here in the administration of public utilities."[35] Murdock insisted that the federal legislation was constitutional, though he did admit that the Department of Justice had at times expressed doubts about whether the *IDIA* applied where the utility was controlled by a municipality.[36]

Church alluded consistently to several public comments made by Murdock (who was not a lawyer), in which Murdock seemed to admit that the constitutionality of the *IDIA* was in question. In the House of Commons, Murdock had explained the federal government's unwillingness to use the *IDIA* to ensure an equitable end to the labour troubles in Nova Scotia by invoking constitutional concerns. He claimed that "the federal government under the *British North America Act* has jurisdiction to determine certain questions, but it has not been considered that we have authority even under the *Industrial Disputes Investigation Act* to go so far as to deal with some particular concern in a particular province."[37] Murdock also said that in some cases boards had not been granted out of fear that the Dominion government lacked jurisdiction. Thus, it had "been seriously questioned whether the [A]ct is not *ultra vires* — I think that is the legal term — of the Dominion authority entirely."[38]

The union was displeased with the Electric Commissioners' decision to challenge the *IDIA*. The union asserted the reasonableness of its actions: "The Canadian Electrical Trades Union is one of the most conservative labor organizations in Toronto, having waited over six months, in the present case, in trying to get their trouble settled."[39] The union claimed to have contacted the provincial minister of labour, Walter Rollo, in March, to point out that there was provincial legislation allowing for the appointment of a conciliation board, but nothing had been done, and thus the union had been forced to appeal to the federal government.[40] The union also called a meeting at Moose Hall in Toronto at which approximately 200 employees of Toronto Hydro and the Toronto Transportation Commission met to discuss the actions of the Electric Commissioners. The employees prepared another statement, this time reaffirming their "legal and constitutional right to a Conciliation Board." The employees also lamented Church's legal advice to the Commission, expressing their "regret that a member of Parliament should advise his clients to fight and violate laws passed by the House of Commons of which he is a member, and laws which he has not endeavored to alter, if he believed them wrong."[41]

Despite the opposition of Toronto Hydro, the federal government proceeded to establish a conciliation board. The union appointed John G. O'Donoghue, a Toronto lawyer and sometime Labour Party politician. When Toronto Hydro refused to select a member, the Minister of Labour appointed F.H. McGuigan, a Toronto contractor who had served previously on conciliation boards as a business representative. O'Donoghue and McGuigan then recommended that the Minister of Labour appoint Colin George Snider to chair the board. Snider was the county court judge for Wentworth, and had extensive experience chairing conciliation boards. Between 1919 and 1924, he chaired fourteen such boards, more than any other individual. He also had some knowledge of the past acrimony between the parties: in 1914 he had served on a conciliation board that had recommended an increase in the wages of Toronto Hydro's electrical workers.[42]

Legal Proceedings

THE CONCILIATION BOARD HELD a preliminary meeting with the representatives of the two sides on 7 August 1923. Lawyer George Kilmer represented Toronto Hydro, while F.A. Cramp and James Gunn, the business manager of the electrical workers' union, represented the employees.[43] Gunn would remain the public face of the employees through most of the dispute. He responded in the press to Church's telegram to Prime Minister King, calling it "Tommy rot."[44] Gunn was an experienced labour leader, though he was no radical. He had served as the secretary of the Canadian Federation of Labour, and he delivered public lectures on labour relations at the University of Toronto. The *Globe* described him as a "guild Socialist."[45]

The constitutional jurisdiction of the federal government came immediately to the fore. Kilmer argued that the *IDIA* interfered with provincial legislative jurisdiction. Gunn noted that sustaining Kilmer's objections would affect the Dominion's ability to help settle industrial disputes. The conciliation board adjourned until August 20, by which time it hoped to hear from the federal government as to whether the *IDIA* applied to the current situation. When the board reconvened on August 20, the leaders of Toronto Hydro and the union attended along with several lawyers, a clear indication that both employees and employer recognized the seriousness of the legal questions to be decided. The federal government also took an interest, dispatching lawyer Lewis Duncan to represent the board. The board decided to proceed under the *IDIA*, despite the objection of Toronto Hydro. Judge Snider revealed that Labour Minister Murdock had contacted the board regarding whether the *IDIA* applied to the dispute, although he refused to reveal the details of the Minister's correspondence. The board scheduled a meeting for the following week to hear evidence. Toronto Hydro reacted swiftly to prevent the board from beginning its work. On August 21, its lawyers applied for an interim injunction at the High Court Division of the Supreme Court of Ontario against the three members of the conciliation board. Hydro asserted that the board members were acting without lawful authority and must not proceed.[46]

Justice John Fosberry Orde heard the application. Orde was a Conservative in his politics, and had become a judge in 1920. Kilmer argued that the *IDIA* interfered with provincial jurisdiction over property and civil rights under section 92(13) of the *BNA Act*, municipal institutions (s. 92(8)), and local works or undertakings (s. 92(10)). Ontario decided to intervene in the dispute on the side of Toronto Hydro, and Edward Bayly, the provincial deputy-Attorney General, also appeared before Justice Orde. Bayly claimed that the province had no interest in taking sides, but simply wished to pursue the issue as a question of constitutional jurisdiction.[47]

Duncan represented the members of the conciliation board. He offered legal and policy arguments. He explained to Orde that the federal government had appointed a conciliation board in part to avoid a strike during the Canadian National Exhibition. He also asserted the necessity of the board on the ground that a strike might spread to other industries, just as had happened in the Winnipeg General Strike. Further, Duncan noted that the Quebec Superior Court had upheld the constitutionality of the *IDIA*. He suggested that *BNA Act*'s section 91 provisions stipulating the federal government's jurisdiction over trade and commerce (section 91(2)) and the criminal law (section 91(27)) made the *IDIA* constitutional, as did the provision in the preamble to section 91 that Ottawa was to "make laws for the peace, order, and good government of Canada" (POGG) in relation to all matters not coming within the subjects assigned exclusively to the provinces.[48]

Trends in the judicial interpretation of the *BNA Act* in the early-twentieth century made Duncan's arguments somewhat tenuous. The Judicial Committee of the Privy Council, especially through the decisions of Lord Richard Haldane, had tended to limit the scope of the federal government's authority to legislate for trade and commerce, criminal law, and for "peace, order, and good government."[49] Lord Haldane dominated the Judicial Committee with respect to Canadian appeals. During his time on the Privy Council, the Committee decided nine appeals that were pivotal to Canadian federalism. Haldane sat on all of these appeals and wrote the decision in all but one.[50] His influential federalism decisions all addressed the regulatory authority of the federal government. Haldane's judgments reflected his political view of Canadian federalism. John Saywell argues that Haldane "diminished the residual clause [POGG], and the power and scope of the enumerations, and elaborated a conception of federalism based on the theoretical, historical, and legal supremacy of the provinces."[51]

Several key cases support this analysis. In the 1921 *Board of Commerce* decision, the Privy Council held *ultra vires* federal legislation designed to supervise and prohibit unfair post-World War I price increases.[52] Haldane said that the federal jurisdiction over trade and commerce could not, by itself, allow the Dominion to interfere in the provinces' jurisdiction over property and civil rights. The federal power over criminal law was similarly restricted in *Board of Commerce* as Haldane insisted that it could only apply where the matter was inherently criminal in nature and could not sustain interference with provincial jurisdiction merely by taking the form of criminal prohibitions and penalties. Haldane also limited the ability of the Dominion to legislate for peace, order, and good government in the *Fort Frances Pulp and Paper Co. v. Manitoba Free Press Company* case of 1923; he held that the federal government could continue to regulate newsprint prices after the end of the Great War under POGG, but also insisted that POGG was limited to temporary emergency situations.[53]

Justice Orde granted an interim injunction on August 29.[54] In doing so, he did not find the entire *IDIA* unconstitutional, but held that the provisions of the *IDIA* that had a compulsory aspect infringed upon property and civil rights within the province. Thus, the board could not compel parties to testify or produce evidence. Orde was especially concerned about the damage done to freedom of contract, noting that once an application for a board of conciliation was made, then neither the employer nor the employee can put an end to the existing situation. The employee must still be retained in his employment and the employer must still pay the same wages, and the employee may not discontinue his employment, the result being that the civil rights of both parties to the dispute are seriously interfered with. Their hands are tied. They continue to be bound by a bargain which they never made until the Board has made its report. It can hardly be suggested for a moment that these provisions are not a direct interference with the civil rights of the parties.[55]

Orde took a dim view of Duncan's argument that the *IDIA*'s interference with property and civil rights was merely ancillary to the main purpose of the Act, that being, the prevention of strikes and lock outs, which, Duncan had argued, fell under Ottawa's authority to regulate for peace, order, and good government. In light of recent Privy Council decisions, Orde doubted that the prevention of strikes and lock outs was of such national importance that the legislation could be found constitutional under POGG:

Here there is nothing abnormal or necessarily of national importance in an industrial dispute or in a threatened strike or lock out [*sic*], and the desire of the Dominion Parliament to prevent strikes and lock outs [*sic*], however laudable it may be, and however effective the machinery devised for the purpose might be if Parliament were not hampered by a divided field of legislative power, cannot empower Parliament to invade either directly, or indirectly, under the guise of ancillary legislation . . . to legislate as to municipal institutions.[56]

Orde claimed that he came to this conclusion "with reluctance," for though he was dealing with a "bald question of law" he admitted that it was "generally [recognized] that the *Industrial Disputes Investigation Act* has been a beneficial one and has facilitated the settlement of numerous disputes." He therefore hoped that it would "be found possible to pass legislation, either federal or provincial or both, which will maintain the efficiency of the scheme of the Act."[57]

All those involved immediately appreciated the importance of the ruling. The federal government announced that it would appeal Orde's decision. The Attorney General of Ontario, W.F. Nickle, noted that the decision meant that the board was nothing more than a voluntary body. The union expressed its displeasure that its particular dispute had been turned into a constitutional question. Other members of the labour movement asserted that Orde's decision meant that employers now had a right to lock out *and* employees had a right to strike, whenever they liked.[58] Judge Snider stated that Orde's decision "goes much further than the question of municipal rights," for it "seriously questions the whole of the operation of the *Industrial Dispute Investigation Act.*"[59] The conciliation board, after some debate, decided to continue by hearing evidence given voluntarily, but not to issue any recommendations. Witnesses for the union appeared, including James Gunn.[60]

Justice Herbert Macdonald Mowat heard the subsequent application for a permanent injunction in November 1923. Mowat had run and lost as a Liberal in the 1911 federal election, but served in the Unionist government of Robert Borden after winning a seat in Toronto in 1917. He only sat briefly in Parliament for he joined the Ontario Supreme Court in 1921. The press coverage of the interim injunction and Orde's ruling stoked public interest in the permanent injunction hearing. The *Globe* suggested that the case's importance was reflected by the decision of both the federal and Ontario governments to be represented by counsel, and by the fact that the last witness to appear before Mowat was none other than Minister of Labour Murdock. A number of other high-profile witnesses gave evidence. Gunn supported the argument under POGG that an "emergency" may have resulted if the federal government had not appointed a conciliation board. Herbert Henry Couzens, the general manager of the Toronto Transportation Commission and Toronto Hydro, painted a different picture, telling the court that a strike had been unlikely even if the federal government had taken no action. The lawyers followed the witnesses with legal arguments.[61]

From the outset, Mowat seemed predisposed to find the *IDIA* constitutional, and in his decision delivered on December 15 he held that Orde had erred.[62] Mowat found the Act constitutional by reasoning that labour did not fall clearly under any enumerated head of legislative jurisdiction in sections 91 and 92 of the *BNA Act*. This absence of "labour" from the division of powers, he believed, stemmed from the inability of those framing the *BNA Act* to foresee the future importance of unions. The development of the labour movement meant that the regulation of labour was now an issue of national concern that fell under Ottawa's power to legislate for the peace, order, and good government of Canada in times of emergency. In making this determination, Mowat invoked the memory of the Winnipeg General Strike to cast "big labour" as a threatening phenomenon. He asserted that the Winnipeg strike "was only brought to an end through the voluntary efforts of the non-industrial citizens to break it and to prevent the misery and underfeeding of children which seemed likely to ensue." If it had spread, Mowat warned, "as at one time feared[,] ruinous conditions would have ensued to trade and stable industry." Such crises, he believed, were too serious to be left to the provinces: "In such a case provincial lines are obliterated and the Provinces not having the means of free and instant communication with each other or for concert could ill avert Dominion wide trouble." Ottawa thus had to defuse labour troubles because the small labour organizations that existed in 1867 had been replaced by "Brotherhoods composed in some instances of hundreds of thousands, and Dominion wide in their operations and probably beyond the resources of each Province to deal with."[63] Therefore, Mowat found the *IDIA* constitutional by casting labour unions as threatening organizations and thus of national concern.

The Ontario *Judicature Act* held that a judge could not depart from a prior known decision of another judge of coordinate authority on any point of law without the concurrence of the other judge, and because of this, Mowat referred the *Snider* case to the Appellate Division of the Supreme Court of Ontario.[64] The conciliation board did not sit while the case was under appeal. The Appellate Division heard the case in late January 1924, and the legal arguments were similar to those put before Orde and Mowat. For example, Duncan argued that in 1867 labour unions were organized locally, and there were no national or international unions. In the twentieth century, however, the creation of large unions meant that a central power was needed to ensure that a strike in Toronto did not spread across Canada.[65]

Surprisingly, given the weight of recent precedent, the Appellate Division held the *IDIA* constitutional. The decision was divided four to one with Justice William Nassau Ferguson writing the majority decision. Ferguson had joined the bar in 1894 and practiced in Toronto prior to his appointment to the appeal court in 1916. The three concurring justices were the Chief Justice of Ontario, William Mulock, a former Liberal member of Parliament, James Magee, who had been a judge since 1904, and Robert Smith, a former Liberal member of the House of Commons who became a member of the Supreme Court of Canada in 1927.[66]

Ferguson not only held the *IDIA* constitutional but also ruled that Ottawa could find fertile soil in many heads of federal power including criminal law, trade and commerce, and the residual POGG clause. He reasoned that the *IDIA* was designed to inquire into industrial disputes which "in some cases may, and in other cases will, develop into disputes affecting not merely the immediate parties thereto, but the national welfare, peace, order and safety, and the national trade and business." In his view, it could not "be disputed that to deprive the City of Toronto of electric power, on which it depends for light, heat and power, is to disturb and hinder the national trade and commerce and to endanger public peace, order and safety." Like Mowat, Ferguson emphasized that large international trade unions posed a special danger to Canadian peace and stability. Ferguson suggested that disputes involving such unions frequently developed into quarrels in which "public wrongs are done and crimes are committed, and the safety of the public and the public peace are endangered and broken, and the national trade and commerce is disturbed and hindered by strikes and lock outs [sic] extending, not only throughout the Dominion, but frequently to the United States, where most of our trade unions have their headquarters."[67] Ferguson came to his conclusions only after a full consideration of the relevant JCPC precedents, most notably the decisions of Lord Haldane. Ferguson's decision was a direct rejection of Haldane's revision of Canadian federalism. It begged his response, which would come when Lord Haldane presided over the *Snider* appeal to the Judicial Committee.

Frank Egerton Hodgins dissented, believing that the *IDIA* clearly encroached on areas of provincial jurisdiction. He also found unconvincing the argument that Ottawa's right to pass the *IDIA* could be grounded in POGG, and he noted that if a fear of a national labour emergency truly existed, "much more drastic and effective legislation than the present would be necessary." The *IDIA* was designed to deal with the "normal working of industrial relations, which often require time and patience and some restraint, to afford protection against dislocation or disturbance in the usual conduct of business as between employer and employees." Like Orde, Hodgins expressed "much regret" at having to reach his conclusions, for the *IDIA* had "been a successful experiment in warding off industrial difficulties."[68]

The appellate court's decision greatly pleased federal Minister of Labour Murdock. "The decision is very satisfactory," he declared, for the ruling "defines the scope of our powers under the [A]ct on a reasonable basis."[69] The certainty provided by the Court of Appeal was short lived, however, for Toronto Hydro decided to bypass the Supreme Court and Canada and appeal directly to the Privy Council. Parties had been able to appeal decisions of provincial appellate courts directly to the Privy Council since the creation of the Supreme Court of Canada in 1875. A majority of the cases that went to the Privy Council from Canada skipped the Supreme Court of Canada, often to save on one level of expensive litigation.[70] The cost factor may explain Toronto Hydro's decision to take the case to the Pricy Council. The conciliation board, which had remained constituted but inactive, met at Osgoode Hall in May 1924, but adjourned when it found out that the Electric Commissioners were appealing the Appellate Division's decision to the Privy Council.

Most of Canada's labour groups expressed hope that the Privy Council would hold the *IDIA* constitutional. The Canadian Trade and Labour Congress recognized that the result would have "have far reaching results," for if "the [A]ct is declared *ultra vires*, then the Mines, Street Car Companies and others, now under the [A]ct but holding provincial charters of incorporation will be released from its provisions."[71] P.M. Draper, the secretary-treasurer of the Trades and Labor Congress, also expressed his hope that the legislation would be upheld. He believed that the Act stood for a principle "that Labor cannot oppose, and is one that Labor has never objected to, that is, that the parties involved should endeavor to get together before a breach occurs."[72]

Oral arguments at the Privy Council took place over five days in November 1924 before Viscount Haldane, Lord Dunedin, Lord Atkinson, Lord Wrensbury, and Lord Salvesen. *Snider* would be Haldane's final important federalism decision and among his best known and most lasting decisions.[73] As might be expected, given his stake in Canadian federalism and the affront the Appellate decision represented to his vision of it, Haldane dominated the proceedings, aggressively challenging the lawyers defending the constitutionality of the *IDIA*, and even cutting off his fellow judges who offered remarks with which he disagreed.[74] Duncan continued to argue that the nature of modern industrial disputes required national legislation. He again explained that the Dominion government had decided to use the *IDIA* in Toronto because of the labour emergency occurring concurrently in Nova Scotia. The strike by steel and coal workers in Nova Scotia had required that the Dominion send every available member of the permanent militia east of Winnipeg to Nova Scotia. Therefore, Toronto was "standing there without troops at all" and labour unions across the country were protesting against the deployment of troops in Nova Scotia and "threatening strikes in other parts of Canada." Duncan portrayed the union's leadership as threatening and heartless. He described Gunn as a "ruthless agitator" who had engineered a police strike in Toronto and organized an earlier strike of electrical workers that forced 100,000 people stranded at the National Exhibition to walk home. He then invoked the fear of communism, explaining that Minister of Labour Murdock had acted because he "knew about the Winnipeg general strike, which was a strike at the very existence of Canada, engineered by the Communist and Soviet people and very nearly successful."

Duncan argued that the Winnipeg strike amply demonstrated the dangers of unions and the need for national regulation. He told the Privy Council that "emergency always is inherent in this matter because of the labour unions being all over Canada, controlled in many cases outside of Canada," and, he asked, "what Government other than the Canadian Government can deal with the situation?"[75] While most Canadian labour organizations supported the attempt to defend the *IDIA*, they did not comment on the fact that doing so required Ottawa to portray unions as a menace that threatened the very existence of the state.

Haldane rejected the Dominion's arguments. In the oral arguments, Haldane consistently expressed concern that the *IDIA* interfered with the property and civil rights of citizens. This meant the right of an employer to act freely in dealing with employees. He asked "What is my civil right if it is not to lock out?" He also downplayed the need for Dominion legislation to regulate labour, suggesting that the provinces could pass the necessary legislation. The *BNA Act* gave the provinces "complete autonomy as regards certain heads of legislative power," such that each province was "treated as a most important entity, as a country by itself." Haldane's questioning frustrated Lewis Duncan, who suggested that the Privy Council's interpretation of the "property and civil rights" was too broad. He asked "what legislation could possibly be passed by the Dominion which does not interfere with property or the civil right of the inhabitant of the provinces to do as he pleases?"[76]

Haldane was unmoved. The *IDIA*'s provisions "were concerned directly with the civil rights of both employers and employed in the Province," and there was little in the *IDIA* that the provinces could not have enacted. In Haldane's view, the rights of employers and employees to enter (and exit) contractual relationships fell within the ambit of property and civil rights. Relying on his own *Board of Commerce* decision, Haldane held that the federal government could not enact the *IDIA* based on its power to pass laws relating to the criminal law. He emphasized that the Act gave boards the power to render it "unlawful for an employer to lock-out or for a workman to strike." The Dominion could not impose "merely ancillary penalties" to make a law dealing with such civil rights fall within federal jurisdiction over the criminal law. Haldane also rejected the argument that the legislation could be grounded on Ottawa's jurisdiction over trade and commerce. He asserted that trade and commerce allowed the Dominion to pass regulations "relating to general trade and commerce," but not for the "contracts of a particular trade or business." Finally, he asserted that the *IDIA* could not be upheld under POGG. Citing his *Fort Frances* decision, he noted that only the most serious circumstances — those which threatened the national life of Canada, such as war — allowed the federal government to employ POGG to interfere in areas of provincial jurisdiction.[77]

Reaction and Responses

THE DECISION OF THE Privy Council displeased Murdock. He first suggested that it "looks as if the entire [A]ct is out of business."[78] "It is to be deeply regretted," he said, "that after employers and employed had through the workings of the [A]ct attained to a broader and fairer view of their relations, the [A]ct should be upset. I do not know what other machinery can take its place." The Toronto press also reacted negatively to the Privy Council's decision. The *Star*, for example, noted that the decision "will have a far reaching effect in respect of federal jurisdiction generally." The *IDIA* could be replaced by provincial acts, but "complete uniformity is regarded as impossible."[79]

The labour movement also expressed its displeasure. James Gunn lamented that the decision "leaves us in a state of confusion," for "there will be an awkward condition of affairs if an industrial dispute now cuts across provincial boundaries."[80] The executive of the Trades and Labor Congress hoped for an amendment to the *BNA Act* to make the *IDIA* constitutional, and expressed hope that *Snider* would not lead to extensive provincial legislation in this area since this would "create confusion and lack of uniformity in the application of such laws," and would "leave the door open for the enactment of legislation that would not be to the benefit of the workers."[81] Tom Moore, president of the Trades and Labor Congress, offered dire predictions, asserting that the Privy Council had "set the clock back for at least a decade" for it forced "Labor into the position of relying on its own numerical and financial strength to secure just treatment and betterment of conditions, instead of being able to rely on the justice of its claims and the force of its arguments." He also warned that the decision would be "welcomed by a minority section of the Labor movement, composed of Communists, etc., who like to be known as the 'Left Wing,' as it will give them the opportunity to develop to the full their propaganda of class conflict by promoting the calling of sudden strikes, etc., in vital or key industries."[82] Moore was not wrong on this point. While many labour groups believed that the *IDIA* encouraged fair negotiations between employees and employers, some labour voices claimed that the Act encouraged results biased toward business.[83] This was the view taken by *The Left Wing,* a radical labour publication, which railed against the Privy Council's decision, and suggested that it stood as a warning for unions to avoid becoming entwined in the law. It said that "capitalist 'justice' as peddled by the 'Noble Lords' of the privy council" had "decided AGAINST THE MEN." The whole case was "very disgusting, and should provide the Electrical workers with a valuable lesson on the folly of relying upon the bosses' laws, interpreted by the bosses' servants, instead of relying upon our own organized might."[84]

Much of the initial reaction of the legal profession focused on the ruling's implications for constitutional interpretation generally, and paid little attention to the implications of the decision for Canadian labour relations.[85] *Snider* also ignited a fierce debate in Parliament on whether to abolish appeals to the Privy Council.[86] It also forced the governing Liberals to defend their decision to appoint a board. Conservative leader Arthur Meighen blamed the ineptitude of the federal government for the result. "One would have thought if there was any single case where the application of the [A]ct was on a very, very weak legal footing, it would be there," said Meighen.[87] Murdock responded by again describing the context of the dispute, including the labour strife in Nova Scotia that required the use of the army. He also defended the government's actions by saying that it was "true that the Labour department could in 1923 have evaded its responsibility and sought, as it had been done admittedly in numerous similar cases for years, to sidestep, dodge and keep out of trouble." But, according to Murdock, "the department decided that the proper course to take was to insist on the formation of a board" even though "our authority so to do might by some be questioned." While "both sides of the House regret the final outcome," Murdock asserted that "surely it was better for us to ascertain what authority we had."[88]

While the debate in the House of Commons revolved around who to blame, the federal government and the provinces went about attempting to repair the tear in the fabric of the legal regulation of labour relations. Ottawa passed an Act that limited the application of the *IDIA* to areas that were clearly within the legislative jurisdiction of the Dominion government. The new legislation applied only to works carried on in connection with shipping, steam railways, telegraphs, and canals extending beyond any one province; ferries between provinces; works operated by aliens; works declared to be for the advantage of Canada; or works operated by a corporation holding a charter from the Dominion government. The new Act also stated that in any case of real or apprehended emergency, the Governor in Council could declare a dispute to be within the purview of the Act. In addition, the Act provided that provinces could transfer to the federal government the right to deal with disputes that would otherwise be handled by the provinces exclusively.[89]

By 1926, five provinces — British Columbia, Saskatchewan, Manitoba, New Brunswick, and Nova Scotia — had passed legislation making the *IDIA* applicable to all disputes that were within the exclusive jurisdiction of the provinces. By 1932, all provinces except Prince Edward Island had brought the *IDIA* into force in their respective jurisdictions.[90] This cohesion was short lived, however. The *Snider* case empowered the provinces to regulate labour relations, and beginning in the late 1930s, provincial legislation resulted in the fragmentation of labour regulation, thus making future institutional reform on a national scale more difficult.[91]

Conclusion

THE *SNIDER* CASE EMERGED out of a confluence of events. It was prompted by weaknesses in the procedures established by the *IDIA*. The failure of many conciliation boards to agree on a chair angered the managers of Toronto Hydro, who felt that the federal government's power to appoint a chair in such situations meant that Ottawa had too much of a say in determining outcomes. Other key factors that contributed to the litigation included the decrease in the cost of living after the Great War, the desire to avoid interrupting the Canadian National Exhibition, and the perceived inability of the federal government to suppress two concurrent labour revolts. These factors led the Department of Labour to appoint a board of conciliation despite strong concerns over the *IDIA*'s constitutionality. Peter Hogg suggests that the Privy Council's *Snider* decision "seems to have been both unexpected and unwelcome."[92] Hogg is half correct. While many Canadians found the *Snider* decision distasteful, the federal government was well aware that the courts might find the *IDIA* unconstitutional. For some time, the Dominion government had attempted to avoid having anyone challenge the constitutionality of the *IDIA*, but the trends in constitutional jurisprudence had only made such delaying tactics more dangerous. One can speculate that the federal government might have had more success defending the Act had the government sought to define jurisdictional boundaries in the immediate aftermath of the Great War and the Winnipeg General Strike since, as has been shown, fear of labour played a role in the reasoning of the five Canadian judges who held the *IDIA* constitutional. Fear and distrust might have saved the *IDIA* if the federal government had acted earlier. The level of concern with revolution was at its highest in the immediate aftermath of the Great War. By the time the *Snider* case went before the Privy Council in late 1924, the acuteness of the perceived danger had waned. *Snider* is thus a reminder of the contingency involved in any case. Most labour groups, employers, and governments supported the *IDIA*, yet, when tested, it failed to pass constitutional muster because of the particular combination of events, litigants, and ideas about constitutional interpretation at a specific time and place.

Snider also demonstrates how different elements of the liberal state could come into conflict. On the one hand, the *IDIA* was meant to entice labour into a legal regime which prevented social conflict. It created a system of dispute resolution that bestowed legitimacy on unions' demands for wage increases in exchange for limiting the ability of labour to strike. It was thus designed to grind the perceived dangerous edges off of industrial labour movements. The *IDIA*, however, used means that ran counter to other aspects of the liberal state. Liberal legal thought emphasized the importance of private property and freedom of contract. The *IDIA*'s provisions allowing boards of conciliation to compel the production of evidence and to force employees to continue working (and companies to continue employing the workers) after contracts had expired was at conflict with the attitude that property and contract rights should be protected at all costs. In the end, the judges who supported the constitutionality of the *IDIA* ground their reasoning on the liberal state's desire to ensure public safety. The judges who found the Act unconstitutional trumpeted the *BNA Act*'s ability to protect against interference in property and civil rights, which to judges such as Orde, Hodgins, and Haldane meant property rights and the freedom of contract. In this context, the *IDIA* could only have been saved if the judiciary believed that public disorder was so rife that the coercive aspects of the *IDIA* overwhelmed the desire to protect "civil rights." Therefore, *The Left Wing* had it right when it said that the *Snider* case was "capitalist 'justice' as peddled by the 'Noble Lords.'"[93] There was no possible "pro-labour" result. The structure of constitutional argument meant that either the *IDIA* would be found unconstitutional (to the chagrin of most labour groups) or the courts would brand unions as dangerous and thus in need of federal regulation.

Notes

1   Peter W. Hogg, *Constitutional Law of Canada*, 5th ed., looseleaf (Toronto: Thompson Carswell, 2007) vol. 1 at para. 21.8.

2   John Saywell, for example, employs *Snider* as a prime example of Lord Richard Haldane's desire to further his provincial rights agenda. John T. Saywell, *The Lawmakers: Judicial Power and the Shaping of Canadian Federalism* (Toronto: University of Toronto Press and the Osgoode Society for Canadian Legal History, 2002) at 179–83. On the other hand, Paul Romney notes that the case "ignited the centralist revolution" in the interpretation of the *BNA Act*. This centralist interpretation, Romney believes, wrongly concludes that the Privy Council had deviated from the original meaning of the *BNA Act*. Paul Romney, *Getting it Wrong: How Canadians Forgot Their Past and Imperilled Confederation* (Toronto: University of Toronto Press, 1999) at 164.

3   See, for example, Judy Fudge & Eric Tucker, *Labour Before the Law: The Regulation of Workers' Collective Action in Canada, 1900–1948* (Toronto: Oxford University Press, 2001) at 138.

4   Christopher Armstrong & H.V. Nelles, *Monopoly's Moment: The Organization and Regulation of Canadian Utilities, 1830–1930* (Philadelphia: Temple University Press, 1986) at 154–57 and 190–92. On the development of hydro-electric power in Ontario see H.V. Nelles, *The Politics of Development: Forests, Mines & Hydro-Electric Power in Ontario, 1849–1941*, 2d ed. (Montreal: McGill-Queen's University Press, 2005); Neil B. Freeman, *The Politics of Power: Ontario Hydro and Its Government, 1906–1995* (Toronto: University of Toronto Press, 1996); Ian M. Drummond, *Progress without Planning: The Economic History of Ontario from Confederation to the Second World War* (Toronto: University of Toronto Press, 1987) at 134–47.

5   *Toronto Globe* (1 July 1914) 2; "Electrical Workers' Success," *Toronto Star* (27 June 1914) 17; "Fear Strike among Local Hydro Workers," *Toronto Star* (16 July 1914) 1 ["Fear Strike"]; "Talk of Strike by Hydro Men is Premature," *Toronto Star* (17 July 1914) 1, 18; "Hydro Accepts Award Men Return to Work," *Toronto Star* (22 July 1914) 1; "Hydro Dispute at Last Cleared off the Slate," *Toronto Star* (23 July 1914) 3; "Electrical Workers Active," *Toronto Star* (30 March 1917) 13; "Electrical Workers' Increase," *Toronto Star* (3 May 1917) 10; "Electrical Workers' Increase," *Toronto Star* (11 May 1917) 11; "Hydro Settlement Expected," *Toronto Star* (17 July 1919) 20; "Conciliation Report not made Public Yet," *Toronto Globe* (8 July 1920) 8; "Board Awards Good Increase," *Toronto Globe* (9 July 1920) 8; "Hydro Board Talks Award," *Toronto Globe* (10 July 1920) 6; "Not satisfied with Increase of 15 Per Cent," *Toronto Globe* (12 July 1920) 8; "Hydro Men Agree to Accept Award," *Toronto Globe* (19 July 1920) 6; "The Toronto Hydro-Electric System," *Toronto World* (21 July 1920) 3.

6   *Industrial Disputes Investigation Act*, S.C. 1907, c. 20 [*IDIA*]; Paul Craven, *An Impartial Umpire: Industrial Relations and the Canadian State, 1900–1911* (Toronto: University of Toronto Press, 1980).

7   *IDIA, ibid.*, at s. 2.

8   *An Act to Amend the Industrial Disputes Investigation Act, 1907*, S.C. 1918, c. 27; *An Act to Amend the Industrial Disputes Investigation Act, 1907*, S.C. 1920, c. 29.

9 C.E. Dankert, "The Canadian Industrial Disputes Investigation Act" (1928) 36:1 Journal of Political Economy 141 at 143.

10 "Electrical Men now Ask for Conciliation Board," *Toronto Star* (30 April 1921) 30; "Commissioners Oppose a Board on Wage Scales," *Toronto Star* (20 May 1921) 1; Armstrong & Nelles, above note 4 at 246 and 266.

11 Department of Labour memorandum, LAC, MG26-J1, vol. 121, 102790; Fudge & Tucker, above note 3 at 136; Saywell, above note 2 at 180.

12 *Montreal Street Railway Co. v. Board of Reconciliation and Investigation* (1913), 44 Q.R. 350; Dankert, above note 9 at 158–59; Department of Labour memorandum, LAC, MG26-J1, vol. 121, 102789.

13 Somewhat ironically, this judicial hostility toward the heads of power supporting the *IDIA* emerged at the same time that the Act's popularity grew amongst most labour groups, federal political leaders, and business groups (though each had complaints). Gordon DiGiacomo, "Support for a Centralist Vision of Labour Policy in Early Canada" (2004) 38:3 Journal of Canadian Studies 171 at 184–86, 188–91, & 192–200; Ben E. Selekman, *Postponing Strikes: A Study of the Industrial Disputes Investigation Act of Canada* (New York: Russell Sage Foundation, 1927) at 147-81; F.R. Scott, "Federal Jurisdiction over Labour Relations — A New Look" (1960) 6 McGill L.J. 156 at 156.

14 Department of Labour memorandum, LAC, MG26-J1, vol. 121, 102788-89; "Proceedings under the Industrial Disputes Investigation Act during September, 1917" (1917) 17 Labour Gazette 790; "Trade Disputes during September, 1917" (1917) 17 Labour Gazette 817; "Other Proceedings under Act" (1917) 17 Labour Gazette 898.

15 OA, RG 8-20, file 100.776, "Toronto Electric Commissioners v. Snider, 1923"; Dankert, above note 9 at 158.

16 Margaret Mackintosh, "Government Intervention in Labour Disputes in Canada" (1924) 31 Queen's Quarterly 321.

17 Fudge & Tucker, above note 3 at 136.

18 "Increase in Wages Asked by Workers," *Toronto Globe* (17 January 1923) 12.

19 OA, RG 8-20, file 100.776, "Toronto Electric Commissioners v. Snider, 1923"; "Decision Tomorrow on Arbitration Plan," *Toronto Globe* (2 August 1923) 11 ["Decision Tomorrow"].

20 Fudge & Tucker, above note 3 at 62; B.M. Greene, ed., *Who's Who in Canada, 1930–1931* (Toronto: International Press Limited, 1932) at 1238 [*Who's Who in Canada, 1930–1931*].

21 "Provinces Must now Pass own Legislation," *Toronto Star* (22 January 1925) 3 ["Provinces Must now Pass"]; *House of Commons Debates* (13 May 1925) at 3152 (Hon. James Murdock).

22 Fudge & Tucker, above note 3 at 125-29; David Frank, "Class Conflict in the Coal Industry, Cape Breton 1922" in Gregory S. Kealey & Peter Warrian, eds., *Essays in Canadian Working Class History* (Toronto: McClelland and Stewart, 1976) at 161; Craig Heron, *Working in Steel: The Early Years in Canada, 1883–1935* (Toronto: McClelland and Stewart, 1988) at 153–59; Paul MacEwan, *Miners and Steelworkers: Labour in Cape Breton* (Toronto: S. Stevens, 1976) at 91–110.

23 *Once Upon a Century: 100 Year History of the 'Ex'* (Toronto: J.H. Robinson Co., 1978) at 38.

24 "Provinces Must now Pass," above note 21.

25 The figure of 118 Liberal MPs includes one "independent Liberal." R. MacGregor Dawson, *William Lyon Mackenzie King: A Political Biography, 1874–1923* (Toronto: University of Toronto Press, 1958) at 356.

26 "Provinces Must now Pass," above note 21. Also see *House of Commons Debates* (13 May 1925) at 3152 (Hon. James Murdock).

27 OA, RG 8-20, file 100.776, "Toronto Electric Commissioners v. Snider, 1923."

28 Edward M. Ashworth, *Toronto Hydro Recollections* (Toronto: University of Toronto Press, 1955) at 223.

29 "Want no Arbitration under Lemieux Act" *Toronto Star* (2 August 1923) 3 ["Want no Arbitration"].

30 Dankert, above note 9 at 146. Also see Selekman, above note 13 at 183–89.

31 "Want no Arbitration," above note 29; "Decision Tomorrow," above note 19.

32 "Decision Tomorrow," *ibid.*

33 "Toronto Hydro is to test Legality of Lemieux Act," *Toronto Star* (3 August 1923) 1.

34 *Who's Who in Canada, 1930–1931*, 1006; *House of Commons Debates,* (25 March 1924) at 638–40 (Thomas Langton Church); "Electrical Union Affirms Attitude at Mass Meeting," *Toronto Globe* (6 August 1923) 11 ["Electrical Union Affirms"].

35 "Tommy Rot, says Gunn Describing T.L.'s Wire," *Toronto Star* (8 August 1923) 3 ["Tommy Rot"].

36 *Ibid.* Also see "Hydro Arbitrators Commence Sittings on Wages Question," *Toronto Globe* (8 August, 1923) 12 ["Hydro Arbitrators Commence Sittings"].

37 *House of Commons Debates,* (28 March 1923) at 1646 (Hon. James Murdock).

38 *House of Commons Debates,* (10 April 1923) at 1704 (Hon. James Murdock).

39 "Hydro Employees Leave Final Word for Mass Meeting," *Toronto Globe* (4 August 1923) 13.

40 *Ibid.*

41 "Electrical Union Affirms," above note 34.

42 "Board is Appointed to Adjust Dispute," *Toronto Globe* (25 July 1923) 12; "McGuigan Appointed to Represent Hydro," *Toronto Globe* (1 August 1923) 12; Charles George Douglas Roberts, ed., *The Canadian Who's Who,* vol. 1 (Toronto: Trans-Canada Press, 1910) at 156; Selekman, above note 13 at 110; OA, RG 8-20, file 100.776, "Toronto Electric Commissioners v. Snider, 1923"; "Proceedings under the Industrial Disputes Investigation Act, 1907, During the Month of July, 1923" (1923) 23 Labour Gazette 837–38; "Judge Colin G. Snider Heads Hydro Board," *Toronto Star* (2 August 1923) 3; Barnet M. Greene, ed., *Who's Who in Canada, 1923–1924* (Toronto: International Press, 1923) at 536 [*Who's Who in Canada, 1923–24*]; "Fear Strike," above note 5.

43 OA, RG 8-20, file 100.776, "Toronto Electric Commissioners v. Snider, 1923"; "Hydro Arbitrators Commence Sittings," above note 36; "Proceedings under the Industrial Disputes Investigation Act, 1907, During the Month of August, 1923" (1923) 23 Labour Gazette 985–86.

44 "Tommy Rot," above note 35.

45 "Industrial Ethics Subject of Lectures," *Toronto Globe* (5 January 1923) 9. On Gunn, also see "Labor Affairs Discussed Before University Forum," *Toronto Globe* (1 Febru-

ary 1923) 9; "Labor Candidates at Sparse Meeting tell Party's Aims," *Toronto Globe* (14 June 1923) 13.

46 OA, RG 8-20, file 100.776, "Toronto Electric Commissioners v. Snider, 1923"; "Standing of Board Subject of Debate," *Toronto Globe* (10 August 1923) 9; "Hydro Board held to be Subject to Conciliation Act," *Toronto Star* (20 August 1923) 17; "Hydro Stands Pat on its Resolution not to Arbitrate," *Toronto Globe* (21 August 1923) 11; "City Hydro Serves Writ on Conciliation Board," *Toronto Star* (22 August 1923) 3.

47 "Hydro Hearing for Injunction Again Delayed," *Toronto Star* (23 August 1923) 17 [Hydro Hearing]; "Board's Contention will be Supported by Ontario Official," *Toronto Globe* (25 August 1923) 23; *Who's Who in Canada, 1923–24*, above note 42 at 307.

48 "Hydro Hearing," *ibid.*; "The Disputes Act not Property One is Duncan's Stand," *Toronto Star* (27 August 1923) 1.

49 R.C.B. Risk, "Canadian Courts under the Influence" (1990) 40 U.T.L.J. 687. On Haldane see Saywell, above note 2 at 150–86; Jonathan Robinson, "Lord Haldane and the British North America Act" (1970) 20 U.T.L.J. at 55; Stephen Wexler, "The Urge to Idealize: Viscount Haldane and the Constitution of Canada" (1984) 29 McGill L.J. 608.

50 Saywell, above note 2 at 155.

51 *Ibid.*, at 160.

52 *In re The Board of Commerce Act, 1919, and the Combines and Fair Prices Act, 1919,* (1921), [1922] A.C. 191; Bernard J. Hibbitts, "A Bridle for Leviathan: The Supreme Court and the Board of Commerce" (1989) 21 Ottawa L. Rev. 65.

53 *Fort Frances Pulp and Paper Co. v. Manitoba Free Press Company* [1923], A.C. 695, [1923] 3 D.L.R. 629.

54 *Toronto Electric Commissioners v. Snider* (1923), [1923–4] 25 O.W.N. 64; "Validity of Industrial Disputes Investigation Act, 1907" (1924) 24 Labour Gazette 384 ["Validity"].

55 Quoted in *Toronto Commissioners v. Snider* [1924], 2 D.L.R. 761 (C.A.) at para. 17 ["ONCA"].

56 *Ibid.* at para. 21.

57 *Ibid.*, at para. 24.

58 "Decision Reached by Justice Orde hits Lemieux Act," *Toronto Globe* (30 August 1923) 13; "Dispute Act Useless if Orde Decision Holds," *Toronto Star* (30 August 1923) 1–2 ["Dispute Act Useless"]; "Voluntary Evidence will be Continued Before Snider Board," *Toronto Globe* (31 August 1923) 11 ["Voluntary Evidence"]; "Electrical Workers Would Avoid Strike," *Toronto Globe* (31 August 1923) 11.

59 "Dispute Act Useless," *ibid.*

60 *Ibid.*; "Board will Approve no Seniority Clause" *Toronto Star* (31 August 1923) 3; "Voluntary Evidence," above note 58.

61 "Confirmatory Law may be Necessary to Strengthen Act," *Toronto Globe* (20 November 1923) 13, 15; "Evidence Concluded in Hydro-Labor Case," *Toronto Globe* (23 November 1923) 15; "Argument goes on over Labor Dispute," *Toronto Globe* (30 November 1923) 12; *Who's Who in Canada, 1923–24*, above note 42 at 428.

62 "Judgment Respecting Legality of Industrial Disputes Investigation Act, 1907" (1923) 23 Labour Gazette 1452; *Toronto Electric Com'rs v. Snider*, [1924] 1 D.L.R. 101 (Ont. Sup. Ct.) ["Mowat J."].

63 "Mowat J.," *ibid.* at 105.

64 *Judicature Act*, R.S.O. c. 56, s. 32.

65 "Need 'Central' Power to Deal with Labor," *Toronto Star* (30 January 1924) 7; "Argument Begins Over Lemieux Act," *Toronto Globe* (30 January 1924) 10.

66 "Validity," above note 54; "ONCA," above note 55.

67 "ONCA," *ibid.* at paras. 57, 74, and 76.

68 *Ibid.*, at paras. 86 and 134.

69 "Says Lemieux Act is Within Powers of Federal House," *Toronto Globe* (23 April 1924) 14.

70 Peter James McCormick, *Supreme at Last: The Evolution of the Supreme Court of Canada* (Toronto: J. Lorimer, 2000), 9; Ian Bushnell, *The Captive Court: A Study of the Supreme Court of Canada* (Montreal & Kingston: McGill-Queen's University Press, 1992), 14–27.

71 *Report of the Proceedings of the Fortieth Annual Convention of the Trades and Labour Congress of Canada, 1924* (Montreal: n.p., 1924) at 49.

72 P.M. Draper, "The Industrial Disputes Investigation Act, 1907" (1923) 2:12 Canadian Congress Journal 22 at 22.

73 Saywell, above note 2 at 175.

74 *Ibid*, at 181.

75 *Judicial Proceedings respecting Constitutional Validity of the Industrial Disputes Investigation Act, 1907* (Ottawa: F.A. Acland, 1925) 170 & 171.

76 *Ibid.*, at 139, 166, and 178.

77 *Toronto Electric Commissioners v. Snider* [1925], A.C. 396, 2 D.L.R. 5 (J.C.P.C.) at paras. 8, 19, 22, & 23–25.

78 "Lemieux Act Wiped out is Opinion of London," *Toronto Star* (21 January 1925) 2.

79 "Provinces Must now Pass," above note 21.

80 "James Gunn Fearful of Knots now Lemieux Act is Killed," *Toronto Star* (22 January 1925) 1.

81 "Industrial Disputes Legislation" *Report of the Proceedings of the Forty-first Annual Convention of the Trades and Labour Congress of Canada, 1925* (Montreal: n.p., 1925) at 54.

82 "Clock Set Back Ten Years, Says Head of Labor Congress," *Toronto Globe* (22 January 1925) 2. Prime Minister King took some pride that labour supported the *IDIA*. See Letter from W. L. Mackenzie King to Dr. Charles W. Elliot (30 January 1925), LAC, MG26-J1, vol. 114, 97312.

83 Ian McKay, *Reasoning Otherwise: Leftists and the People's Enlightenment in Canada, 1890–1920* (Toronto: Between the Lines, 2008) at 152.

84 "That Privy Council Bunk" *The Left Wing* (February 1925) 4 ["Privy Council Bunk"].

85 See, for example, R.W.S., "Editorial," (1925) 3 Can. Bar Rev. 212.; R.W.S., "Industrial Disputes Act," (1925) 4 Can. Bar Rev. 214; H.A.S., "The Lemieux Act Decision" (1925) 3 Can. Bar Rev. 217; F.E.H., "Lord Haldane and the Russell Case" (1925) 3 Can. Bar Rev. 265; A Berriedale Keith, "The Privy Council and the Canadian Constitution," (1925) 7:1 Journal of Comparative Legislation and International Law, 3d series, 65–6.

86 See *House of Commons Debates,* (19 February 1925) at 307–41.

87 *House of Commons Debates,* (13 May 1925) at 3155 (Arthur Meighen).

42 • R. Blake Brown and Jennifer J. Llewellyn

88 *House of Commons Debates*, (13 May 1925) at 3156 (Hon. James Murdock).
89 *An Act to amend The Industrial Disputes Investigation Act, 1907*, S.C. 1925, c. 14; Letter from W.L. Mackenzie King to Dr. Charles W. Elliott (30 January 1925), LAC, MG26-J1, vol. 114, 97312; Letter from W.L. Mackenzie King to Lord Askwith (30 November 1925) Ottawa, Library and Archives Canada (MG26-J1, vol. 111 at 94663); Department of Labour memorandum, LAC, MG26-J1, vol. 121, 102792; "Commons Revives the Lemieux Act," *Toronto Globe* (14 May 1925) 5.
90 *Industrial Disputes Investigation Act (Saskatchewan)*, S.S. 1925–26, c. 58; *Industrial Disputes Investigation Act (British Columbia)*, S.B.C. 1925, c. 19; *An Act Respecting the Investigation of Industrial Disputes within the Province*, S.N.S. 1926, c. 5; *The Labour Disputes Act*, S.A. 1926, c. 53; *Industrial Disputes Investigation Act (Manitoba)*, S.M. 1926, c. 21; *Industrial Disputes Investigation Act (New Brunswick)*, S.N.B. 1926, c. 17; *An Act respecting investigations into industrial disputes*, S.Q. 1932, c. 46; *Industrial Disputes Investigation Act, 1932*, S.O. 1932, c. 20.
91 Fudge & Tucker, above note 3 at 192–227.
92 Hogg, above note 1.
93 "That Privy Council Bunk," above note 84.

John East Iron Works v. Saskatchewan Labour Relations Board: A Test for the Infant Administrative State

Beth Bilson

Introduction

THE MID-1940S SAW JURISDICTIONS across Canada adopt new statutory regimes which extended collective bargaining rights to workers who wished to be represented by trade unions. Though in many ways the legislation reflected Canadian concerns, it was modelled in form and structure on the *Wagner Act* passed in 1935 as part of the New Deal legislative program of Franklin D. Roosevelt.[1] To a large extent, the political support necessary to ensure the passage of that statute was cultivated not on the basis that it would provide broad-based worker rights to self-determination, but on the more pragmatic ground that it would foster industrial harmony and promote commerce.[2]

The authority for the *Wagner Act* was ostensibly found in the interstate commerce clause of the American constitution. This constitutional justification was not available to Canadian legislators, but the Canadian statutes were largely based on the same pragmatic foundation. The lingering example of wartime governance of labour relations in *Privy Council Act 1003* (PC 1003) was clearly focused on the maintenance of industrial peace as a matter of policy. Though there was reference in some of these statutes to workers "rights" in relation to collective bargaining, the language of rights was muted.[3] The *Wagner Act* model provided a legal foundation for the exercise of rights to organize and associate, and for the use by employees of collective economic power in their dealings with employers, but the statutory scheme was also designed to regulate conflict and enhance productivity.[4]

Canadian collective bargaining legislation also shared with the *Wagner Act* roots in the new administrative state, and erected a system in which a key role would be played by labour relations boards consisting of neither judges nor public servants, but of persons with experience in the labour relations field. That hallmark of the administrative state, the administrative tribunal, was a particularly vital component of legislative collective bargaining regimes on both sides of the border, given the perceived hostility of the common law courts to "combination" by workers, and the conviction of worker representatives that the principles of freedom of contract developed in the courts had proved to be an instrument for worker subjugation.

In some respects, the courts saw these new administrative agencies as a threat to the values articulated through the common law. Through their power of judicial review, the courts of the 1940s attempted to place limits on the scope and impact of tribunal decisions. The creation of labour relations boards represented an acknowledgment of worker suspicion of the traditional role of the courts, and posed an explicit challenge to common law tenets concerning the sanctity of property and employer prerogative. The contest between courts and labour boards was a particularly fierce one.[5] This seems to have been more the case in Saskatchewan than elsewhere.[6]

This paper tells the story of one test faced by a Canadian collective bargaining statute, the Saskatchewan *Trade Union Act*, and by the Saskatchewan Labour Relations Board, the administrative agency responsible for administering that legislation. The 1947 decision of the Board in the case of *United Steelworkers of America v. John East Iron Works*[7] concerned the now entirely unremarkable question of compensation for lost wages for five employees whose dismissal was found to constitute an unfair labour practice. The responses of successive levels of court to the employer's application for judicial review, and the aftermath of those responses, provide insight into the early progress of the post-war Canadian administrative state, and into the relationship between courts and administrative tribunals, a relationship which has not always been harmonious.

Saskatchewan and the *Trade Union Act*

SASKATCHEWAN WAS THE FIRST province to pass post-war collective bargaining legislation patterned on the *Wagner Act*.[8] In many respects, this seemed to be a natural consequence of the spring 1944 landslide election of a social democratic Co-operative Commonwealth Federation (CCF) government led by T.C. Douglas. The CCF had roots in the labour movement and in organizations of social democratic intellectuals and activists like the League for Social Reconstruction; many associated with these groups saw the advent of a CCF government in Saskatchewan as a golden opportunity for putting in place a legislative scheme which would support the aspirations of labour.

Furthermore, the structural features of *Wagner Act*-type labour legislation made sense to a government which seized vigorously the ideas underlying a more technocratic form of public administration. New forms of political organization, a group of key advisors with specialized qualifications in various fields, mechanisms for economic and administrative planning, the creation of a non-partisan civil service — all of these were prominent features of the new government, and were reflected in an ambitious legislative program which saw 196 statutes enacted in the space of 500 days. This body of legislation was to be the framework for an entirely different approach to government, based on the idea that the levers of legislative — and particularly executive — authority could be used in an intentional and coherent way to bring about social and economic betterment for citizens still reeling from the effects of depression and war. Though there was a revolutionary streak in CCF thought, the emphasis was on competent and innovative government.[9]

Though the views and interests of workers had been a key consideration in the founding of the CCF, Saskatchewan was not a heavily industrial province, and the interests of agriculture had a much higher priority on the government agenda that those of labour. Douglas himself had famously visited strikers in the coalfields of southeast Saskatchewan in the days before the Estevan riot, but it seems likely that this was largely an expression of his commitment to the religious ideas of the "social gospel" and to the desperate conditions of coalminers' families, rather than a gesture of solidarity with labour. The premier also expressed on occasion some ambivalence about certain common features of collective bargaining legislation.[10]

Nonetheless, collective bargaining legislation was seen as an important initiative for a socialist government. A labour relations board to determine issues under PC 1003 was set up in May 1944, and a bill was introduced into the legislature on 7 November 1944, eight months after the CCF was first elected. Though Douglas denied that the bill had been "prepared in Toronto and fussed up a bit in Regina," the legislation was apparently drafted primarily by F. Andrew Brewin, a Toronto lawyer. Brewin, who was born in

England and sent to public school there, came to the democratic socialism of
the CCF through the outreach work of his father's Anglican parish in Toronto, and through the League for Social Reconstruction, which he described as
a "half-way house for 'middle class intellectuals' to join the movement."[11]

The legislation does not appear to have engendered extensive public debate, although the newspapers in Regina and Saskatoon — not notable supporters of the CCF government — did register a number of comments once
the bill had been alluded to in the Speech from the Throne. This commentary was woven around a number of themes which were or became familiar: the authoritarian tendencies of the new government; the risks posed to
farmers by the government's friendliness to labour; the unfairness of moving forward with new arrangements for labour without waiting for veterans
to return home; the origins of trade union legislation in CCF ambitions in
Ontario and Quebec; and the startling nature of the provision — no doubt
later much regretted by the government — which would permit the labour
relations board to assume trusteeship of enterprises which repeatedly failed
to comply with the *Trade Union Act*.[12]

For my purposes, however, the most interesting aspect of this discussion
was the concern expressed about the violence that would be done to legal
tradition by placing responsibility for administering the legislation in the
hands of an administrative agency, the labour relations board. The issue was
clearly joined over the extent to which government could confer quasi-judicial tasks on tribunals. The editors of Regina's *Leader-Post* said the following
about the prospective trade union legislation:

> This draft bill, according to intimations made earlier by the minister of labor,
> departs in several drastic respects from any labor legislation so far adopted
> in Canada. There are indications that it is planned to arm a government-
> appointed board with powers equivalent to those of a court, powers not only
> remedial but actually punitive and from whose orders there can be no appeal
> to the courts.[13]

In a later editorial, they continued in the same vein:

> Of the many objectionable features of the new Saskatchewan *Trade[s] Union
> Act*, the most objectionable and dangerous is that which confers upon the
> politically appointed board the powers of the courts and requires the courts
> to enforce the orders of the board without right of reviewing them or con-
> sidering the foundation for their issuance . . . There can be no resort to the
> courts for protection against injustice or oppression.[14]

The editors also noted:

> [This type of legislation] substitutes boards for courts as the authority to issue legal judgments and reduces the courts to the level of enforcement officers or policemen.[15]

The *Leader-Post* also printed a statement from the Saskatchewan Employers' Association, which observed that "[t]he bill outrages every principle of British justice," and complained that the board would not consist of "judges trained in sifting evidence and reaching judicial conclusions."[16]

Though there is no way of drawing a direct line from these sentiments to the views expressed by Saskatchewan judges when they were invited to examine the work of the Labour Relations Board, it is interesting that the concern that the Board would be trespassing on the authority of the courts, so prominent in what limited public debate there was on the legislation, should provide the courts with a rationale for overturning the Board's decision on review.

John East Iron Works at the Labour Relations Board

THE LABOUR RELATIONS BOARD appointed in 1945 consisted of seven members, including two representatives of employers, two representatives of unions, and two "public" representatives.[17] The chair was W.K. Bryden, an Ontario lawyer and CCF adherent who had been brought to Saskatchewan in September 1944 to assist with the development of labour legislation.[18]

The United Steelworkers of America applied to the Board in June, 1947, alleging that six employees — Harold Craigmile, Peter Troobitscoff, J.E. Boryski, Nick Troobitscoff, G.M. Svendsen, and T.J. Germaine — had been dismissed from their jobs at John East Iron Works for involvement in union activity, contrary to the *Trade Union Act*.[19]

John East Iron Works had been founded in 1910 by John East, who worked in a number of cities in Canada and the United States, and homesteaded briefly in Alberta before identifying Saskatoon as a promising place to set up his own foundry and machine shop venture.[20] By the 1940s, though John East remained involved in the business of John East Iron Works and its sister company Blanchard Foundry Ltd., primary management of the firm had passed into the hands of his son, Mel East.[21]

The Easts made no secret of their distaste for union organizing among their employees; in his testimony, Mel East said that "generally speaking" he would prefer not to have a union officer or active union member in his shop.[22]

The John East staff celebrating the thirtieth anniversary of the iron works
Photograph a795 courtesy Saskatoon Public Library—Local History Room

The Board found that since 1942, there had been efforts made by two different unions to organize this workplace and during that time, three union
presidents had been dismissed; the Easts, father and son, had addressed
employees on a number of occasions to persuade them not to support the
union; individual employees had been asked to sign requests (authored by
Mel East) to withdraw their support cards; and a number of employees had
resigned from negotiating committees on Mel East's advice. Mel East clearly
followed proceedings involving the Board closely; on one occasion he drew
his employees' attention to the fact that, after lengthy proceedings before the
Board and the courts, the employees of Acme Machine and Electric Company in Saskatoon had opted to rescind their support for their union and
deal directly with their employer.[23]

The dismissal of the six employees who were the subject of the application
before the Board occurred shortly after Mel East had presented employees
with an opportunity to withdraw their support from the Steelworkers union
by signing a "petition" and a "ballot"; this ballot, which the employees all
returned unsigned, indicated that in fact the majority of the employees continued to support the union. The dismissals also followed a further meeting
at which Mel East announced to employees his intention to mount a judicial
challenge to the union security provisions of the *Trade Union Act*.[24]

The Board concluded that the dismissals, seen against the pattern of conduct on the part of the Easts, were no coincidence and noted that—with the exception of Nick Troobitscoff, who seems to have been branded by his association with his son Peter—these employees had been active in the union.[25] The Board held that the employer had failed to displace the presumption that the dismissals were linked to the exercise by the employees of their rights under the Act, and ordered that they be reinstated with compensation for lost wages.

It is hard to imagine, from the Board's point of view, a situation more directly linked to the purposes of the *Trade Union Act* than one in which it was alleged that an employer had dismissed employees who were trying to avail themselves of their choice to support a union. It is also hard to imagine that the Board could carry out its statutory mandate effectively if its authority to address this situation were to be eliminated.

John East Iron Works in the Saskatchewan Court of Appeal

The employer applied to the Saskatchewan Court of Appeal for judicial review of the Board's orders,[26] which moved the dispute into an arena of quite a different kind. Where the Board assumed the legitimacy of the legislation, and saw its job as protecting the rights of employees to choose to support unions and participate in bargaining collectively with their employers, the preoccupation of the Court was with whether the legislation itself breached constitutional boundaries and trespassed on the sphere of authority dedicated to the superior courts. In these proceedings, unlike the hearing before the Board, the union was not a participant.

That both the *Trade Union Act* and the Board itself were targets was evident from the grounds cited for review: (1) that the Board erred in assuming that the only question for determination in fixing monetary loss was the amount of wages the employees would have earned had they remained employed; (2) that the chairman of the Board was disqualified by bias or a reasonable apprehension of bias from taking part in the case and that this taint extended to the other members of the Board; and (3) that the *Trade Union Act* was *ultra vires* insofar as it purported to (a) make orders of the Board enforceable as orders of the Court of King's Bench, and (b) allow the Board to make orders requiring reinstatement and fixing monetary loss under section 5(e).[27]

The Court of Appeal elected not to deal with the bias question or the question of whether the enforceability of Board orders as court orders rendered sections 9 and 10 of the *Trade Union Act ultra vires*,[28] but concentrated on the contention of John East counsel that "[s.] 5(e) is *ultra vires* because it is legislation conferring upon the Labour Relations Board judicial powers with respect to contracts of hiring and breaches thereof, powers which have always been exercised by the superior, district and county courts,"[29] whose members are appointed in accordance with section 96 of the *British North America Act 1867*, by the Governor in Council.[30]

Section 96 provides that the Governor General "shall appoint the judges of the Superior, District and County Courts in each Province," and thus on the face of it seems simply to clarify that the power to appoint these judges rests at the federal level — that is, it seems to carry the assignment of federal and provincial powers [31] into the judicial system. The courts, however, interpreted section 96 as more than a procedural provision; it was understood to provide constitutional protection to the scope of the jurisdiction of the superior courts as it existed in 1867.[32] The Judicial Committee of the Privy Council itself had concluded that a provincial commission considering expropriation could perform "ministerial" but not "judicial" functions.[33] The Committee saw the restrictions on the appointment of judges as safeguarding the independence of the judiciary.[34] The question of whether the new generation of administrative agencies was acting like "section 96 courts" was therefore a vital one, and certainly the centre of attention in the *John East Iron Works* case.

Chief Justice of Saskatchewan Martin followed the trail which conferred upon Saskatchewan superior courts the jurisdiction of English common law courts, and in particular identified the interpretation and enforcement of "contracts for hiring" as falling within this jurisdiction. The Court conceded that "The Labour Relations Board is primarily an administrative body and so far as it is an administrative body its constitution is within provincial powers . . ." The Court went on, however, to hold that the important question was whether the *Trade Union Act* purported to confer judicial power on the Board.[35]

Chief Justice Martin found assistance in the decision of the Supreme Court of Canada in *Reference re Adoption Act* in which Duff, C.J.C. described the implications of permitting a province to confer judicial powers on an administrative body: "That, in effect, would not be distinguishable from constituting a new court as, for example, a Superior Court, within the scope of section 96 and assuming power to appoint a judge of it."[36]

It is clear that in drawing this firm line between administrative and judicial functions, the Court of Appeal was not prepared to contemplate the notion — now trite — that "judicial" functions might legitimately be performed by decision makers who were not judges. This was not because this idea was not being articulated at the time. For example, in 1941 J.A. Corry had written of administrative tribunals:

> One of the most persistent criticisms of these boards in their work of apply-
> ing legislative standards to particular cases is that they are usurping judicial
> functions which should only be performed by the Courts under the safe-
> guards provided by judicial procedure and a tradition of judicial independ-
> ence and impartiality. In one sense, the function is judicial; in another sense,
> it is not. Any authority which decides questions affecting the rights of in-
> dividuals ought, under all circumstances, to act judicially in the sense of
> maintaining a fair and impartial attitude throughout the proceeding. But the
> function is not judicial in the sense that controversies are to be decided in ac-
> cordance with a pre-existing law which determines the decision.[37]

The Court of Appeal did not accept that the dismissals of the six John East employees might give rise to a completely different set of questions under the *Trade Union Act* than those dismissals would raise in the context of a common law action for wrongful dismissal, or that the remedial pow-ers given to the Board under the Act would be focused on the amelioration of a different harm — the impairment of the ability of John East employees to exercise their right to bargain collectively through a union — than that addressed by the common law remedy of reasonable notice. The finding of the Court that section 5(e) of the Act was *ultra vires* the province was thus founded in a refusal to differentiate between dismissal in the context of the law of master and servant, and dismissal in the context of unfair labour prac-tice provisions of collective bargaining legislation.[38]

The Court of Appeal did, however, regard the issues raised in the case as of "great general or public importance" and granted leave to the Labour Relations Board to appeal to the Judicial Committee of the Privy Council.[39]

John East Iron Works in the Privy Council

THE GROUNDS STATED FOR appeal by the Saskatchewan Labour Relations Board raised the issue of whether a modern administrative tribunal was barred from carrying out judicial functions. The Board argued that its substantive responsibilities under the *Trade Union Act* concerned labour relations, a mat-ter clearly under provincial jurisdiction. Any "judicial functions" performed by the Board were of a wholly different nature than those associated with courts, as they were not founded on the common law contract of employment, but on a complete new model for conducting the employment relationship.[40] E.C. Leslie, counsel for the respondent John East Iron Works, reiterated the grounds on which they had sought judicial review, including the grounds of bias and of error in assessing monetary loss.[41]

The Judicial Committee of the Privy Council was by this time in the twilight of its life as the court of last resort for Canada. A recent decision had upheld the view of the Supreme Court of Canada that Parliament had the authority to abolish appeals to the Privy Council in civil matters.[42] The new autonomy granted to the Dominion of Canada under the *Statute of Westminster* had led to increasing sentiment supporting the abolition of appeals to a "foreign" court, a court whose judges could not be expected to have a profound understanding of Canadian tradition or circumstance.[43]

The panel of judges who sat to hear the *John East Iron Works* case consisted of Lord Porter, a judge of long experience who came originally from Yorkshire; Lord Morton, a Scot who later chaired a well-known royal commission on marriage and divorce; Lord Oaksey, who had presided over the British judges at the Nuremberg trials; Lord MacDermott, shortly to be appointed as Lord Chief Justice of Northern Ireland;[44] and, of course, Lord Simonds, who wrote the Judicial Committee's judgment in the case. The character and orientation of Lord Simonds raise some interesting questions about how he came to write the decision he did.[45]

An influential member of the bench, Lord Simonds was described, along with Lord Reid and Lord Radcliffe, as one of the "triumvirate of legal giants whose shadow has loomed so large as to dominate the course of judicial business in the House of Lords."[46] He was renowned for his conservative approach to statutory interpretation, and for his characterization of the judicial task as "to consider what the law is, *not* what it ought to be."[47] In one of the decisions more or less overtly aimed at the expansive interpretive tendencies of Lord Denning, Lord Simonds observed, "to me heterodoxy, or, as some might say, heresy, is not the more attractive because it is dignified by the name of reform."[48]

A corollary of this acontextual approach to statutory interpretation was that it was not part of the judge's role to evaluate or modify the "policy" of elected legislatures; rather, the focus should be on giving effect to the "law" as stated in the statute. Notwithstanding his "conservative" view on many things, Lord Simonds understood that society was changing, and to the question whether the "Welfare State" is "essentially compatible with the freedom that we cherish," he gave the answer, "Let me say at once that I see here no fatal antinomy."[49] While still a practising barrister, he had been a member of the Committee on Ministers' Powers, the Donoughmore Committee, which had been struck to preempt the Diceyan thunderclap anticipated with the publication of Lord Chief Justice Hewart's book *The New Despotism.* Indeed, he had a "substantial share" in writing the report of that Committee. The work of the Committee entailed extensive consideration of the significance of categorizing powers as "judicial" or "quasi-judicial" and concluded that there was nothing constitutionally problematic about the assignment of judicial powers to tribunals.[50] Though Lord Simonds was much more widely noted for his stature as a judge and his subsequent spell as Lord Chancellor in Churchill's post-war government, it is possibly the Donoughmore Committee experience in analyzing the nature of judicial functions that had a more direct connection with his judgment in the *John East Iron Works* case.

The argument before the Judicial Committee with Lord Porter presiding took three days, with considerable interaction between the judges and counsel.[51] Counsel for the Board were Morris C. Shumiatcher, a native of Alberta who had been invited by Premier Douglas to join the Attorney General's department in Regina; and Andrew Brewin, the Toronto lawyer who had helped to draft the *Trade Union Act.* Brewin presented the major arguments, the essence of which was made clear in the following exchange:

LORD PORTER: I am afraid I was truncating mine too much. I was not trying to say judicial powers in general. Certain courts may be appointed with judicial powers, but it is superior courts['] judicial powers or county courts and the various courts mentioned.

MR. BREWIN: I think I may be in a good deal of trouble if I had to establish that no judicial powers could be conferred on a properly established board.

LORD OAKSEY: It would not be enough to say the actual judicial powers now conferred had been conferred at the time on superior courts. You would have to show the powers now conferred were not of the same character as powers which might have been conferred at the time.

MR. BREWIN: Yes. I think I might accept that proposition, although I say we get considerable help from the fact that they were not in fact conferred. I concede that there might be some judicial power created by some new legislation strictly similar to that exercised by superior courts and it may be that jurisdiction could only be conferred upon a court appointed by [s]ection 96.

LORD SIMONDS: This is going to come down to a nice question of what is similar or analogous.

MR. BREWIN: I think your Lordship has hit on the point and my contention of course will be that the power conferred here is neither similar nor analogous to any of the powers exercised by any of the named courts.[52]

In a further exchange Brewin elaborated on the significance to his argument of the characterization of the functions performed by the Board under section 5(e) as "judicial"; although he felt his argument would stand whether or not the functions were found to be judicial, the main thrust of his argument was that "whether or not judicial, they were not analogous or did not constitute this tribunal into a court."[53] He argued that these functions were "linked to something that is purely administrative by nature"—indeed, "the word 'reinstatement' itself provides a remedy which must include elements of policy, and is certainly not a judicial remedy."[54] At a later point, he emphasized, "[T]his statute looks at things not from the point of view of the individual rights of the employee but from the point of view of public policy, that certain industrial policies shall prevail."[55] He also observed:

> This particular power under [s]ection 5(e) is only one of a group of remedies designed to safeguard the general policy of protecting industrial peace within the province by encouraging collective bargaining. It does not stand out by itself. We find it allied to and associated with a number of other remedies which are of an administrative nature and clearly in my submission the purpose or point of view . . . is that in order that you may have this collective bargaining of the type contemplated by the Act you say that the employer shall not nullify that policy by threats of intimidation or discrimination against people active in the collective bargaining agency.[56]

Leaving aside the question of whether reinstatement was a remedy available to the common law courts under the law of contract,[57] Brewin pointed out that nearly every jurisdiction in Canada, including the federal government, had chosen to confide similar powers to a labour relations board rather than a court.[58]

Brewin attempted to create a picture of a new statutory regime for collective bargaining, one which rested on different premises and assumptions than those reflected in the law of master and servant.[59] He acknowledged that the powers exercised by the Board under section 5(e) could be described as judicial. This did not, in itself, mean that the Board was trespassing on turf occupied by the superior courts; the policy framework established by the *Trade Union Act* signalled a whole new direction for labour relations and laid out a scheme which was not derived from or dependent on common law understandings of the employment relationship.

Brewin's argument was supported by counsel for the intervening Attorneys General of Nova Scotia and Ontario. J.C. Currie, K.C., counsel for the Attorney General of Nova Scotia, agreed essentially with the way Brewin had put the argument, adding some historical detail pertinent to the issue.[60] C.R. Magone, K.C., counsel for the Attorney General of Ontario, devoted much of his argument to distinguishing between various kinds of courts and to exploring circumstances in which redefining the mandate of a judicial body would change its character.[61]

In his argument on behalf of John East Iron Works, E.C. Leslie, K.C., emphasized heavily the argument that had prevailed in the Court of Appeal — that any legislative consignment of judicial functions to an administrative tribunal was unconstitutional.[62] In an exchange with Lord Morton, Leslie agreed that counsel for the Board and supporting interveners had accepted that the functions exercised by the Board under section 5(e) were judicial functions.[63] The nub of his argument, however, was that the effect of section 96 was that judicial functions could not be assigned to administrative tribunals, at least to those established after 1867. The impact of the impugned legislative provisions was to "take away from the superior court a very vital and important part of the powers which a superior court has always exercised." In other words, he suggested that the Judicial Committee should not accept the argument that the authority of the Board rested on a completely new paradigm of labour relations.

When Lord Morton raised the question of whether the *Trade Union Act* could be viewed as creating an entirely new set of statutory conditions for the employment relationship, Leslie responded that "every time those conditions are imposed there still remains the contract of employment substratum upon which the jurisdiction of the court rests."

Following his argument on this point, Leslie was discouraged by the Committee from making submissions on the other grounds cited in the appeal documents, on the basis that the Saskatchewan Court of Appeal had not thought it necessary to determine those issues.[64]

The federal government might be taken to have some interest in creating administrative agencies with "judicial" functions as a vehicle of public policy. On this occasion, however, the government opted to defend an interpretation of section 96 that would prevent the exercise of such powers by anyone but judges. B.J. McKenna, counsel for the intervening Attorney General of Canada, reinforced the argument made by Leslie that judicial functions could not properly be conferred on a tribunal. He acknowledged that the *Trade Union Act* expressed provincial public policy with respect to collective bargaining, but said:

> [M]y submission is that if as one of the instruments for giving effect to that public policy the province interferes with the civil rights and creates new courts to determine those civil rights then the province may find itself in conflict with [s]ection 96 as much as it may in any other case.[65]

The arguments put by Leslie and McKenna rested on the premise that in essence the statutory provisions which had been the basis of the Labour Relations Board decision concerned the "dismissal" of "employees" who were party to "contracts of employment," and that the nature of the dispute could be aligned with disputes invoking the common law jurisdiction of section 96 courts. Though this argument did not deny that the Board could carry out administrative functions under statute, it did draw the line at permitting a tribunal to be given judicial powers.

One of the arguments made on behalf of John East Iron Works cited the privative clause in section 15 of the Act as an indicator that the Labour Relations Board was constructed like a court; this clause prevented appeal from the decisions of the Board or judicial review. In rebuttal, M.C. Shumiatcher, K.C., co-counsel for the Board, observed that some previous decisions of the Board had been reviewed by way of certiorari—the instant case being an example. Shumiatcher said there could be no objection to this, as in a confederation where legislative powers are divided, judicial review must always be available. Pressed about the wording of section 15—which apparently purported to bar access to the writ of certiorari—he described the privative provision as "largely redundant."[66] He went on to explain that it was his position that on jurisdictional issues, judicial review could never be foreclosed completely.[67]

This is, of course, a fairly orthodox principle of administrative law, but Shumiatcher's decision to make this concession in the closing moments of his argument presumably sprang from a wish to ensure that all aspects of the respondents' submission had been addressed. It did, however, form a weaker accompaniment to the argument originally put in by Brewin, which rested on the creation of a coherent statutory scheme for promoting and regulating collective bargaining, a scheme in which was manifest a legislative intention to have certain kinds of judicial functions carried out, not by judges, but by the Labour Relations Board. The privative clause might be viewed in this context as a sign that the regime under the *Trade Union Act* was intended to be self-contained and that responsibility for interpreting the Act should rest exclusively with the Board.[68] To equivocate about the wording of the statute or to suggest that this provision could be viewed as "redundant" seems to sap that argument.

In the judgment written by Lord Simonds, the Judicial Committee reversed the Saskatchewan Court of Appeal and concluded that the jurisdiction exercisable by the Board did not make it a court within section 96.[69] Notwithstanding the apparent agreement of the parties that the powers exercised by the Board were in some sense judicial, and their seeming willingness to stand or fall by whether that attribute made the Board a court, the Judicial Committee hedged on the question of what the definition of "judicial power" might entail, and whether the Board was in fact exercising such power. They accepted that the "broad features" of a definition were found in earlier cases, and noted that "any combination of such features will fail to establish judicial power if, as is a common characteristic of so-called administrative tribunals, the ultimate decision may be determined not merely by the application of legal principles to ascertained facts but by considerations of policy also."[70]

This reference to policy is tantalizing, as the proposition of which it is a part seems to be that a body whose decisions are influenced by policy considerations, no matter what judicial trappings it may possess, cannot be a court. Given what I have said earlier about Lord Simonds' insistence about excluding policy as a factor in statutory interpretation by judges, it stands to reason that he would view overt consideration of policy by a decision maker as an indication that the decision maker is not acting as a judge. The implication of this statement is that the Committee would have regarded this law/policy distinction by itself as an adequate basis for separating courts from non-courts.[71]

The Committee did not rely on this as the basis of their decision, however. Instead, they focused on the scope of section 96 through a historical lens and framed the issue as one of whether the jurisdiction of those courts in existence in 1867 extended to the questions asked of the Labour Relations Board under the *Trade Union Act* or to "analogous" questions. The Committee conceded that there might be certain points of resemblance between the

issues put forward for determination under the *Trade Union Act* and the principles of contract, but felt this distant cousinship was not determinative:

> It may be possible to describe an issue thus raised as a *lis* and to regard its de-
> termination as the exercise of judicial power. But it appears to their Lordships
> that such an issue is indeed remote from those which at the time of Confed-
> eration occupied the Superior, District or County Courts of Upper Canada.[72]

In any case, the Committee rejected the idea that the points of resemblance should be used to assimilate the framework of the *Trade Union Act*
to the principles of contract at common law. The work of the Board must be
seen in the context of a new legislative approach to the relationship between
an employee and an employer:

> The jurisdiction of the Board under s. 5(e) is not invoked by the employee for
> the enforcement of his contractual rights; those, whatever they may be, he
> can assert elsewhere. But his reinstatement, which the terms of his contract
> of employment might not by themselves justify, is the means by which labour
> practices regarded as unfair are frustrated and the policy of collective bar-
> gaining as a road to industrial peace is secured. It is in the light of this new
> conception of industrial relations that the question to be determined by the
> Board must be viewed, and, even if the issue so raised can be regarded as a
> justiciable one, it finds no analogy in those issues which were familiar to the
> Courts of 1867.[73]

The Committee was prepared to carry its speculation about the jurisdictional picture in 1867 even further. A murky question that was put forward
in argument—if they had been familiar with such a concept, would the
drafters of the *BNA Act* in 1867 have thought that the subject matter of section 5(e) fell within the traditional jurisdiction of the courts? — was taken up
in the decision:

> It is legitimate therefore to ask whether if trade unions had in 1867 been rec-
> ognized by the law, if collective bargaining had then been the accepted pos-
> tulate of industrial peace, if, in a word, the economic and social outlook had
> been the same in 1867 as it became in 1944, it would not have been expedient
> to establish just such a specialized tribunal . . . . It is as good a test as another
> of "analogy" to ask whether the subject-matter of the assumed justiciable
> issue makes it desirable that the Judges should have the same qualifications
> as those which distinguish the Judges of Superior or other courts. And it ap-

pears to their Lordships that to this question only one answer can be given. For wide experience has shown that although an independent President of the tribunal may in certain cases be advisable, it is essential that its other members should bring an experience and knowledge acquired extra-judicially to the solution of their problems.[74]

With respect to the privative clause, the Committee commented that the same rationale for setting up a tribunal in the first place may make it "inexpedient that the tribunal's decisions should be reviewed by an ordinary Court."[75]

It seems ironic that the cramped canons of interpretation favoured by Lord Simonds, along with a division between law and policy which we would now regard as unsustainable, should be the basis on which the Committee, in bold strokes, declared the distinctiveness of the organs of the administrative state and described not only their differences from courts, but the grounds for deference to them. The modern tribunal — charged with responsibility to advance legislative policy, characterized by expertise distinct from the qualifications of judges, making decisions in a framework unlike the common law — is portrayed here, and the Committee clearly accepted that, though the roles of courts and tribunals were different, this did not derogate from the importance and legitimacy of tribunals.

While in this case the decision of the Judicial Committee has largely been noted for these propositions concerning administrative decision making, it was also significant for its recognition that statutes protecting collective bargaining represented a new model for the employment relationship, a model which did not need to be aligned with common law contractual principles and values.

John East Iron Works **Back in the Court of Appeal**

THOUGH THE JUDICIAL COMMITTEE upheld the decision of the Board in *John East Iron Works* on constitutional grounds, they did not entertain argument about the other two bases for review advanced by John East: that the Board had erred in law in the calculation of monetary loss, and that the conduct of the chair had given rise to a reasonable apprehension of bias. The case was therefore remitted to the Saskatchewan Court of Appeal so that those issues could be addressed.

If those victorious in the Privy Council supposed that the expansive language of Lord Simonds would herald a new receptiveness in the Court of

Appeal to the idea of greater deference to the work of administrative tribunals, this hope would have been ended by the second decision of the Saskatchewan Court.[76]

In dealing with the issue of whether the Board had made a legal error in calculating the amount of monetary loss payable to the employees, the Court continued to base its fundamental approach to the question on the premise that the common law principles of contract provided the paradigm for evaluating the decision of the Labour Relations Board.[77] In the judgment written by Lord Simonds, the Judicial Committee had, as we have seen, commented that an employee coming before the Board was not asserting contractual rights, and said, "these, whatever they may be . . . can [be] assert[ed] elsewhere."[78] This observation must, of course, be seen in the context of a passage which largely rejected the utility of efforts to fit the familiar constructs of the common law into the new environment created by sweeping legislative schemes in specialized areas. In the hands of the Saskatchewan Court of Appeal, however, it gave an opening to use contractual analysis as the basis for overturning the decision of the Labour Relations Board — again.

The Court held that the Labour Relations Board had failed to adequately examine whether the employees had taken steps to mitigate their damages, a question which fell to the Board members as commissioners under the *Public Inquiries Act*.[79] For this reason alone, MacDonald J.A. concluded that the Board had committed a legal error which warranted quashing the decision. The Court went further, however, and examined the question of whether the Board had jurisdiction under the *Trade Union Act* to determine the amount of monetary loss which should be paid. The Act clearly said that the Board could order the employer to pay monetary loss, but did not explicitly say that the Board could determine the amount to be paid.[80] Since the Judicial Committee had suggested that an employee could assert contractual rights "elsewhere" than the Board, the Court stated:

> It seems to me that this means that while the Board may require an employer to pay the monetary loss suffered by a discharged employee, yet in order to fix, determine and recover the amount thereof, the employee must have recourse to the Courts. This construction is, to say the least, consistent with the view that, under s. 5(e) of the Act, the Board is not exercising a jurisdiction possessed, or analogous to that possessed by the Courts, and affords a reason why the provision in question should be held *intra vires*.[81]

The interpretation given by the Court to the Judicial Committee's comment that an employee before the Board was not asserting contractual rights seems, in fact, to turn the observation on its head. Read in context, the decision of the Judicial Committee suggests that common law contract considerations are entirely irrelevant to questions raised before the Board under the *Trade Union Act*. The Court of Appeal chose to pluck out a single phrase from the judgment as the basis for holding that determination of these questions in common law contract terms should continue to dominate.

The Court of Appeal may perhaps be forgiven for alluding to the continued existence of an individual employment contract, and raising questions about what this implies; after all, the terms on which this individual contract survived the advent of a collective bargaining relationship were not fully worked out by Canadian courts until *McGavin Toastmaster v. Ainscough*.[82] What impresses about this portion of the Court of Appeal judgment, however, is the strength of the commitment to an approach which would minimize the scope of the jurisdiction of the Board and safely return as many aspects of the case as possible into the fold of common law principle. This approach yet again, in the words of the Judicial Committee, "ignore[d] the wider aspects" and seemed oblivious to the Judicial Committee's description of the purpose and role of modern administrative tribunals.

This approach seems particularly well-illustrated by the final comments of MacDonald J.A. on an argument for review which the Court itself contributed — and on which they therefore made no ruling. In the final paragraphs of the decision, the Court pointed out that the *Trade Union Act* did not specifically remove the power of an employer to dismiss an employee, though it did allude to circumstances under which dismissal related to union activity might constitute an unfair labour practice. The Court suggested that an employer might still choose to dismiss an employee with notice; since cause is irrelevant to this form of termination of an employment contract, it would not be touched by a statutory provision addressing dismissal for a particular kind of motive.[83]

The Court also addressed the allegation that the conduct of the chair of the Board, W.K. Bryden, had given rise to a reasonable apprehension of bias. Although it was not necessary to come to a definitive conclusion given their finding on the other issue, the length of the commentary on this point is perhaps an affirmation of the Court's general wariness about the Board. The allegation was that Bryden, in the course of a hearing, had produced from his briefcase documents concerning John East Iron Works from the provincial corporation registry, and handed them to P.G. Makaroff, counsel for the union, who used them as evidence; Bryden's explanation was that he was simply delivering documents at the request of a lawyer in the Attorney General's office. The Court commented that if the proceedings were more trial-like than inquisitorial in nature — a question they did not answer — this conduct *would* create a reasonable apprehension of bias.[84]

The Board subsequently applied to the Court for leave to appeal this decision to the Supreme Court of Canada. The application was accompanied by an affidavit from counsel for the Board,[85] which cited statistics about the number of Saskatchewan workers represented by trade unions as a basis for claiming the issues raised by the case as being of "great public importance." In denying the application, Martin C.J.S. alluded to the following statement which had been given by the chair of the Board to the newspapers as a comment on the decision of the Judicial Committee:

> We have never had much doubt as to the constitutionality of the *Trade Union Act* and naturally we are pleased that the Privy Council has upheld our view. While two points in this case are being referred back to the Saskatchewan Court of Appeal these are of decidedly minor consequence and the essential point has been conclusively determined.[86]

The Court concluded that this statement did not square with the claim in the application that the issues were of "great public importance."

The Board made further application for leave to appeal directly to the Supreme Court of Canada. In a ruling issued on 24 June 1949,[87] that Court denied leave on the basis that the matter did not fall within the grounds of appeal set out in section 41(c) or (f) of the *Supreme Court Act*.[88]

Though one would not expect to find any extensive interpretive observations in a ruling of this kind, and though the *Supreme Court Act* defined the jurisdiction of the Court in quite narrow terms, it is still striking how unequipped the Court seems to have been to deal with an application emerging from an administrative tribunal working under a new kind of statutory scheme. It is particularly striking when one considers that the formulation of judicial review principles has become one of the major tasks of Canada's highest Court. At a time when the judges of the Judicial Committee of the Privy Council were clearly familiar with the contours of a post-war administrative state, the Supreme Court of Canada seemed less ready to embark on a consideration of the scope of activity of the new organs of legislative authority.

Afterword

THE DENIAL OF LEAVE to appeal brought the John East Iron Works saga to a close. As we have seen, the Saskatchewan Court of Appeal did not read in the Judicial Committee's decision a message that led them to make any accommodation of Labour Relations Board decisions.

In this context, it is instructive to look briefly at a subsequent instance where Saskatchewan courts were called upon to review a decision of the Labour Relations Board, a decision which also concerned the application of section 5(e) of the *Trade Union Act*.[89] The case concerned an allegation that several employees of a hospital run by a Catholic religious order had been dismissed for union activity. In the Court of King's Bench, Taylor J. expressed a number of criticisms of the proceedings before the Board, and it is not necessary to examine them all here.[90] Justice Taylor inveighed against the admission of evidence which would be inadmissible in court and against the reverse onus provision in section 8(1)(e) of the *Trade Union Act*.[91] He accepted the argument [92] that it was open to the hospital to dismiss employees with notice, and that this would not engage the prohibition in section 8(1)(e) against dismissing employees for their involvement in union activity. He concluded:

> The Board is partisan favouring labour, as it is constituted. It lacks the knowledge of fundamental principles and the practice that has been the foundation of British justice for centuries.[93]

On appeal, the Saskatchewan Court of Appeal used more temperate language in a decision which largely focused on the standing of the union representative who had signed the application.[94] However, the Court did state:

> On the other hand the *Trade Union Act* gives to the Labour Relations Board powers so extensive that rights usually regarded as fundamental in democratic states are severely curtailed, and in particular a citizen's right of access to the courts to protect himself from injustice or hardship, purport to be taken away. In such cases the Act must be construed strictly.[95]

In this and other cases, Saskatchewan courts in this period demonstrated a lack of understanding of the labour relations objectives underlying the *Trade Union Act*,[96] and an unwillingness to trust the decisions of an administrative tribunal.[97] Though gradually there was an acknowledgment that legislatures had placed certain kinds of questions within the jurisdiction of such tribunals and had charged them with some kinds of judicial functions,[98] the courts were wary about the possible derogation of this kind of decision making from traditional judicial values.

There is no doubt that in the long run, the judgment of the Judicial Committee in the *John East Iron Works* case helped to establish a framework of more respectful judicial review of the decisions of tribunals and communicated a strong message about the legitimacy of the administrative state, the specialized expertise of tribunals, and the appropriate boundaries of administrative and judicial roles.[99]

As we have seen, however, the message was not immediately clasped to the bosom of Saskatchewan courts. Downplaying the language in the Judicial Committee's decision that invited a more generous characterization of the place of administrative decision making in a modern state — and an acknowledgement of the possibility of a new paradigm for employment relationships — the Saskatchewan Court of Appeal, when this case returned for their consideration, reiterated a restrictive and untrusting view of tribunal adjudication. Though the Court on occasion showed some grasp of the distinctive roles of courts and tribunals,[100] when the arguments in *John East* concerning section 96 raised the issue of those respective roles in a direct way, the Court fell back on a narrow and defensive set of principles.

In a province where the construction of the administrative state was proceeding further and faster than elsewhere, this obduracy on the part of the Court of Appeal was a reminder of the legal obstacles to the full attainment of legislative goals. Those favouring the substitution of specialized labour board jurisprudence for common law principles may have been briefly heartened by the victory in the Privy Council in *John East Iron Works*, but this decision, whatever its long-term impact, did little in the short run to alter the direction of judicial review in Saskatchewan. Changes were ultimately brought about by other forces,[101] and the Saskatchewan Court of Appeal eventually articulated a posture of deference to administrative bodies, and in particular to the Saskatchewan Labour Relations Board, which was certainly equivalent to the deference shown by courts in other jurisdictions.[102] It is possible that the remarks of the Judicial Committee in *John East Iron Works* contributed in time to this shift, but there was seemingly no direct link. The *John East Iron Works* moment was important in the history of Canadian judicial review, but — in Saskatchewan at least — it soon elapsed and left little behind.

Notes

1   *National Labour Relations Act*, C. 372, 49 Stat. (1935) [*Wagner Act*].

2   In the run up to the passage of the *Wagner Act*, a dispute arose between proponents of the Act who favoured a rationale based on the "free labour" provisions of the US Constitution, and those who supported a narrower rationale based on the interstate commerce clause; see for example, James Gray Pope, "The Thirteenth Amendment Versus the Commerce Clause: Labor and the Shaping of American Constitutional Law, 1921–1957" (2002) 102 Colum. L. Rev. 1.

3   Saskatchewan *Trade Union Act*, S.S. 1944, c. 69, s. 3. Unless otherwise noted, references in this paper are to the 1944 version of the Act. Following the decision in *Toronto Electric Commissioners v. Snider*, [1925] 2 D.L.R. 5 (P.C.), labour relations was considered to fall under provincial jurisdiction. For a discussion of the tension between protection of workers' rights and the preservation of industrial order as themes in the political origins of collective bargaining legislation in Canada, see Alfred W.R. Carrothers, *Collective Bargaining Law in Canada* (Toronto: Butterworths, 1965) at 43–59.

4   There has been considerable research on how "institutionalized" or regulated collective bargaining channels worker dissatisfaction. See Alan Campbell, Nina Fishman, & John McIlroy, "The Post-War Compromise: Mapping Industrial Politics, 1945–64" and John Kelly, "Social Democracy and Anti-Communism: Allan Flanders and British Industrial Relations in the Early Post-War Period," both in Alan Campbell, Nina Fishman, & John McIlroy, eds., *British Trade Unions and Industrial Politics: The Post-War Compromise, 1945–64* (Aldershot: Ashgate, 1999) at 69–113 and 192–221, respectively.

5   See, for example, Bora Laskin, "Certiorari to Labour Boards: The Apparent Futility of Privative Clauses" (1952) 30 Can. Bar Rev. 986. See also R. Blake Brown, "'To Err is Human, to Forgive Divine': The Labour Relations Board and the Supreme Court of Nova Scotia, 1947–1965" in Philip Girard, Jim Phillips, & Barry Cahill, *The Supreme Court of Nova Scotia, 1754–2004: From Imperial Bastion to Provincial Oracle* (Toronto: University of Toronto Press for the Osgoode Society for Canadian Legal History, 2004) at 448.

6   Laskin, *ibid.* at 993, where he notes that half the cases identified in his research came from Saskatchewan.

7   *United Steelworkers of America, Local 3493 v. John East Iron Works Ltd.* (1945–54) 1 Decisions of the Saskatchewan Labour Relations Board and Court Cases Arising Therefrom 301 [*John East LRB*].

8   Similar legislation passed in Ontario in 1943 had been shelved to bring that province under the umbrella of the federal wartime legislation known as P.C. 1003; see *Ontario Collective Bargaining Act, 1943*, S.O. 1943, c. 4; *Wartime Labour Relations Regulations*, P.C. 1003.

9   Albert W. Johnson, *Dream No Little Dreams: A Biography of the Douglas Government of Saskatchewan, 1944–1961* (Toronto: University of Toronto Press, 2004) at 36–149.

10 The influence of the "social gospel" — the belief that a political program was an important manifestation of Christian religious belief — is, of course a study in itself, and the religious convictions of CCF supporters had a profound effect on the formulation of party and government policies; see Scott Pittendrigh, *The Religious Perspective of T.C. Douglas: Social Gospel Theology and Pragmatism* (M.A. Thesis, University of Regina, 1997) [unpublished]; see also John F. Brewin, *Francis Andrew Brewin: "He Who Would Valiant Be" — The Makings of a Canadian Anglican Christian Socialist* (M.T.S. Thesis, Vancouver School of Theology, 1999) [unpublished], for an interesting discussion of the religious influences on one of the major players in the history of the *Trade Union Act* and the *John East Iron Works* case. For a discussion of the labour policies of the CCF government under Douglas, see Thomas H. McLeod & Ian McLeod, *Tommy Douglas: The Road to Jerusalem* (Edmonton: Hurtig, 1987) at 156–74.

11 "Union Bill Approved after 5-Hour Debate," [Regina] *Leader-Post* (10 November 1944) 16; "Patterson Says 'Musts' in Speech," *Leader-Post* (24 October 1944) 2. The former Liberal Premier, William Patterson, now leader of the five-member opposition, returned often to the theme that the Saskatchewan government was being taken over by "carpet-baggers"; see Beth Bilson, "William J. Patterson, 1935–1944" in Gordon L. Barnhart, ed., *Saskatchewan Premiers of the Twentieth Century* (Regina: Canadian Plains Research Centre, 2004) at 153. See Brewin, above note 10 at 28, 62, and 70. Andrew Brewin practised law in the firm of a future Chief Justice of Ontario, James C. McRuer; see Patrick Boyer, *A Passion for Justice: The Legacy of James Chalmers McRuer* (Toronto: The Osgoode Society, 1994) at 81 and 164–65. In 1946 he was retained by the Douglas government to oppose the efforts of the federal government to deport Japanese-Canadians; see Carmela Patrias, "Socialists, Jews and the 1947 Saskatchewan Bill of Rights" (2006) 87 Can. Hist. Rev. 265 at 270.

12 "Responsibilities of Office," Editorial, *Leader-Post* (19 October 1944) 11; "Haste Makes Waste," Editorial, *Leader-Post* (21 October 1944) 11; "Labor Laws and the Armed Forces," Editorial, *Leader-Post* (31 October 1944) 9; "Contentious Trade Union Act Given First Reading in Provincial House," *Leader-Post* (7 November 1944) 1.

13 "Haste Makes Waste," *ibid.*

14 "The Attack on Justice," Editorial, *Leader-Post* (9 November 1944) 11.

15 *Ibid.* The Law Society of Saskatchewan also commented, in a letter from their Legislation Committee to the Minister of Labour, on the "ousting of the jurisdiction of the courts in matters pertaining to the rights and liberties of the subject;" see "Powers Protested by Law Society," *Leader-Post* (10 November 1944) 1 and 19.

16 "Employers Call Bill 'Class' Law," *Leader-Post* (7 November 1944) 1.

17 The public representatives were Marjorie Cooper, who had strong connections with community organizations such as the YWCA, and Elsie Hart, who was involved in the United Farmers of Canada. Cooper was later a CCF Member of the Legislative Assembly.

18 Interview with W.K. Bryden, Toronto, June 1995. Bryden was appointed Deputy Minister of Labour in March 1946, and was in that position at the time of the *John East Iron Works* decision. His double role suggests that neither governments nor courts were as sensitive as they have since become about the independence of tribu-

nals, and that this consideration was outweighed by the concern of the government that government policy be faithfully implemented.

19 The application was withdrawn as it concerned Mr. Germaine, who had left the province by the time the application was heard.

20 Eric Knowles, "A 'Boomer' Settled in Saskatoon and Built" *Western Business & Industry* (January 1946) Cuttings Files J-KIL, Local History Room, Saskatoon Public Library; Alan L. Morton, "John East — Saskatoon's Foundry Pioneer!" *Optimistic View* (December 2007) Cuttings Files J-KIL, Local History Room, Saskatoon Public Library. Both of these items can be found in the collection of the Local History Room of the Saskatoon Public Library. They both state that John East made his final decision after noticing that there was not a local foundry making manhole covers and no company had secured a commitment from the City of Saskatoon for a contract to make them.

21 Two of John East's brothers, Bus and Frank, as well as Mel's sons, Bill and Jack, were involved in the management of the company over the period before the business was sold in 1975.

22 *John East LRB*, above note 7 at 302.

23 *Ibid.* at 304.

24 *Ibid.* at 306.

25 *Ibid.* at 308.

26 The decision of the Court of Appeal was written by Martin, C.J.S., himself a former Liberal premier of the province; see Ted Regehr, "William Martin, 1916–1922," in Barnhart, above note 11 at 39. Two other members of the Court, H.Y. MacDonald and P.H. Gordon, had practised law in the same Regina law firm, established by Gordon's brother A.L. Gordon; the father of these Gordon brothers had also been a Regina lawyer. See W. Howard McConnell, *Prairie Justice* (Calgary: Burroughs, 1980). John East Iron Works Ltd. was represented by E.C. Leslie, K.C., and the Saskatchewan Labour Relations Board by Morris C. Shumiatcher, both of whom would appear before the Judicial Committee of the Privy Council. The Attorney General of Saskatchewan was represented by Peter G. Makaroff, Canada's first Doukhobor lawyer, who had represented the United Steelworkers of America before the Labour Relations Board. Mr. Makaroff succeeded W.K. Bryden as chair of the Labour Relations Board.

27 *John East Iron Works Ltd. v. Local 3493, United Steelworkers of America*, [1948] 1 W.W.R. 81 (Sask. C.A.) [*John East CA*]. For a discussion of the general orientation of the Court of Appeal to review of decisions of the Saskatchewan Labour Relations Board, see Gene Anne Smith, "Judicial Review of Saskatchewan Labour Relations Board Proceedings" (1974–75) 39 Sask. L. Rev. 1; Smith (now herself a justice of the Court of Appeal) traces the beginning of a more open attitude to Board decisions to the appointment of Culliton J.A. in 1951.

28 *John East CA, ibid.* at 95.

29 *Ibid.* at 85.

30 *British North America Act, 1867*, 30 & 31 Vict., c. 3 (U.K.).

31 Sections 91 and 92 of this Act represent the most comprehensive example of this allocation of authority to provincial and federal levels of government.

32 It is interesting to note that M.C. Shumiatcher, one of the counsel for the Labour Relations Board in *John East Iron Works*, contributed to the academic analysis of this issue in Morris C. Shumiatcher, "Section 96 of the *British North America Act*" (1940) 18 Can. Bar Rev. 517.

33 *O. Martineau and Sons Ltd. v. Montreal City*, [1932] A.C. 113.

34 *Toronto Corporation v. York Corporation*, [1938] A.C. 415.

35 *John East CA*, above note 27 at 86–88.

36 [1938] S.C.R. 398 at 414.

37 J.A. Corry, "The Genesis and Nature of Boards," in John Willis, ed. *Canadian Boards at Work* (Toronto: MacMillan, 1941) at xxxv. Earlier in this piece, Corry recounted the reasons underlying a general loss of faith in *laissez-faire* as a basis for resolving social problems, and the adoption, instead, of a "collectivist ideal." The instruments for advancing this ideal, including administrative tribunals, needed room to make their expert decisions on how government policies should be pursued. Comparing these bodies to generals combating external enemies, Corry saw limited scope for judicial review, observing at xxi:

> Because Parliament cannot lay down any detailed rules in advance, the Courts are deprived of any fixed standard against which to measure the conduct of officials and lacking these, the degree of control which they can exercise without substituting their lay judgment for the expert judgment of general staff is subject to narrow limits. Vigorous action is wanted and not merely restraints upon action.

Corry was not arguing that there was no function for the courts in reviewing the decisions of administrative bodies, but he did not think the relevant division of labour began at the boundary between administrative and judicial functions.

38 A point which was made in an editorial note at the beginning of the reported version of *John East CA*, above note 27.

39 [1948] 1 D.L.R. 771 (Sask. C.A.).

40 *Labour Relations Board of Saskatchewan v. John East Iron Works Ltd.*, "Case for the Appellant, the Labour Relations Board of Saskatchewan," Regina, Saskatchewan Archives Board (Morris C. Shumiatcher fonds, R-1728, File not. 12.2.6) at 8. The intervenant Attorney General of Ontario took a slightly different tack, arguing that the Saskatchewan Labour Relations Board did not in fact perform any judicial functions; see "Case for the Attorney-General of Ontario" in *ibid.* at 3.

41 "Case for the Respondent," in *ibid.* at 6.

42 *Attorney-General of Ontario v. Attorney-General of Canada*, [1947] 1 All E.R. 137 (P.C.). The issue of the power of Parliament to abolish criminal appeals had been determined in *British Coal Corporation v. The King*, [1935] A.C. 484; see H.H. Marshall, "The Judicial Committee of the Privy Council: A Waning Jurisdiction" (1964) I.C.L.Q. 697 at 699–702. See also *Reference re Privy Council Appeals*, [1940] S.C.R. 49, 1 D.L.R. 289; "Decline of the Judicial Committee of the Privy Council — Current Status of Appeals from the British Dominions" (1947) 60 Harv L. Rev. 1138.

43 22 & 23 Geo. V., c. 4, 11 December 1931. For an assessment of the role of the Judicial Committee in Canadian constitutional affairs, see for example, Alan C. Cairns, "The Judicial Committee and its Critics" (1971) 4 Can. J.Pol. Sci. 301. An important theme of the criticism of the Judicial Committee's decisions had to do with the apparent adherence of the Law Lords to an interpretation of the *British North America Act, 1867* favouring a highly-centralized Canada. Their decision in *John East Iron Works* would seem anomalous in this respect, though clearly the focus on s. 96 presented issues of federalism in a slightly different way.

44 H.G. Hanbury, "Porter, Samuel Lowry," in *Oxford Dictionary of National Biography* (Oxford: Oxford University Press, 2004–08) [DNB]; Denys B. Buckley, "Morton, Fergus Dunlop," in DNB, *ibid.*; R.F.V. Heuston, "Lawrence, Geoffrey," in DNB, *ibid.*; Lowry, "MacDermott, John Clarke," in DNB, *ibid.*

45 [1948] 4 D.L.R. 673 (P.C.) [*John East PC*]. Prior to the 1960s, it was the custom of the Judicial Committee to provide a single decision, without dissent.

46 Louis Blom-Cooper & Gavin Drewry, *Final Appeal: A Study of the House of Lords in its Judicial Capacity* (New York: Oxford University Press, 1972) at 156.

47 *Jacobs v. London County Council*, [1950] A.C. 361 (H.L.) at 373.

48 *Scruttons Ltd. v. Midland Silicones Ltd.*, [1962] A.C. 446 (H.L.) at 447. See Robert Stevens, *Law and Politics: The House of Lords as a Judicial Body, 1800–1976* (London: Weidenfeld and Nicholson, 1979) at 341–54 for a discussion of the role of Lord Simonds in the House of Lords and as Lord Chancellor.

49 Lord Simonds, "'Liberty Within the Law:' The Lord High Chancellor's Address" (1953) 39 A.B.A. J. 1059 at 1115. He continued,

> The radical changes which have taken place in our social structure have necessarily meant the imposition of restrictions upon the ownership of property and the freedom of contract, but there is nothing new or revolutionary in this.

50 G.R. Rubin, "Simonds, Gavin Turnbull," in DNB, above note 44; Lord Hewart, *The New Despotism* (London: Ernest Benn, 1929). Lord Hewart had his Canadian supporters; see J.J. Fraser Winslow, "Bureaucracy" (1930) 4 Can. Bar Rev. 278. For the link between the publication of the Hewart book and the appointment of a committee to consider the constitutional consequences of delegating legislative and judicial functions to the executive, see W. Ivor Jennings, "The Report on Ministers' Powers" (1932) 10 Public Administration 333 at 333–34; John Willis, *The Parliamentary Powers of English Government Departments* (Cambridge: Harvard University Press, 1933) at 174. See also William A. Robson, "The Report of the Committee on Ministers' Powers" (1932) 3 Political Quarterly 346 at 347, where the author asserts that Dicey (and Hewart) fundamentally misunderstood the centrality of administrative institutions to the British constitutional structure. He went on to say (at 349) that the ubiquity of Diceyan thought had prevented the "upper middle-class, Forsytic and conservative legal mind" from appreciating that the activities of the executive were not only "essential to the well-being of the great mass of the people, but also the most significant expressions of democracy in our time." If this description of the "legal mind"

is accurate, Lord Simonds' grasp of a broader role for government activity comes to appear more radical.

51 *The Labour Relations Board of Saskatchewan v. John East Iron Works Ltd.*, transcript of proceedings in the Privy Council, Regina, Saskatchewan Archives Board (Morris C. Shumiatcher fonds, R-1728, File No. 12.2.4) [Transcript].

52 "First Day" at 3–4 in *ibid*.

53 *Ibid.* at 18.

54 *Ibid.* at 19.

55 *Ibid.* at 24; see also *ibid.* at 28.

56 *Ibid.* at 12.

57 "Second Day" in Transcript, above note 51 at 5.

58 *Ibid.* at 9–10. Brewin here also argued that there is no reason to suppose that had this kind of subject matter occurred to the drafters of the 1867 Act, they would not have considered it appropriate to confer decision-making power upon a tribunal.

59 The Supreme Court of Canada ultimately threw itself behind this conceptual description of collective bargaining legislation in decisions like *McGavin Toastmaster v. Ainscough*, [1976] 1 S.C.R. 718; and *St. Anne Nackawic Pulp & Paper Co. Ltd. v. Canadian Paper Workers Union, Local 219*, [1986] 1 S.C.R. 704.

60 "Second Day" in Transcript, above note 51 at 30–38. Currie said at 31:

> We say further that not only did s. 96 not lay down any new principle, but also that it was enacted against a background of legislative custom and practice whereby particular purposes were served by conferring powers in whole or in part on bodies or persons not within s. 96.

61 *Ibid.* at 19–29.

62 Leslie, a native of Nova Scotia, attended law school in Saskatchewan, drawn to the dry climate as relief for pulmonary ailments resulting from exposure to gas during World War I. He was a member of one of Saskatchewan's historic law firms, now called MacPherson Leslie Tyerman. See McConnell, above note 26 at 91–94.

63 "Second Day" in Transcript above note 51 at 48. Lord Morton tartly commented "It does not follow that you win because of that."

64 "Third Day" in Transcript, *ibid.* at 5, 11, 13, and 16.

65 *Ibid.* at 21.

66 *Ibid.* at 37–38.

67 *Ibid.* at 39.

68 The courts have been quite firm about the idea that judicial review can never be excluded altogether; see for example, *Crévier v. Quebec (Attorney General)*, [1981] 2 S.C.R. 220. However, the relative strength in the wording of such clauses has become an important indicator of the degree of deference which a reviewing court should accord to a tribunal; see *Dunsmuir v. New Brunswick*, 2008 SCC 9, [2008] S.C.J. No. 9.

69 *John East PC*, above note 45 at 683.

70 *Ibid.* at 680.

71 An unworkable test, no doubt, as subsequent generations of judges engaged in statutory interpretation have found it increasingly difficult to ignore policy altogether.

The evolution of the concept of "reasonable notice" in the law of the employment contract is itself an illustration of how difficult it is for judges to disentangle "law" from "policy"; see, for example, *Wallace v. United Grain Growers*, [1997] 3 S.C.R. 701.

72 *John East PC*, above note 45 at 681.

73 *Ibid.* The Committee did not consider it necessary to make specific comparisons with the functions in 1867 of justices of the peace; see *ibid.* at 683.

74 *Ibid.* at 682.

75 *Ibid.* at 683.

76 That expansive language — rather than the sequel (or *sequelae*) in the Court of Appeal — is what the *John East Iron Works* case is largely remembered for outside Saskatchewan.

77 *John East Iron Works Ltd. v. Labour Relations Board of Saskatchewan*, [1949] 3 D.L.R. 51 (Sask. C.A.) [*John East CA2*].

78 *John East PC*, above note 45 at 681.

79 *Trade Union Act*, above note 3 at s. 14.

80 This omission was remedied in subsequent version of the Act; see *An Act to Amend the Trade Union Act*, S.S. 1950, c. 92, s. 3(2) (Board given express authority to "fix and determine the monetary loss").

81 *John East CA2*, above note 77 at 61.

82 Above note 59.

83 *John East CA2*, above note 77 at 63–64.

84 For a recent discussion of the institutional independence of the Board, see *Saskatchewan Federation of Labour v. Saskatchewan (Attorney General, Department of Advanced Education, Employment and Labour)*, 2009 SKQB 20, (2009), 323 Sask. R. 115 (Q.B.).

85 *Labour Relations Board of Saskatchewan v. John East Iron Works Ltd. and Local 3493 United Steelworkers of America*, [1949] 3 D.L.R. 488 (Sask. C.A.) at 491 [*John East CA3*]. The affidavit in part contested certain findings of the Court in *John East CA2* about the factors considered by the Board in assessing monetary loss; the Court reiterated these findings.

86 *Ibid.*

87 *Saskatchewan (Labour Relations Board) v. John East Iron Works Ltd.*, [1949] S.C.R. 677 [*John East SCC*].

88 *Supreme Court Act*, R.S.C. 1927, c. 35, ss. 41(c) and 41(f), which listed as grounds on which leave might be granted:

> c) the taking of any annual rent, customary or other fee, or, other matters by which rights in future of the parties may be affected; or
>
> . . .
>
> f) in cases which originated in a court of which the judges are appointed by the Governor General and in which the amount or value of the matter in controversy in the appeal will exceed the amount of one thousand dollars.

The Supreme Court interpreted these sections to mean that the Board itself, as the party bringing the appeal, would have to show an economic interest.

89 *Textile Workers' Union of America v. Sisters of Charity Providence Hospital*, January 12, 1950 (1945–54) 1 Decisions of the Saskatchewan Labour Relations Board and Court Cases Arising Therefrom 412.

90 The Court was of the view, for example, that the Board had not sufficiently considered that hospitals of this kind were an expression of benevolence founded on religious belief; see *Sisters of Charity, Providence Hospital v. Labour Relations Board (Sask.)*, [1951] 1 D.L.R. 502 (Sask. K.B.) at 503–4 [*Providence Hospital KB*]. The comments of Taylor J. were reported extensively in "Judge Makes Blistering Attack on Labor Board" *Leader-Post* (9 November 1950). In an editorial commenting on the response of Labour Relations Board chair Peter Makaroff to the judgment, the *Leader-Post* said that, though some of the Board's decisions had no doubt been "fair and wise," to the extent that it was biased in favour of a particular class, "it has been an undemocratic, even dictatorial operation . . . the class-biased nature of its administration clearly has been heightened by the board's own conception of what it calls 'the main object and intention of the act'"; see "An 'Intolerable Situation,'" *Leader-Post* (25 November 1950) 11.

91 *Providence Hospital KB*, ibid. at 505.

92 Drawn apparently from the ruminations of MacDonald J. in *John East CA2*, above note 77 at 63–64.

93 *Providence Hospital KB*, above note 90 at 511.

94 *Sisters of Charity, Providence Hospital v. Labour Relations Board*, [1951] 3 D.L.R. 735 (Sask. C.A.) [*Providence Hospital CA*].

95 *Ibid.* at 745.

96 In *F.W. Woolworth Co. Ltd. v. Labour Relations Board* (1954), 13 W.W.R. (N.S.) 1 (Sask. C.A.), Gordon J.A. asked at 17:

> Am I to banish from my consideration the facts which are notorious, such as the difficulty of getting help in towns and small cities of the province and the rapid turnover of such help? Why should girls, who are only taking a position for a few months, be forced to join a union at all? The duty of explaining this fact to new untrained help is on the employer. One of the orders made against this employer for "unfair labour practices" we are told was its failure to discharge an employee who would not join the union.

97 See, for example, *Capital Cabs Ltd. v. Canadian Brotherhood of Railway Employees and Other Transport Workers*, [1949] 2 W.W.R. 481 (Sask. K.B.).

98 See, for example, *Bruton v. Regina City Policemen's Association, Local No. 155*, [1945] 2 W.W.R. 273 (Sask. C.A.); for an example of a similar view on the Supreme Court of Canada see *Labour Relations Board of Saskatchewan v. Dominion Fire Brick & Clay Products* (1947), 3 D.L.R. 1 (S.C.C.).

99 In *Yeomans v. Sobeys Stores Ltd.*, [1989] 1 S.C.R. 238, an unsuccessful challenge to the statutory authority of a labour standards tribunal in Nova Scotia was based on a s. 96 argument similar to that advanced on behalf of John East; see also *Canadian Imperial Bank of Commerce v. Rifou*, [1986] 3 F.C. 486 (F.C.A.).

100 See some of the comments in the dissenting judgment of Martin C.J.S. in *Bruton*, above note 98 at 284.
101 Such as changes in the membership of the Court; see Smith, above note 27.
102 See *Saskatchewan Joint Board Retail, Wholesale and Department Store Union v. Dairy Producers Cooperative Ltd.* (1990), 74 D.L.R. (4th) 694 (Sask. C.A.).

PART TWO

Responsible Unions: Security, Orderly Production, and Dissent

How Justice Rand Devised His Famous Formula

William Kaplan

The Ford Strike

AT TEN IN THE morning on 12 September 1945, the 10,000 workers at the Ford plant in Windsor, Ontario walked out, bringing the assembly line to a halt. The timing, just weeks after Japan's surrender, was not unexpected. During World War II, organized labour had won the right to collectively bargain and union membership had soared. In the giant automobile plants and the smaller feeder factories, employees knew that there would be a period of adjustment, a slowdown as the industry retooled to meet the demands of a peacetime market. They also expected, with war's end, that the federal government would vacate the labour relations field, leaving the regulation of most industrial activity to the provinces. What, then, would become of all the hard-won wartime labour gains? Having helped to win the war, organized labour was determined to win the peace.

Since November 1941, the workers at Ford, Windsor's largest employer, had been represented by a big and powerful trade union, the International Union of United Automobile, Aircraft and Agricultural Implement Workers of America (the UAW). Earlier that year, the UAW had taken on the world's biggest automobile plant — Ford's Rouge Plant in Dearborn, Michigan — and won two key demands: the union shop (everyone had to join the union as a condition of employment) and the union check-off (management deducted union dues from the wages of every employee and forwarded them to the union).[1] This was exactly what the UAW wanted to achieve at the Ford plant in Windsor. During the war, Ford's Windsor operations had been hit by walkouts three times — but the federal government had declared the plant an "essential service," so these disruptions were illegal.

Tensions simmered on the assembly line, as negotiations began early in 1945 for a new collective agreement geared to peacetime. Ford offered improvements to the grievance procedure and "fair" rules for determining the seniority of "employee-veterans." Everything else was to remain status quo "because the present collective agreement has worked out fairly well."[2] The UAW rejected management's offer: it was time for catch-up. Their counter-proposal was a comprehensive package for a new and improved collective agreement. As the stalemate continued, the National War Labour Board and the Department of Labour made several attempts to mediate through conciliation boards and an industrial disputes commission, all to no avail. Meanwhile, more than 3,000 Ford Canada workers had already received layoff notices. "We will take action," promised Roy England, the president of Local 200 at Ford Canada.[3]

Ford of Canada was not alone in facing labour unrest. In the United States, Ford had laid off more than 50,000 employees, and the number was growing because of disputes at automotive parts suppliers. Henry Ford II knew who to blame: Communists, he claimed, were deliberately impeding the progress of reconversion. Communists were a convenient target, and indeed, in the 1940s, domestic Communists were a force to be reckoned with. Many Communists were extremely active in the labour movement, especially in the leadership of the Windsor UAW and its Ford local.[4] Canadian UAW director George Burt was "soft" on party members. He claimed that "[m]ost people didn't know communism from rheumatism," but Burt knew the difference.[5]

A Toronto native, born in 1903, Burt started work in General Motor's body shop in Oshawa, where he quickly gravitated toward union politics. He helped organize Local 222, participated in the famous 1937 strike, and was the local's first treasurer. In 1939, Burt threw his hat into the election ring for Canadian Regional Director, the top position in the UAW in Canada. His opponent was none other then Charlie Millard, the incumbent and one of Canada's most powerful union officials. Backed by Communists, Canadian nationalists, militant trade unionists, and left-wing social democrats, Burt beat Millard. Burt did not forget his friends and how they had helped in his rise to power. While not a Communist himself, he followed the communist philosophy in much of his dealings, except when it threatened his personal and professional survival, in which cases he pragmatically backed off.[6]

While Burt was sympathetic to communist goals, the executive of Local 200 was under Communist control, and Roy England was a secret party member.[7] These connections greatly muddied the waters, and it was often unclear whose interests Communist union members put first — those of organized labour or of Moscow. On the one hand, what better way to renew the class struggle than to take 10,000 men and women out on strike and precipitate a crisis in capitalism? On the other, the UAW and its members were well within their rights to withdraw their labour from Ford in pursuit of legitimate collective bargaining demands. Most UAW members were not Communists. They did, however, want to preserve wartime gains. And, after many months of unsuccessful negotiations and a democratic election, the union and its members decided to pull the plug. When the whistle blew to signal the mid-morning break on 12 September, they walked out.

Reverberations were quickly felt. Ford's union payroll was huge, and the 10,000 striking auto workers were, on the second day of the strike, joined by 1,200 more Ford employees: office workers who belonged to a different UAW local, but who were prevented by the picketers from going to work. While not required to do so, Ford continued to pay the office workers during the dispute. The strikers were a different matter, however, and the UAW established a soup kitchen for those who presented an up-to-date union card and had served on the picket line. Only about 8,000 strikers could even ask for union assistance, as it was for members only. There was no strike pay, only grocery vouchers. And there was nothing for the thousands of workers sent home when Ford feeder plants began to close down days after the strike began.

Most of the action and excitement was at the enormous Ford plant, located on the banks of the Detroit River. Pickets were established at all sixteen gates — 1,000 men assigned to duty at all times. When company president Wallace Campbell arrived at work on day two of the strike, he was not allowed in. He immediately settled into a suite at the Prince Edward Hotel, the city's finest hotel. He also called on the police and its chief constable, Claude Renaud, to enforce the law. The law was clear — picketers are not entitled to prevent non-striking employees from crossing the line. Renaud, however, instructed his officers to keep their hands off — a sentiment echoed by Mayor Art Reaume.[8] Union towns are often like that.

On 7 October, the union made its next move. Ford generated its own electricity, but the more than 100 union men who maintained the power plant walked out. The lights went dark, the heat was turned off, and the water stopped running. In previous strikes, a skeleton powerhouse crew had been kept in place. Now, once the strike was settled, it would take weeks to fully restore services, extending the time spent without work — and wages. In the meantime, there was a real risk of the hundreds of miles of water pipes freezing in the event of a cold snap. Untended machinery would seize and rust, and might, eventually, have to be junked. The source of everyone's livelihood was at risk. And what would happen if there was a fire?

The strike was often discussed in the House of Commons. During the war, the government had, in the midst of intractable labour disputes, sent in controllers to run industries and plants, justifiably sacrificing property rights to the national interest. But the government had no intention of taking that step now. So long as a negotiated solution was being sought, a lighter touch was in order, and Labour Minister Humphrey Mitchell set out to get the parties together. Before Ford would talk, however, Campbell insisted that the lawbreakers blocking entrance to the plant leave and allow powerhouse operations to resume. Moreover, he made clear, unless it became law, Ford would never force anyone to join a union as a condition of employment.

At the end of October, Mitchell presented a four-point plan: dismantle the pickets and reopen the powerhouse, call the men back to work in order of seniority, send the non-monetary issues to an arbitrator, and let the National War Labour Board set the wage rate. Ford rejected the proposal, angered by the union's latest move: non-union watchmen were no longer allowed to cross the line. The physical plant was huge and needed to be patrolled, strike or no strike. The company was enraged. It became even more intransigent and decided to go on the offensive.

Calling on Chief Constable Renaud, Campbell demanded immediate action. Initially, Renaud vacillated, but on 2 November he tried to lead a contingent of officers across the picket line, opening the way for security guards and office employees to return to work. But the strikers had been tipped off, and they were ready for the "flying wedge." Renaud and his officers were pushed across the street to the tune of catcalls and loud boos.[9]

For the strikers, it was terrific fun, and morale was high. The carnival atmosphere got even better the next day with the arrival of a brass band and groups of young women to join in the street dancing. England promised the men that any further outside interference would be met with a city-wide strike, as he led them in singing "Solidarity Forever." Mayor Reaume also arrived to show his support. From the union's point of view, the company had been dealt a major blow. This meant that the timing was right to escalate matters further. There was another large UAW local in Windsor, Local 195, composed of UAW members working at more than thirty Windsor-area automotive industries led by Alex Parent, the MPP for Essex North, and a well-known Communist anxiously awaiting an opportunity to lead the class struggle.[10] None of these employees had any dispute with their employers, but Parent, in solidarity with England and Local 200, decided to take 8,000 more men and women out on strike. Parent was not acting alone. As Burt later explained, "I closed all the plants then in Local 195 . . . I closed them down and broke their contracts. To hell with it."[11]

All this activity played right into Ford's hands. With the agreement of Ontario premier George Drew and acting Prime Minister J.L. Ilsley, hundreds of Ontario Provincial Police (OPP) and Royal Canadian Mounted Police (RCMP) officers began arriving in town. An army unit in nearby Chatham was placed on standby.[12] Attorney General Leslie Blackwell declared that the people of Windsor were at risk in this "state of emergency."[13]

The arrival of massive police reinforcements should have been sobering, but the union decided instead to provoke a major confrontation. On 5 November, UAW members, along with some of their friends (widely believed to have been imported from Detroit especially for this purpose), stole approximately 1,000 cars and buses from the streets of Windsor, beating uncooperative drivers with lengths of rubber hose. They then abandoned the vehicles around the perimeter of the Ford plant, completely blocking all sidewalks and streets. It was a defensive action, some unionists claimed, in anticipation of a police attack. The union was demanding its rights, but what about the rights of others? Union president England expressed regret that private vehicles were caught up in the melee. He was, he added, "extremely sorry."[14]

Clearly, the parties were at an impasse, so Mitchell decided to take another crack at breaking the log-jam. From his suite at the Prince Edward Hotel, he called Henry Ford II across the river and invited him over for a chat. Ford arrived that night and explained to the minister that he had no control over Ford of Canada. He also told Mitchell that nothing would change until the blockade was removed and the union allowed the powerhouse to be reopened and the non-striking employees to return to work. It was a matter of "safety and sanity."

Ford's claim that the Canadian branch plant was run independently was nonsense. The company bore considerable responsibility for the dispute. Its

Ford, UAW, 1945 Strike, Windsor, Ontario
Walter Reuther Library, Wayne State University

delay tactics were notorious, and refusing to yield in Canada on a matter already settled in the United States was bad business and bad labour relations. Still, coming to Windsor had been a sage move for the experienced Mitchell. As he told reporters, "I never give up in labour disputes."[15] Within days, he persuaded the union leaders to dismantle the barricade in return for an understanding that the government would encourage Ford to resume negotiations and, should the negotiations fail, to proceed to arbitration on any outstanding issues.[16] Mitchell's quiet diplomacy provided the parties with an opening, allowing them to step back and avert a major showdown. As Burt now belatedly realized, if the union did not return the cars to their owners, the troops would be called in and the future existence of the union threatened.[17] The need for a settlement was urgent.

On Mitchell's urging, following a visit to Ford headquarters in Dearborn, the company proposed that the strike end, the powerhouse reopen, and the plant prepare for resumption of work. Once the employees returned to work "without discrimination," all issues in dispute would be referred to an arbitrator chosen by Mitchell. Privately, the union leaders were not entirely displeased — a lost strike would be settled on reasonable terms, the men would get back to work and, possibly, union security would be favourably addressed at arbitration. But the rank and file resoundingly rejected the proposal and called on all unions in Canada to show solidarity. Expectations had been raised by the union leadership, and many members regarded anything less than complete victory as a defeat.

Dutifully, England and Parent sent telegrams to unions across the country, asking them to join in a one-day "solidarity strike," but they were quickly disappointed.[18] The local union leaders failed to appreciate that threatening the establishment with mob rule, penalizing employers and employees not involved in the dispute, and threatening public safety could never advance the union's goals. Canadians would not support any threat to peace, order, and good government. And what about the collective agreements the Local 195 union had breached by calling illegal strikes? If unions could ignore their contracts, so too could employers.

Disgusted, Mitchell packed his bags and left for Ottawa, telling reporters he had "no plans for returning to Windsor."[19] He had put the power of his position on the line, interceded directly with Henry Ford II, and succeeded in obtaining a commitment from management for the arbitration of the key outstanding issues. Obviously, union members needed more time on the picket line. An accordionist was brought in to entertain the strikers, but the

numbers of picketers, on what was now a sixty-day strike, began to notice-
ably thin.

Mitchell continued to work hard at resolving the dispute. He summoned
the UAW leaders to the capital on 13 November and told them frankly that
the union had little chance of success if it remained on its present course. For
the first time, Mitchell sensed "a conciliatory attitude" — the realization that
the fight was probably lost was made even more pronounced by the failure
of organized labour across the country to positively respond to the call for
a one-day sympathy strike. The leaders also finally realized that any escala-
tion of the dispute beyond Windsor would trigger a forceful governmental
response. They now openly signalled their desire to conclude the strike and
agreed to recommend to members that the powerhouse be reopened and that
non-union employees no longer be prevented from going to work. To allow
the union to save face, the Police Commission announced that the outside
police forces would be withdrawn from Windsor if the powerhouse was reopened and security personnel was allowed access to the plant. Proclaiming
victory, the union leadership urged members to approve the proposal, which
they did at a meeting on 15 November.

Now Ford announced that this agreement was not good enough — all the
pickets must be removed. The company's response was problematic. "If the
emergency was so great," the *Windsor Star* pointed out in an editorial, "the
powerhouse should be put into operation without delay."[20] Still, the union's
softened position opened the door for a resumption of negotiations.

On 19 November, the parties met for the second time since the strike
began. The employer had no intention of negotiating anything other than
some minor issues and a return-to-work protocol. The union wanted to talk
about all the issues in dispute. The only thing both sides could agree on
was that negotiations were unlikely to resolve the outstanding issues and
that arbitration was the only answer. As the strike entered its eleventh week,
Mitchell observed, "I would like to think that the company and the union
are about to shake hands, but they have not reached out yet."[21]

In short order, the union promised management that once reopened, the
power plant would not be closed. This had been a long-standing sticking
point as Ford was concerned that if the powerhouse equipment was put back
in operation and then suddenly shut down a second time, the damage would
be even greater than if it was left as it was because winter had arrived in
Windsor. Management accepted the offer, and on 23 November, powerhouse
workers returned to their jobs. Mitchell continued to work at keeping the

lines of communication open and, on 27 November, he announced that an agreement had been reached in Ottawa. It provided that, until a new collective agreement was reached, an "umpire" would be appointed to deal with any issues that arose; that further collective bargaining would take place under the supervision of an arbitrator; and that all unresolved issues would be referred for final decision to that arbitrator, who was to be a judge of the Supreme Court of Canada. The next day, 28 November, Ford accepted the proposal. So too did the union leaders. Once again, however, the rank and file narrowly rejected it after a raucous and most irregular ratification meeting.[22] The strike went into its twelfth week.

Fortunately, Mitchell figured out an exit strategy: he recommended a new secret and supervised ballot to the union leaders. They agreed, and the vote took place on two days in mid-December. This time, 72 percent of the union members voted in favour of ending the walkout. After ninety-nine days, the strike was over.

Settling Controversies

SPECULATION QUICKLY BEGAN TO focus on which Supreme Court judge would be appointed to arbitrate the outstanding issues in dispute, and, finally, the job went to Ivan C. Rand. Born in Moncton, New Brunswick, in 1884, he was a Harvard Law School graduate. He had served briefly as New Brunswick's Attorney General in the mid-1920s, before becoming regional counsel for Canadian National Railways (CNR) and then Commission Counsel — the company's top law job. When the maritime seat on the Supreme Court became vacant in April 1943, Rand, a frugal, brusque son of a railway master mechanic, got the nod. "I am greatly pleased that the Supreme Court has been strengthened to this extent," Prime Minister William Lyon Mackenzie King confided to his diary. King was an excellent judge of character, but he had no idea how much of an activist judge Rand would become on the court.[23] Arbitrating the Ford Strike was Rand's first real opportunity to demonstrate his commitment to judicial activism in support of social justice.

Paul Martin, a Windsor MP and recently-appointed secretary of state, lobbied behind the scenes to get Rand assigned to the Ford dispute. Hard working, ambitious, and well educated, the left-leaning Martin always had his eye on the bandwagon, and considering all the elections in his future, that meant retaining UAW support. As he observed in his memoirs, "it was fairly obvious that the executives of the car plants could influence only

a tiny number of voters."²⁴ Rand, Martin later recalled, "was a man who
knew the evolution that was taking place in social thinking . . . and it just
happened that I was in a position to help bring about his appointment."²⁵
Martin never understated his contribution to events, but his opinion about
how to handle a legal and political problem in his own backyard was not
taken lightly in Ottawa. There was opposition in Cabinet as some ministers, such as acting Prime Minister J.L. Ilsley and the "minister of everything" C.D. Howe, believed that the parties should work out their problems
without the government getting involved, but Martin was convinced that
official intervention was necessary. The strike had gone on for far too long,
he said, and only the appointment of an eminent jurist as arbitrator would
end it. Meanwhile, he privately assured the union leadership that Rand
had "progressive ideas."²⁶

It did not take long for Humphrey Mitchell, the labour minister, to an-
nounce that Rand was the government choice. For umpire, Mitchell selected
Horace R. Pettigrove, an industrial relations officer from the federal Department of Labour who was also its most experienced negotiator and concili-
ator. Before leaving for Windsor, Rand met privately with Mitchell's deputy,
Arthur MacNamara, who soon followed up with a "secret" letter in which
he made the government's position clear: there should not be something for
nothing. Union security, if implemented, would come at a cost.²⁷ After Rand
arrived in Windsor on 27 December, the last of the auxiliary provincial police and RCMP officers were pulled out. Pettigrove showed up two days later
and, for the first time, met Justice Rand.

Pettigrove had been born in 1899 in Marysville, New Brunswick. He
began working when he was eleven, spending his summers sweeping in a
local mill. When he was fourteen, with his grade eight diploma in hand, he
signed on full-time and, for the next eighteen years, toiled in that crowded,
dirty, and unsafe mill. A bit of a radical, he enjoyed challenging authority
and developed a reputation as someone who stood up for the workers. In
1936, he was appointed one of the province's fair wage officers, and then the
first full-time employee in the Labour Division of the Department of Health
and Labour, where he played a key role in drafting much of New Brunswick's early labour law. In 1942, he was appointed industrial relations officer
for the Maritime Provinces in the federal Department of Labour. Pettigrove
knew first hand that, without legal protection for the right to join a union
and to participate in its lawful activities, even the most dogged unionists
would be defeated by a determined employer.²⁸

Pettigrove's task in Windsor was to facilitate the reopening of the Ford plant and the return to work of the striking employees. He was also given the responsibility, as umpire, of dealing with any disputes that arose until the new collective agreement was settled, either by negotiations or by arbitration. Rand's job was to supervise those negotiations and, only if they were unsuccessful, to impose a collective agreement by arbitration. The two men had two distinct but interrelated jobs — and they got off to a bad start.

"I met Mr. Justice Rand," Pettigrove later recalled, "and we didn't click it off at all." Convinced that Rand, the former CNR lawyer, would never be able "to see the other side of it," Pettigrove told him that "he didn't want to get involved in his work, and he [Rand] shouldn't get involved in mine." Rand moved quickly to change Pettigrove's mind: "I would like to have you act as an advisor to me, as a consultant," he explained to the umpire. But still, the answer was no. "Don't you think," Rand replied, "that you are a little unbending?" When Pettigrove reported the conversation to his boss, M.M. Maclean, the director of industrial relations properly let Pettigrove have it: "My God, Horace, a member of the Supreme Court of Canada asks you to act as an advisor to him. Why, you can't refuse." That should have been obvious, and the two men got to work.[29] The supervised negotiations began on 27 December.

The talks lasted until 8 January 1946, and a number of outstanding issues were resolved through mediation. No one had ever believed, however, that there was any realistic prospect of reaching a complete settlement through negotiations alone. Some cases must be heard, and this one, according to the terms of the order-in-council, included "points of difference between the Ford Motor Company of Canada and the UAW." The hearing began at two in the afternoon on 9 January, with John B. Aylesworth, K.C., one of the best corporate lawyers in the province and a future judge of the Court of Appeal, representing Ford. George Burt, the director of the Canadian branch of the UAW, and Pat Conroy, the secretary-treasurer of the Canadian Congress of Labour, were there on behalf of the union, together with a committee that included local president Roy England.

The first order of business was to deal with a request that Rand had received for representation by a group of employees who did not believe the union was acting on their behalf. Within minutes of the start of the hearing, Rand had to face the principal issue before him — reconciling majoritarianism, as reflected in the vote by a majority of employees that the UAW represent them in negotiating the terms and conditions of employment with the employer, versus the assertion by a minority of employees that they had the right to be heard independently of their elected representatives. Without asking for any representations on point, Rand gave his answer.

Rand stated at the outset that he had "always been habituated to the principle that nobody should have compulsion placed upon him without his being heard. On the other hand, this is an arbitration between two recognized parties." The disputing employees were not a party to the proceeding. This was the right call to make: the union represented the employees and was one of two parties to the collective agreement; the other party was the employer. There was no place at the table for employees acting in opposition to their legally recognized bargaining unit. The dispute was solely between the union and the employer, and, as Rand expressed it, "This arbitration is yours and I am in your hands."[30]

Attention then focused on the main issue in dispute: union security. There was no ambiguity about what the union sought — a classic union shop. Everyone presently working at Ford who was not a union member had to become one, and anyone hired to work at Ford had to join the union. Continued membership was to be a condition of employment. The employer would also institute a check-off — deducting union dues from everyone's pay and remitting these funds to the union. Union security provisions — and the more comprehensive the better — are important to unions for many obvious reasons. They provide the union with membership support and financial stability, leaving it free to focus its efforts on collective bargaining and the representation of employees, not on collecting dues. Moreover, the argument goes, it is equitable to require everyone, union member and non-member alike to pay dues, because everyone benefits from the activities of the union.

For its part, management naturally reacted negatively to any restrictions on its rights, especially to exercising discretion in the running of the enterprise. The existence of a union and a collective agreement are two of the main fetters on management's right to operate its business. In addition, there are principled reasons for opposing the union shop: no one should be forced to join a union, or any other organization, in order to remain employed. Even more important, there are practical and self-interested reasons for employers to be against the union shop and check-off: stronger unions are better able to achieve gains for their members, some of which might be in the short-term interests of employees but, over the long term, contrary to the best interests of the business and its shareholders.

Rand had no difficulty understanding what the union was after. It was obvious why the UAW wanted a union shop and check-off, but did that mean it should have either? Rand told Burt that he had "asserted the desirability of a union shop, but [he was] not making it clear just what objectives will be served by it which cannot be served by a powerful union which attracts membership by its own qualities and other inducements."[31] Put another way, why, if the union was any good, could it not succeed on its own? The question was a fair one, and Burt had an answer to it. Don't forget, he told the judge, that the automobile industry in Canada has been uniformly hostile to unionization for years. Surely, Rand interjected, that would stiffen the backbone of the men and strengthen the union. That was true in some cases, Burt replied, but while some unions were strong, others were weak, and a union shop would give employees confidence in collective bargaining. After a meandering discussion between the two men about Canadian labour law, Rand announced, to Burt's obvious pleasure and Aylesworth's noticeable discomfort, that he would proceed "on the basis of the desirability of the social policy of the maintenance of unionism among employees."[32] Given that desirability, a way had to be found to make it work. Within an hour, Rand had a suggestion: Why not let employees refrain from joining the union but require them to pay dues? He asked Burt how he felt about that option.

Burt's answer was, predictably, not much. But when asked to explain why, the union official floundered. Rand moved on, temporarily, coming back to the question later in the afternoon. Now Burt understood and answered Rand's question with a question. He replied, "If it is recognized that collective bargaining is a matter of public policy, that is accepted by the government and they have passed laws about it, then what is the best way to make sure that collective bargaining works?"[33] What about the power of the group over the individual? Rand asked. Don't get carried away, Burt replied. There was power, but it was nothing to worry about, and, besides, any employee with a complaint about the union had a mechanism for redress: internal appeal ultimately to the international convention. It was not dissimilar, he pointed out, to the rights of Canadian citizens to have their case ultimately heard at the Judicial Committee of the Privy Council. Safeguards were not only appropriate but present.

Rand was being asked to issue an award making every Ford employee join the union, requiring the employer to deduct from the wages earned by that employee, and then turn that money over to the union. He was understandably interested in the relationship between the union and its members — and its non-members, an issue he returned to several times over the six days of hearing. What position, Rand inquired, did the union take with non-members?

They were, Burt explained, entitled to the benefits of the collective agreement, but if they had a dispute with the employer, they were on their own. If a man was fired, and if he was not a union member, he was out of luck. Even if he ran to the union hall and joined up, he would not get any official assistance because union rules demanded that an employee be a member in good standing for three months before the union would take up his grievance.

Rand's follow-up questions to Burt suggested that he believed that this was an outlandish situation. If the collective agreement confers benefits on all employees, how can the union deny them representation when they need to have their complaints brought to the attention of management? According to Burt, the answer was simple,. It was not good policy to provide this type of assistance, for doing so would discourage employees from joining the union. Rand still had trouble understanding. He pointed out that the union bargained with management on behalf of everyone, and that the collective agreement was for the benefit of the collective. If the collective agreement provided for a grievance procedure, that procedure should, he suggested, surely apply to everyone. No, Burt explained, if you are not a member and you are not paying dues, you are not entitled to representation. What happened to these employees was not the union's concern.

Individual welfare was, however, one of Rand's main concerns. He stated, "I confess that I have a very great regard for that individual, because I picture myself as that individual."[34] Nevertheless, he felt that everyone should "pull his share in the boat."[35] Rand wanted to know on what basis did unions discipline members. For "conduct unbecoming," replied Burt. But what was that? Rand asked — and off they went, with Rand struggling to understand the protections afforded individuals who were in conflict with the union, especially in a union shop where loss of union membership meant loss of employment. Employees could, therefore, be at "the mercy of the union."[36] While the employer also possessed the power to terminate employment, that power, Rand observed, was checked by the protection of the union.

Be serious, Burt told Rand. Just because we have the power doesn't mean we are going to use it. "You have to give us some leeway as far as authority is concerned."[37] Rand was concerned — prophetically so (as the paper in this volume by Mark Leier, "Dissent, Democracy, and Discipline: The Case of *Kuzych v. White et al.*" makes very clear).[38] What if a man spoke out against his union, and the union determined that this was conduct unbecoming and terminated his membership, ending, in a closed shop, his employment? Well, he asked, what then? When Burt again attempted to draw a parallel between the trial the UAW would offer to dissenters, including ultimate appeal to the union's international convention, with the appellate review available from an independent judiciary, Rand just cut him off. But before he could move on to another subject, Patrick Conroy, the secretary-treasurer of the Canadian Congress of Labour (known as the CCL, it was the central labour body with which the UAW was affiliated), jumped in, debunking all the company's arguments in advance and, as Rand's highlights on the transcript suggest, using language the Supreme Court judge found appealing.

Conroy was a Scot, born in 1900 in Bailieston, a mining town near Glasgow. He was eight years old when his father, a coal miner, died. He and his two older brothers all went into the mines in their early teens and, around 1919, they moved to Drumheller, Alberta, to work in the mines there. Three years later, Conroy was elected to the local union office, and by 1940, he was vice-president of the United Mine Workers in western Canada. That year, he was elected as vice-president of the CCL and, the following year, he became secretary-treasurer of the CCL, its chief administrative position. "Domineering and intransigent," Conroy was also a fierce democrat and generally "thought to be the most accomplished trade unionist in Canada; he was certainly the best informed."[39]

Don't lose sight of the ball, Conroy told Rand. The collective agreement was no ordinary commercial agreement: "The contract is an instrument, it is a mechanism of relationship, good, bad or indifferent, that in the larger and broader sense is an obligation to the community, to the citizens of Canada, to run the business in a civilized manner. By civilized I mean in an intelligent, decent and restrained fashion."[40] Conroy asserted that the union would earn the respect of the community, though even that was not enough — there had to be self-respect as well:

> That self-respect is conditioned by the degree of responsibility that we exercise in living up to our obligation. So the relationship of a small minority to the company, on one side, and of the union on the other, a union which comprises the vast majority of the employees, goes beyond the whims . . . . They are wrapped up in the requirements of good citizenship . . . . To be a good industrial citizen means something fundamentally more than standing aloof in our own pride and our own ego and our own prejudice from the true dominating agency that runs the industry. By dominating agency I mean the invested capital, on the one hand, and invested labour, on the other hand. The one makes up the company and the other makes up the union.[41]

Conroy argued that no industry could succeed if the relationship between the two parties was bad. But, likewise, no industry could succeed if there was an imbalance of power between the two parties. Minority groups had no place in this formulation — they could not be tolerated because they sought the benefits of the agreement in opposition to the group, which has given them better terms and conditions of employment. That situation was, in a word, "absurd." Conroy submitted that there was "no industry that [could] function on that basis."[42] It was simply wrong that a man could say, "I will take the higher wages. I will take my seniority. I will take the grievance procedure. But I will not pay a penny for any of it." Conroy urged in language sure to appeal to Rand that no one "should be above the law."[43] Economic progress demanded no less than the union shop. Reason demanded no less.

On the topic of economic progress and the role of legitimate trade unions in promoting it, Rand wanted to know what role the Communist Party played in the dispute. Conroy began his response by asserting that, while he personally was not a Communist, he did not "condemn the whole communistic credo" because he thought that there were "some good elements in it." Rand remarked that he found that very interesting, but what he really wanted to know was whether the Reds were behind the strike. Conroy refused to give a direct response, though he clearly thought they were. "Frankly," he said, referring to Communist control of the strike, "I cannot prove that," but "I may say to myself that the communists have an objective in controlling the union in the Ford strike."[44] Rand asked if that suggested that the union leadership might have been motivated by factors other than legitimate industrial objectives. Conroy was in no position to answer that question, though he had attended many meetings and only legitimate trade union issues had been discussed. Rand decided to get at the issue another way by interrogating various members of the union committee.

"Where were you born?" he asked one of them. "Scotland" was the answer. "And do you believe in free enterprise or Communism?" The man refused to answer the question. Rand moved on to the next man, another one of the local delegates. "Scotland," and another refusal. Then "England," and refusal again. Then to the next man. "Canada" was the answer to the first question. "You ought to be pretty safe," Rand observed out loud, but instead of asking the second question, he asked whether Conroy had got it right when he said that only legitimate union objectives were behind the strike. The answer, of course, was yes, although Rand realized that his question was ridiculous "because, if there were other motives, they would not be revealed."[45] Eventually, it was the company's turn to speak to the main issue separating the parties.

Lawyer John Aylesworth stated that Ford perfectly understood that unions were an important part of our economic system — that they possessed, as they should, significant powers that imposed on them considerable responsibilities. But there was no reason to conclude that the relationship of union members to their union was anything like the relationship of a citizen to the state. To be sure, citizens had no choice about paying taxes, but no matter who was elected to office, citizens had freedom within the state. That could not be said about compulsory union membership, where the union could deprive employees of their livelihood. It was apples and oranges. Make no mistake, Aylesworth warned, union security gave the union financial security, protected it against membership raids from other unions, and, most objectionable of all, gave the union undisputed control over the lives and destinies of the employees, including their very right to work.[46] This was, of course, the key to the employer's opposition to a union shop. If the union could deprive an employee of his or her job by revoking union membership, then the union could control that employee at work and while out on strike.

The employer did not have any current objection to the union, although Aylesworth candidly admitted that, in the beginning, management went out of its way to frustrate collective bargaining. Nor was Ford at all interested in assisting a rival trade union. Ford was satisfied that UAW Local 200 represented a majority of its employees. These matters were established, and a union security provision was not necessary. The company was completely opposed to union security. Obviously, the union did not require it to bargain — or bargain well — on behalf of the Ford employees. If the union had the power to deprive men and women of their jobs in a union or closed shop, it would do so. At that, Aylesworth provided Rand with a recent example from across the river where twelve employees had been terminated at a union's behest when they had the temerity to disagree with some internal policy of their local.

Other problems were forecast as well. If the union had enhanced security, one could expect that next time around, the damage to plant and equipment would be greater; that more men and women not involved in the labour dispute would be prevented from attending their work; and that episodes like the near revolt on 5 November would start earlier, last longer, and cause greater destruction. All of these events, Aylesworth told Rand, could be predicted with near certainty unless there was an adequate system of checks and balances; unless there was no union shop; unless there were real, substantial, and judicially enforceable fetters on the union's exercise of power, including the right to sue and be sued for damages for breach of its contractual obligations; and unless individuals had access to an impartial tribunal should they come into conflict with their union. Aylesworth did not believe that these safeguards needed to be static: "If it were demonstrated that the counter checks were too extensive or not extensive enough . . . well and good; those are matters of progress and are matters that are not necessarily static but which can be changed as progress demands it."[47]

At this point Rand interjected: what about making everyone pay union dues and, at the same time, allowing everyone, whether member or not, an equal vote on the question of going out on strike? Aylesworth, though surprised, liked that idea very much: "This is a new idea to me," he exulted, "and I must confess that I am somewhat struck with it. I am rather inclined to kick myself because I did not perceive it myself."[48] Ford would support such a scheme, he hinted: "To approach it in that way will be going quite a measure along the lines of setting up regulations and counter checks such as we have been talking about."[49] After the lunch recess, Aylesworth told Rand what he required. A method had to be introduced in law in which the union could be held liable for a contractual breach which caused damages. In the Ford dispute, for instance, Local 200 had lawfully gone on strike. It was a perfectly legal strike. However, the same could not be said of Local 195. That amalgamated local had collective agreements with dozens of employers and it had no collective bargaining disputes with any of them. Yet, in solidarity with Local 200, it had pulled thousands of men and women from their jobs and kept them away from work for a month. In each case, the collective agreement had contained a covenant not to strike during the life of the agreement, and in each case, the union had ignored that legal obligation. If Rand was giving any thought to any type of check-off, Aylesworth argued that it was incumbent on him to ensure that any growth in union strength resulting from union security be accompanied by a growth in enforceable union responsibility. Just like anyone else, unions must be responsible for breach of contract.

Burt agreed that was a good point — everyone should be liable for breach of contract. After reviewing the tremendous opposition Ford had raised to unionization in the early years, and after agreeing with Aylesworth that matters had improved substantially in recent years — the fall strike being the exception to the rule — Burt pointed out that even though Ford was bound by custom and agreement to arbitrate disputes and then accept the result, there were a number of cases where it had refused to implement awards that went against it. We, too, the union suggested, need a legal mechanism to enforce our legal rights.

Aylesworth explained that the only problem, at least from management's view, was that Burt had got it all wrong. Refusing to implement an award was one thing; raising a jurisdictional objection and then defending oneself from an application to prosecute before the Labour Board on the basis of having raised that objection was quite another. More to the point, the Ford lawyer continued, there had never been any lockouts when the employer did not get its way. The employer did not deprive everyone of their jobs in order to prove a point or force an issue. In marked contrast, the union had condoned several illegal, wildcat, strikes.

While union security was the focus of the arbitration, the parties touched on other issues such as picketing — a topic of particular interest to Rand. How was it done? What were its legal limits? What were its purposes? And what about the practice of "taking motor cars"? What did the union leadership think of that? Rand said he could not conceive of a circumstance where it would be justified, and the union did not disagree. But it had done nothing to prevent the thefts and nothing, immediately, to remedy that wrong. And what about shutting down the powerhouse? Did that not hurt the union too? The answer was obvious, but Burt took the line that it was only through the union's efforts that the powerhouse was put back into operation. Rand lectured that both of these acts were "not only idiotic, but illegal."[50]

When the parties began to consider, clause by clause, the other outstanding matters in dispute, Rand was quite effective, gently prodding one party or the other into agreement on actual contractual language. The process was an education for Rand in how both sides operated — how management ran the plant and the union went about its work. True, Rand had been the chief legal officer of one of the biggest companies in the country with many unionized employees. Rand had also been steeped in the progressive attitudes toward labour relations of Canadian National Railway's enlightened president, Sir Henry Thornton.[51] But a modern assembly line with 10,000 employees was completely beyond his experience. He was a fast learner, quickly absorbing the details of modern industrial life, and he was doing so to the evident satisfaction of the parties.

Rand's views on some matters were conservative: it was, he suggested, really up to management to decide what industrial penalty fit what industrial crime; on other matters, he was progressive. For example, he suggested it would be best if management called in a union representative before dismissing a man, one who might mention something that the company had overlooked. "Why can't you agree on this?" he asked, referring to one intractable question that was occupying too much attention, adding, "You have agreed on nearly everything else." The answer was clear: the parties had been able to agree on much, because, in Burt's words, "you are here."[52] That was true. In this environment, the parties actually engaged and, after the submissions on union security were completed, began talking about critical issues such as employing and re-employing veterans; the need for the union to repudiate unlawful strikes; the necessity of maintaining the powerhouse in the event of a future labour dispute; and clauses dealing with the daily administration of a collective agreement covering as many as 16,000 employees — once the plant got up to full speed, and assuming a good North American market. They were all key issues, but also detailed complex matters requiring careful attention. To a remarkable degree, these points were settled or refined as Rand was educated about what was *really* important and why.

Despite Pettigrove's earlier misgivings, Rand could see both points of view. After almost six full days of evidence, the hearing came to an end and it was up to Rand to write the award. Not surprisingly, the matter of union security had to be dealt with first. Rand asked Pettigrove what he thought about an associate membership. When Pettigrove asked what he meant, Rand explained: "If you belong to a club and you have an associate membership, you would not have any right to vote or anything like that, but you would pay your dues and you would have the facilities of the club." The same could be true with associate union membership. "That's a mighty rare bird — original thinking," Pettigrove recalled years later. But when Rand then speculated that, if union dues were around $1 per month, associate members might pay 60¢, the umpire responded "Absolutely not, that's union busting tactics." "I am not here to bust unions," Rand retorted, and he agreed to think about what Pettigrove had said.[53]

The next day, the discussion between the two men resumed. "I've been thinking about what you said," Rand announced. "About this check-off thing, I think that if they pay anything, they pay it all. Now they won't have to pay any initiation fees or that sort of thing, but they will pay the dues, the regular dues." That was fine with Pettigrove, who stated, "I could go along with that." That left the question of how the money was to be collected. Not only could there be no free riders, Pettigrove explained, but, if men refused to pay, "something would fall on their head, or a truck would run into them." Pettigrove suggested that this was the way that voluntary check-offs were enforced. "Well, they can't do that," Rand asserted. "They do do it," replied Pettigrove, who had been around the block more than once.[54] What this meant was that the responsibility for collecting the dues had to be placed on the employer. There would, however, be no union shop — that, Rand confided to Pettigrove, would give the union too much power over its members.[55]

The "Rand Formula" was announced on 29 January 1946, at Toronto's Royal York Hotel. As he handed out his 6,000 word "report," Rand said that he hoped "this may prove to be the beginning of cooperation . . . that will be to the benefit of the entire industry." The negotiations, he added, had been "on a most pleasant plane, there were good tempers, good manners and a good spirit."[56] Balancing the respective interests of the parties was Rand's objective: "I do not want anybody here to look upon anything as a victory. We are trying to arrive at a rationalization of arrangements that are essential to the industry . . . We are just settling controversies and that is all there is to it." Or, as one of the union representatives correctly put it, they were merely "getting down to business."[57]

The Rand Formula

HIS ASSIGNMENT, RAND NOTED at the outset of his award, was not a conventional arbitration — a right arising under a contract or some other legal relationship. No legal right was being claimed, no legal entitlement had been violated. Instead, what was at stake was the resolution of a series of competing interests arising out of modern industrial life. Rand stated, "Here, the work generally is the repetition of limited operations; the psychological effects . . . under the best conditions would require a sympathetic handling; in a hostile atmosphere they could be deplorable." There were "strains and frictions" arising out of the "anomaly of a magnificent engineering plant, machines and functions coexisting with a human engineering." These strains and frictions had to be addressed — and in the context of private enterprise, where capital would always hold the dominant power. "Against the consequence of that, as the history of the past century has demonstrated, the power of organized labour, the necessary co-partner of capital, must be available to redress the balance of what is called social justice: the just protection of all interests in an activity which the social order approves of and encourages."

Rand continued: "The organization of labour must be elaborated and strengthened for its essential function in an economy of private enterprise."

To that end, there had to be "enlightened leadership at the top and democratic control at the bottom." The same logic applied to capital. "The absolutist notion of property" had to be modified, and "the social involvement of industry" had to be "the setting in which reconciliation with the interests of labour and public takes place." Conflict between these interests was inevitable, but, given "their real mutuality of interest in this enterprise," it should not lead inevitably to labour strikes.

"Certain actions which took place during the strike appeared to the public mind as extraordinary," he admitted. "Beyond doubt, picketing was carried on in an illegal manner. The resistance to preservation of plant property was from the standpoint of the strikers a supreme stupidity. The filling of the street alongside the plant with vehicles and the interference with innocent members of the public was an insolent flouting of civil order." But he admitted that, "there was exasperation and provocation . . . No one attempts to justify these actions, but a strike is not a tea party and, when passions are deeply aroused, civilized restraints go by the board unless the powers of order are summoned to vindicate them." Of course, that is exactly what had happened during the ninety-nine-day strike. But Rand, like the union and the employer, was "desirous of avoiding futile recriminations," and he hoped his repositioning of the parties would provide "for the future protection of the industry as a whole."

Were they up to it? "An irresponsible labour organization has no claim to be clothed with authority over persons or interests," he intoned. "But I am dealing with a body recognized as the bargaining agent for approximately 9,500 employees and, while their abuse of striking power cannot be excused, much less justified, we cannot disregard the complex of hostile attitudes and resulting exasperations from which that abuse in fact arose." So, Rand seemed to admit, the strike was justified. But, as he saw it, that was a matter of only historical interest. Ford employees could change their bargaining agent if it continued to act irresponsibly, though he was satisfied that George Burt and others had the best interests of Ford at heart: "They conducted themselves in negotiation with intelligence and reasonableness," Rand said. "I have no doubt . . . that their object is to attain for those employees and their families a secure and self-respecting living, which seem to be the object of most Canadians."

There was, in fact, no need to worry about excessive union power: "It has been suggested that the union officers, as other labour leaders, are primarily concerned with the maintenance of their positions and power," Rand continued. "But union organization is admittedly necessary in the present set-up of our society and we cannot expect these men who have gifts of leadership ... to be quite free of those human frailties from which only a few saints escape. The only effective remedy for abuse of this nature is a greater democratization of the union."

Likewise, he said, the communist threat was overstated. It had been clear, when questioning some of the union delegates, that they were party members. "There may be such a group among the automobile workers in and about Windsor," he agreed, but "the employees who would be susceptible to one-sided teachings of that sort would not in general have the remotest understanding of communist ideology and would grasp at its premise as an escape from what is vaguely felt to be a dictatorship of capital." Rand was probably right, but it still had not stopped the 8,000 members of Local 195 from following their Communist union leaders and going out on a sympathy strike, even though their collective agreement committed them to work and even though they had no dispute whatsoever with Ford.

But that was then, said Rand. "I should say on principle that a leadership which is opposed to communistic ends and methods, as I think this is, should be supported in a democratic economy; it is the failure of that leadership that furnishes the opportunity for strengthening the position of its opponents." And so Rand proposed *his* compromise of union security — his singular, inventive, and creative solution to the dispute. "Union security is simply security in the maintenance of the strength and integrity of the union," he said. The UAW wanted a union shop with a union check-off. This union, however, did not need it: "The negotiating union is unchallenged in the organization of workers of automobile and affiliated industries." Moreover, awarding a union shop was inconsistent with "the principles which I think the large majority of Canadians accept ... and it would deny the individual Canadian the right to seek work and to work independently of personal associations with any organized group." It was not the Canadian way. "On the other hand," Rand declared, "the employees as a whole become the beneficiaries of union action, and I doubt if any circumstance provokes more resentment in a plant than this sharing of the fruits of unionist work and courage by the non-member." Ford was on record, admitting that "substantial benefits for the employees have been obtained by the union, some in negotiation and some over the opposition of the Company." "It would not then as a general proposition be inequitable," Rand continued, "to require of all employees a contribution toward the expense of maintaining the administration of employee interests, of administering the law of their employment." And there it was — the Rand Formula. No one would be forced to join the union, but everybody would be equally required to help support it financially.

This solution was particularly suited, Rand believed, to mass industry:

> The employees are coordinated with mechanical functions, which, in large measure, require only semi-skilled operators. No long apprenticeship is necessary to acquire those skills . . . it is essentially the utilization of concentrated manpower in a framework of machines in which the initiative and artistry of the individual is either non-existent or becomes stereotyped. The large body of employees . . . [is] inescapably of a class that must be governed . . . by mass techniques, and one chief object of the plant law is to diffuse authority among the labour representatives to make administration as flexible as possible.

The old connection with the craft unions was broken. Moreover, with the aggravation of an annual layoff, the union was subject to a periodic disorganizing tendency. Then, too, the union had little to offer the men except its plant law. And so, in Rand's opinion, it became "essential to the larger concerns of the industry" that the relationship between employer and employee be treated in one mass agreement for "the primary protection of their interests."

All employees, Rand continued, should share in the financial cost: "[T]hey must take the burden along with the benefit." Moreover, in his view, making the check-off mandatory would induce membership and encourage union democracy. "It may be argued that it is unjust to compel non-members of a union to contribute to funds over the expenditure of which they have no direct voice," he conceded; and it might even be said "that it is dangerous to place such money power in the control of an unregulated union." But, he continued, "the dues are only those which members are satisfied to pay for substantially the same benefits, and, as any employee can join the union and still retain his independence in employment, I see no serious objection in this circumstance . . . Much more important to the employee will be the right which is being secured to him in the conditions to be attached to the check off, to have a voice in that of which he is now a victim, the decision to strike."

Rand, therefore, ordered the check-off of union dues from all employees, whether members or not, during the term of the collective agreement:

> I should perhaps add that I do not for a moment suggest that this is a device of general applicability. Its object is primarily to enable the union to function

properly. In other cases it might defeat that objective by lessening the necessity for self-development. In dealing with each labour situation we must pay regard to its special features and circumstances.[58]

The UAW did not, however, get something for nothing. Rand also ordered that all strike votes be supervised by officials from the Department of Labour and that all employees, whether union members or not, be entitled to vote. Illegal strikes were prohibited. Illegal strikers would be fined and lose one year's seniority for every week's absence. And there was more. If the union itself was involved in any illegal strike, or if it failed to immediately repudiate an illegal strike commenced without its involvement, the check-off would be suspended. Rand also introduced an "open period," ten to twelve months after the date of the agreement, when, at the request of 25 percent of all employees, the department would hold a vote where the employees could, if they wished, vote the UAW out or some other union in.

Pettigrove, on instructions from Ottawa, took special steps to ensure that the award was intelligible.[59] His challenge was great, given that Rand's turn of phrase was often difficult to follow. The government knew what was coming, however, as Rand had sent a draft to Ottawa. The director of industrial relations, M.M. Maclean, wholeheartedly approved, telling Pettigrove that the draft award was "a masterly document of historical and social significance."[60] Though the award was clearly intended to apply only to Ford, Maclean predicted that it "would become a state document of lasting importance in the history of labour jurisprudence." As he explained:

> I am impressed with Justice Rand's profound understanding of the forces which operate in our private enterprise economy, especially the predominance of power which resides in the control exercised by Capital. Rand's observation that responsibilities are co-relatives of rights points up a blind spot in the vision of the average employer. The employer expects the union to enforce the provisions of the collective agreement and discipline its refractory members but does not accord it the means by which that can be done.[61]

Rand believed that the formula would have a positive effect on unions and would, indeed, promote internal democracy by encouraging member participation.

Rand's award institutionalized the existing trend in conciliation board reports that had, in the years before the Ford strike, generally recommended some form of union security.[62] Yet Rand went one step further in satisfying both union and employer concerns with his particular "formula," and he did so by imposing important concessions on the union in return for union and financial security. The union was now required to conduct a secret ballot before calling a strike, just as it was obliged to repudiate any wildcat strike that arose during the term of the collective agreement. The secret supervised ballot of all the employees within a unit would guarantee union democracy. Implicit in all of this was Rand's understanding that strong unions were necessary to act as a bulwark against communist influence in the workplace. The Communist Party was no longer illegal as it had been during much of World War II. As a judge, Rand would stand up for communist free speech. He also would not disentitle someone from union office simply for having a Communist Party membership. However, he intuitively understood, as did organized labour in time, that Communists and communism represented a real threat to democracy and free trade unions. The counterweight to communist influence was the rule of law, reflected in a collective agreement negotiated in a legal framework imposing contractual obligations on employers, unions, and employees. Since "the union was granted security in order to better exercise its function — the peaceful administration of the collective agreement — it was responsible for taking steps to ensure that its function was not hampered."[63]

It was all part of a piece, one set into motion several years earlier in PC 1003 and the regulatory prohibition of industrial action during the life of a collective agreement. Illegal work stoppages would still be a matter for the courts and the labour board, but there was now a new power to hit the unions where it hurt — in the pocketbook. If the union failed to respect the contract, it, along with the membership, would be punished. In addition to bargaining for employees, unions would also exercise control over those employees within a contractual context. And, as a number of post-war arbitration and judicial decisions soon established, unions *would* be held responsible for illegal work stoppages during the term of a collective agreement. The Rand Formula can and should be seen as part of the federal government's post-war settlement, an important part of which was institutionalized collective bargaining, statutory recognition, and financial security for unions in exchange for organized labour's continued commitment to free enterprise and, to a considerable extent, commitment to the Liberal Party.[64]

The beauty of the formula was its simplicity. It avoided the union shop but provided the union with real financial security. At $1 per employee per month, the union would have, assuming current employment levels, $120,000 a year to administer and enforce the collective agreement as soon as it reached its pre-strike strength. There was also a lot in the award for the employer. The workers at this plant had a history of wildcat strikes, and Rand's award made it clear that the union was required to repudiate any illegal strike, declare any picket line unlawful, and make sure its members reported to work. Anyone participating in an illegal strike would be subject to fines of $3 a day and the loss of one year's seniority for every week on strike. Non-compliance meant suspension of the check-off. Moreover, Rand introduced a provision allowing employees to vote in favour of a new union — and it is interesting that he did not provide for the option of no union representation at all. Every employee was entitled to join the union by paying the entrance fee.

Of all the checks and balances, the loss of seniority was particularly significant. More than 5,000 Ford employees had enlisted in the Canadian forces and had continued to accrue Ford seniority while in uniform. Ford had treated these men well — most of them received allowances and other contributions from the company while they served, and more than $1 million had been paid out in all. On their return, many of them had displacement rights over newer hires with less seniority. Any truncation of seniority would have had a direct impact on job security, as more men came back to work and also during the layoffs that would accompany reconversion. If the economy tanked, seniority would be even more important. Moreover, buried deep in the award were other provisions that cemented the union's position in the workplace. Plant "committee men and negotiating committee men," notwithstanding their seniority status, were, in the case of layoff, to be kept at work as long as there was work in their classification. Fifty years from the date of Rand's award, many unions remain unsuccessful in negotiating "super seniority" for stewards and other local officials.

For the parties, the Rand Formula signaled the end of one era, characterized by confrontation, and the start of another, marked by negotiation. Both parties, it seemed, needed the strike: the union to obtain the security measures it required to represent its members, and the employer to accept that unions were here to stay and that the UAW was the legitimate representative of its industrial workers. In the aftermath of the strike, grievances — often a useful barometer about the state of the world — declined. Rand was privately pleased in the honeymoon period following the release of his award to be told by both labour and management that relations between the two sides were in a "heavenly harmony."[65] Peace prevailed until 1954, when the union again went on strike — in another bitterly fought but ultimately successful battle for company-paid health and welfare benefits.

John Aylesworth said that Rand's union security provision "went quite a way to meeting his objections to a union shop."[66] But it really did much more than that, as he well knew. In fact, as early as 1943, two years before the strike, Aylesworth had testified before the select committee of the Ontario Legislative Assembly holding hearings into proposed collective bargaining legislation. If there was going to be an Act, the canny corporate lawyer told the elected officials, it was necessary to ensure that it actually improved industrial relations, and one way of doing that was imposing greater responsibility on the "bargaining agencies."[67] As Rand himself had observed when he first toured the Ford plant, "there seems to be a lot of mechanical engineering around here but not much *human* engineering."[68] The Rand Formula fixed that. It put the brakes on union militancy by legalizing the rights and obligations of the parties, and initiating a regime of industrial legality in which all disputes were channelled to arbitration, the labour boards, or the courts. It is no accident that a new professional class of labour and management lawyers arose in its aftermath.

Not everyone was enamored with the award. The Rand Formula, some unionists believed, was at best a mixed blessing: "Previous to Rand, the stewards had to go round every payday and collect the dues. The union and the stewards had to be doing a good job to get those dues. Not so today. The Rand Formula turned the unions into big businesses."[69] The Rand Formula put an end to the idea that union militancy, at Ford or anywhere else, was truly an expression from the rank and file or reflected some kind of class consciousness that might one day lead to a general strike and social change. Simply put, unions and their leaders became the guarantors of industrial peace. There would still be strikes, but they would usually be lawful and mostly about money.

Of course, on a more careful examination, there were unanswered questions about Rand's overall enterprise. Rand expressed a need for "some sort of law or convention" regarding industrial relations. He may have been right, and, if so, was it his job to provide it? He thought it was — and, to a large extent, that became the objective of his formula. Others, minority voices in the hoopla surrounding the award, were concerned that, assuming there was this need, it should be Parliament that provided it, not an arbitrator assigned to adjudicate an *ad hoc* dispute.[70] Public policy, traditionalists claimed, should be set by Parliament. At the root of the concern was this question: was Rand, in deciding a case between Ford and the UAW, entitled to direct the employer to deduct wages from third parties without their consent and to give those wages to a union they did not belong to or support?

Conversely, others said that democracy is based on majoritarianism, so the union, which enjoyed the support of the majority of Ford employees, had the right to take employee money, just as the government took taxpayer money as directed by the majority. Indeed, to secure recognition, a union, unlike the situation in our first-past-the-post electoral system, must attract the support of a majority of employees in the bargaining unit strengthening the legitimacy of mandatory union dues: majority rules. The only difference, however, is that once a bargaining agent has been chosen, employees, unlike in the broader political realm where there are recognized avenues for opposition and dissent, must become members of the union if they wish to participate in the government of their industrial life.

The 1945 Ford strike never seriously threatened the social order. Unlike the situation in 1919, when state action successfully crushed labour unrest during the Winnipeg General Strike, the landscape had profoundly changed — as England and Parent realized when their calls for a general sympathy strike fell on deaf ears. Disputes were now about wages and working conditions, and they were largely confined to single industries, preceded by lengthy negotiations under a legal umbrella, and monitored and mediated by expert government officials. Industrial conflict would be carefully managed.

Rand knew that his award on union security might be far-reaching: "A great many people are looking to the issue of this arbitration as indicating some basis or principle upon which controversies of this sort may be settled," he said.[71] And Burt also declared his satisfaction: "It is a work of literary craftsmanship as well as a legal document that will have repercussions affecting all future relations between employee and employer in the auto industry, if not in other fields."[72] He was right: the Rand Formula soon became the default provision of Canadian labour law, although it would take time for Parliament and the provincial legislatures to catch up. But by the early 1980s, legislation was in place in just about every jurisdiction in Canada requiring an employer, on receipt of a request from its union, to deduct union dues for all employees and remit them to the union.

Aftermath

THE FORMULA EASILY SURVIVED the enactment of the *Bill of Rights*. The advent of the *Charter of Rights and Freedoms*, however, was a different matter. Did freedom of association, one of the *Charter* guarantees, also include freedom from association? Under the Rand Formula, no one was forced to join a union, but everyone, with some limited statutory exceptions for persons asserting a religious objection to unions, was required to pay a share of its support. What was really at issue, of course, was how the money was being spent. The test case was framed somewhat differently: were mandatory union dues inconsistent with the *Charter*?

At first, a judge said yes, buying the argument of community college teacher Francis Edmund Mervyn Lavigne who, with the backing of the National Citizens' Coalition, challenged the constitutionality of the Rand Formula. Lavigne was required by the Rand Formula to pay union dues to the Ontario Public Service Employees Union (OPSEU). Under the OPSEU constitution, monies collected could be used toward the advancement of the members' "common interests, economic, social and political." Lavigne was not a union member and he objected, among other things, to the union directing a fraction — $2 of his $338 annual payment — to causes with which he disagreed, most particularly abortion rights, a union of health care workers in Nicaragua, disarmament campaigns such as Operation Dismantle, and the New Democratic Party. Simply put, Lavigne claimed that he had a right not to be forced into association with "socialists" and "fellow travelers." He argued that the money should be exclusively spent for collective bargaining. He claimed that his *Charter* right to associate also gave him the right not to associate, and that compulsory union dues interfered with his rights.

When the case finally got to the Supreme Court of Canada, the Rand Formula was upheld in a 1991 decision.[73] While two of the judges concluded that Lavigne's *Charter* freedom of association rights had been infringed, they also found that that the violation was justified under section 1 of the *Charter*. That meant that the infringement was a reasonable limit, prescribed by law and demonstrably justified in a free and democratic society. The rest of the Court, for different reasons, concluded that there was no violation at all. Decades after the Ford strike had been settled by Rand's Formula, that compromise and settlement was confirmed by the Supreme Court as one of the defining features of Canadian labour law.

Notes

1   There are a number of different types of union security provisions. The closed shop requires all employees to be union members as a condition of employment. The union shop requires all employees to join the union as a condition of becoming and remaining employed. The Agency shop allows employees to join a union or not, but requires all employees to pay union dues unless granted an exemption, for example, because of a religious objection.

2   *Windsor Star* (16 June 1945). A much more detailed account of the background to the strike and the development of the Rand Formula can be found in *Canadian Maverick: The Life and Times of Ivan C. Rand* (Toronto: University of Toronto Press for the Osgoode Society, 2009).

3   *Windsor Star* (4 September 1945).

4   "Subversive Activity in UAW, Canada," Ottawa, National Archives of Canada (RCMP Security Service files, NA, RG 146).

5   Gloria Montero, *We Stood Together* (Toronto: James Lorimer, 1979) at 103–4 [Montero].

6   Burt belatedly came to see that the Communists were the enemy, and he helped drive them from the UAW. See Morden Lazarus, ed., *Up From the Ranks* (Toronto: Cooperative Press Associates, 1977) at 21; Charlotte A.B. Yates, *From Plants to Power: The Autoworkers Union in Postwar Canada* (Philadelphia: Temple University Press, 1993) at 27–30, 66–67, and 132–34; John T. Morley, *Secular Socialists: The CCF/NDP in Ontario: A Biography* (Kingston and Montreal: Montreal-Queen's University Press, 1984) at 178; Irving Abella, *Nationalism, Communism and Canadian Labour* (Toronto: University of Toronto Press, 1973) at 32, 38, 50, 62, 77, and 164–67 [Abella, *Nationalism*].

7   Stephen Charles Cako, *Labour's Struggle for Union Security: The Ford of Canada Strike, Windsor, 1945,* (M.A. Thesis, University of Guelph, 1971) at 18 and 110 [Cako]. This thesis was extremely valuable in reconstructing the background to the dispute and in the preparation of this narrative. On the communist issue, Cako states at 105 that the UAW was "a union whose principal officials were Communists or men influenced by Communist political policies." See Montero, above note 5 at 103–4 and James S. Napier, *Memories of Building the UAW* (Toronto: Canadian Party of Labour, 1976) at 56–64 [Napier].

8   Affidavits of Ford officials, Toronto, Archives of Ontario (NA, RG G 23, Series 4-02, Box 36, file 36.6). Affidavits filed by Ford officials clearly indicate that police officers were instructed not to offer assistance to Ford employees attempting to enter the plant. "I cannot break that picket line sir," was the typical police response when a Ford executive attempted to drive to work.

9   There was a definite tension about the appropriate approach. See, for example, Mayor of Windsor, Arthur Reaume to Ontario's Attorney-General, Leslie Blackwell, (14 September 1945), Toronto, Archives of Ontario (NA, RG 23, Series 4-02, File 36.6, Box 36).

10 "List of Communists Elected in Canada," online: ndp.wikia.com/wiki/List_of_Communists_elected_in_Canada.

11 Montero, above note 5 at 104.

12 RCMP *Access to Information Act* Request (19 September 1990).

13 *Windsor Star* (3 November 1945).

14 *Windsor Star* (6 November 1945).

15 Herb Colling, *Ninety-Nine Days: The Ford Strike in Windsor, 1945* (Toronto: NC Press, 1995) at 96 and 122 [Colling].

16 Cabinet Conclusions (14 November 1945), Toronto, Archives of Ontario (NA, RG 2, A-5-a, Vol. 2637, Reel T-2364.

17 *Windsor Star* (7 November 1945); Cako, above note 7 at 85.

18 Doris Jantzi, "Ford Strike in Windsor, 1945" in Paul Craven & Gary Teeple, eds., *Union organization and strikes* (Toronto: OISE, 1978) at 54.

19 *Windsor Star* (10 November 1945).

20 *Windsor Star* (17 November 1945).

21 *House of Commons Debates* (16 November 1945) at 2182.

22 *Windsor Star* (5 December 1945).

23 W.L.M. King, *William Lyon McKenzie King's Diary*, Ottawa, National Archives of Canada (MG26-J13) at 294 and 301.

24 Paul Martin, *A Very Public Life*, vol. 1 (Ottawa: Deneau, 1983) at 214 [Martin].

25 David Moulton, "Ford Windsor 1945" in Irving Abella, ed., *On Strike: Six Key Labour Struggles in Canada, 1919–1949* (Toronto: James Lewis & Samuel, 1974) 129 at 147. See Martin, above note 24 at 395.

26 Colling, above note 15 at 138. On Martin's role, see Martin, above note 24 at 388–97; interview of Paul Martin (11 May 1989).

27 Deputy Minister of Labour Arthur MacNamara to Ivan Rand (18 December 1945), Ottawa, National Archives of Canada (NA, RG 30 E77, vol. 1.).

28 Gary N. Chaison & Edward D. Maher, *An Interview with Horace Pettigrove* (University of New Brunswick, 1974 [unpublished]) at 12 [Chaison & Maher].

29 *Ibid.* at n. 88.

30 Transcript of Evidence (9 January 1946) at 3–4.

31 *Ibid.* at 25.

32 *Ibid.* at 32.

33 *Ibid.* at 42–43.

34 Transcript (11 January 1947) at 197.

35 *Ibid.*

36 Transcript (10 January 1946) at 66.

37 *Ibid.* at 70.

38 See James Mark Leier, "Dissent, Democracy, and Discipline: The Case of *Kuzych v. White et al.*" this volume.

39 See Morden Lazarus, *Years of Hard Labour* (Don Mills: Ontario Federation of Labour, 1974) at 50; Martin, above note 24 at 296; Abella, *Nationalism*, above note 6 at 66–85, 95, 98, 120, 160, 174–75, 179, 204, and 214.

40 Transcript of Evidence (10 January 1946) at 72.

41 *Ibid.* at 80–81.

42 *Ibid.* at 83.

43 *Ibid.* at 89.

44 *Ibid.* at 128–29.

45 *Ibid.* at 142.
46 *Ibid.* at 154.
47 *Ibid.* at 194.
48 *Ibid.* at 204.
49 *Ibid.*
50 *Ibid.*; Transcript (12 January 1946) at 386–87.
51 See D'Arcy Marsh, *The Tragedy of Henry Thornton* (Toronto: Macmillan, 1935); G.R. Stevens, *History of the Canadian National Railways* (New York: Macmillan, 1973); and Donald McKay, *The People's Railway: A History of Canadian National* (Vancouver: Douglas & McIntyre, 1992).
52 Transcript (14 January 1946) at 519, 525, and 531.
53 Interview of Horace Pettigrove (27 November 1989).
54 Chaison & Maher, above note 28 at 39.
55 Interview of Horace Pettigrove (27 October 1989) [Pettigrove interview, 27 October]. According to Pettigrove, Rand was influenced by Herbert Agar and his book, *A Time for Greatness* (Boston: Little, Brown & Co., 1942).
56 *Windsor Star* (29 January 1946).
57 Transcript of Evidence, 15 January 1946 at 689.
58 "Award on Issue of Union Security in Ford Dispute" (1947) 46 *Labour Gazette* at 123–29.
59 Pettigrove to Marshall Pollock (9 April 1976), Pettigrove Papers.
60 Memo re Ford Co. and UAW, Pettigrove Papers.
61 Memo re Ford Co. and UAW, Pettigrove Papers.
62 Canadian Congress of Labour, *The Case for Union Security and the Check-off* (Ottawa: 1951) at 41.
63 Judy Fudge, "Voluntarism and Compulsion: The Canadian Federal Government's Intervention in Collective Bargaining from 1900 to 1946" (Ph.D. Thesis, University of Oxford 1988) [unpublished] at 338–39 [Fudge, "Voluntarism"].
64 Fudge, "Voluntarism," *ibid.* at 344.
65 Rand to Pettigrove (13 March 1946), Pettigrove Papers.
66 Colling, above note 15 at 175.
67 Cited in Tucker, in this volume at note 84.
68 Pettigrove interview, 27 October, above note 55.
69 Napier, above note 7 at 60. See Don Wells, "The Impact of the Postwar Compromise on Canadian Unionism: The Formation of Auto Worker Local in the 1950s" (1995) 36 Labour/Le Travail 147.
70 See, for example, *Globe and Mail*, "Editorial," published in the *Windsor Star* (1 February 1946).
71 Transcript of Evidence (9 January 1946) at 5–6.
72 *Windsor Star* (30 January 1946).
73 *Lavigne v. Ontario Public Service Employees Union* (1991), 81 D.L.R. (4th) 545 (S.C.C.).

Dissent, Democracy, and Discipline: The Case of *Kuzych v. White et al.*

*Mark Leier**

On the Waterfront: The Setting of *Kuzych v. White*

STRIKE WAVES, MASS STRIKES, sit-ins, and radical politics during World War II pushed Canadian legislators to make sweeping changes to labour law in the 1940s. As other essays in this collection point out, the intent, meaning, and results of the new labour codes were contested at the time and are still contested today. They have been characterized as consensus, as modernization, and as co-optation. The effects have also been argued over, as the new industrial relations regime is credited both for labour's relative successes in the 1950s and 1960s and for its failures in the 1980s and 1990s.[1]

Among those critical of the post-war settlement, a key issue has been the role of the union, or more precisely, the union leadership. As early as 1948, American sociologist C. Wright Mills warned that the union leaders were responsible for policing the collective agreement, and that cut two ways: employers are held, at least in theory, to the wages and conditions of the contract; and workers are forced by the union to resolve all disputes within the carefully structured and limited regime of industrial legality that narrows the kinds of issues that can be contested, restricts the right to strike, and keeps production going. As a result, the union leader may become a "manager of discontent" who "holds back rebellion."[2] This function has been recognized by labour leaders and by employers, both of whom often agree that it is useful and legitimate even when they differ over how that function should be

—John Steel
KUZYCH: *Unionists to jail.*

Myron Kuzych
Photo by John Steele, Vancouver Sun

WILLIAM L. WHITE
. . . discrimination?

Bill White
Vancouver Sun

exercised. It is also recognized by critics on the Left and Right, where the Left condemns it as crippling union democracy and militancy and the Right condemns it as sacrificing the rights of the individual in favour of the collective.[3]

Kuzych v. White was primarily a fight over the right of unions to discipline members and as such, it touches on the concerns about the industrial relations framework that was emerging in the 1940s. As a result, it has become a staple in labour law and labour law classes. From its beginnings in 1944, it was pitched in the courts and the press as a David and Goliath struggle between a single worker, Myron Kuzych, and a Communist-led union, headed by powerful labour boss, Bill White, though that was a misleading characterization. It wound through the Canadian legal system until 1951, when it became one of the last Canadian cases heard by the Privy Council. Even the law lords could not resolve the case and it lingered in the Canadian courts until the mid-1950s. Nor was the battle restricted to legal wrangling: Kuzych was threatened with a makeshift firebomb and White was convicted of assault. The case reached back to the nineteenth century for precedents and is still cited in the twenty-first century.[4] Yet for all of the attention paid to the case, it bears re-examination now as the case offers insight into the dilemmas, contradictions, and consequences that labour faced while the new industrial relations regime was forming.

Kuzych v. White grew out of the specific conditions that transformed Canadian labour relations during World War II. The war created a huge demand for ships and for workers to build them. Shipyards developed new techniques to increase production, reduce costs, and maximize profits from the lucrative government contracts. Welding largely replaced the riveting of ships, and special government courses taught rudimentary skills to men and women in six weeks. In Vancouver and North Vancouver, many of these new workers became members of the Boilermakers and Iron Ship Builders Union of Canada (BISU), Local 1. Formerly Local 194 of the American International Brotherhood of Boilermakers, the BISU broke from the International Brotherhood in 1927, and in 1928 became a directly chartered member of the All-Canadian Congress of Labour (ACCL). In 1940, the ACCL merged with the Canadian branches of the Congress of Industrial Organizations (CIO) to form the Canadian Congress of Labour (CCL). Headed by Aaron Mosher, the CCL was firmly in the hands of union leaders who supported the Cooperative Commonwealth Federation (CCF), the precursor to the New Democratic Party and the Liberal party. The BISU grew rapidly during war: in 1939 there were about 200 members, and by 1942 it swelled to approximately 13,000 members and represented over 50 percent of the unionized workforce in the Vancouver ship and repair yards. The largest union in the CCL and by far its biggest financial contributor, the BISU was a prize worth fighting for. Thus when the BISU members elected a communist slate to its executive in December 1942, the avowedly anti-Communist Mosher launched a ferocious counter-attack on the new left-wing leadership.[5]

Panicked by BISU's "capture" by the Communists, Mosher declared the election null and void and appointed an old colleague, Alex McAuslane, as trustee. The elected Left leadership, however, refused to accept Mosher's actions and took office on 1 January 1943 in a well-publicized swearing-in ceremony that had several prominent BC labour leaders in attendance. The elected BISU officers issued a proclamation that Mosher's actions were illegal, and that they would take their instructions from the rank and file who elected them, not the CCL president or his appointed trustee. The new leaders staked their claim to legitimacy on two principles: the grassroots support of the rank and file and the militant pursuit of better wages and conditions for their members.[6]

Certainly they were able to demonstrate that they had considerable rank and file support. When Mosher and McAuslane obtained a court injunction to keep the Left leaders out of the union offices, a battalion of shop stewards seized the hall and held the trustee at bay. At a large open-air meeting, 3,500 BISU members overwhelmingly endorsed the action of the shop stewards and the leadership of Communist Party (CP) members.[7] When the CCL recommended that the BISU charter be suspended and the union broken up into several small locals, the BISU voted to secede from the CCL. It then confirmed the Left leadership in a open-air vote by about 6,000 members, accompanied by pipe and brass bands. By the end of 1943, the CCL conceded defeat and the courts turned over the assets of the union to the Left leadership. The BISU remained in the CCL, but as an independent national union affiliated with it, not a chartered creation of the Congress. In 1945, the BISU merged with other unions to create the Marine Workers and Boilermakers Industrial Union Local 1 (Marine Workers).[8]

Despite the new leadership's pledge to fight for the members, wartime regulation of the industry made it difficult to negotiate better wages or conditions. Bill White, the named defendant in *Kuzych v. White*, a business agent for the BISU, member of the CP, and president of the Marine Workers, noted that "us working stiffs were frozen on the job, our wages were pegged and we were forced to work under conditions that were inhuman . . . . We could occasionally pull off a sit[-]down but we were under tremendous pressure not to interrupt war production."[9] The most glaring example of the union's inability to improve conditions was its grudging acceptance of the recommendation of the Royal Commission on Production of Ships in the Shipyards of British Columbia (the Richards Commission) for a scheme of continuous production in the shipyards. That meant scheduling work for twenty-four hours a day, seven days a week, with a six-day work week instead of the customary five and a half, an alternating day off instead of the regular Sunday, and reductions in shift premiums and overtime pay. In short, the Commission called for significant changes in work and pay that unilaterally changed the collective agreement for the worse. Despite its pledge to improve conditions, the new Left executive recommended acceptance of the continuous production schedule. While a majority of the members who voted supported the executive's recommendation, most union members did not cast a ballot, and a significant minority voted against it.[10]

That gave the CCL a wedge to split the Left executive from the membership. As a labour representative on the commission, McAuslane had opposed continuous production. In doing so, he reflected the concerns of many of the rank and file in the shipyards and could paint the new contract as a failure of the Left to deliver on its promises. McAuslane's opposition to continuous production won him some support among the rank and file and meant the Left leadership needed to find another defining issue in which it could clearly position itself as an alternative to McAuslane and the CCL.[11]

The closed shop became that defining issue. Strictly speaking, in Canadian usage, the closed shop is a work place where the employer agrees to hire only union workers who are supplied by the union, usually through a hiring hall. This has been a longstanding practice in the construction industry and longshoring. However, the term "closed shop" is also used more generally to include the "union shop," where the employer may hire anyone, but all employees are compelled to join the union as a term of continuing employment. In *Kuzych v. White*, the closed shop was defined more loosely, conforming to McCarthy's later, broad definition, as "a situation in which employees come realize that a particular job is only to be obtained and retained if they become and remain members of one of a specified number of unions." The closed shop is considered a form of union security, that is, a measure to ensure that the union is able to maintain itself in the workplace, help correct the preponderance of power the employer holds, and give the union stability of membership and funds.[12]

There were good reasons to fight for the closed shop. Most of Canada's longest strikes had the right to organize and bargain as key issues. Given that painful, often bloody history, union security was a crucial issue at the bargaining table as it would let labour hold onto its hard-won gains and engage in real collective bargaining. Perhaps the most compelling recent example of the failure to obtain union security is the Canadian Auto Workers' organizing campaign at a McDonald's fast food franchise in Squamish, BC. The lengthy battle to certify the union and obtain a collective agreement was ultimately defeated when enough anti-union workers were hired and voted to decertify the union.[13] The closed shop was one of the critical demands of the strike wave of World War II and the immediate post-war period as Canada moved toward its "new regime of industrial legality" in the 1940s and 1950s.[14] It was a key demand of the 1945 Ford strike at Windsor, Ontario, and while workers there did not win the closed shop, their efforts led to the creation of the Rand Formula. Under the Rand Formula, workers do not have to join the union but must pay dues to the union in a compromised form of union security.[15] In March 1943, North Vancouver Ship Repair (Norvan) hired seventy non-union workers in violation of the closed shop agreement it had signed with the BISU, and the Left leadership called a wildcat strike in protest. McAuslane vocally opposed the wildcat. The CP executive then accused McAuslane of helping companies fight the closed shop and taking the side of the employer. The CCL, it argued, was essentially an ally of the boss that could not be counted on to fight for workers. In contrast, the Communist leadership argued that it would use any weapon, legal or illegal, to fight for trade union principles, and the closed shop became the most sacred of principles. Thus CP stalwart and BISU president William Stewart would insist that "the closed shop clause is the only guarantee that an employer will live up to the other clauses in the agreement. Without a closed shop clause, the agreement is useless." At the same time, the closed shop would let the Left leadership use the contract to end the faction fight with the CCL, establish itself in firm control of the BISU, and establish the BISU as the dominant union in the shipyards. Communist organizer and BISU business agent Malcolm MacLeod put it clearly. Obviously aiming at the efforts of the CCL to pull the BISU charter and replace the union, MacLeod insisted that "there will be no peace and harmony in the yards so long as a company leaves the door open for another group to start up an opposition union."[16] The closed shop would shut that door.

Enter Myron Kuzych

THUS WHEN ONE UNION member objected to the closed shop, first within the union and then publicly, the Left leadership could not regard him as a minor annoyance or a principled dissenter. Instead, Myron Kuzych was regarded as a serious threat to the union leadership's legitimacy and to fundamental trade union principles and his opposition to the closed shop was constructed as anti-union and anti-worker. The union responded immediately and aggressively to Kuzych's challenge, and in doing so, prompted the legal battle that would ultimately cost the union the equivalent of $1 million in 2008.

Kuzych had completed a six-week government welding course and was assigned by Selective Service to a BISU shop, Norvan, in November 1942. He started work, made a donation to the union, and attended union meetings, but did not sign the membership card, join the union, or pay dues. Early in 1943 the union announced that it would inspect union cards at the shipyard gates to ensure all the workers were paid-up union members. Those without cards could join then and there; if they refused or were delinquent in their dues, they would be barred from going to work. Kuzych was stopped at the gate and was asked to sign up. He refused. Shop stewards pointed out to him that his continued employment was conditional on his joining the union, and gave him time to reconsider. Kuzych then went to the management of the yard, who told him they would indeed terminate Kuzych's employment if he did not join the union. At that point, Kuzych signed the application and became a member. One of the conditions of union membership, noted on the application and membership card, was to accept and to follow the bylaws and constitution of the union. These included provisions that bound the member to refrain from attacking the union and union policy in public, to refrain from personal attacks on union officers and members, and to try to resolve any disputes with the union according to the constitution's provisions before taking court action against the union. These provisions would be the key to how the union would frame its response to Kuzych.[17]

Kuzych soon proved to be an obstreperous and disruptive union member, at least as far as the leadership was concerned. During the March 1943 wildcat strike at Norvan called to protest the hiring of non-union workers, Kuzych decried the illegal walk-out. He was unhappy at having to take part in an illegal shutdown before arbitration had been tried, and was unwilling to engage in any strike activity that had been called by a small group of union officers and stewards rather than voted on by the entire membership. He made his views known to other workers during the wildcat until someone stopped him and warned him that "if you know what is good for you, you will keep your mouth shut, see?" Kuzych decided discretion was the better part of valour, but he was determined to speak against the union and in particular against the closed shop.[18]

His next opportunity came a few months later. Since 1942, the BISU had been engaged in a struggle to win the closed shop at West Coast Shipbuilders, the only Vancouver steel shipyard that remained an open shop. As the fight with the CCL developed, winning the closed shop at West Coast became more urgent. By May 1943, William Stewart announced that while "we are in agreement on all other points such as wages and working conditions . . . laid down in the Richards Commission report," the union insisted that West Coast concede the closed shop.[19]

But the employer remained intransigent and negotiations were stalled by August 1943. To resolve the issue, a conciliation board, headed by Justice John Wilson, was convened. Kuzych addressed the board at a public hearing on 12 October 1943. He launched into a critique of the closed shop as undemocratic, denounced the BISU as "spurious" and a "fake," and opined that it did not deserve to be awarded the closed shop.

From the union's perspective, Kuzych's testimony was particularly damning. The union leadership claimed to represent workers, not just in the legal sense of being responsible for negotiating for the group, but as the united voice of the workers. Kuzych was a voice from the rank and file that attacked the union. He was apparent proof that the union leaders did not accurately represent workers and that there was division within the union. It did not help that Kuzych was an expressive speaker who impressed the conciliation board and captured the imagination of the press. "Shipyard Welder's Eloquence 'Wows' Arbitration Board," read the headline in the *Vancouver Sun*. The paper billed Kuzych as "a son of the Ukraine" who "amazed the bench, the bar, and the Boilermakers' union with his version of democracy and apt quotations from Shakespeare and Edgar Allen Poe." According to the paper, Kuzych's arguments, erudition, and wit "brought admiring comments from the legal talent at the hearing." The *Province* newspaper, more sedate, more anti-union, and less inclined to strike a populist tone, headlined its coverage, "Welder Doubts Value of Closed Shop," and hinted in its sub-heads of shop "Stewards' Despotism," "Glaring Mismanagement," and "Members Threatened" by the union. Citing the earlier Norvan wildcat as an example, Kuzych maintained that the BISU and the closed shop itself were undemocratic. Kuzych insisted that others in the shipyards thought the way he did, and suggested that if most workers supported the closed shop, they did so not on its merits but because they reasoned that "if the employer opposes it so much it must be good for the workingman." Furthermore, union leaders were "'whooping up things' which befuddled the workers and merely made him [sic] follow blindly." Nor was the wildcat strike an unequivocal indication of mass support for the leadership or the closed shop, Kuzych continued, for "during the sit-down, some of the men played poker or craps and were so successful that they were in favour of a strike every day."[20]

The Kuzych Expulsion: Round 1

WHILE IT IS IMPOSSIBLE to know how much Kuzych may have swayed the board, he was now on record as publicly opposing the BISU, its leadership, and one of its most important principles, the closed shop. When the conciliation board handed down its decision to maintain the open shop at West Coast Shipping, the union lost little time in disciplining Kuzych. Charges of "conduct unbecoming a member of the union and contrary to its policy" of the closed shop were launched by four union members, at least two of whom had strong connections to the union executive. A committee was struck to investigate and try Kuzych, and it recommended at a union meeting that he be expelled from the union. The meeting supported the recommendation, Kuzych was expelled, a letter was sent to the employer pointing out that Kuzych was no longer a member in good standing, and on 9 December 1943, Kuzych was dismissed from Norvan. He then launched legal action against the union to have his expulsion overturned.[21]

On the advice of its attorney, John Stanton, the BISU resolved to settle the issue quickly to rid itself of a minor nuisance. It reinstated Kuzych on 21 June 1944. He continued his suit, however, seeking damages for the time at work he had lost. The case was heard before BC Supreme Court Judge Wallace Farris in October 1944. The union admitted that Kuzych had, technically, been wrongfully suspended from the union, as a change in his mailing address delayed his mail and gave him only six days' notice before the union trial, not the seven called for in the union bylaws. The judge awarded Kuzych damages of $1,000, largely representing wages he had lost during the time he could not work at Norvan.[22]

But Stanton and the union had miscalculated; Kuzych was much more than a nuisance. He continued his attacks on the union leadership and the closed shop at union meetings, in a campaign of letters to the editor of Vancouver's daily newspapers and a series of radio broadcasts. In December 1944, Kuzych ran for the presidency of the union, but at the last minute, asked his supporters to vote for another candidate to avoid splitting the vote against the CP incumbent. This candidate, C.A. Henderson, was successful, largely because of the widespread dislike of the continuous production schedule, and he replaced CP member William Stewart as president of the union; three other non-CP activists won seats on the executive. Henderson, however, proved unable to conduct the business of the union, probably in the face of organized resistance by the CP cadre, and soon all four of the protest candidates resigned. Bill White, a CP member, was then elected to head the union, and other CP members won the open positions on the union executive.

This executive, smarting from its recent electoral defeat, triumphant in its return to power, annoyed by Kuzych's continued denunciations of the leadership, and keen to make a test case for the closed shop and union discipline, was determined to expel Kuzych from the union once and for all. As Bill White put it in his memoirs,

there was some feeling that we should go on appeasing him and not be bait-
ed into more litigation, but I figured what the hell, we were in the right and
there was no reason we should have to put up with this kind of bullshit. If
the CMA [Canadian Manufacturers Association] wanted to take Labour on
in the courts, we couldn't run away forever. Better we meet them head on and
get it settled . . . . We're going to give this fella what he's asking for but we're
going to do it by the letter of the law.

Charles W. Caron, a staunch CP member and newly elected secretary-treasurer of the union, declared in early February 1945 in the union newspaper,
the *Main Deck*, that while the earlier expulsion was technically flawed, it
"was correct in principle." Therefore, "new charges are now pending against
Myron Kuzych." More was at stake than punishing a political opponent, or
so Caron argued: "[I]f Myron Kuzych intends to take us to court again he
will be placing the entire trade union movement on trial, as to whether a
trade union has the right to discipline its members for violation of union
policies and individual members' obligations."

Kuzych Expulsion: Round 2

A UNION COMMITTEE HELD a trial on 13 March 1945, charging that Kuzych had
violated the contract he signed when he joined the union. Specifically, the
union application contained a pledge to follow the bylaws and constitution
of the union. These included refraining from attacking the union, union
policy, union officers, and union members in public. Kuzych, the committee charged, had violated this obligation in three ways. The first was that
Kuzych had called an unauthorized public meeting to discuss private union
business, a reference to a meeting held to discuss strategy and tactics before the election in which Henderson defeated Stewart. The second charge
was that Kuzych had spoken publicly against the closed shop and the dues
check-off, a principle of the union explicitly outlined in its constitution. The
third charge was that Kuzych had failed to repudiate slanderous remarks
that he had made or were made on his behalf against William Stewart, during Kuzych's radio broadcasts. The committee found Kuzych guilty on all
three charges and recommended his expulsion from the union. A union
meeting voted in favour of the recommendation, Kuzych was expelled, the
union notified the company, and on 29 March 1945, Kuzych was again fired
by Norvan. Kuzych returned to the courts to be reinstated, and *Kuzych v.
White* began its decade-long journey through the courts.[23]

Bill White summed up the union leadership's position on the case. If a union did not have the legal right to discipline its members, including the right to expel them, it meant that "[y]ou could have a union, in other words, but you had to let everyone in and you couldn't throw anyone out. If you went on strike the company could bring in an army of scabs, and not only would you have to let them take your jobs, you'd have to welcome them into your union!"[24]

Who Was Myron Kuzych?

WHITE'S ANALYSIS, HOWEVER, WAS misleading. Kuzych was not a scab. There was no strike; he was not crossing a picket line. He was a dissident, a critic, and undoubtedly an irritant, but he was not even opposed to unions in principle; indeed, at this point, he was fighting to remain a union member. Nonetheless, his opposition to the closed shop and to the CP union leadership was constructed by the leadership as an attack on trade unionism, the union, and the rank and file. Kuzych was painted as a class traitor. Caron's article in the *Main Deck*, for example, insisted that "the action of Myron Kuzych, testifying against a closed shop, contrary to the policy of our union, was not the action of a trade unionist." Subsequent attacks on Kuzych made similar claims, and these have largely been taken at face value by participants and historians. Bill White maintains that whether Kuzych was a "professional agitator . . . . picked out by the Canadian Manufacturers' Association to make trouble for us" or "was acting entirely on his own" made little difference. "So maybe Kuzych wasn't pro," White concludes, "but he couldn't have served the bosses better if he was." Communist activist Jack Scott argues that "there was [*sic*] powerful interests — the Chamber of Commerce and the Board of Trade for instance — that were backing him [Kuzych] and giving him money." More recently, historian Benjamin Isitt, working from Labour and Communist Party newspapers, argues that Kuzych's legal case was financed by business, and so implies that Kuzych was anti-union, while Chris Madsen more cautiously suggests that "Kuzych conveniently fulfilled the purpose for which the company needed him."[25]

A closer examination of what Kuzych actually said, however, reveals a different story. For Kuzych was not simply a right-wing opponent of unions. He was born Miroslav Kuzych in 1911, in a small village near Kolomiya, Ukraine, which came under the control of Poland in 1918. As part of the school curriculum, he had learned the poetry of the liberal nationalist Taras

Shevchenko, and more importantly, the work of Ivan Franko, who embraced Marxism for a time and imbued Ukrainian nationalism with a critical, social democratic consciousness. In 1926, Kuzych emigrated with his twin brother to Canada to avoid conscription into the Polish army. He worked as a farm labourer in Manitoba and as a railway navvy, and attended Point Grey Junior High School in Vancouver as an older student, graduating in 1930, at age 19. A voracious reader, he was fond of quoting the classics and debating; the school yearbook, *The Explorer*, noted that "Myron is tough, but we hold great hopes of him becoming a famous author someday." He worked at various jobs during the depression, and became interested in Socialism. He went to open meetings held by the Communist Party, and met Richard "Lefty" Morgan, an anti-Communist Socialist and member of the anarcho-syndicalist Industrial Workers of the World, or the Wobblies, who was active in organizing in the relief camps and was beaten by police at the Battle of Ballantyne Pier in 1935, when police attacked a demonstration of longshoremen. Morgan was a member of the Young Socialist League and later the Cooperative Commonwealth Federation, though he was always on the extreme left of the CCF and remained highly critical of its constant slide to the right. The two men became fast friends and remained close until Morgan's death in 1987. Kuzych's own political trajectory was somewhat different. He was briefly a member of the Young Communist League, but joined the Socialist Labor Party (SLP) in the 1930s after hearing its organizer and later head of the party, Eric Hass, speak at an open-air meeting in Vancouver. Formed in 1877, the SLP was an avowedly Marxist party that embraced the ideas of Daniel De Leon, the party leader from 1890 until his death in 1914. The SLP was highly critical of the bureaucratic nature of the labour movement in both its trade union American Federation of Labor and industrial union CIO incarnations and of the Communist Party, insisting that the labour and Socialist movements had to be democratic and rational. The party distrusted emotional appeals and romanticism, arguing instead that worker militancy had to be the result of rational analysis and persuasion rather than demagoguery or adventurism, and was highly critical of the Communist Party idea that a militant minority could, or should, make the revolution on behalf of workers.[26]

Kuzych, however, was too cantankerous for the SLP, and in 1937, he resigned shortly before being thrown out of the party. He continued to hold many of the views of the SLP, and his critique of labour imposters and the closed shop echoed that of De Leon and the party. In particular, he opposed the closed shop because it was not democratic and furthered the creation of a labour bureaucracy that could afford to ignore the rank and file once its income had been safeguarded by the closed shop and the dues check-off.[27]

At the 1943 West Coast conciliation board hearing, Kuzych pointed out that far from being democratic, the BISU had used coercion to pull workers off the job during the wildcat strike at Norvan. He maintained that the CP leaders and shop stewards intimidated others to go on strike, and that the decision to go on strike had not been decided democratically and openly by the members. He argued that historically the closed shop had often supported company unionism. Indeed, the closed shop had long been the policy of the conservative American Federation of Labor and had been used to keep out more radical unions from the Knights of Labor to the Industrial Workers of the World to the CIO, and Kuzych drew attention to the irony of the radical and revolutionary CP giving it support. Cross-examined by the BISU president William Stewart, Kuzych continued to score rhetorical points at the hearing. Throughout the proceedings, Stewart insisted that the closed shop was essential for unions. Arguing that the employer's fierce opposition to the closed shop was proof that it was in the workers' interest, Stewart asked Kuzych, "Do you think an employer is foolish in not wanting a closed shop?" Kuzych replied, "No, I wouldn't say that." He then continued, "But most employers unfortunately belong to the Conservative party. They fight things from sheer habit," drawing laughter from the audience. At the same time, Kuzych denounced the Communist leadership for coming to an accommodation with the employer. Under questioning from Justice Wilson during the conciliation board hearings, Kuzych made an analogy to the Munich Pact of 1938, when Britain and Germany carved up Czechoslovakia as Britain desperately sought to avoid war. "Who's who in this analogy?" the judge asked Kuzych. "Do you regard Mr. Walkem [managing director of West Coast] as Hitler?" Kuzych responded, "I would say Stewart was Chamberlain," the British Prime Minister who had appeased Hitler, promising "peace in our time." Moreover, Kuzych insisted that there was no "form of collective bargaining that could be of benefit to both employer and employee," echoing the radical observation that capitalism was essentially a zero-sum game in which one side gained at the expense of the other.[28]

The only surviving transcript of his radio broadcasts, made after Kuzych had been expelled from the union, gives further evidence of his views. In it, Kuzych, speaking on behalf of the "Genuine Socialist Industrial Unionists of British Columbia," an organization he founded and named to distinguish it from the socialist industrial unionism the SLP espoused, examined the Ford strike then underway in Windsor. Broadcasting only four days before the strike ended, Kuzych noted that "We sympathise with the economic position of the Windsor Strikers. It is, more or less, our own economic position. It is, more or less, the economic position of every Canadian worker. No more. No less. We also admire their fighting spirit. Workingmen who will not bend their knee to oppression, but will take a manly stand against it, are to be admired." But if he were fighting for the wrong cause, Kuzych continued, "then a man's spirit — though noble and admirable — is wantonly wasted." Such was the case in the Windsor strike. While he agreed that workers were entitled to higher wages, shorter hours, paid vacations, "and a great deal more," in ninety-four days of strike action, the Ford workers had lost $7.5 million in wages. A settlement could have been reached much earlier, Kuzych argued; the only sticking point was the union's insistence on the closed shop and the dues check-off. While the strike leaders insisted that these measures were "good, sound Unionism," Kuzych maintained that they had not backed up their claim with convincing arguments. They could not, he suggested, because "the closed shop and the check-off in no way helps, or can help, to advance the cause of genuine Industrial Unionism." They would not benefit workers, in his opinion, but they would surely benefit the labour bosses. "A better set-up for procuring a comfortable living, without doing any work, can hardly be invented!" he maintained. "Once the workingmen are properly yoked into the closed shop and union dues and all the many extra assessments are checked off by the company time-keepers every month, regularly as death and taxes, the labor-dictator's worries are over! For them, at any rate, the millennium has been reached!" The strike, he concluded, was unnecessary and wasteful; it was not an example of rank-and-file militancy but of manipulation by union leaders for their own ends.[29]

Kuzych also had some evidence that the Communists in control of the Boilermakers were more opportunistic and less radical than they liked to think. As he pointed out at the West Coast commission, the salaries for the executive had not been published in the January 1943 financial reports, and this, he believed, indicated that they were hiding large salaries that would not sit well with the membership. When the union purchased a hall and used it as a meeting and recreation centre for workers, unions, and the Communist Party, Kuzych obtained the "Memorandum of Association" filed with the provincial government for Marine Workers Holding Limited, the named owner of the hall, capitalized to the amount of $75,000. Among the objects of the company was listed, "to carry on business as investors, capitalists, and financiers," with William Stewart and Thomas MacKenzie, another CP stalwart, listed as the directors. This was proof that the CP was little different from the capitalists it claimed to deplore. In some ways, it was worse, for in 1944, the manager of the hall was fined for hiring an underage boy to work as a pinsetter in the hall's bowling alley. For Kuzych, the notion of the Communist Party employing child labour was a Dickensian irony too delicious to let pass, and the story became part of his repertoire as he stumped the country in the 1950s trying to raise money to continue his legal appeal. His claims that the Boilermakers, and later the Marine Workers union that subsumed the Boilermakers, were "fake" and "spurious" unions too had some validity, in a political sense and in a narrow legal sense. Politically, Kuzych maintained that since they were not democratic or radical, the unions could not address workers' concerns properly. Nor was the CP leadership particularly democratic. The membership had not voted on the new bylaws and constitution; as the union went through its changes from being a CCL branch to an independent affiliate and inserted clauses that made the closed shop policy, no mass votes were taken. As Bill White revealed in his memoirs, in the 1944 election that saw Stewart defeated, the other CP executives only held onto their positions by stuffing the ballot boxes at the last minute. Legally, the internecine wrangling had put the union in a judicial limbo; while later courts ruled that the union was a legally constituted body, that was not clear when Kuzych began his battle and at least one BC judge would support his contention that the union had no legal existence.[30] All of this is to say that Kuzych had a case, and it was more profound than his critics allowed.

Litigating the Second Expulsion

It was a case he would soon take again to the courts. In *Kuzych v. White et al.*, No. 1, Kuzych argued that the expulsion was illegal because the new union, its constitution, and its bylaws had not been properly adopted and so were invalid. BC Supreme Court Justice Macfarlane, however, found that the new union and its constitution were valid, that Kuzych had been expelled in accordance with the constitution, and that the appeal process provided in the constitution, not the courts, was the appropriate venue for Kuzych to press his claim for redress. His action was dismissed with costs.[31]

Kuzych appealed Macfarlane's ruling to the BC Court of Appeal. There he found a great deal of support from a judiciary largely concerned with protecting individual rights and reluctant to support the collective rights asserted by unions. In its defence, the union, in an ironic, even bizarre, twist, argued since it sought the closed shop to raise the wages of its members, it was an organization illegally engaged in the restraint of trade. As an organization operating illegally, it could have no legal contract with Kuzych and so the court had no jurisdiction to intervene. This argument had not been advanced in the Supreme Court, and so the Court of Appeal ordered a new trial in the BC Supreme Court to determine a conclusion of fact and law.[32]

This time Kuzych found relief in the Supreme Court. The union again argued that its policies and objectives, particularly the demand for the closed shop, were in illegal restraint of trade and thus its contracts of membership were null and void. Justice Whittaker rejected this argument on several grounds, including the fact that the entering of a closed shop agreement was explicitly declared not to be an offence in BC and federal labour legislation. To the union's argument that the courts had no jurisdiction to intervene in the operation of an association or society, Whittaker held that the courts did have such a jurisdiction when a right of property was vested in the member of the society and when that member had been unjustly deprived of that right. Further, he held Kuzych did have rights of property based on union membership. These included sickness and death benefits, the right to vote, rights of members, and in particular, a preferred position in the matter of employment granted, ironically, by the very closed shop that Kuzych opposed. This was a very broad interpretation of property rights, so broad as to suggest that Whittaker was stretching mightily to find a legal justification to rule in favour of Kuzych.[33]

Contrary to Kuzych's argument, Whittaker agreed with Justice Macfarlane's earlier decision that the bylaws and constitution of the new union had been properly adopted and were in effect. However, he also held that the union committee that tried Kuzych was not constituted in accordance with the union's bylaws, citing an irregularity in its election. In matters as important as expulsion, it was crucial that an organization act in strict conformity with its rules. Since it had been improperly selected, the committee had no authority to try Kuzych. Therefore, the judge ruled, in essence, there had been no trial. That meant that Kuzych was not compelled to appeal within the union before seeking remedy from the courts as the bylaws stated and the union argued; there was, the judge held, nothing to appeal. It followed that Kuzych was entitled to succeed in his action against the union on this basis.[34]

Furthermore, the judge ruled that Kuzych was entitled to succeed on the grounds that "it cannot, by any stretch of the imagination, be said that the trial within the union was one that was free from prejudice and bias." Citing the testimony of William Stewart, who acknowledged that Kuzych was "a marked man" from the time he first refused to join the union; the union executive's refusal to let Kuzych attend meetings after he was reinstated in 1944; the threats made against Kuzych and his supporters; the article in the union paper, the *Main Deck,* that accused Kuzych of wasting $1,600 of the union's money and of "placing the entire trade movement on trial"; and the testimony of a witness who said that the names of those who voted against Kuzych's expulsion were called out and written down, Whittaker concluded that "the purported expulsion of the plaintiff was contrary to natural justice." The failure to properly select the committee and the campaign against Kuzych made it unnecessary, he continued, to decide whether Kuzych had in fact violated the union's bylaws and constitution, but Whittaker added that none of the three charges was adequately proved.[35]

Whittaker then commented on the larger question of the closed shop and trade unions. He began by asking, "ought a trade union which has a closed shop agreement with an employer under *any* circumstances (other than for non-payment of dues) have the right to expel a member?" The closed shop, he observed, was "a powerful weapon in the hands of organized labour," and as such, came with "corresponding duties and obligations." Chief among these were the "duty and obligation not to deprive a member of that membership which may have been acquired solely because employment could not be otherwise obtained." Other, "less drastic methods" of disciplining workers, such as fines and short suspensions, were readily available, Whittaker observed, and the obvious inference is that he did not believe the union had the right to expel members. Quoting a decision from Lord Justice Younger, he wrote, "even where there is no closed shop agreement, expulsion . . . means 'little less than a sentence of industrial death.'" Clearly, Whittaker continued, "these words have added force where the workman is in danger not only of being ostracized by his fellow workmen but of necessity by the employer as well." In his opinion, "it is alarming to think that the happiness and well being of the subject may rest in the hands of a tribunal which exercises power not conferred upon it by Parliament," particularly when the safeguards provided in a court of law, such as rules of evidence and the assistance of counsel, were absent. And in yet another ironic twist, Whittaker suggested that the federal and provincial laws that gave every employee the right to be a member of a trade union, generally seen as laws protecting pro-union employees from anti-union employers, should be interpreted as offering protection to employees from expulsion from the union. Whittaker then ruled that the expulsion of Kuzych from the BISU was illegal and void and that he was a member in good standing of the Marine Workers union that had absorbed it. He granted an injunction restraining the union from giving effect to its resolution expelling Kuzych, and granted Kuzych costs and damages of $5,000.[36]

Thus to White's insistence that the issue was whether and to what extent a union could discipline its members, Whittaker determined that the right to a job — and not just any job, but a union job — was paramount. In this conception, collective rights of workers expressed in and through unions took a back seat to individual rights, and the courts saw themselves as upholding the rights of the individual in the face of tyrannical organizations. Of course the courts upheld the "right" to a job only when this was threatened by unions, never when threatened by employers.

The union then appealed to the BC Court of Appeal. In a 3:2 decision, the majority upheld the essence of Whittaker's judgement, though it rejected some of his arguments and elaborated on others as it held that Kuzych did not have to exhaust all the internal remedies before turning to the courts. Justice O'Halloran, who along with Justices Robertson and Sidney Smith formed the majority, noted that it was Kuzych's "persistent advocacy of the open shop principle within and without the union" that led to his expulsion. The "almost religious zeal" of the union in enforcing the closed shop led the union leaders to conclude, "unjustifiably," in the justice's opinion, that Kuzych was "an enemy of organized labour" and "anti-working class." The leadership had convinced union members that opposition to the closed shop was tantamount to being anti-union, and as a result, it was impossible for Kuzych to receive a fair trial. In the judge's opinion, once it was proven that Kuzych was opposed to the closed shop, the verdict was a foregone conclusion. Since the verdict was "inevitably prejudiced and virtually decided before the trial was held . . . in essence there was no trial at all. The trial committee was simply carrying out the declared policy of the union as announced by its leaders at the time." To the union's defence that the conduct of a person might create an intense animus against him such that bias and prejudice were almost inevitable, the judge agreed, but inverted the argument to offer it as further proof that the trial committee was "inherently incapable of giving the respondent a fair trial." Since the "so-called [trial]" was "no trial at all and hence a nullity," there was nothing for Kuzych to appeal against, and so he was not required to go through the union's appeal process. Such an appeal would be meaningless in any case, for the Shipyard General Workers' Federation to whom Kuzych could appeal would not, and could not, by the judge's reading of its constitution, interfere with the union's autonomy, including its declaration in its bylaws that one of its purposes was to consummate closed shop agreements. That is, the judge believed that the verdict of the appellate tribunal too would be "a foregone conclusion"; it could only carry out established policy, not give a fair hearing.[37]

As had Whittaker in the BC Supreme Court, O'Halloran held that expulsion from the union was a sentence of "industrial death." As such, it was a violation of Kuzych's civil rights. "A man has a right to work at his trade," the judge wrote, and thus it followed that if union membership were required for that work, "then he has an indefeasible right to belong to that union." No union could have the right to be the sole arbiter of who could join and remain in the union and at the same time decree that only union members could be employed. No doubt influenced by the rhetoric of the Cold War and cognizant of the CP leadership of the union, O'Halloran felt obliged to hold that "such interference with individual liberty and coercion may be done under a totalitarian system, but not under any system which takes its inspiration from the common law." In addition, O'Halloran argued that the expulsion denied Kuzych's common law rights to freedom of legitimate speech and action, rights that were far beyond the power of any union to decide. That, the judge noted, "is the prerogative of the constituted Courts of the country." That the union had acted beyond its competence was yet another reason Kuzych did not have to go through the union's appeal process before going to the courts.[38]

Justice Robertson rejected Whittaker's conclusion that the union committee had not been elected properly; noting the irregularities in the first election, he nonetheless was able to "assume that the second committee was duly elected." However, he agreed with Whittaker that the expulsion "was contrary to natural justice." Furthermore, the bias displayed before the trial by one of the union committee members that tried Kuzych was so extreme "as to render him unfit to act" on the committee. Citing several precedents regarding judges and bias, Robertson concluded that having such a biased member on the quasi-judicial committee meant that the committee "was not competent to hear the charges" against Kuzych. Since the committee was incompetent, the union had failed to hold the proper investigation and so Kuzych was not compelled to appeal a verdict that, in effect, had never been rendered.[39]

Perhaps the most subtle arguments for dismissing the union's appeal came from Justice Sidney Smith. He first rejected the union's argument that

Kuzych was bound by his membership in the union to abide by the constitution and appeal to the Shipyard General Workers' Federation before going to the courts. If that principle applied to fraternal orders, Sidney Smith doubted that it should apply when the consequences of expulsion were as great as they were in the Kuzych case. He did, however, hold that the union committee was properly constituted, and so rejected Whittaker's finding that the process was invalid because the union had not followed its own rules. He also rejected the standard of "natural justice" that Whittaker and Robertson had applied, arguing that "natural justice" had "little meaning and that little [was] misleading." If it had any meaning at all, it must mean some common law principle, and so violations of natural justice had remedies in common law "without involving any special brand of justice."[40]

Unlike O'Halloran, Sidney Smith gave some credence to the union's argument that Kuzych's behaviour had made some bias against him inevitable, and that bias alone did not necessarily invalidate a committee's decision. He acknowledged that

> the plaintiff has not only proved a turbulent and unruly member, but had indulged in acrimonious criticism and even abuse of the union and its policies generally, so that personal bias and strong dislike from the committee was nothing more than he could expect. I appreciate this to the full, and agree that if the result of this had simply been that the committee and general executive had simply detested him and had dealt with his actions officially with straightforward indignation, we could not and should not interfere.

But in this case, he continued, the committee and the union executive had gone much further. The actions of union officials before and during the trial went "far beyond what can be excused as mere expressions of honest and justifiable resentment. They disclose attempts to prevent anything like a fair trial by either the committee or the general meeting." The justice held that the expulsion of Kuzych was invalid, and went on to suggest that the legislature give the courts better tools with which to intervene in union affairs, for it was by no means clear "whether membership on which men's livelihood depends should be left entirely at the mercy of committees and similar domestic tribunals. Things seemed to have advanced past the state when principles that originally only governed membership for social amusements should be allowed to prevail where men's livelihood is at stake."[41]

Justices Bird and Sloan dissented from the majority opinion. Bird, writing for them both, acknowledged that the election of the trial committee had not strictly conformed to the letter of the appropriate article in the bylaws, but held that "it was in accord with . . . the spirit of that article," and was "a bona fide attempt to resolve the difficulty" caused by the discovery that one of the elected members was not eligible to hold office. Since the trial committee was valid, Kuzych was bound to exhaust all the remedies and appeals provided in the bylaws and constitution before turning to the courts to exhaust all the remedies. Finally, Bird argued that there was no reason to doubt that Kuzych would have had an opportunity for a fair hearing before the union appeal tribunal.[42]

While the court upheld Whittaker's verdict, the 3:2 split left the union some room to hope that an appeal might be successful. The union decided to appeal directly to the Privy Council, believing, as White put it much later, that "the judicial system in this country isn't set up to dispense justice, it's set up to protect the established order."[43] While this may sound naïve — the Privy Council could hardly be called the cutting edge of the revolution — it reflects White's sense that the BC courts were directly influenced by local business and political leaders. The Privy Council heard the union's appeal over eight days in April, May, and June 1951. While the law lords spoke to several of the issues raised by Kuzych and the union, they declared two questions to be paramount. The first was whether the trial committee was improperly constituted. If it were, its decisions were legal nullities and thus Kuzych was freed from the obligation to appeal within the union before going to the courts. The second was whether the process was so contrary to natural justice that it could not produce a meaningful decision; again, that would make appeal through the union's processes irrelevant and unnecessary. On the first question, the law lords concurred with the dissenting opinions of Bird and Sloan and concluded that the union committee was validly constituted. On the second question, they held that "the whole difficulty is to put the proper construction on the word 'decision' when the [bylaw] gives a right of appeal . . . when a member found guilty or penalised . . . 'feels that the decision is unfair or the penalty too severe.'" The law lords again concurred with Bird and Sloan, though only "after anxious reflection." Noting that the purpose of the relevant union bylaws was to attempt to settle disputes between members and the unions "to the exclusion of the law courts," a "decision" meant a "conclusion" that could be appealed rather than a decision reached through an impartial, untainted process in accord with principles of natural justice. Such a decision had been rendered, even though the law lords agreed that "severe condemnation of the methods followed in the proceedings under review is fully justified." Since the trial committee was valid and it had come to a decision, Kuzych was bound to go through the appeal process before taking to the courts.[44]

The union had won its legal challenge and was awarded costs. But while White and others hailed the decision as a vindication of the right of unions to discipline members and the closed shop, it was not as sweeping and clear as union leaders suggested. Indeed, Kuzych maintained, accurately enough, that nothing in the ruling supported the closed shop; the law lords were highly critical of the process of expelling Kuzcyh; and the decision had hinged on technical grounds rather than principles. The end result was simply that the Privy Council decision allowed Kuzych to begin his case all over again. Ultimately, he was stopped not by the court ruling but by the requirement that he post a $15,000 bond for costs before proceeding with further action. Unable to raise the money, he finally quit.[45]

Furthermore, there are several versions of the union's response to Kuzych's return to the BC courts, none of which redound to the union's credit. Bill White maintains that when Kuzych applied to the BC Court of Appeal to proceed without posting the $15,000 bond, White gave Gordon Wismer, a notorious Liberal bagman, $5,000 to fix the case. According to White, the case was to be heard by two anti-union judges and one pro-union judge, but after a short adjournment, three pro-union judges returned and gave a unanimous verdict that required Kuzych to post the $15,000 bond before continuing his action. "How Wismer set that up I don't know," White concludes, "and I made a point never to ask." Sam Jenkins, who succeeded White as president of the union, claims that he was given a letter that listed the names of several corporations and people who were trying to raise money for Kuzych. Jenkins then warned Phil Gaglardi, a minister in W.A.C. Bennett's Social Credit government, that he would take the letter to the press unless Gaglardi used his political muscle to force the companies to cease and desist, and the minister complied. William Stewart tells a similar story, claiming that the union spread a rumour that it was going to sue the people named in the letter and this threat had the desired effect of making them drop support for Kuzych. Jack Scott on the other hand, holds that the union, which Scott belonged to at the time, passed a motion to reinstate Kuzych and post him to work to avoid further litigation and the possibility of having to pay damages that could include time lost from work for more than ten years.[46] However it happened, through some combination of exhaustion, penury, bribery, or threats, it was a shabby end to a case that had ostensibly begun as a matter of principle, politics, and power.

Conclusion

WHAT ARE WE TO make of this case? The strictly legal lessons are inconclusive, for the decision essentially left Kuzych and the union where they had started and resolved none of the substantive issues of the closed shop, union discipline, and union democracy that propelled the case. While *Kuzych v. White* is still widely cited, it is usually restricted to the relatively simple issue of exhausting internal appeals before seeking recourse through the courts.

Thus the most important lessons to be drawn from *Kuzych v. White* may be political and historical, not legal, in nature. Most obviously, the case is a reminder that justice can be a commodity, for it shows how costs can be an insurmountable barrier for an individual worker and a formidable barrier for a union seeking to enforce common law rights in courts. The case is also an important reminder that the post-war labour relations regime, often called the "post-war consensus" and the "post-war settlement" between capital and labour was contested and patched together; it was a complicated affair, and one in which workers were rarely consulted directly.

Kuzych v. White also demonstrates how ethical and political concerns become transformed by the courts into more legalistic battles that can become far removed from the original issues. Taking the matter to the judicial system guaranteed that Kuzych's principles would be transformed into much narrower legal claims that bore little relation to his stated concern for union democracy and socialism: whether union constitutions are justiciable, whether the union followed its stipulated procedures, whether those procedures met the requirements of "natural justice" as defined by the courts, and whether Kuzych had to go through the union appeal process before turning to the legal system. While Kuzych undoubtedly had politics and principles that were much more profound than those attributed to him by his opponents, his decision to fight the union through the courts virtually ensured that his beliefs would be ignored or distorted and that unionism itself would be put on trial.

Certainly the court cases and the publicity surrounding *Kuzych v. White* focused on Kuzych's attacks on the union and ignored his critique of capital and the state. By casting the dispute as a contest between an embattled but principled working stiff and a powerful union led by Communists, the judicial system and the media used Kuzych's banner of "individual rights" to attack the union movement. Thus there is some truth to White's charge that whether he knew it or not, Kuzych's attacks on the union aided the employer by weakening the union's legal position, draining its treasury, and influencing public opinion.

At the same time, since no organization or collective agreement is perfect, some dissatisfaction is probably inevitable, and unions rely on majorities, not unanimity, to resolve differences. That means controversy and dissent are inevitable, and how union officials choose to handle dissidents poses new difficulties and opportunities. In this case, the CP union executive counted on the closed shop as a club to control dissidents. It is not difficult to see why. The union had been in the ring facing two opponents, the CCL and the employer, with the courts and government as the allegedly impartial referees who threw sand in the union's eyes. The union leaders had taken part in important struggles and had been red-baited and harassed by other labour officials who would use any trick they could to secure their positions. Having won a victory over the CCL and having won considerable, if not universal, support from the membership, it was easy to assume that the rank and file had repudiated the old trade unionists and given the new leaders a meaningful mandate to fight for the closed shop and better conditions. At the same time, the new executive faced the three-pronged challenge every union faces. Unions achieve their aims only through struggle; they are "fighting organizations," as Robert Michels put it many years ago.[47] But they are also democratic institutions, which means that the command structures of armies, governments, and businesses do not exist: unions have few ways to compel members to do the right thing. Finally, unions need unity, or solidarity, to accomplish anything, and building that solidarity is time-consuming and difficult. Perhaps there is a healthy formula to resolve this often contradictory situation, but no union has found an ideal, permanent solution. The BISU and the Marine Workers were no exception.

The union's defence of the closed shop as a crucial tool for labour, however, was disingenuous. While many employers have fought the closed shop as a restriction on management's rights, or, hypocritically, as an affront to workers' democratic rights, others have found it useful. The closed shop usually means a single union bargains for all the workers, and if this gives the union more strength, it also makes labour relations easier for the company. The closed shop turns the union into a labour contractor that dispatches competent workers. This reduces the effort the company must expend in training and selecting personnel. As it diverts the attention of the union from representing workers to supplying the employer with labour, it may cause a real conflict of interest. The closed shop also means that issues arising from the shop floor are presented to the company in an orderly fashion by a union representative who understands the rules and the compromises necessary to handle things within the rules. Chris Madsen points out that most BC shipyards found it advantageous to have the closed shop, precisely because it brought the harmony William Stewart promised it would. As C. Wright Mills put it, "the closed shop makes for peace and stability," not democracy and militancy, as Kuzych warned.[48]

Kuzych v. White also helps us refine our assessment of the Communist Party and its work in the union movement. The militant action of CP union organizers and union leaders was crucial to their success. Unlike Kuzych, the CP activists understood that workers' struggles, even when they are lost, play a critical role in building unions and movements that cannot be replaced with logic and programmatic correctness. At the same time, by the 1940s the unions headed by CP members resembled other unions more than they did a revolutionary movement in their quest for better wages and conditions and their actions as a labour bureaucracy. Understanding Kuzych's politics shows that there were currents in the Canadian Left and labour movements that were more principled and more radical than the CP, though they were much weaker and have not been explored adequately by historians.

Thus Jack Scott, who later broke with the CP, maintains that the union reaction "was overblown," and that Kuzych's attack on the closed shop and the dues check-off was essentially correct from a radical's perspective. Instead of taking on Kuzych directly about the issues of the closed shop and union discipline, Scott suggests the union could have fined him for testifying for the boss during the West Coast commission and let the matter stop there. Ironically, the same process of defining loyalty and dissent, expelling members from the union, and using the closed shop to force them out of their jobs was used by the "Whites" to purge CP leaders from the trade union movement in the 1940s and 1950s.

Perhaps the ultimate consequences of *Kuzych v. White* were summed up brusquely and ironically by one activist in 1983, as labour in BC was under attack from a Social Credit government:

> When I see the face of a labour leader on the TV now it's always fat. All jowls like hogs ready for the knife, it's hard to imagine the sight of any of them striking fear in the capitalists' hearts. It's bad enough not being able to tell the bosses from the labour leaders by looking at them but the worst of it is half the time you can't tell when they talk either . . . . Now the leadership

can lay back in the head office and pay themselves big salaries because they know the dues are going to come rolling in anyway. Much as I hate to say it the closed shop has a lot to do with this.

The author of the above lines is Bill White.[49]

While the evolving industrial relations framework in Canada gave unions some rights and protections, these rights came with a price: bureaucracy and an industrial peace treaty that ultimately rendered workers unarmed while capital rearmed at a ferocious pace. For a North American labour movement in crisis and transition, *Kuzych v. White* may serve as a reminder that unions need militancy and democracy if they are to thrive and present a meaningful, radical challenge to capital and the state.[50]

Notes

* The author would like to thank Aisling Murphy and Eryk Martin for their help and suggestions.

1 See David Roth, "A Union on the Hill: The International Union of Mine, Mill and Smelter Workers and the Organization of Trail Smelter and Chemical Workers, 1938–1945" (M.A. Thesis, Simon Fraser University, 1991) for an examination of how the legislation was welcomed by one union and was the key to its organizing success. Peter S. McInnis, *Harnessing Labour Confrontation: Shaping the Postwar Settlement in Canada, 1943–1950* (Toronto: University of Toronto Press, 2002) gives a less optimistic analysis.

2 C. Wright Mills, *The New Men of Power: America's Labor Leaders*, 1948 (Reprint, Urbana: University of Illinois Press, 2001), see especially 7–9 and 224–29.

3 For an examination of these issues and how they apply specifically to the closed shop, see W.E.J. McCarthy, *The Closed Shop in Britain* (Oxford: Basil Blackwell, 1964). See also Michael Goldfield, *The Decline of Organized Labor in the United States* (Chicago: University of Chicago Press, 1987) and Kim Moody, *US Labor in Trouble and Transition: The Failure of Reform from Above, the Promise of Renewal from Below* (New York: Verso, 2007) for critiques of labour and the law.

4 *Mainland Sawmills Ltd. v. IWA-Canada, Local I-3567 Society* (2004), 33 B.C.L.R. 4th 110 (SC).

5 *A History of Shipbuilding in British Columbia* (Vancouver: Marine Retirees Association, 1977) at 25–27 and 52–61 [*A History of Shipbuilding in BC*]; Howard White, *A Hard Man to Beat: The Story of Bill White, Labour Leader, Historian, Shipyard Worker, Raconteur* (Vancouver: Pulp Press, 1983) at 20–73 [White, *Hard Man to Beat*]; Chris Madsen, "Continuous Production in British Columbia Shipyards during the Second World War" (July 2004) 14:3 The Northern Mariner 1 [Madsen, "Continuous Production"]; Chris Madsen, "Organizing a Wartime Shipyard: The Union Struggle for a Closed Shop at West Coast Shipbuilders Limited 1941–44" (Spring 2010) 65 Labour/Le Travail 75–108 [Madsen, "Organizing a Wartime Shipyard]; Jan Drent, "Labour and the Unions in a Wartime Essential Industry: Shipyard Workers in BC, 1939–1945" (October 1996) 6:4 Northern Mariner 47; Royal Commission to Inquire into the Most Effective Methods to Secure Maximum Production in the Shipyards of British Columbia, "Report of the Royal Commission on Production of Ships in the Shipyards of British Columbia," 1942 ["Production of Ships"]; Irving Abella, *Nationalism, Communism, and Canadian Labour: The CIO, the Communist Party, and the Canadian Congress of Labour, 1935–1956* (Toronto: University of Toronto Press, 1973) at 80–85; John Stanton, *Never Say Die! The Life and Times of John Stanton, A Pioneer Labour Lawyer* (Ottawa: Steel Rail Publishing, 1987) at 187–196.

6 *A History of Shipbuilding in BC*, ibid. at 52–68; Stanton, ibid. at 187–96; Abella, ibid. at 80–85; White, *Hard Man to Beat*, ibid. at 176–77.

7 The Communist Party of Canada was renamed the Labour-Progressive Party from 1943 to 1959, but I refer to it here as the Communist Party for simplicity and clarity.

8 *A History of Shipbuilding in BC*, above note 5 at 52–64 and 108; Stanton, above note 5 at 187–96; White, *Hard Man to Beat*, above note 5 at 29–31.

9 White, *Hard Man to Beat*, ibid. at 26 and 34.

10 "Production of Ships," above note 5; Madsen, "Organizing a Wartime Shipyard," above note 5 at 93–96; *A History of Shipbuilding in BC*, above note 5 at 62.

11 "Production of Ships," above note 5 (reports of C. Pritchard and Alex McAuslane); Madsen, "Continuous Production," above note 5 at 18–19; for opposition to continuous production and voting, see *A History of Shipbuilding in BC*, above note 5 at 60–67.

12 See McCarthy, above note 3 at 3.

13 For the McDonald's case, see Jeremy Milloy, "Fast Food Alienation: Service Work and Unionism in British Columbia, 1968–1998" (M.A. Thesis, Simon Fraser University, 2007) at 65–86.

14 See Judy Fudge & Eric Tucker, *Labour before the Law: The Regulation of Workers' Collective Action in Canada, 1900–1948* (Toronto: Oxford University Press, 2001) Part II; Peter S. McInnis, above note 1.

15 For the Ford strike, see Fudge & Tucker, *ibid.* at 283–85; David Moulton, "Ford Windsor 1945" in Irving Abella, ed., *On Strike: Six Key Labour Struggles in Canada, 1919–1949* (Toronto: J. Lewis & Samuel, 1974); William Kaplan, this volume.

16 *A History of Shipbuilding in BC*, above note 5 at 52–64; Stanton, above note 5 at 187–96; Madsen, "Continuous Production," above note 5; for Stewart and MacLeod, see *Vancouver Sun* (18 May 1943). For the closed shop as a way to keep competing unions in shipyards at bay, see Madsen, "Organizing a Wartime Shipyard," above note 5 at 4–5.

17 *A History of Shipbuilding in BC, ibid.* at 123–27; White, *A Hard Man to Beat*, above note 5 at 133. Interview of Myron Kuzych with author (9 April 2001, 21 July 2001, transcript in author's possession) [Kuzych interviews]; E.F. Whitmore, "Judicial Control of Union Discipline: The *Kuzych* Case" (January 1952) 30:1 Can. Bar Rev. 1; H.J. Clawson, "Union Security Clauses and the Right to Work" (February 1952) 30:2 Can. Bar Rev. 137; Marine Workers and Boilermakers Industrial Union Local No. 1, "On Appeal from the Supreme Court of British Columbia, from the judgement of the Honorable Mr. Justice Whittaker, 22 September 1949" (Appeal Book, Volume 1) (Myron D. Kuzych Collection, Simon Fraser University, Special Collections [Kuzych Collection]) at 63–64 [Appeal Book]; Bill White, "The History and Outline of the Case, Kuzych versus the Boilermakers' Union," typescript, 8 June 1950, Kuzych Collection [White, "History and Outline of the Case"]; *Vancouver Sun* (13 October 1943); *(Vancouver) Province* (13 October 1943); *Vancouver News-Herald* (13 October 1943).

18 *Vancouver Sun* (13 October 1943); *(Vancouver) Province* (13 October 1943); *Vancouver News-Herald* (13 October 1943).

19 *Vancouver Sun* (18 May 1943).

20 Kuzych interviews, above note 17; Whitmore, above note 17 at 2; Appeal Book, above note 17; White, "The History and Outline of the Case," above note 17; *Vancouver Sun* (13 October 1943); *Vancouver Province* (13 October 1943); *Vancouver News-Herald* (13 October 1943).

21 *A History of Shipbuilding in BC*, above note 5 at 123; White, *A Hard Man to Beat*, above note 5 at 122; Whitmore, above note 17.

22 *Kuzych v. Stewart et al.*, [1994] 4 D.L.R. at 775–79. This suit was launched against William Stewart, then president of the BISU; the other cases named Bill White, who replaced Stewart as head of the new Marine Workers Union that absorbed the BISU.

23 *A History of Shipbuilding in BC,* above note 5 at 67–68 and 123–27; White, *A Hard Man to Beat,* above note 5 at 122; White, "The History and Outline of the Case," above note 17; *The Main Deck,* 2 February 1945, Kuzych collection, above note 17; Marine Workers and Boilermakers Industrial Union No. 1, "Trial Report of Proceedings, Myron Kuzych," 12–13 March 1945, (UBC Special Collections, Box 9, Folder 1); White, *A Hard Man to Beat,* above note 5 at 121–23 and 133; Proceedings at Trial, BC Court of Appeal, *Kuzych v. White et al.,* 3 May 1950, transcript, Kuzych Collection, above note 17 at 45–68.

24 White, *A Hard Man to Beat,* above note 5.

25 White, *A Hard Man to Beat, ibid.* at 120–21; Jack Scott, *A Communist Life: Jack Scott and the Canadian Workers Movement, 1927–1985* (St. John's: Committee on Canadian Labour History, 1988) at 114–17; Benjamin Isitt, "Moscow on the Fraser: The Communist Party in Cold War British Columbia," (unpublished paper, delivered to the Canadian Historical Association, Vancouver, BC, 4 June 2008) at 26–27; Madsen, "Organizing a Wartime Shipyard," above note 5.

26 Kuzych interviews, above note 17. For a short biography of Lefty Morgan, see the introduction to R.E. (Lefty) Morgan in G.R. Pool & D.J. Young, eds., *Workers' Control on The Railroad: A Practical Example "Right Under Your Nose"* (St. John's: Canadian Committee on Labour History, 1994) and Gail R. Pool, Jim Stanley, & Donna Young, "Biography of Richard E. (Lefty) Morgan" (Spring 1991) 27 Labour/Le Travail 215. The SLP has not been well treated by historians, but see Stephen Coleman, *Daniel De Leon* (Manchester: Manchester University Press, 1990); James B. Stalvey, "Daniel De Leon: A Study of Marxian Orthodoxy in the United States" (PhD Thesis, University of Illinois, 1947); James A. Stevenson, "Daniel De Leon: The Relationship of the Socialist Labor Party and European Marxism, 1890–1914" (PhD thesis, University of Wisconsin, 1977); Roger O'Toole, *The Precipitous Path: Studies in Political Sects* (Toronto: P. Martin Associates, 1977); Frank Girard & Ben Perry, *The Socialist Labor Party, 1876-1991: A Short History* (Philadelphia: Livra Books, 1991).

27 Kuzych interviews, above note 17; BC Court of Appeal, *Kuzych v. White et al.,* 3 May 1950 (Marine Workers and Boilermakers Industrial Union Local No. 1 Collection at 63–64).

28 Madsen, "Organizing a Wartime Shipyard," above note 5; *A History of Shipbuilding in BC,* above note 5 at 123–27; Madsen, "Continuous Production in British Columbia Shipyards," above note 5; Kuzych interviews, above note 17; Whitmore, above note 17 at 2; Appeal Book, above note 17 at 116–19; White, "The History and Outline of the Case," above note 17; *Vancouver Sun* (13 October 1943); *(Vancouver) Province* (13 October 1943); *Vancouver News-Herald* (13 October 1943).

29 Myron Kuzych, "Fifth Address" (transcript delivered over the CKWX, 15 December 1945); Marine Workers and Boilermakers, above note 23.

30 Myron Kuzych, speech delivered to the Department of Industrial Relations, Queen's University, October 1954, copy in author's possession. Kuzych cites the *Vancouver Sun* (29 December 1944) for the fine levied against the manager of the bowling alley. A copy of the "Memorandum of Association" dated 10 July 1943 with the stamp of the BC Registrar of Companies is in the Kuzych Collection, above note 17. So too

is a letter dated 5 March 1943 from a BISU member noting that the financial report for 6–31 January 1943 did not disclose officers' salaries. White, *A Hard Man to Beat*, above note 5 at 41–42.

31 *Kuzych v. White et al.*, No. 1 (1947), 1 W.W.R. 323.

32 This judgment was not reported. Reference is made to it in *Kuzych v. White et al.*, No. 2 (1948) 2 W.W.R. 732 (BCCA), where the union failed in its appeal from the order directing a new trial.

33 *Kuzych v. White et al.*, No 3 (1949), 2 W.W.R. 558.

34 *Ibid.*

35 *Ibid.*

36 *Ibid.*

37 *Kuzych v. White et al.*, No 3 (1949), 2 W.W.R. 558, aff'd No. 3 (1950), 2 W.W.R. 193 (BCCA).

38 *Ibid.*

39 *Ibid.*

40 *Ibid.*

41 *Ibid.*

42 *Ibid.*

43 White, *A Hard Man to Beat*, above note 5 at 144. Two other cases, *Kuzych v. White et al.* Nos. 4 and 5, were heard in Canadian courts before the Privy Council appeal. In No. 4, Bill White and William Stewart were found guilty of contempt of court for refusing to grant Kuzych membership in the new Marine Workers' and Boilermakers' Industrial Union that had succeeded the BISU. That conviction was overturned by the BC Court of Appeals. Kuzych received leave to appeal to the Supreme Court of Canada, but in *Kuzych v. White et al.*, No 5, Kuzych was denied his motion to the BC Court of Appeals to forego paying costs of $1,200 before launching that appeal. See *Kuzych v. White et al.*, No. 4 (1950), 1 W.W.R. 325; the overturning of the contempt conviction is in (1950), 2 W.W.R. 255; see (1950), 2 W.W.R. 1069 for *Kuzych v. White et al.* No. 5.

44 *White and Others v. Kuzych*, [1951] 2 All ER 435.

45 *Kuzych v. White et al.*, No. 6 concerned Kuzych's attempt to have the BISU's merger with the Marine Workers declared invalid or to have the court declare he was entitled to membership in the Marine Workers. The union's application to stop Kuzych's further action was denied. *Kuzych v. White et al.*, No. 7 and its appeal concerned Kuzych's attempts to continue his action without first paying the costs awarded to the union by the Privy Council. He lost, and the decision was upheld on appeal. See (1952), 6 W.W.R. 567 (NS); (1953), 10 W.W.R. (NS) 106; and (1953), 11 W.W.R. (NS) 44.

46 White, *A Hard Man to Beat*, above note 5 at 145–46; *A History of Shipbuilding in BC*, above note 5 at 126–27; Scott, above note 25 at 116.

47 Robert Michels, *Political Parties: A Sociological Study of the Oligarchical Tendencies of Modern Democracy*, 1915 (Reprint, Glencoe: Free Press, 1948) at 30–47.

48 Madsen, "Organizing a Wartime Shipyard," above note 5; Mills, above note 2, see especially 7–9 and 224–29. See Mark Leier, *Red Flags and Red Tape: The Making of a*

Labour Bureaucracy (Toronto: University of Toronto Press, 1995) for a discussion of bureaucracy. See Christopher L. Tomlins, *The State and the Unions: Labor Relations, Law, and the Organized Labor Movement in America, 1880-1960* (Cambridge: Cambridge University Press, 1985), especially Chapter 6 and Part III.

49 Scott, above note 25 at 116–17. White, *A Hard Man to Beat,* above note 5 at 210.

50 See, for example, Goldfield, above note 3 and Moody, above note 3 for a critique of labour's move to the right over the last two decades and the need for union democracy to revitalize the labour movement.

Organizing Offshore: Labour Relations, Industrial Pluralism, and Order in the Newfoundland and Labrador Oil Industry, 1997–2006

Sean T. Cadigan

THROUGHOUT THE SUMMER AND early fall of 2001, the Newfoundland and Labrador Labour Relations Board (NLRB) made a series of decisions that allowed organized labour to gain a foothold among workers in the province's offshore oil industry, which was notoriously resistant to union organization. On 11 July, the board ruled that the Communications, Energy and Paperworkers Union of Canada (CEP) was legally entitled to apply for certification of a bargaining unit for workers on the Hibernia offshore drilling platform. The union won a certification vote on 24 September by a significant majority. On 12 October, the board dismissed an attempt by the employer, the Hibernia Management and Development Company (HMDC), to challenge the composition of the bargaining unit, affirming the CEP's victory in the fight to organize and certify the union.

The NLRB appeared to be routinely sorting out a union's struggle with a determined opponent in HMDC, and its rivalry with a competitor, the Canadian Auto Workers — Fish, Food, and Allied Workers (CAW-FFAW), which had also tried to organize the platform's workers. However, the board's decisions are an important example of the persistence and ambiguities of industrial pluralism in the particular case of Newfoundland and Labrador. One of the main features of post-1945 Canadian industrial legality was state recognition of skilled workers' collective bargaining rights to promote economic growth in manufacturing. Canadian unions generally did not participate in tripartite industrial management in partnership with capitalists and governments, but tripartism was essential to industrial pluralism in the offshore oil industry. In Newfoundland and Labrador, natural-resource sector workers enjoyed few of the rights of industrial legality. The post-1945 experience was usually of employer and state opposition to such workers' rights to bargain collectively. From the International Woodworkers of America (IWA) strike of 1958–1959 to the *Ocean Ranger* tragedy of 1982, workers in the province's natural-resource sectors could take for granted few of the state's and enterprise's post-1945 bargains with organized labour that affected industrial legality.[1] Throughout the 1980s, economic recession created an exceptionally hostile environment for unions in the province. Antagonistic relations between the labour movement and the provincial government suggested that unions would face state opposition to their efforts to organize the offshore oil sector.

It might seem odd that the provincial government actually amended legislation to facilitate the organization of workers on the Hibernia oil production platform. The province's actions took place before more recent battles with the Canadian government over revenue sharing under the Atlantic Accord or its struggles with oil corporations for an equity stake in future oil field development. Consequently, there is no reason to think that the government acted because it sympathized with local workers' effort to secure better employment conditions in an industry controlled by outside interests. This paper argues that the Newfoundland and Labrador government amended the Newfoundland *Labour Relations Act* (*NLRA*) to facilitate unionization offshore because of two factors. First, the *Ocean Ranger* disaster had made safety in the offshore oil sector a public priority, including a stable labour relations environment that would secure operations. Second, by the late 1980s, worsening economic conditions had forced unions, employer representatives, and the provincial government to consider cooperative action in fostering economic development. By 1996, representatives of the three groups flirted with tripartism in a Labour Relations Working Group (LRWG). In the same year, the province appointed Morgan C. Cooper to make recommendations on the future of labour relations in the offshore oil industry. While the work of the LRWG had little impact on provincial labour policy, it did influence Cooper's work. Cooper's report advocated offshore workers' rights to collective bargaining and recommended new regulations for the offshore sector. Cooper's recommendations led the government to amend the *NLRA*.[2] The amendment accommodated the unionization of workers on the Hibernia offshore production platform.

The provincial government's statements on Cooper's report and the subsequent actions of the NLRB suggest that the government's priority was not collective bargaining for workers. Instead, the province recognized that it and oil corporations had to accept but restrain unions to secure a safe industrial environment and attract more capital investment. The new consensus held that union certification and a "mature" approach to collective bargaining were necessary to foster strategic industries such as offshore oil. For unions, this "mature" approach meant giving up the right to strike in first-contract situations, limiting autonomy, and accepting a supporting role in advancing the goals of the state and capital in the development of the offshore oil industry. The provincial government's legislative changes and the NLRB's rulings were in keeping with the broader pattern of industrial pluralism: to ensure labour peace that would promote economic development.

Historical Context

INDUSTRIAL LEGALITY BEGAN TO take shape in Newfoundland as the government sought union support for its war effort during World War II. During his successful fight for Newfoundland's entry into Confederation in 1949, J.R. Smallwood led people to believe that he would advance the cause of industrial legality; the Newfoundland *Labour Relations Act* of 1949, which emulated the American *Wagner Act* (1935) and the Canadian *Industrial Relations Disputes Investigation Act* (1948), was one of his provincial government's first measures. While employers of skilled workers, such as those in the industrial enclaves of pulp and paper towns Grand Falls and Corner Brook, recognized their right to collective bargaining, employers of unskilled workers, such as poorly paid loggers, made no such concessions. The Industrial Woodworkers of America (IWA) began to organize loggers in 1958 and led a strike in 1959 for higher wages and better living conditions in the on-site camps. The bitter struggle that followed led to violent confrontations between loggers and the police in central Newfoundland, Smallwood's personal public campaign against the IWA, the passage of the *Trade Union (Emergency Provisions) Act* on 6 March 1959 to revoke certification of the IWA as the bargaining agent for the loggers, and the government's appointment of a Liberal Party loyalist as president of a more conciliatory union. The federal Conservative government, the International Labor Organization (ILO), and the Canadian Labour Congress (CLC) condemned the provincial government's actions, but Smallwood succeeded in forcing the IWA out of the province.[3]

Smallwood opposed the IWA primarily because he feared that stronger unions among resource harvesters would be a deterrent to foreign investment in natural-resource development. The premier's intimidation of organized labour revealed that the rights of industrial pluralism could be dismissed with a legislative flourish if unions dared to oppose his government's policies. In the short-term, Smallwood mollified people by instigating public battles for provincial rights with the federal government. Throughout the 1960s, the difficult position of the labour movement in Newfoundland continued to be apparent, such as when the Smallwood government ignored most of the recommendations made by a Royal Commission it had appointed to investigate industrial disease among St. Lawrence miners in 1967. By the early 1970s, unions representing diverse workers such as teachers, fishers, miners, and hospital workers became more militant, finally rejecting Smallwood and joining unions.[4]

By the late 1970s, unionized workers hoped that prosperity might emerge from Progressive Conservative Premier Brian Peckford's battles with the federal government over which order of government would control the rapid expansion in oil and gas exploration off the province's coasts. In their rush for development and jurisdictional fights, the federal and provincial governments overlooked offshore workers' safety. This inattention took on tragic dimensions on Valentine's Day, 1982, when a winter storm led to the sinking of the exploratory drilling rig *Ocean Ranger*. All eighty-four crew members aboard the rig lost their lives. The tragedy was part of a rapid increase in major mishaps involving oil rigs in the offshore oil sector globally as exploratory drilling boomed throughout the 1970s and 1980s. Subsequent investigations, including a Royal Commission, attributed the disaster to rig design problems, poor training for the crew, and the offshore oil companies' insufficient attention to workers' safety and related complaints.[5]

The *Ocean Ranger* disaster was a tragic example of how courting investment in natural resource development had greater priority than workers' rights for the provincial government. As the recession of the late 1970s deepened and extended throughout the 1980s, the Peckford government passed Bill 37 in 1984. This bill deprived workers in the mining, fishing, and forestry industries of rights to layoff notices and compensation when companies closed and sold out to new corporate interests. In the public sector, the province had passed Bill 59 in 1983. This bill permitted the government to designate up to 49 percent of public-sector union members as essential public employees, and limited their right to strike, especially by outlawing rotating strikes. The Peckford government earned the criticism of the ILO, but it hoped that offshore oil development under the Atlantic Accord with the federal government in 1985 would improve the province's fortunes. The Progressive Conservatives nonetheless lost to Clyde Wells' Liberals in the provincial election of 1989. The Wells government embraced retrenchment and battles with public-sector unions, but it prohibited "double-breasting" (a practice plaguing the building and construction trades whereby unscrupulous contractors would shut down unionized companies, and then reopen as non-union organizations to avoid their obligations to collective agreements). A consortium of oil companies began to develop the Hibernia offshore oil field amid a barely improved local labour relations scene.[6]

Over-expansion in fishing and forestry produced over-capacity and severe economic and social problems by the early 1990s. By 1992, northern cod stocks collapsed, and the federal government declared moratoria on ground fisheries. Employment declined dramatically in the fishing industry from about 16,000 full-time fishers in 1988, especially as federal adjustment programs and regulations confined much of the right to fish commercially to what it defined as "core fishers" (just over 4,000 in 2004). Employment also declined in fish processing from about 11,300 in 1986 to about 8,400 in 2001, in an area notorious for the extremely short duration of work and lower pay. In the forestry sector, pulp and paper production depended on a shrinking resource base and drastically reduced levels of employment. Employment in pulp and paper production has fluctuated more; the total number of people employed dropped from 2,800 in 1996 to 1,400 in 2006, a trend worsened by the permanent closure of the mill in Stephenville and the shutdown of one of two paper machines operating at the mill in Grand Falls-Windsor.[7]

Unions and Industrial Stability

IN THE 1980s AND 1990s, offshore oil development was a beacon on what was otherwise a bleak economic horizon for the province. The Newfoundland government and industrial partners in the Hibernia project had agreed that a gravity-base structure (GBS) would be used for oil production. The GBS, a massive platform that would be fixed to the ocean floor, was to be fabricated at a new facility built for this purpose at Bull Arm, Trinity Bay. While the GBS was well suited to the harsh weather of the North Atlantic, it required much more capital investment than floating production platforms. Fabrication required hundreds of workers from a variety of trades, many of whom lived on the construction site. The project consequently required other workers to house and care for the construction force.

The Newfoundland government hoped that the fabrication of the GBS would begin an oil-related construction sector in the province. Such a development would be unlikely if labour unrest disrupted the production schedule and added to the cost of the GBS. From the beginning, the Hibernia partners recognized the need for a reliable labour relations framework for dealing with so many different types of workers and their unions. At the same time, labour leaders had come to believe that union cooperation was essential to the success of the GBS project. By January 1989, twelve building and construction unions, together with representatives of the Teamsters and the Hotel and Restaurant Workers had formed an Oil Development Council (ODC) and were ready to organize the fabrication facility. The owners of the Hibernia project and their contractors formed the Hibernia Employers' Association (HEA) and, by July 1990, concluded an agreement with the ODC with government support.[8] The provincial government placed all workers at the construction site under the agreement by a special project order. The most important provision of the agreement was that there would be no strikes, lockouts, or other job actions by either party, who would submit disputes for expedited settlement or arbitration. Through NL Reg. 97/91, the Newfoundland government later placed the offshore start-up phase of the Hibernia platform under the same special project designation.[9]

Initially, the relationship between the ODC and the HEA appeared to ensure that informal resolution or expedited arbitration would prevent labour disputes between the multiple unions and subcontractors on the Bull Arm site from igniting into work stoppages that would throw off the fabrication schedule. However, internal disputes within both the ODC and the HEA eventually led to delays at the worksite, which disrupted production. The building trades unions had played a leading role in ensuring that Bull Arm workers had full rights to collective bargaining. Over time, the difficulties of sorting out union jurisdictions in matters of dues and in contributions to self-insured health plans and pension funds meant that these unions were not interested in fighting for a similar council of unions for offshore facilities. The historical trend among employers and unions in the construction industry across Canada had been a lack of cooperation in their approach to labour relations.[10] By the late 1970s, unions in the construction trades had responded to greater employer cooperation and poor economic conditions by forming provincial councils. However, the unions remained suspicious that broader-based collective bargaining might weaken them individually. In the case of the ODC, the logistical problems of overseeing a collective agreement were more important than mistrust between unions. The building trade unions decided to support the larger unions such as the CAW-FFAW or the CEP in their efforts to organize offshore. The oil companies, otherwise resistant to unions offshore, wanted their future oil production facilities to be considered single bargaining units to avoid the disruptions that developed at Bull Arm.[11]

The GBS was ready for towing to the drilling site on the Grand Banks in 1997. While there would be subcontractors and skilled workers involved in its operation, the platform provided a well-defined community of interest among the employees. A number of unions such as the CEP and the CAW-FFAW wanted to organize the platform workers alone rather than working together in a council of unions. Both unions were the result of the merger movement of the 1990s. Most unions had suffered internationally from membership losses and declining influence in collective bargaining and politics throughout the 1980s and 1990s. The CEP and CAW-FFAW faced added local problems in the fishery and forestry, and hoped to regroup their forces by mergers with other unions and by marshalling their resources to organize new groups of workers.[12]

The FFAW became a subsidiary of the CAW in 1987 as part of a larger merger process. From 1985 to 1995, sixteen unions joined the CAW's embrace of Canadian nationalism and social democracy in opposition to affiliation with American-based international unions. CAW support helped the FFAW negotiate federal programs to assist fishers and plant workers who had been hurt by the moratoria on Atlantic ground fisheries in 1992. However, the CAW-FFAW's structure most suited organizing small-boat fishers, deep-sea fishers, and fish-processing workers. More experienced in organizing previously unrepresented workers in new industrial sectors, the CEP had formed in 1992 from the merger of the Communications and Electrical Workers of Canada, the Energy and Chemical Workers Union (ECWU), and the Canadian Paperworkers Union (CPU), which had absorbed Newfoundland loggers in 1988. The merger created a union with deep roots in the Newfoundland forestry sector, but which was also experienced in organizing petroleum workers elsewhere in Canada.[13]

The CEP's composition and background in the province ideally positioned it to organize Hibernia platform workers. Local CEP leaders Ray Cluny, the union's organizer in Grand Falls, along with Ron Smith, the CEP's national representative in the province, Brian Campbell, and Keith Klein-wachter, an energy worker who had previously organized the Nanticoke, Ontario oil refinery, spearheaded the CEP effort, almost immediately facing a culture of "paternalism and manic anti-union attitude of multinational oil companies bigger than most countries."[14] Well paid by provincial standards, the Hibernia workers were encouraged by their employers to say as little as possible about their work to outsiders. The offshore workers were difficult to organize because they came from communities spread out around Newfoundland and Labrador. On the other hand, the arbitrariness of offshore management had not changed much from the days of the *Ocean Ranger* and stories abounded among platform workers of management attempts to dismiss workers with medical problems. Also, many workers disliked management favouritism in the "personal development program," a system by which workers received different rates of pay for the same work, depending on their supervisors' personal reviews. Overall, Hibernia platform workers had begun to appreciate the importance of union representation and collective bargaining to job security, although they did not seem to be overtly concerned about occupational health and safety issues.[15]

By early 1997, there were few local opportunities for the CAW-FFAW or the CEP to grow except by expansion into the offshore oil sector. Organizing that sector was daunting. The American firms that dominated the offshore sector were well-known for their hostility to unions aboard their rigs and platforms. In the United Kingdom (UK), for example, American corporations and their UK partners had opposed unions for years.[16] Operators in the offshore sector felt that unions would interfere with production partially by diverting effort into health and safety. Unions affiliated with the Trades Union Congress (TUC) played into operators' hands by divisive efforts to extend their accepted onshore "spheres of interest" to the offshore. Only in the wake of the 1988 *Piper Alpha* oil rig disaster, which killed 167 men, did offshore workers begin to acquire collective bargaining rights. An Offshore Industry Liaison Committee (OILC) developed as offshore workers believed that the TUC unions did not appreciate the centrality of health and safety measures to the offshore labour relations environment. Fearful of OILC influence, the offshore operators welcomed the more conservative and business-friendly TUC unions under the auspices of the UK *Employment Relations Act* (1999). The UK Act permitted partnership agreements between employers and unions to determine who represented workers rather than providing for employees' choice through certification votes.[17]

Although the Newfoundland and Labrador industry appeared set to follow the British pattern, it actually followed a path that more resembled Norwegian tripartism. The Norwegian industry, especially the publicly owned Statoil, had accepted unions. These unions participated on safety committees for oil rigs with management and consulted with employers and government about the management of the industry.[18] In Newfoundland and Labrador, the Liberal government of Brian Tobin appointed Morgan C. Cooper to investigate offshore labour relations in 1996. The Tobin government was disinterested in labour matters, but recognized the importance of offshore development in an otherwise troubled economy. Cooper was a prominent local specialist in labour and employment law who had taught labour law at Memorial University, served as an arbitrator, and who had no close relationships with unions or employers. Union leaders such as Bill Parsons considered him to be a proactive, impartial voice in facilitating a better labour relations climate in Newfoundland. Cooper agreed to make recommendations "to facilitate a harmonious labour relations climate on offshore oil production platforms that will optimize labour stability, health and safety and productivity."[19] He requested written submissions from interested parties from labour, management, and other backgrounds and met with selected representatives from government, industry, and the labour movement. Cooper also consulted representatives of the Canada-Newfoundland Offshore Petroleum Board (C-NOPB) and the Canada-Nova Scotia Offshore Petroleum Board (C-NSOPB), and representatives of the oil and gas industry in Alberta, Nova Scotia, Norway, and the UK.[20]

The oil companies involved in the Newfoundland and Labrador offshore sector had well-established reputations for being anti-union, and the labour relations climate had chilled considerably over more than twenty years of economic recession and government retrenchment. However, organized labour, employers' groups, and provincial officials were desperate to attract more capital investment in natural resource development by ensuring a peaceable labour relations climate. In 1996, thirteen senior representatives of labour such as Bill Parsons and Elaine Price, then president of the Newfoundland and Labrador Federation of Labour (NLFL), and employers such as John Peddle, then Executive Director of the Newfoundland and Labrador Health Boards Association, had come together in a Labour Relations Working Group (LRWG) to recommend overall legislative changes to facilitate collective bargaining. In return, unions would cooperate with employers and government in producing a secure environment conducive to private-sector growth. While the provincial government largely ignored the LRWG, its tripartist perspective was not lost on Cooper, who argued that the group's recommendations "offer significant potential to facilitate harmonious labour relations as well as productivity and stability for all work establishments, including provincially regulated establishments in the offshore petroleum industry."[21]

While there would be no sweeping reform of labour legislation in Newfoundland and Labrador, the government wanted Cooper to make specific recommendations that would promote the development of the offshore sector. Federal-provincial negotiations over offshore jurisdiction resulted in section 152 of the *Canada-Newfoundland Atlantic Accord Implementation Newfoundland Act*.[22] This section allowed the province to apply the *NLRA* to any rig that was to be permanently attached or anchored to the seabed or subsoil of the offshore area. Labour organizations differed on whether or not individual unions or councils of unions would best represent Hibernia platform workers. Nonetheless, most unions felt that the current procedures for certification and the designation of bargaining units favoured multi-employer and multi-union bargaining. Such bargaining risked the jurisdictional disputes and delays that had developed at the Bull Arm fabrication facility. The NLFL endorsed the LRWG's position that strikes and lockouts could be avoided through compulsory interest arbitration for a first collective agreement if the provincial government developed special legislation that would designate the Hibernia platform as a unionized project. The unions maintained that such designation would guarantee a safer workplace that would be more likely to avoid the fate of the *Ocean Ranger*. Industry representatives argued for voluntary implementation of better government regulations, although there had been very limited development of a regulatory framework for health and safety offshore since the tragedy under the C-NOPB. Furthermore, the lost-time accidents during the oil exploration of the later 1980s remained high, and safety incentive schemes put into effect by the oil industry during construction of the Hibernia platform may have encouraged under-reporting rather than reduction of accidents and other safety incidents. It is not surprising, therefore, that labour organizations emphasized the importance of union representation in the implementation of better regulations in the provincial industry, and Cooper agreed that platform workers must be involved in such.[23]

Cooper proposed that the management structure adopted by the owners of the platform, an overarching HMDC, provided for more centralized employer control over work and avoided the fragmentation of the building trades in the construction phase of the Hibernia project. The industry preferred that one bargaining unit be established for the sake of stability, and the unions agreed because they felt it was the best way to organize as many workers as possible. Many unions argued why they would be best designated as representatives of the platform workers, but Cooper maintained that "the employees who make up the workforce must be the ultimate judge of their interests on the issue of unionization as well as choice of bargaining agent."[24] Cooper asserted that the "team work, multi-skilling and functional integration" of platform work favoured a platform-based bargaining unit of all workers. He wanted the NLRB to have the authority to designate such a unit upon an application for certification. The board would have to require HMDC to organize all contractors and subcontractors for the purposes of collective bargaining. The special project designation for the construction and start-up of the Hibernia platform excluded construction and start-up workers aboard the platform and left the NLRB to sort out who was eligible for membership in the bargaining unit. Cooper further recommended that the NLRB should have the power to order "reasonable" and "economical" access by unions to the platform.[25]

Cooper advised against legislating compulsory arbitration for the Hibernia platform because of the "mature outlook on the role of industrial conflict in the offshore petroleum industry" in written submissions from the CAW, CEP, NLFL, and the Offshore Development Council. These submissions favoured first-agreement compulsory interest arbitration. The CAW-FFAW, which represented crew members aboard shuttle tankers that service the Hibernia platform, had already agreed with the employer, Cancrew, on a twenty-five year collective agreement in exchange for wage indexing and the submission of disputes to interest arbitration. Such voluntary relinquishment of the right to strike, Cooper argued, was the best way for the union movement "to seek improvements in terms and conditions of employment." Although the CAW-FFAW contract, a "life of field" agreement, suggested that the "mature" unions might effectively surrender their right to strike, it is clear that Cooper was referring primarily to first-contract situations. Cooper acknowledged that organized labour had little choice because of the prospect of the provincial government introducing "legislation on either a permanent or *ad hoc* basis restricting or prohibiting strikes or lockouts in the offshore." If the government adopted such measures, "the potential to capitalize on the commitment associated with the voluntary relinquishment of economic sanctions will never be realized." However, to be sure that no strike or lockout would be used to produce a first collective agreement in the event of certification, Cooper recommended that interest arbitration be required by law as the means of resolving impasses in negotiations.[26]

The provincial government welcomed what became known as the Morgan Cooper report and, in December 1997, amended the *NLRA* to provide "a labour relations regime to govern oil production platforms in the Newfoundland offshore industry."[27] Charles Furey, then Minister of Mines and Energy, stated that the government was acting "to ensure harmonious labour relations in the offshore oil industry," which would "greatly contribute to the province's ability to be globally competitive in the offshore oil industry"[28] The government amended section 41 to recognize and regulate councils of trade unions as well as single unions that might apply for the right to represent offshore oil production platform workers. Amendments to section 56 required that employers form a council to deal with a single union or council that had been certified to represent platform workers. Additions to section 81 provided for arbitration of a first collective agreement through the board's appointment of an arbitration board upon notice from either party that they were unable to reach agreement. An amended section 100 provided that the parties to a collective agreement might not authorize a strike or lockout until procedures had been put in place to ensure the safe shutdown and maintenance of the platform. The most important amendments proved to be

> 38.1 (1) Where the board receives an application with respect to employees employed on an offshore petroleum production platform, the unit appropriate for collective bargaining is the unit comprising all the employees employed on the platform except those employees the board determines are employed in construction and start up on the platform. . . .
>
> (3) For the purpose of an application for certification with respect to employees employed on an offshore petroleum production platform, the licensed operator of the platform shall be considered to be the employer of the employees for the purpose of the board's consideration of the application.[29]

The amendments to section 38 provided the NLRB with the authority to designate HMDC as the single employer of record for the Hibernia platform.

The NLRB and Hibernia Certification

THE AMENDMENT TO SECTION 38 of the *NLRA* proved indispensable to the CEP's organization of the Hibernia platform workers. The union was lucky in that HMDC mistakenly left an employee list in files it had submitted to a government review of design and safety issues related to the platform. This list gave the CEP valuable contacts and a core group of workers to sign union cards. The rules and procedures of the NLRB, as in many other Canadian jurisdictions, allowed the platform workers to indicate their desire for a vote on union certification by signing membership cards, an expedited process that inhibited anti-union campaigns by employers.[30] For certification purposes, a signed union card was only good for ninety days from the date of its signature, so the CEP not only had to constantly find new workers who were not on the list, but it also had to re-sign those workers whose cards were about to expire. Ron Smith did much of this work by networking over the telephone, expensive home visits to workers, media advertising, and a web-based campaign. Smith used these techniques because HMDC successfully used legal challenges, contrary to the spirit and intent of the Cooper report, to inhibit the unions' ready access to the Hibernia platform.[31]

While the CEP expected resistance from the employer, it did not expect the CAW-FFAW's attempt to piggyback on its effort to organize Hibernia platform workers. Early in 1997, the CEP had gained the blessing of a meeting of unions called by the NLFL to decide which one should organize the Hibernia platform. The CAW-FFAW, which absented itself from this effort to avoid a jurisdictional dispute, stepped in with an application for certification on 12 November 1999. In the CEP's opinion, the FFAW "were looking to reap where the CEP had sown." The CEP's Local 97 followed six days later with an application, although it did not feel that the union was ready for a certification vote. Ron Smith felt that the FFAW had probably been acting on behalf of the CAW, which had been trying to bolster the sagging membership of its CAW-Marine Workers Federation Local 20, which represents workers at the Marystown shipyard on the Burin Peninsula of Newfoundland.[32]

Caught unaware of the strength of both unions' organizing efforts, HMDC offered stiff resistance that relied heavily on a litigation strategy (see Appendix: Board and Court Decisions).[33] In 2000, CEP Local 97 and the FFAW complained to the NLRB that HMDC and its subcontractors had laid off twenty-five workers in violation of section 45 of the *NLRA*. This section prohibited employers' alteration of the wages, terms, and/or conditions of employment until the outcomes of applications for certification were known. HMDC's action likely aided the CEP's cause because the affected workers included supporters of the FFAW certification drive.[34] HMDC claimed that, although it had received the notice of application for certification, the actual contractors that employed the workers had not. Consequently, HMDC argued, the statutory freeze on working conditions did not apply to HMDC and its subcontracting firms. The NLRB disagreed with HMDC's position. The board reiterated the amendments to section 38; as the licensed operator of the Hibernia platform, HMDC was the sole relevant employer that required notice of the certification application. The board's decision clarified how the NLRA simplified the process of defining the proper bargaining unit and employer for the unions that wished to organize platform workers. It chose not to decide at that time about whether the layoffs had violated the NLRA. Resolution of the fate of the twenty-five workers would take almost another six years of board hearings, judicial reviews, and appeals.[35]

Although the amended NLRA had simplified the issue of identifying the proper employer of record and bargaining unit, the NLRB had to establish procedures for two unions applying separately to certify the Hibernia workers at the same time. The board decided there would be two separate but concurrent votes in which each Hibernia worker received two separate ballots. One ballot asked whether or not the worker wished to be represented by the FFAW and the other asked the same question about the CEP. The workers cast each ballot in a separate ballot box, but the ballots were held on the Hibernia platform, the Airport Plaza Hotel (which is close to the heliport workers use to go to and from the platform), and by mail in December 1999. The NLRB ordered that the ballots be segregated and the ballot boxes be sealed until a hearing on the unions' applications could be held. The hearing began on 24 June 2000 and lasted until 16 February 2001.[36]

HMDC fought the applications partially by contesting the eligibility of many of the workers who had originally signed the membership cards that led to the votes. Citing the special project order exclusion of construction and start-up workers on the platform from certification, HMDC argued that any work related to the replacement of equipment that had not been performed as originally specified was start-up work. Such capital expenditure (or "Capex") work, HMDC maintained, would continue throughout the operation of the Hibernia platform, and would demand the ad hoc hiring of workers on short-term contracts, who should be ineligible for membership in a bargaining unit.

The NLRB did not accept HMDC's position. It noted the CEP's and the CAW-FFAW's position that "construction and start up" work arose specifically from the towing of the Hibernia platform to its drilling location, and from the work required to bring the platform into production. To accept

HMDC's position about Capex work would have the effect of allowing a substantial group of workers to be employed on the Hibernia platform without representation in a bargaining unit. The NLRB argued that the amendments to the *NLRA* specified that HMDC would be the employer of record for purposes of collective bargaining and prohibited the proliferation of many small bargaining units aboard the platform. These changes had to be considered in light of the amendment to section 100, which provided for no strikes or lockouts until an agreement was put in place for a safe and orderly shutdown of the platform's operations. These provisions existed to ensure that labour relations aboard the platform would not threaten safety. Conceding HMDC's position on Capex workers would provoke more uncertain and potentially disruptive relations, accomplishing the opposite of the amended *NLRA*'s intentions. The NLRB ruled that none of the platform workers would be excluded from a bargaining unit as desired by HMDC. The board also ruled that a variety of highly specialized coordinators, operators, and engineers should be members.[37]

By the time of the board's ruling on HMDC's struggle against the certification applications, Morgan Cooper had become its chair, and he held the position until 28 February 2003.[38] It is difficult to be certain about how much influence he personally exerted on the board's subsequent deliberations. Almost all of the subsequent applications and interventions to the board came before panels of board members that did not include Cooper, and the vice chairs of the board wrote its rulings. Nevertheless, the NLRB's application of the amended section 38 of the *NLRA* was consistent with the views of the Cooper report. The ruling made clear the NLRB's view that the need for overall stability on the platform overrode the individual prerogatives of the various contracting and subcontracting employers on board. The NLRB, in keeping with the Cooper report, was not safeguarding employer rights, as is the usual practice in Canada, or employee rights for that matter. Its main concern was a "public" interest, which the board defined as a provincial commitment to the safest, most stable environment in which offshore oil production might be carried out and attract further capital investment. The amendments to the *NLRA* put aside, as a special case for the offshore oil industry, the usual commitment of boards in most Canadian jurisdictions to minor modification of "the anarchic competitive-market model" boards assume should prevail in the determination of union certification. Labour relations boards usually approach certification with the intent to contain the potential for industrial disputes to disrupt production and to "enhance stability for individual employers." In the Hibernia case, the NLRB considered the stability and safety of production as paramount.[39]

The NLRB's dismissal of HMDC's main argument against the applications of certification was a victory for the unions, but neither the CEP nor the CAW-FFAW succeeded in their first bid to certify a bargaining unit for the Hibernia workers. Both unions failed to demonstrate that they had the support of at least 40 percent of the workers eligible for membership in a bargaining unit, the minimum threshold under the NLRB's rules for allowing certification votes.[40]

The labour relations environment of the province, however, was tipping even more in favour of unionization. By 2001, the serious economic problems that continued to face Newfoundland and Labrador led officials from the provincial government into partnership with representatives of the business community and of the province's major labour organizations, including the NLFL, the Newfoundland and Labrador Nurses Union, the Newfoundland and Labrador Teachers Association, and the Newfoundland and Labrador Building and Construction Trades Council. These representatives constituted a "Strategic Partnership Study Group," which developed a Strategic Partnership Initiative (SPI). The goal of the SPI was to promote collaboration rather than confrontation between government, business, and organized labour by focusing on strategic policy rather than collective bargaining as the way to improve society and the economy. One member of the NLRB, Bill Parsons, had served in the SPI as he had with the LRWG.[41]

Undaunted by its initial failure to secure certification, the CEP reapplied for certification within a month with Local 60N, the local which represented forestry workers in Newfoundland, as the bargaining unit for the Hibernia platform workers. Expecting to have to wait out the minimum six-month cooling-off period, the FFAW was taken by surprise. The CEP's Ron Smith remembered how, during the IWA Strike, the NLRA had specified that, to be a considered a union in the province, an organization must be a "local or provincial organization of or association of employees, or a local or provincial branch of a national or international organization or association of employees within the province." Each local of the same national or international group was a distinct legal entity in Newfoundland and Labrador. Smith reviewed the NLRA and found that the provision still existed. He convinced the CEP's doubtful lawyer that Local 60N was a pre-existing multi-bargaining unit local that might not be taken as an alter ego of Local 97.[42] The CAW-FFAW's legal advisors did not accept the CEP's premise; it supported

HMDC's protest to the NLRB on 28 March 2001, that the CEP's action violated the board's Rules of Procedure, which specified that unions that failed in a certification application had to wait at least six months before applying again. The NLRB agreed with the CEP. The board ruled that Local 60N was a separate and distinct legal entity from Local 97 and its national parent. Local 60N could apply for certification without waiting for six months from the time of the NLRB ruling on the earlier application. The board set aside any questions about the validity of union membership cards held by the CEP until it made a decision on the local's application for certification.[43]

In the only ruling on the subject to be written by Morgan Cooper as chair of the NLRB, the board finally decided on CEP Local 60N's application on 12 October 2001 following a 19 September challenge of the bargaining unit's composition by HMDC. The board disagreed with HMDC's claim that the signed membership cards presented by Local 60N were "an insufficient proxy" for evidence of membership in the local. Citing a previous decision of the Newfoundland Court of Appeal, the board argued that its rules allowed the board "a broad and liberal construction of membership evidence in keeping with the remedial nature of the certification provisions" of the *NLRA*. The board also ruled that HMDC was wrong to contend that the memberships of many of the workers presented by the CEP were invalid because they violated the CEP's bylaws, which prohibited members from joining two unions, in this case concurrent memberships in Local 97 and Local 60N. Again, the NLRB maintained its own broad discretionary powers in determining the eligibility of membership in accordance with the view that the collective representation of workers was in the public interest. Upon reviewing CEP Local 60N's application, the NLRB had found that it had 191 members of a possible 400 workers signing cards, or 47.75 percent. The CEP had crossed the threshold that allowed it to proceed to a certification vote, which it won by obtaining a two-thirds majority of the votes that were cast on shore or by mail-in ballots and counted on 24 September 2001. This majority was far more than the simple majority required for certification and gave the CEP the right to represent the Hibernia platform workers.[44]

The intervention by HMDC resembled a common method used by employers throughout North America to thwart union drives since the 1980s: using legal procedural delays to wear down support for certification. While the NLRB's ruling thwarted the effort, it failed to prevent the possible use of "illegal discharge of union supporters," another common anti-certification tactic used by employers.[45] Certification was not a complete victory for the workers involved. The CEP and the FFAW had fought to have reinstated the twenty-five workers who had been laid off in 2000. The unions emphasized HMDC's rhetoric about treating workers like family and that it offered its permanent or "steady state" workers security for the life of the project. The laid off workers, who had been permanent employees, had a right to expect such security as members of the HMDC "family." The NLRB agreed, but found more compelling the CEP's argument that HMDC had violated the statutory freeze on changing the conditions of employment for workers involved in a certification drive. HMDC had defended the layoffs by claiming they were part of a normal restructuring process as the platform moved from start-up to steady-state operations. In the board's opinion, the question of how restructuring would affect workers was a reasonable subject for first-contract negotiations. The board further suggested that laying off the workers was an antagonistic step that would damage the relationships between workers and their employer before negotiations even began, and ordered that the workers be reinstated with compensation for lost income.[46]

HMDC did not accept the board's decisions on the Local 60N application for certification or for the laid off workers. It applied for judicial review to the Newfoundland and Labrador Supreme Court. Although the court affirmed in 2004 the NLRB decision on the Local 60N application, it overturned the board's decisions about the laid off workers.[47] On 12 July 2002, Justice LeBlanc ruled that the NLRB had improperly applied a subjective rather than an objective test to determine whether or not HMDC had breached the freeze period specified by section 45 of the *NLRA*. In LeBlanc's view, caselaw supported considering whether the layoffs were in keeping with the general "pattern of employment relationship" that had existed before the CEP and CAW-FFAW applications for certification.[48] He found that the HMDC's productivity incentive program, called "Gainshare," clearly outlined the possibility of layoffs for temporary and permanent employees. Consequently, it had been improper for the NLRB to consider whether permanent employees' subjective perspectives on the likelihood of being laid off had any bearing on the objective condition that such layoffs had clearly been possible.[49] The CEP appealed the review, which resulted in the Court of Appeal ordering the NLRB to reconsider the matter again by a "proper application" of an objective test to whether or not the layoffs violated the freeze period.[50]

The NLRB reconsidered but reaffirmed its decision, and refused to assent to HMDC's request that it reconsider the order that the employer rehire the workers.[51] HMDC again applied for judicial review, and Justice Halley ruled that the board's reinstatement order was a punitive measure that extended a remedy beyond the freeze period for certification applications provided in section 45 of the *NLRA*. He overturned the NLRB's order that the workers be rehired, a decision confirmed by the CEP's failed appeal.[52] While courts normally defer to administrative boards in judicial review, the provincial Supreme Court concentrated on questioning the process by which the NLRB had attempted to preserve the best labour relations environment possible from the damage caused by suspicions that the layoffs had been retaliatory actions by the employer in the face of certification applications.

Conclusion

WHILE LABOUR RELATIONS STATUTES across Canada have facilitated collective bargaining, they have carefully circumscribed workers' right to strike.[53] The process that led to Hibernia workers gaining collective bargaining rights, including Cooper's assessment of local unions' "maturity," rested on the notion that such bargaining would forswear completely the right to strike or, for that matter, employers' right to lock out at least in first-contract situations.[54] However, the CEP was unable to come to terms with the Hibernia Platform Employers' Organization by 2004. Joseph Gargiso, the national bargaining coordinator for the CEP, stated that the union preferred "to negotiate terms but employer resistance is forcing us into following the mandatory first contract arbitration procedure," provided for in the amendment to section 81 of the *NLRA* in 1997.[55] The CEP invoked the amended section 81 of the *NLRA*, which required arbitration of a first collective agreement on the request of either party, and achieved a collective agreement that covered the period from 1 May 2006 to 30 June 2009.[56]

Despite giving up the right to strike for a first contract, the CEP had achieved a significant victory in its organization of the Hibernia platform partially by being able to take advantage of the amendments to the *NLRA* and the interpretations of the NLRB. Although the CEP's mergers are part of a pan-Canadian trend that has witnessed relatively stable union density since the 1970s, the reinvigoration of the organized labour movement depends partially on representing workers in economic sectors such as the offshore that are difficult for unions to organize or feature relatively well-paid workers in strategic sectors such as in energy. While many unions have stagnated through the merger process, real growth may be measured in terms of becoming certified to represent new workers in collective bargaining. Offshore oil production workers remain largely unorganized in North America; however, the CEP's victory at Hibernia has paved the way for Local 60N to organize expeditiously the nearby Terra Nova field workers.[57] Whether certification and collective agreements for Hibernia and Terra Nova workers are the beachhead for unionization of offshore platforms and rigs along the American seaboard, as hoped for by the CEP, remains to be seen.

The significance of the developments in labour law in Newfoundland and Labrador should not be underestimated. Elsewhere in Canada, few jurisdictions have been interested in the development of new legislation that would assist workers in gaining the right to organize. The overall trend has been toward making it more difficult for unions to win certification battles. The amendments to the *NLRA* in 1997 and subsequent application by the NLRB simplified the process of collective bargaining for the CEP. The government was primarily interested in rationalizing what would otherwise have been a potentially divisive and confusing multi-employer and multi-bargaining unit industry in the interest of safety. However, such bargaining units have been associated with relatively weak unionization elsewhere.[58]

The "discursive power" of labour law in this case was both in the nature of the revisions of the *NLRA* and the willingness of the NLRB to interpret the actions of the HMDC (although within limits set by judicial review) in terms of what would secure the environment aboard the Hibernia platform through good employee-employer relations and a mutually acceptable collective agreement.[59] Nevertheless, the amendment to the *NLRA* and the decisions of the NLRB also reflect the provincial labour movement's interest in tripartism, abandonment of its right to strike, and embrace of compulsory first-contract arbitration.[60] While the SPI represented an effort by the labour movement to become more influential in public policy, it also suggests indifference to an independent political voice for organized labour that might otherwise be a key to a more vigorous union movement.[60] The shift in provincial labour law was not merely discursive; it arose from a political-economic context in which positive economic development has continued to be elusive in Newfoundland and Labrador outside of key industrial staples, especially offshore oil. Desperate for better times, provincial unions have accepted a labour relations process that continues to harness it to the development imperatives of capitalism. The amendments of the *NLRA* and their interpretation by the NLRB, as such are the culmination, not the abrogation, of the province's much slower movement toward the post-war settlement.

Appendix: Board and Court Decisions by Date

Date of Decision	Body	Legal Citation	Issue	Outcome
20 Dec. 2000	NL Labour Relations Board	CEP L97, First Applicant, and FFAW/CAW, Second Applicant, and HMDC, First Respondent, NLRB file 118:508, 118:510.	Whether or not HMDC was employer of record in matter of layoff of twenty-five workers	HMDC confirmed as employer of record under *Labour Relations Act*, R.S.N.L., 1990, c. 44, s. 38.
30 March 2001	NL Labour Relations Board	FFAW/CAW, Applicant, and HMDC., Respondent, and CEP L97, Applicant, and HMDC, Respondent, NLRB file 712:2784, 712: 2788.	HMDC challenges composition of possible platform bargaining unit membership	Board confirms membership but rules unions failed to sign enough members to warrant certification votes.
11 July 2001	NL Labour Relations Board	HMDC, Applicant, and CEP, Respondent, and CEP L60N, FFAW/CAW, Intervenor, NLRB file 2207.	HMDC argues CEP L60N application for certification violated six-month freeze of *Labour Relations Act*, R.S.N.L., 1990, c. 44. s. 45	Board rules that CEP L60N was legally distinct entity and had a right to apply for certification.
11 July 2001	NL Labour Relations Board	CEP L60N, Applicant, and HMDC, Respondent, FFAW/CAW, Intervenor, NLRB file 2228.	NLRB's jurisdiction in the above questioned by FFAW/CAW	NLRB confirms its jurisdiction.
12 Oct. 2001	NL Labour Relations Board	CEP L60N, Applicant, and HMDC, Respondent, FFAW/CAW, Intervenor, NLRB file 2228, 12 October 2001.	Did L60N have support of 40 percent of members of possible bargaining unit?	NLRB confirms and orders certification vote.
4 Dec. 2001	NL Labour Relations Board	FFAW/CAW, Applicant, and HMDC, Respondent, and CEP L97, Applicant, and HMDC, Respondent, NLRB file 118:508, 118:510.	Whether or not HMDC layoffs of twenty-five employees violated *Labour Relations Act*, R.S.N.L., 1990, c. 44, s.45	Confirms violation and NLRB order to reinstate and compensate the twenty-five workers.
4 Dec. 2001	NL Labour Relations Board	CEP L 97, First Applicant, and FFAW/CAW, Second Applicant, and HMDC, First Respondent, NLRB file 118:508, 118:510.	Reasons for above decision	Established that employees' "reasonable expectation" about job security must be considered in the application of *Labour Relations Act*, R.S.N.L., 1990, c. 44. s.45.

Date of Decision	Body	Legal Citation	Issue	Outcome
12 July 2002	NL Supreme Court (Trial Division)	HMDC v. F.F.A.W.-C.A.W., 215 Nfld. & P.E.I.R. 280, 644 A.P.R. 280, 44 Admin. L.R. (3d) 132, 93 C.L.R.B.R. (2d) 262, 2002 CarswellNfld 193 (WLeC).	Judicial review of NLRB decisions of 4 Dec. 2001	Overturns the NLRB order as erroneous application of subjective test.
4 Sept. 2003	NL Court of Appeal	HMDC v. F.F.A.W.-C.A.W., 2003 NLCA 43, 93 C.L.R.B.R. (2d) 239, 229 Nfld. & P.E.I.R. 204, 679 A.P.R. 204, 5 Admin. L.R. (4th) 140, 2003 CarswellNfld 195 (WLeC).	Appeal of 12 July 2002 judicial review	Orders case returned to NLRB for application of objective test.
2 Oct. 2003	NL Labour Relations Board	FFAW/CAW, Applicant, and HMDC, Respondent, and CEP 97, Applicant, and HMDC, Respondent, NLRB file 118:508, 118:510.	NLRB reapplication of test	Confirms earlier decisions about HMDC violations of Labour Relations Act, R.S.N.L., 1990, c. 44, s.45.
16 Dec. 2003	NL Labour Relations Board	FFAW/CAW, Applicant, and HMDC, Respondent, and CEP, L97, Applicant, and HMDC, Respondent, NLRB file 118:508, 118:510.	NLRB reapplication of test	NLRB provides reasons for decision above.
28 April 2004	NL Supreme Court (Trial Division)	C.E.P., L60N v. HMDC, 2004 NLSCTD 80, 237 Nfld. & P.E.I.R. 1, 703 A.P.R. 1, 103 C.L.R.B.R. (2d) 37, 15 Admin. L.R. (4th) 171, 2004 CarswellNfld 121 (WLeC).	Judicial review of NLRB decision on L60N application for certification as explained 11 July 2001	NLRB decision upheld.
21 Sept. 2004	NL Supreme Court (Trial Division)	HMDC. v. C.E.P., L97, 2004 NLSCTD 174, 2004 C.L.L.C. 220-063, 241 Nfld. & P.E.I.R. 305, 716 A.P.R. 305, 106 C.L.R.B.R. (2d) 303, 2004 CarswellNfld 280 (WLeC).	Judicial review of NLRB decision of 2 Oct. 2003	Overturns NLRB order for reinstatement of laid off workers.

Date of Decision	Body	Legal Citation	Issue	Outcome
15 March 2006	NL Court of Appeal	*HMDC v. C.E.P., L97*, 2006 NLCA 19, 2006 C.L.L.C. 220-027, 254 Nfld. & P.E.I.R. 185, 764 A.P.R. 185, 266 D.L.R. (4th) 740, 125 C.L.R.B.R. (2d) 230, 2006 CarswellNfld 86 (WLeC).	Appeal of above	Appeal dismissed.

Notes

1   On industrial pluralism, see Judy Fudge & Eric Tucker, *Labour Before the Law: The Regulation of Workers' Collective Action in Canada, 1900–1948* (Toronto: University of Toronto Press, 2004) at 302–15 [Fudge & Tucker]. My view of the post-war settlement reflects Bryan D. Palmer, *Working-Class Experience: Rethinking the History of Canadian Labour, 1800–1991* (Toronto: McClelland & Stewart, 1992) at 278–84 and 336–39 [Palmer]; Peter S. McInnis, *Harnessing Labour Confrontation: Shaping the Postwar Settlement in Canada, 1943–1950* (Toronto: University of Toronto Press, 2002). See also Daniel Drache and Harry Glasbeek, *The Changing Workplace: Reshaping Canada's Industrial Relations System* (Toronto: Lorimer, 1992) [Drache]; Leo Panitch & Donald Swartz, *From Consent to Coercion: The Assault on Trade Union Freedoms*, 3d ed. (Aurora, ON: Garamond Press, 2003). On the CEP, see Jamie Swift, *Walking the Union Walk: Stories from CEP's First Ten Years* (Toronto: Between The Lines, 2003) at 28–29 [Swift].

2   R.S.N.L. 1990, Chapter L-1.

3   Andrew A. Luchak, "Newfoundland and Labrador: Shifting Tides," in Mark Thompson, Joseph B. Rose, & Anthony E. Smith, *Beyond the National Divide: Regional Dimensions of Industrial Relations* (Montreal and Kingston: McGill-Queen's University Press, 2003) at 201 [Luchak]; Bill Gillespie, *A Class Act: An Illustrated History of the Labour Movement in Newfoundland and Labrador* (St. John's: Newfoundland and Labrador Federation of Labour, 1986) at 53–83, 85–90, and 107–18 [Gillespie]; Glen Norcliffe, *Global Game, Local Arena: Restructuring in Corner Brook, Newfoundland* (St. John's: ISER, 2005) at 69–78 [Norcliffe]; Richard Gwyn, *Smallwood: The Unlikely Revolutionary* (Toronto: McClelland & Stewart, 1962, 1972) at 199–222 [Gwyn]; Jerry Lembcke & William M. Tattam, *One Union in Wood: A Political History of the International Woodworkers of America* (New York: International Publishers, 1984) at 155–76.

4   Gwyn, *ibid.* at 303–24; Gordon Inglis, *More Than Just a Union: The Story of the NF-FAWU.* (St. John's: Jespersen Press, 1985) at 143–239; Gillespie, *ibid.* at 121–26.

5   Canada, Royal Commission on the Ocean Ranger Marine Disaster, *Report*, vol. 1 (St. John's: Royal Commission on the Ocean Ranger Marine Disaster, 1984–1985) at 151–52; Rob Nishman, *Through the Portlights of the Ocean Ranger: Federalism, Energy, and the American Development of the Canadian Eastern Offshore, 1955–1985* (MA thesis, Queen's University, 1991) at 157–68 [unpublished]; Brian O'Neill, "Mobil and the Canadian Offshore: A Study of Context and Purpose" (1987) 3:1 *Newfoundland Studies* 71; J.D. House, *But Who Cares Now? The Tragedy of the Ocean Ranger*, ed. by Cle Newhook (St. John's: Breakwater Books, 1987) at 49.

6   Gregory S. Kealey, *The History and Structure of the Newfoundland Labour Movement* (St. John's: Royal Commission on Employment and Unemployment, 1986) at 202–9; Norcliffe, above note 3 at 97–104; Luchak, above note 3 at 204; Claire Hoy, *Clyde Wells: A Political Biography* (Toronto: Stoddart Publishing, 1992) at 297–314.

7   Fisheries and Oceans Canada, *Canadian Fisheries Annual Statistical Review*, 1982–2001 (Ottawa: Fisheries and Oceans Canada); Fisheries and Oceans Canada, *Canadian Fisheries Statistics 2004* (Ottawa: Fisheries and Oceans Canada, 2007); Natural Resources Canada, *Canada's Forests: Statistical Data, Newfoundland and Labrador, Domes-*

tic Economic Impact, online: canadaforests.nrcan.gc.ca/statsprofile/economicimpact/ nl; Rosemary E. Ommer, *Coasts Under Stress: Restructuring and Social-Ecological Health* (Montreal and Kingston: McGill-Queen's University Press, 2007) at 33–67 and 94–110.The situation has become worse in the forestry sector as Abitibi-Bowater shut down its pulp and paper mill in Grand Falls-Windsor in December 2008.

8   The Hibernia offshore oil production platform is owned by a partnership of oil and energy companies with varying degrees of shares in the enterprise: Mobil Oil Canada (33.125 percent), Chevron Canada Resources (26.125 percent), Petro-Canada Hibernia Partnership (20 percent), Canada Hibernia Holding Corporation (8.5 percent), Murphy Atlantic Offshore Oil Company (6.5 percent), and Norsk Hydro (5 percent).

9   Gregory S. Kealey and Gene Long, *Labour and Hibernia: Conflict Resolution at Bull Arm, 1990–92* (St. John's: ISER, 1993); Robert Hatfield, "Extreme Organising: A Case Study of Hibernia" (2003) 2 *Just Labour* 19 [Hatfield].

10   Joseph B. Rose, "The Construction Labour Relations Association of British Columbia: A Case Study" (1976) 27:2 Lab. L.J. 407–19; "Canadian Efforts to Stabilize Collective Bargaining in Construction" (1977) 100: 4 *Monthly Labor Review* 76–78; "A Canadian View of Labor Relations in Construction" (1979) 18:2 *Industrial Relations* 156–72; *Public Policy, Bargaining Structure and the Construction Identity* (Toronto: Butterworth, 1980).

11   Interview of Mr. Bill Parsons (14 July 2008) Victoria, NL [Parsons interview]; Interview of Mr. Ron Smith (28 July 2008) Grand Falls, NL [Smith interview]. Parsons became a regular representative of the NLRB from 1995 through 2004 in a series of two-year appointments. Over the course of his thirty-year career in the labour movement, Parsons had served as a vice-president of the Canadian Communications Workers' Union, organizing director of the Fish, Food and Allied Workers Union, an international representative of the United Steelworkers of America, past president of the NLFL and past vice-president of the CLC. See Newfoundland and Labrador, Labour Relations Board, *2003 Annual Report* (St. John's: Labour Relations Board, 2003) at 5–6. Ron Smith is the CEP national representative in Grand Falls-Windsor.

12   Gary N. Chaison, *Union Mergers in Hard Times: The View from Five Countries* (Ithaca, NY: ILR Press, 1996) at 2–23 [Chaison, *Union Mergers*].

13   The CAW's proper name is the National Automobile, Aerospace, Transportation and General Workers' Union of Canada. Charlotte A.B. Yates, "Unity and Diversity: Challenges to an Expanding Canadian Autoworkers' Union" (1998) 35:1 *The Canadian Review of Sociology and Anthropology* 93; Chaison, *Union Mergers, ibid.* at 59–75. FFAW/CAW, *Sectors*, online: www.ffaw.nf.ca/Sectors.asp; Swift, above note 1 at 3–5.

14   Swift, *ibid.* at 25–26 and 30–31.

15   Smith interview, above note 11.

16   Jonathan Kitchen, *Labour Law and Off-shore Oil* (London: Croom Helm, 1977) at 99–106.

17   Charles Woolfson & Matthias Beck, "Union Recognition in Britain's Offshore Oil and Gas Industry: Implications of the *Employment Relations Act 1999*" (2004) 35:4 Industrial Relations Journal 343. The *Piper Alpha* was a production platform in the North Sea oil industry that was destroyed by an explosion and fire in 1988, with a loss of 167 people. The tragedy stands as the worst disaster in the history of the

global offshore oil and gas industry. See Charles Woolfson, John Foster, & Matthias Beck, *Paying for the Piper: Capital and Labour in Britain's Offshore Oil Industry* (London: Mansell, 1997).

18 Susan M. Hart, "Norwegian Workforce Involvement in Safety Offshore: Regulatory Framework and Participants' Perspectives" (2002) 24:5 Employee Relations 486–99; Hart, "Industry, Labour and Government in Norwegian Offshore Oil and Gas Safety: What Lessons Can We Learn?" (November 2007) Workplace Review 21–29.

19 Morgan C. Cooper, *Labour Relations Processes on Offshore Oil Production Platforms* (St. John's: M. C. Cooper, 1997) at 2 [Cooper].

20 Parsons interview, above note 11; Smith interview, above note 11. The C-NOPB and the C-NSOPB are the joint federal-provincial bodies that regulate offshore oil and gas development.

21 Cooper, above note 19. The Canadian labour movement had flirted unsuccessfully with tripartism in the 1980s. See Palmer, above note 1 at 370–77; Craig Heron, *The Canadian Labour Movement: A Short History*, 2d ed. (Toronto: J. Lorimer, 1996) at 116–19; Stephen McBride, "Public Policy as a Determinant of Interest Group Behaviour: The Canadian Labour Congress' Corporatist Initiative, 1976–1978" (1983) 16:3 Canadian Journal of Political Science 501. For the LRWG's recommendations, see *New Century-New Realities: Creating a Framework Together, Executive Summary* (St. John's: Labour Relations Working Group, 1996). The other members of the labour movement on the LRWG included Earl McCurdy (FFAW), Ron Smith (CEP), and Dave Curtis (NAPE).

22 R.S.N. 1990, c. C-2.

23 Cooper, above note 19 at 8–65 and 78; Susan M. Hart, "Safety and Industrial Relations in the Newfoundland Offshore Oil Industry Since the Ocean Ranger Disaster in 1982" in Charles Woolfson & Mathias Beck, eds., *Corporate Social Responsibility Failures in the Oil Industry* (Amityville, NY: Baywood, 2005) at 65–117. Bill Parsons maintains that it is inappropriate for the C-NOPB to administer occupational health and safety regulations for the offshore industry because its primary goal is to promote economic development. Parsons interview, above note 11.

24 Cooper, *ibid.* at 20.

25 Cooper, *ibid.* at 16–56.

26 Cooper, *ibid.* at 62–65 and 85. Bill Parsons suggested that, by referring to their "mature" outlook, Cooper recognized a basic principle of the administration of most unions in Canada: union leaders do not want to see their members strike for what is obtainable through fair and reasonable negotiation and subsequent administration of collective agreements by unions and employers. Parsons interview, above note 11.

27 R.S.N. 1990, c. L-1.

28 Government of Newfoundland and Labrador, News Release, "Government Unveils Labour Relations Regime for Offshore Oil Production Platforms" (15 December 1997); online: www.releases.gov.nl.ca/releases/1997/envlab/1215n02.htm.

29 *Labour Relations Act*, R.S.N.L. 1990, c. 44, online: Statutes of Newfoundland 1997, Chapter 44 www.assembly.nl.ca/legislation/sr/annualstatutes/1997/9744.chp.htm [*Labour Relations Act*].

30 Chaison, *Union Mergers*, above note 12 at 52–53.

31 While this paper supports the CEP view that HMDC did its best to oppose certification, other research blames the struggle between the CEP and the CAW-FFAW and the complexities of organizing an offshore platform for the obstacles the CEP faced in winning the right to represent Hibernia workers. See Marilyn Shortall, "The History of Unionization of the Hibernia Offshore Production Platform" (Paper prepared for Master of Employment Relations seminar on Advanced Studies in Labour and Working-Class History, Memorial University, 2005) [unpublished].

32 Swift, above note 1 at 26–27, 30, and 32; Hatfield, above note 9 at 18. Smith expressed nothing but admiration for the FFAW's work. Smith interview above note 11. Repeated efforts to interview an FFAW representative for this study have failed.

33 In Bill Parsons' opinion, the CEP and CAW-FFAW applications for certification likely "shocked" HMDC, which was equally or more so dismayed by the subsequent revelation of just how many workers had signed union membership cards. Parsons interview, above note 11. The CEP's Ron Smith argued that HMDC, led by Exxon-Mobil, was committed to using its massive financial resources to do everything it could legally to oppose union certification. Smith interview, above note 11.

34 Swift, above note 1 at 32.

35 *Re the Labour Relations Act, as amended, and applications for certification as bargaining agent* (30 March 2001), NLRB Decision file number 712:2784 and 712:2788 at para. 26, online: Labour Relations Board Decision System http://lrb.gov.nl.ca/docs/712-2784_712-2788.pdf [*Re Labour Relations Act and applications for certification*].

36 Swift, above note 1 at 27.

37 *Re Labour Relations Act and applications for certification*, above note 35.

38 Government of Newfoundland and Labrador, News Release, "Morgan Cooper appointed full-time chair of the Labour Relations Board" (21 March 2001), online: www.releases.gov.nl.ca/releases/2001/labour/0321n06n02.htm. The Minister of Labour, Anna Thistle, cited Cooper's recommendations on offshore labour relations in her announcement of his appointment.

39 The usual practices of LRBs in Canada have been addressed in Drache, above note 1 at 61 and 71–75.

40 *Re Labour Relations Act and applications for certification*, above note 35 at para. 68.

41 NLFA executive members of the time that sat on the SPI's steering committee: President Elaine Price, Vice-President Reg Anstey, and Secretary-Treasurer Margie Hancock. The recommendations for the SPI came from a study group composed of the NLFL, the St. John's Board of Trade, Newfoundland and Labrador Chamber of Commerce, the Newfoundland and Labrador Employer's Council, and the provincial Department of Industry, Trade and Rural Development. See Newfoundland and Labrador, Strategic Partnership Study Group, *Strategic Partnership: How Business, Labour and Government Collaborate to Produce Europe's High Performance Economies* (St. John's: Strategic Partnership Study Group, 2002) at 53–54, online: www.nlfl.nf.ca/Campaigns/StrategicPartnership.aspx.

42 Smith interview, above note 11; *Labour Relations Act*, above note 29, s. 2(1)(w).

43 *Re the Labour Relations Act, as amended* (11 July 2001) NLRB Decision file number 2207 at para. 8, online: lrb.gov.nl.ca/docs/2207.pdf. *Re the Labour Relations Act, as amended*

(12 October 2001) NLRB Decision 2228, online: lrb.gov.nl.ca/docs/2228.pdf [*Re the Labour Relations Act* 2228]. The NLRB referred to *Titan Tool and Die Ltd.* [1997] OLRB Rep. March/April 281 and *UFCW, Local 1977 v. White Rose Crafts & Nursery Sales Ltd.* [1998] OLRB Rep. 755.

44 *Re the Labour Relations Act* file number 2228, *ibid.* at para. 5. "Welcome Hibernia Oil Workers" (2002) 10:1 *CEP Journal* 1 at 12, online: www.cep.ca/journal/2002_winter/ 2002_winter_e.pdf.

45 Chaison, *Union Mergers*, above note 12 at 22–23.

46 *Re Labour Relations Act as amended and a preliminary jurisdictional issue flowing from complaints pursuant to Sections 122 and 45 of the Act* (4 December 2001) NLRB Decision file number 118-:08 and 118:510, online: http://lrb.gov.nl.ca/docs/118-508_118-510.pdf.

47 *C.E.P., Local 60N v. Hibernia Management & Development Co.*, 2004 NLSCTD 80, 237 Nfld. & P.E.I.R. 1, 703 A.P.R. 1, 103 C.L.R.B.R. (2d) 37, 15 Admin. L.R. (4th) 171, 2004 CarswellNfld 121 (WLeC).

48 LeBlanc specified that the objective test should be specified as it had been in *B.F.C.S.D. v. Simpsons Ltd.*, [1985] O.L.R.B. Rep. 594, 85 C.L.L.C. 16,035, 9 C.L.R.B.R. (N.S.) 343, 1985 CarswellOnt 1207 (Ont. L.R.B.).

49 *Hibernia Management & Development Co. v. F.F.A.W.-C.A.W.*, 215 Nfld. & P.E.I.R. 280, 644 A.P.R. 280, 44 Admin. L.R. (3d) 132, 93 C.L.R.B.R. (2d) 262, 2002 CarswellNfld 193 (WLeC).

50 *Hibernia Management & Development Co. v. F.F.A.W.-C.A.W.*, 2003 NLCA 43, 93 C.L.R.B.R. (2d) 239, 229 Nfld. & P.E.I.R. 204, 679 A.P.R. 204, 5 Admin. L.R. (4th) 140, 2003 CarswellNfld 195 (WLeC).

51 *Re Labour Relations Act* file number 118:508 and 118:510, above note 46; *Re the Labour Relations Act, and a complaint pursuant to Section 122 of the Act,* (16 December 2003) NLRB Decision file number 118:508, 118:510, online: lrb.gov.nl.ca/docs/118508remedy. pdf.

52 *Hibernia Management & Development Co. v. C.E.P., Local 97,* 2004 NLSCTD 174, 2004 C.L.L.C. 220-063, 241 Nfld. & P.E.I.R. 305, 716 A.P.R. 305, 106 C.L.R.B.R. (2d) 303, 2004 CarswellNfld 280 (WLeC); *Hibernia Management & Development Co. v. C.E.P., Local 97,* 2006 NLCA 19, 2006 C.L.L.C. 220-027, 254 Nfld. & P.E.I.R. 185, 764 A.P.R. 185, 266 D.L.R. (4th) 740, 125 C.L.R.B.R. (2d) 230, 2006 CarswellNfld 86 (WLeC).

53 Drache, above note 1 at 99.

54 "First Collective Agreement in NA Offshore Sector" *ICEM in Brief* (17 October 2005), online: ICEM in Brief www.icem.org/en/78-ICEM-InBrief/1454-First-Collective-Agreement-in-NA-Offshore-Sector; "Welcome Aboard Terra Nova Workers!" *Around the Region* (May 2003), online: Around the Region www.cep.ca/reg_atlantic/files/bulletin/030501_bulletin_e.pdf. Oil production from the Terra Nova field takes place on a floating production, storage and offloading vessel (FPSO) crewed by ninety workers. The companies participating in the Terra Nova Alliance include ExxonMobil, Norske Hydro, Husky Oil, Murphy Oil, Mosbacher Operating, and Chevron.

55 Communications, Energy and Paperworkers Union of Canada, News Release, "CEP Seeks Arbitration at Hibernia" (20 December 2004), online: www.cep1129.ca/cep_news_releases.htm.

56 Arbitration Award between Communication, Energy and Paperworkers Union of Canada, Local 60N and Hibernia Platform Employers' Organization (21 April 2006).

57 Joseph B. Rose & Gary N. Chaison, "Unionism in Canada and the United States in the 21st Century: The Prospects for Revival" (2001) 56:1 *Relations Industrielles/Industrial Relations* 39 [Rose & Chaison]. Rose and Chaison were pessimistic about the overall prospects for revitalization, although Chaison has more recently stated that much more research and debate is required to understand the impact of mergers. See Chaison, "Union Mergers in the U.S. and Abroad" (2004) 25:1 Journal of Labor Research 97.

58 Rose & Chaison, *ibid.* at 41–42 and 45.

59 For a discussion of discursive elements in the law, see Fudge & Tucker, above note 1 at 7–8.

60 The limits of arbitration for unions are discussed in Drache, above note 1 at 127–48.

61 Rose & Chaison, above note 57 at 58.

PART THREE

Courts and Collective Action
in the Post-War Regime

The Royal York Hotel Case: The "Right" to Strike — And Not Be Fired for Striking[1]

Malcolm E. Davidson[2]

ON 25 JUNE 1962, the Supreme Court of Canada delivered its ruling in *C.P.R. Co. v. Zambri* (*C.P.R. Co.*).[3] The full court, writing three different judgments, unanimously upheld an order of two Ontario appellate courts that a Toronto magistrate reverse himself and enter convictions against the Canadian Pacific Railway (CPR) for unfair labour practices under the *Ontario Labour Relations Act* (*OLRA*).[4] In June 1961, management had threatened to dismiss several hundred striking employees at the Royal York Hotel, a luxury Toronto hotel the company had opened in 1929. The strike was a legal strike under the statute. Management offered no justification for its actions except that the employees were not reporting for work. In July 1961, the company had acted on its threat and fired the strikers.[5]

At the time the Supreme Court ruled, the strike had already ended almost three months earlier. The ruling would not have any immediate effect on the workers who had gone on strike. Almost all of the strikers had gotten their jobs back as part of the negotiated settlement of the strike. It was a mammoth convention in Toronto in early July 1962 of an international fraternity, the Ancient Arabic Order of the Nobles of the Mystic Shrine (Shriners), rather than a Supreme Court of Canada pronouncement, that accelerated the implementation of the negotiated schedule to recall the strikers. The final stage of the Royal York strike litigation was anticlimactic. Despite that, *C.P.R. Co.* continues to endure, almost fifty years on, as a venerable "chestnut" of Canadian labour law.[6]

The case is important because of what it says about the status of unionists carrying on legal strikes under Canada's collective bargaining statutes. The Supreme Court held that the employer-employee relationship continues during lawful strikes. It is illegal both to threaten to fire strikers and to actually fire them solely because they have gone on strike. This holding left it open to conjecture that lawfully striking employees might be dismissed for other reasons, such as criminal or other misconduct inconsistent with the employment relationship, or adverse economic circumstances coinciding with a strike (but not caused by it) which would have warranted staff reductions in any event. Those issues, however, were not specifically addressed at any of the various levels of litigation.[7]

More than this, however, the Royal York case established that there is an actual "right" to strike. It now truly was a right, rather than a "freedom" or "privilege," in that the law now imposed a correlative duty, namely, the employer's duty to abstain from discharging its striking employees.[8] Before this, the common law had recognized the freedom of workers to strike so long as they were pursuing improved wages and working conditions. However, it had not imposed any corresponding obligation on employers to refrain from interference. This was a historic limitation on the prerogative of employers. Remember, however, that this was of immediate benefit only to that minority of Canadian workers which was organized in unions and that the great majority of unionized workers were male and were employed not in the services sector, but in the construction trades; the auto, steel, and rubber industries; mining; and forestry. The Royal York workers were exceptional in that they were service sector employees organized in a union. They were also exceptional in that almost half of them were women.

The case is also remembered for having nibbled at the edges of other issues concerning strikers. What did the enduring employee status entail? Was management entitled to hire strikebreakers? Was management entitled to make strikebreakers permanent employees and displace the strikers? Did workers, in the end, have rights to their jobs? What becomes of seniority, pensions, and diverse employment benefits during and after strikes? For the most part, the judges in the Royal York controversy left those problems unsettled and unclear. So too did the Ontario legislature for several years after the strike. These issues were left for the future, to be brought into focus again by later workplace conflicts. When they eventually were dealt with, the outcomes were not satisfactory from the viewpoint of unions.

The Royal York case also is important because of what it has to say about the place of the common law of individual employment contracts within a collective bargaining regime. At common law, the employer had enjoyed the prerogative to treat the absence of employees from work because of a strike as a breach of contract and grounds for dismissal. Strikes were no different than any other unauthorized absence. *C.P.R. Co.* found that, in the circumstances of a lawful strike, this prerogative had been abrogated by the labour relations statute. By rejecting the antiquated English precedents marshalled on this point by CPR counsel, the Supreme Court took a step toward a labour law jurisprudence rooted in its own time and place.[9] This too is a significant aspect of the Royal York case (though not an aspect pursued in this paper), in that the case had a place in the emergence of Canada's highest court from its long-standing status as a "captive court."[10]

The legal proceedings that sprang from the Royal York strike wound their way from the Ontario Labour Relations Board (OLRB), to summary conviction Magistrate's Court, to the Ontario High Court of Justice, to the Ontario Court of Appeal, then to the Supreme Court of Canada and, finally, back to Magistrate's Court for conviction and sentencing. The events of the strike form the background of this litigation. It is logical, therefore, to look first at the strike and why it became such a long and hard-fought struggle.

Cabbages, Carrots and Royal York Employees: The Prelude to Litigation

THE ROYAL YORK HOTEL opened in June 1929. It was the largest hotel not only in Canada, but anywhere in the British Empire and, in later times, the Commonwealth.[11] The Hotel and Restaurant Employees and Bartenders International Union (HRE) took a keen interest in the celebrated hotel from the beginning. Its organizing efforts initially made progress, but collapsed with the Depression. The full employment of the war years turned the tables, and continued organizing in those years resulted in 1945 in the first collective agreement with the Royal York. Two HRE locals, Local 7 and Local 299, signed this agreement. Local 7 consisted of Toronto and area master chefs, cooks, and pastry cooks. Local 299, Hotel and Club Employees, was a composite local of other service workers, its membership being drawn from several Toronto and area hotels and elite clubs. After this first agreement, nothing more is heard of Local 7 in our sources. Local 299, however, persisted, and, at least at the Royal York, apparently absorbed Local 7. Agreements between Local 299 and the Royal York followed one after another until the 1958 agreement, which expired in August 1960. This was the last agreement before the strike of 1961–62, the first known strike in the hotel's history.[12]

The Royal York workers, like other unionized Canadian workers in the 1950s, sought, and, to a considerable extent, won, better wages and hours, as well as pensions, health and welfare benefits, union security clauses, vacation time, and paid holidays. Perhaps the most significant achievement of this era for the Royal York employees occurred in 1954 with the attainment of the five-day, forty-hour week at no loss of pay. A health and welfare plan, involving equal contributions by employee and employer, followed in 1956. Progress also was made in reducing inequities in wage scales between the hotel's numerous departments. The advances constituted a modest success story for the union. Local 299 considered its agreements, at the Royal York and other major hotels, as the best in the industry in Canada.[13]

By the late 1950s, however, the ground was shifting. In 1957–58 and 1960–61, unemployment in Canada rose to the highest level in the post-war era.[14] The availability of a reservoir of unemployed persons was to play a decisive role for the CPR during the strike. Moreover, the CPR had other reasons to take a tough stand. It was in the throes of modernizing and restructuring, partly to ensure that the corporation's previously neglected non-rail assets (including hotels) paid well.[15] Also, the Royal York was now facing greater competition than ever before. It had long dominated the Canadian market for major conventions. Starting in 1958, it was challenged for that business by a newly-opened Montreal luxury hotel, the Queen Elizabeth. There also was new competition in Toronto. The city was undergoing a hotel construction boom and several new hotels were now competing with the Royal York for lesser conventions and events.[16]

As the CPR approached the 1960 negotiations, its executives eagerly embraced the new doctrines of the day in industrial relations. One of the leaders in that field in Canada was Floyd Henry, the managing director of a firm of consultants to management. Henry urged employers to turn over a new leaf. There was a need, he said in a speech to Canadian stove and furnace manufacturers, for "more calcium in the spine of management when it comes to labour relations." Companies should go to the bargaining table with their *own* "demands." They should, in many cases, "firmly reject" retroactive application of a new collective agreement. After the expiry of a collective agreement, they should continue to operate and take "unilateral action and initiate wage adjustments and changes in seniority and grievance policy." It was time to put an end to the "merry ritual dance around the collective bargaining table that labor has led management in recent years."[17] The CPR agreed. It named Henry as its representative on the tripartite conciliation board appointed after negotiations with Local 299 had stalled.[18]

By mid-April 1961, after several months of back-and-forth and conflicting demands, the issues at the Royal York had been narrowed to wages and layoff notice. On wages, the company proposed an increase of 2.5¢ per hour spread over eighteen months starting 1 April 1961, with no increase at all for the period since the expiry of the 1958–60 contract. The union asked for a 10¢ per hour increase spread over thirty-three months, including a retroactive increase since the expiry of the previous contract. With respect to layoff notice, the CPR wanted to do away with the existing seven-day notice and replace it with four hours' notice. This, the company said, was consistent with competing hotels.[19]

Local 299 rejected both positions. It saw the proposed cut in layoff notice as a return to an outdated system by which the hotel could "order every employee by the day — the way it orders its carrots and cabbages."[20] Furthermore, the HRE believed that acceptance of management's wage position would undermine the pattern that Toronto hotel bargaining had taken in the previous decade. The Royal York had set the pace for wages. The union's view was that, in order to keep wages climbing in hotels and in the services sector generally (which paid notoriously low wages compared to other sectors), it had to force the Royal York firmly out in front again.[21]

A strike still might have been avoided, or it might not have started as soon as it did (24 April 1961), but for the provocative action of management in taking its position directly to the employees, sidestepping the union. This was a key turn of events and one consistent with the position taken by the employer in the subsequent wholesale dismissals and the legal proceedings that followed. Though the company continued to negotiate with the union from time to time through the course of the strike, it otherwise acted as though it was dealing with unrepresented employees on individual employment contracts.

In the heated atmosphere of continuing negotiations on 24 April, the hotel's general manager, Angus P. MacKinnon, called a meeting of Royal York employees in the hotel's Canadian Room. He did so, he said, to inform them fully on the company's latest wage offer — just in case the union had not made it clear. HRE Canadian vice-president Archie Johnstone responded that he would not object to the meeting if the union bargaining team could also attend and present its position. MacKinnon shot back, "we'll meet without you." Johnstone replied that he would do "everything [he could] to make your meeting unsuccessful." The union immediately advised its stewards to strike that afternoon. As MacKinnon started his presentation in the Canadian Room, he was interrupted by Royal York bellman and Local 299 vice-president Charles Ireton, who advised the startled hotel executive that the strike already had begun. A sharp exchange followed between MacKinnon and Ireton. Ireton and all but a few of the several hundred assembled employees then filed out of the hotel and into the streets, on strike.[22]

The strike dragged on for almost a year, until 8 April 1962. Through its many months, the hotel continued to operate, drawing on its own supervisory personnel, newly-hired workers, and increasing numbers of discouraged unionists. The company was unrelenting in its demands for concessions and surrender. Local 299 maintained its picket line and appealed to public opinion to try to embarrass the hotel and hurt its business, but did not engage in "mass" picketing of the hotel or boycotts of other CPR hotels or businesses. Negotiations occurred from time to time over the first nine months of the strike. None of these negotiations, however, including those leading to the settlement proposals of provincial labour minister William Warrender in late January 1962, resulted in a settlement.[23]

The settlement ending the strike was reached through the mediation efforts, at the request of the provincial government, of H. Carl Goldenberg, who was a Montreal-based lawyer and at that time Canada's most prominent labour-management mediator.[24] There was a three-year agreement. Wages rose by 2.5¢ per hour over the first eighteen months and a further 1¢ per hour subsequently. With exceptions according to department, employees of eight years' seniority retained pre-strike seven-day layoff notice, but all others were reduced to four hours. Almost all of the remaining strikers, 447 of them, were to be rehired, in stages, by 30 August 1962. Pre-strike levels of seniority, vacation, and pension benefits were restored, but seniority rights on promotions and layoffs were compromised in the hotel's favour. Mandatory check-off of union dues, which formerly applied to all bargaining unit members, would henceforth apply only to the returning strikers, although other employees could opt in. Approximately seventy job classifications, comprising about 150 employees, were eliminated from the bargaining unit, subject to a union option to apply to the OLRB for a ruling on the excluded classifications.[25]

The litigation in *C.P.R. Co.* had its origin in a subset of strike events beginning on 26 June 1961 and culminating in large-scale dismissals on 16 July 1961. This subset of events again reveals the determination of the CPR to communicate directly with its employees as individuals.

On 26 June 1961, Angus MacKinnon sent all strikers letters setting a deadline of 15 July 1961 for the return of a form indicating that the employee was applying to return to work. If the form was not returned, the striker's employment records would be "closed" and the employee would be dismissed as of 16 July 1961. Upon dismissal, any money owing by the company, such as contributions to the pension fund, would be refunded. The letters emphasized that returning the form would not guarantee reinstatement. MacKinnon warned that returning to work would depend on an individual's qualifications and on the availability of jobs in the individual's classification. In other words, the hotel intended to give full consideration to the strikebreakers for ongoing employment, possibly in preference to the would-be returnees.

On 18 July 1961, MacKinnon sent the strikers another letter, this one confirming the closure of their employment records as of 16 July. He announced to the press that 600 persons had ignored the deadline and had their records closed. He said they could reapply if they wanted to start over as new employees.[26] Local 299 responded by filing an application with the OLRB for consent to prosecute the employer for unfair labour practice offences under the *OLRA*.

Counsel for Local 299 was David Lewis, a partner in the Toronto firm of Jolliffe, Lewis, and Osler, and a prominent counsel for unions.[27] Counsel for the CPR was Wilbur Roy Jackett, who in 1960 had joined the corporation as general counsel after a stellar career with the federal Justice Department, where he had risen to the post of deputy minister.[28]

Overview of the Litigation and the Legal Arguments

BY THE EARLY-TWENTIETH CENTURY, the common law in Canada recognized a sphere of toleration for collective action by workers. The boundaries, however, were always uncertain, and, as Eric Tucker has stated, "narrowly defined."[29] The cases that shaped the law took the form of employers' suits for injunctions and damages. The touchstone of legality was a finding that the purpose of a strike was the workers' own self-betterment rather than an intention to injure their employer or anyone else. This usually was not difficult to demonstrate and, as a result, the real controversy almost always centred on the legality of the actions taken in support of a strike. The state of the judge-made law in the era before the compulsory collective bargaining statutes was summarized as follows by H.W. Arthurs:

This much, at least, appears from the dicta in the cases: absent a nominate tort (e.g. assault, procuring breach, defamation), absent a criminal act, absent an intent to injure, strikes might lawfully be waged or threatened in furtherance of some legitimate economic interest. Those interests sometimes considered legitimate included higher wages, a union shop, the nonemployment of persons with whom the union did not wish to work, and assistance to fellow unionists engaged in some legitimate dispute. Political strikes were beyond the pale, as were gratuitous demonstrations of force, or strikes calculated to injure an employer in the carrying on of his business, by interfering with his contracts with employees or customers, or jurisdictional strikes.[30]

This, however, was as far as the common law would go. It did not interfere with the prerogative of employers to dismiss or refuse to re-employ strikers; to insist on "yellow-dog" contracts as a condition of employment or rehiring;[31] or to hire strikebreakers and try to carry on business as usual. In the 1930s and early 1940s, the result of the employees' freedom to organize unions and conduct strikes, along with the wide-ranging freedom of employers to disrupt and oppose them, was a proliferation of union recognition strikes and picket-line conflict, an increased loss of production because of work stoppages, and a growing demand by organized labour for laws to compel employers to recognize unions and bargain with them. These pressures, along with the rising strength of left-wing political parties, led the Ontario and federal governments to enact compulsory collective bargaining legislation during the war years.[32]

By 1961 in Ontario, this legislation had passed through a succession of statutory embodiments but the scheme of the legislation had basically remained the same.[33] Recognition strikes were replaced by certification of unions by a labour relations board. Once certified, a union had the exclusive bargaining rights for a particular bargaining unit and the employer was not at liberty to contract with employees individually or through another union or employee association. Union and employer were expected to bargain in good faith and reach a collective agreement. Strikes were forbidden during the course of a collective agreement, with all disputes about the interpretation of the agreement to be referred to arbitration. Certain kinds of misconduct were proscribed as "unfair practices," including employer interference in the choice of a union, discrimination against employees for lawful union activities, and unlawful strikes and lockouts. Enforcement measures, which expanded in scope and varied in procedure through the years, included reinstatement for unlawful discharges, declarations of unlawful strikes and lockouts, and summary conviction court prosecutions for violations of the statute. Such prosecutions, initiated and carried forward by the aggrieved employer or union, could be instituted only with the consent of the OLRB.[34] Successful prosecutions resulted in fines, payable to the provincial treasury.

As the *OLRA* stood in 1961, a plain reading of the very first section of the statute might seem to dispel any doubt that striking workers maintained employee status and therefore were not subject to dismissal for striking. In particular, subsection 1(2) of the Act stipulated that,

> [f]or the purposes of this Act, no person shall be deemed to have ceased to be an employee by reason only of his ceasing to work for his employer as the result of a lock-out or strike or by reason only of his being dismissed by his employer contrary to this Act or to a collective agreement.[35]

However, this provision did not fully determine the issue. This was because of its qualifying words "for the purposes of this Act." Strictly construed, the subsection had the effect of conferring on strikers the status of "employees" for the purpose of whatever protections the remainder of the statute conferred on employees. Standing on its own, the provision could not provide a basis for the right to strike and not be fired for striking; it had to be interpreted within the context of the whole statute. Unfortunately for unionists, the statute did not make any explicit statement of a right of employees to go on strike and not be fired for striking. This right had to be extrapolated — by reading together various sections of the statute and by considering the statute's purpose — as one of the "rights under this Act" that belonged to employees and that was protected by the statute's unfair practices provisions.

In the following discussion of the arguments crafted by both counsel, it is essential to keep in mind that neither Lewis nor Jackett made the distinction, as has been made in this essay, between a "right" and a "freedom." Neither did the jurists deciding the case, with the possible exception of Justice Charles Holland Locke in the Supreme Court of Canada. Even in Locke's judgment, however, the distinction is implicit rather than explicit and turns up in only one passage of the judgment.[36] The Royal York case unfolded in an era when bar and bench were less concerned with legal scholarship than a later era would be. In the arguments and the judgments, the overwhelming tendency was to use the term "right to strike" where what was meant, according to the terms employed in this essay, was the "freedom to strike."

The prosecution of the hotel was for breaches of the *OLRA*'s unfair practices provisions. The case turned on proof of three things. First, the strikers had to be shown to be persons eligible for the protection offered by the unfair practices sections. Second, participation in a lawful strike had to be proven to be one of the "rights under this Act" as contemplated by those provisions. Finally, it had to be shown that the MacKinnon letters amounted to offences under the Act. The alleged offences were a threat of dismissal and a subsequent refusal to employ or to continue to employ. They were set out in two separate informations that were tried together.[37]

Proof of the strikers' eligibility for protection under the unfair practices provisions came from the qualifying words in the provisions themselves. Specifically, one of the provisions stipulated that it applied to any "person" who had been refused continued employment because of exercising rights under the Act. Strikers obviously were persons. The other provision specified that it applied to an "employee" who had been threatened with dismissal for exercising rights under the Act.[38] Subsection 1(2) of the *OLRA* made it clear that strikers remained "employees" and thus eligible for the law's protection.

The argument that lawfully striking was a "right" under the Act rested on two alternative foundations. Union counsel contended that either was sufficient to prove the point. One alternative was that the right was inherent within the scheme of the statute. For this argument, Lewis pointed to sections 33 and 54, which set out the procedural preconditions for strikes, and also to other sections which distinguished between "lawful" and "unlawful" strikes and empowered the OLRB to declare certain strikes unlawful. He concluded that, "once certain requirements are fulfilled, strikes are lawful under the Act and . . . therefore, striking is a right recognized by and under the Act." As if to bolster the legitimacy of the right, he argued that the elaborate limitations prescribed by the statute indicated that "the Act does not merely import the common law right . . . but establishes such right on a new basis." The alternative foundation that he proposed was section 3 of the statute, which declared that "every person is free to join a trade union of his own choice and to participate in its lawful activities." A lawful strike, maintained Lewis, qualified as a lawful activity of a trade union and the right to participate in it was guaranteed by that section.[39]

Jackett, for the CPR, conceded that the unionists had complied with the statutory preconditions before striking. The problem, he argued, was that they had breached the common law of master and servant. He contended that, since the collective agreement had ceased to operate before the strike began, all subsequent work was being performed under personal contracts of service. The strikers were not exercising a right under the Act because a refusal to work in accordance with an employment contract was neither a lawful activity under section 3 nor a lawful exercise of a common law right to strike imported into the Act. In order to strike lawfully, the workers first had to terminate their contracts. They had not done so. Jackett continued by stating that MacKinnon's letter of 26 June had constituted reasonable notice that the hotel would treat the contract breaches as cause for dismissal. The company was right, he said, to refuse to continue to employ workers who were no longer performing the duties the hotel had hired them to do.[40]

Jackett supported this position by, among other authorities of similar vintage, two decisions made by the House of Lords in 1906 and 1912, and a 1908 decision of the English Court of Appeal.[41] These cases had their roots in very different historical and legal contexts than Ontario in 1961–62. The real issues in those cases were the liability of central union officials for the actions of local union officials; union officials' liability where they claimed immunity under a 1906 statute; or the enforceability of a union constitution relied on by a deceased union member's widow to claim benefits. The fact that they referred to contracts of employment requiring a fixed period of notice before striking was merely incidental. Moreover, the cases were distinguishable in that they all referred to written contracts. The Royal York employees, whatever their exact legal position at the time of striking, did not have written contracts.

The union did not challenge the CPR's position that the common law of employment applied, at least in part, at the time the strike began. Without a collective agreement, the employees were, the union brief said, "under some form of express or implied contract of personal service."[42] This was a concession that perhaps need not have been made. It was open to union counsel to argue that, in the face of the union's continuing certification, it was no longer accurate to speak of individual contracts as the controlling law, even after a collective agreement had ceased to operate.[43] Lewis, however, accepted the company's position on this point. He argued, in rebuttal, that the common law had measured the legality of a strike only in terms of its purpose, not on the basis of whether or not contracts had been terminated before it began. He also argued that, in any event, the statute operated through subsection 1(2) to abrogate any requirement of the common law, if there really was such a requirement, to terminate contracts in order to strike lawfully. Furthermore, objected Lewis, Jackett's position resulted in an absurdity. At no time could an employee, while remaining an employee, lawfully strike. This, Lewis said, ran against the grain of the statute and erased the commonly-understood distinction between quitting and striking.

Jackett also relied on several other contentions. He argued that the right to strike was not a right "under" the *OLRA* because the statute's intention was to limit and diminish the rights of strikers at common law, rather than augment them. "A right that is curtailed by a statute," Jackett submitted, "does not thereby become a right 'under' that statute."[44] He also argued that striking was not a right under section 3 because striking, in his view, was an activity of individual employees, not of the union. He sought to nullify subsection 1(2) by saying that it was a mere interpretation provision. He argued, in the alternative, that if subsection 1(2) did indeed have the effect of creating a class of "employees" who were not functioning as *real* employees by working, then it could not form the subject of an offence because no employer could terminate a legal status that the statute ordained to continue. Moreover, subsection 1(2) could not mean what it appeared to mean because if it did, the result would be that, by going on strike, an employee would acquire a right not previously enjoyed: that is, to have an employment contract continue indefinitely rather than be terminated on reasonable notice. This was a result, Jackett maintained, that could only come about through clear statutory language which removed the employer's previously-held right — and there was no such language. Finally, he argued that the tortured drafting of one of the unfair practice provisions rendered it incapable of supporting a conviction on the facts.[45]

The prosecution case, as Jackett did not fail to emphasize, was not without its difficulties. The lack of any outright declaration in the statute of a right to strike and not be fired for striking meant that union counsel had to engage in an elaborate exercise of statutory interpretation to demonstrate a right which the legislature might have stated much more directly. Indeed, the outlines and preconditions of the freedom to strike were shrouded in cautious obscurity in the *OLRA*. They had to be deduced from provisions in the statute that were framed negatively, amidst a thicket of qualifiers. A weary reader in 1961 had to persevere to sections 33 and 54 and read them together to determine that an employee could lawfully strike, but only after the expiry of a collective agreement, the completion of conciliation proceedings, the observance of a seven-day "cooling-off" period, and a secret strike vote.[46]

By comparison, however, the CPR's case was much the more difficult one. The company could not get over the hurdle that its basic proposition — the necessity of terminating contracts and formally quitting before lawfully striking — seemed not only artificial and technical, but, as Lewis said, lacking in common sense. The antiquated and readily distinguishable caselaw that the CPR relied upon left it open to ridicule. Additionally, the company could not surmount the further hurdle of subsection 1(2) of the statute. Jackett laboured mightily to nullify that provision, but it had to be given meaning and that meaning, whatever precisely it was, rather obviously did not support the employer. Beyond these considerations, however, there were also the equities of the situation and they did not favour the CPR. One of Canada's richest corporations, in its determination to intimidate the hotel strikers, had blundered. Now, dressed up in barrister's robes, it was clutching at straws to save face.

In casting themselves into the difficult legal position they did, it is not clear whether CPR management failed to anticipate the dismissals would result in litigation; or, alternatively, whether they anticipated litigation but erred in assessing the merits of their position; or, alternatively again, whether they sought the maximum intimidation effect from the dismissals and chose to let the chips fall where they may and cope with the outcome. Any one of these options is consistent with the brashness and self-confidence of the top hats of the day at the CPR. In its president, Norris Roy "Buck" Crump, the company had a hard-nosed career railroader who, during a brief strike in 1957 by train firemen, had announced he would "run the damn railroad" with secretaries if he had to.[47] In Ian David Sinclair, a lawyer and company vice-president for labour relations, the CPR had, as David Lewis recalled, "a tough, combative advocate who had no doubt about the exalted place of the CPR in Canadian society, or about everyone's duty to . . . accept the company's position as righteous and fair, by definition."[48] And in Wilbur Jackett, the CPR had a solicitor who, while a Justice Department lawyer, had a hand in drafting the first federal compulsory bargaining legislation, and who harboured a conviction that neither the federal legislation, nor the Ontario legislation which had followed it, had abrogated the restrictions the common law placed on employees going on strike.[49]

But the case for the CPR was weak not only because of the speciousness of its legal arguments and the blatant unfairness of the dismissal of low-status workers who sought to improve their pay and working conditions through the socially-approved methods of doing so. It was also weak because the management case, based as it was on individual employment contracts, ran against the trend of post-World War II labour law decision making by judges and arbitrators, which was collectivist in orientation. The thrust of this decision making had been to confer on unions a distinct legal personality from their members and to build up unions as financially stable institutions. Along with financial stability and distinct legal personality went responsibility for enforcing trade agreements with employers and, not incidentally, responsibility to pay damages incurred when insufficient measures were taken by union officials to deter "wildcat" strikes.

The foundation of this jurisprudential trend was the judgment, setting out what came to be known as the "Rand Formula" on union security, of Supreme Court of Canada Justice Ivan C. Rand acting as interest arbitrator in the 1945 Ford strike at Windsor.[50] This was followed, in 1958–59, by the grievance arbitration judgments in a dispute between the Oil, Chemical and Atomic Workers International Union and Polymer Corporation. Upheld on judicial review by three appeal courts including the Supreme Court of Canada, these arbitration judgments asserted the authority of the arbitration board to award and assess damages against the union for a breach of the no-strike clause of a collective agreement.[51] The Supreme Court of Canada's judgment in 1959 of the case of *Syndicat Catholique des Employés de Magasins de Québec v. Paquet Ltée.* also forms part of this trend.[52] This, in short, was the jurisprudential context which made the CPR's position in the Royal York Hotel case a very difficult one. The CPR, with its insistently individualist approach to labour relations at the Royal York Hotel, was at odds with the judicial elite about how best to manage Canada's workplaces.

The Litigation

The OLRB Consent-to-Prosecute Application: Legal Questions "Far From Clear"

Local 299 filed its application with the OLRB on 10 July 1961. The application followed the first MacKinnon letter but preceded the dismissals and the letter confirming them. The Board heard the application on 15 August 1961 and ruled on it on 21 September 1961.[53]

It is not certain why Local 299 sought a remedy by way of a Magistrate's Court prosecution rather than by an OLRB order. That issue is not addressed in the sources. The likely answer, however, is that Local 299 counsel feared the Board would be reluctant to exercise the few and recently-conferred remedial powers it had at its disposal in the novel and politically sensitive circumstances of a strike at the Royal York, the preserve of the well-off, well-connected, and powerful. The hotel was the home away from home of Premier Leslie M. Frost and other high-rolling Progressive Conservatives.[54] Moreover, it was only in 1960 that the legislature had transferred to the Board the power previously exercised by the Minister of Labour to investigate complaints of unlawful discharges and order reinstatement.[55] This power was still unproven and it had been focused (by practice, not by legislative requirement) on refereeing the certification process, not on circumstances such as those in the Royal York strike. Secondly, counsel probably considered adjudication by the OLRB too risky because of the limitations inherent within the law governing the review of administrative agencies' decision making. A dismissal of the strikers' application by the OLRB would be reversible in the appellate courts only on the limited jurisdictional grounds canvassed on a judicial review. Furthermore, on a judicial review, the union would find itself in the uncomfortable and uncustomary position (for organized labour) of attacking the statute's privative clause. By contrast, a verdict in Magistrate's Court would be open to a full-fledged appeal and would not entail an attack on the statute.[56] Thirdly, the extent and audacity of the employer misconduct must have seemed to the hotel workers' union to cry out for the censure which might flow from a quasi-criminal proceeding rather than an administrative board proceeding.

The Board tripartite panel which heard the Local 299 application decided it by an endorsement on the record, with a dissent by Colin C. Young. The facts, the majority said, were "clear," but counsel had raised legal questions that were "far from clear." Accordingly, leave was granted to prosecute the alleged violations of the Act. Young's dissent said, simply enough, that no offence was disclosed.[57]

The CPR probably did not strongly oppose the application. Ian Sinclair had already set his sights on the appeal courts. With the Board's ruling still pending, many hours of strike negotiations took place on 19 September 1961. Thomas M. Eberlee, the Ontario Cabinet's assistant secretary, convened the negotiations and Sinclair, among others, was at the table. The CPR insisted on the union's abject surrender, but Local 299 refused to give in. In a report to Premier Frost, Eberlee advised that "Sinclair believes that the Supreme Court of Canada will rule that striking employees no longer are employees after a certain period on strike." With this ruling in hand, the CPR intended to "ask the courts to remove the picket line from outside the Royal York Hotel."[58]

The Trial in Magistrate's Court: Elmore Clears the Track

On 29 September 1961, Onofrio Zambri, Local 299's secretary-business agent, laid two informations, one for each alleged offence. Each named Laura Job, Ann Todd, Robert Boyle, Albert Hetenyi, Raymond Seguin, and Charles Ireton as among the Royal York employees affected by the company's misconduct.[59] The hearing proceeded on 13 October 1961. Toronto's senior magistrate, Thomas S. Elmore, presided. Unlike several magistrates in that era, Elmore had been a lawyer, indeed, he was a Q.C. Nonetheless, he lacked experience in labour cases and he admitted it.[60]

The prosecution's case on the evidence closed after only thirty-five minutes. Lewis called three witnesses. The first was Zambri. The testimony elicited from him was intended to show that the persons named in the informations were Local 299 members working at the Royal York, that all requirements for a lawful strike had been observed, and that it was the union which had organized and was conducting the strike. Strike captain Charles Ireton told of coordinating the pickets. Laura Job, senior dining room cashier and long-term employee, also testified, likely to the receipt of MacKinnon's letters and her dismissal. The Court heard passages from the letters and received them as exhibits. Lewis also filed a three- by two-foot picket sign proclaiming Local 299 on strike at the Royal York Hotel. The company declined to call evidence. Five hours of legal argument followed.[61]

On 18 October 1961, Elmore delivered a written judgment dismissing both charges. He adopted the core of Jackett's argument, if not every detail. Elmore noted that the statute did not have any section specifically pronouncing a right to strike. He accepted, however, that the OLRA had imported the common law right to strike, but had curtailed it. The right could be exercised, he said, only as at common law, unless the statute expressly authorized otherwise. At the time the strike began, the hotel workers had "individual, express contracts or such as the law would presume from their working and receiving wages." There was nothing in the statute which relieved the strikers of complying with the common law requirement, as Elmore saw it, that an employee formally quit the job before striking. The Royal York strikers had not done this and therefore they were not lawfully striking and were subject to dismissal. The judgment acknowledged subsection 1(2) as relevant law, but left uncanvassed the issue of what force, if any, ought to be given to that provision, or why it ought not to be considered an abrogation of the common law.[62]

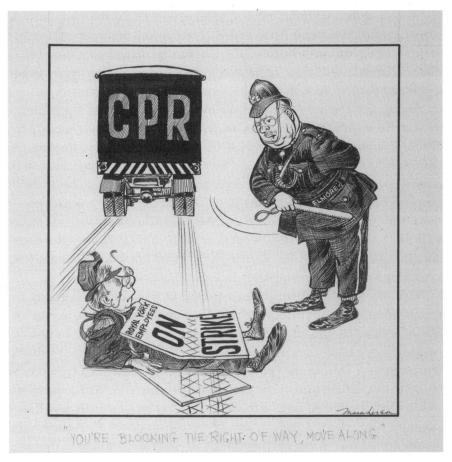

Duncan Macpherson of the *Toronto Star* found colourful subject matter in the Royal York Hotel strike. In this editorial cartoon, published on 20 October 1961, Magistrate Thomas Elmore is rendered as a railway police officer. *Library and Archives Canada, 1987-37-70.*

Appeal to the Ontario High Court of Justice: Goodbye to the Days of 1912

JAMES CHALMERS McRUER, CHIEF Justice of the High Court, heard Local 299's appeal on 7–8 December 1961.[63] The case came before McRuer as a "stated case," meaning that it proceeded entirely as legal argument on a specified set of facts. The alternative appeal route, a trial *de novo*, was not necessary because the facts were straightforward and uncontentious.[64] In a written judgment delivered on 13 December 1961, McRuer allowed the appeal. He set aside the acquittals and ordered the case returned to the lower court to be dealt with according to his findings.[65]

McRuer agreed with Elmore that, although the *OLRA* did not positively pronounce a right to strike, it had implicitly recognized the common law right to strike, albeit in a curtailed form. He went further than Elmore, however, in that he also endorsed Lewis' contention that section 3 (freedom to join a trade union and participate in its lawful activities) was an alternative foundation for finding that the right to participate in a lawful strike was a right under the Act. He also differed from Elmore in that he adopted Lewis' view of the effects of subsection 1(2). The interpretation of that provision, in McRuer's opinion, was the "crux" of the case. He concluded that it created a statutory class of employees on strike. It preserved the employment relationship for all purposes of the Act, including lawful strikes and the unfair practices provisions. The "irresistible" conclusion was that the 26 June letter was a threat of dismissal with loss of all pension rights, solely because strikers were exercising their lawful right to strike. Read together, the 18 July letter and the 26 June letter added up to a dismissal solely for exercising that right.[66]

McRuer's Royal York judgment reflected in part that "philosophy for understanding some of the difficulties of the underdog" which, in oral history interviews in 1978, the then eighty-eight year-old jurist said he had developed from having grown up on a farm and having seen the hard struggle of the farmer.[67] During the hearing, he repeatedly had forced Jackett onto the defensive, telling him in one exchange that he would "hate to think we were back in the days of 1912," a reference to Jackett's caselaw.[68] But McRuer's judgment also reflected the cautious conservatism of the Mackenzie King banner he had waved in a previous life as an electoral candidate.[69] The judgment spelled out the common law jurisprudence since 1851 to show the evolution away from thinking of strikes as unlawful conspiracies. It set out the statutory development since 1894 to show the public purpose in promoting industrial peace. It observed that under the evolving labour law some workers had achieved greater security through pensions, group insurance, and seniority rights. It worried that confirmation of the trial judgment would mean employees would have to swallow wholly unacceptable contract terms laid down by employers unless they were prepared to terminate the employment relationship, lose all benefits, and strike. There effectively would be no right to strike. This, McRuer further worried, ran counter to the historical progression and undercut the preconditions for social stability.

Despite its display of labour law knowledge, McRuer's judgment had a whiff of labour relations naivete about it. The Chief Justice was clearly troubled that, if the employer-employee relationship did not persist during a strike and employees had to terminate individual contracts before striking, workers would lose their workplace benefits. What is not clear, however, is whether he conceived by this that strikers, by virtue of their continuing employment status during strikes, also had a statutory right to reinstatement after a strike ended, and reinstatement with at least the same benefits packages as they had before they struck. Or, alternatively, was he assuming that reinstatement and the continuation of benefits were the ordinary course upon the settlement of strikes? The lack of any expository detail in his judgment to support the prior proposition leads this writer to suspect the latter. It was this aspect of the judgment that suggests labour relations naivete. In the era of the compulsory collective bargaining statutes, reinstatement, with the same or better benefits, was frequently the result of strikes, but it was far from automatic. Returning to work and the terms of returning were contingent, as in the Royal York strike, on the strength of a union to win a negotiated settlement.

Appeal to the Ontario Court of Appeal: "Substantial Agreement" with McRuer

On 9 January 1962, the Court of Appeal granted the CPR leave to appeal. Local 299 did not oppose leave.[70] A bench consisting of Justices Wilfrid Daniel Roach, John Bell Aylesworth, and Frederick George McKay heard the appeal on 12–13 February 1962.[71] Aylesworth was the Court's dominant personality, though not Chief Justice of Ontario. He had acted as counsel for Ford Motor Company on labour-management conciliation boards during World War II and had also represented Ford during the strike at Windsor in 1945 and the ensuing arbitration proceedings before Justice Rand.[72]

In a judgment delivered orally on 13 February 1962, Justice Roach, speaking for a unanimous Court, dismissed the appeal. There was "substantial agreement" with McRuer. The Court amended McRuer's order, however, by specifically instructing Elmore to record a conviction on each count and impose sentence. McRuer had stated his order less directly, ordering Elmore to dispose of the case "according to the law as I have found it to be." This amounted, for practical purposes, to the same thing.[73]

The Court of Appeal judgment was a terse five paragraphs. Even at that short length, it managed to go beyond simply expressing agreement with McRuer to suggest an alternative approach to the same result. McRuer had set out the requirements of a lawful strike at common law (i.e., pursuit of self-betterment rather than intent to injure) and the additional limitation of timeliness which the statute imposed. He had found the Royal York strike to be lawful on both prongs of what he conceived of as a double-pronged test. The Court of Appeal acknowledged the test at common law and also acknowledged that the Royal York strikers' purpose passed that test. It then said that, altogether apart from the common law, the statute had "recognized the lawfulness of a strike called in the circumstances and facts of this case and [had] expressly preserved the status of the striking employees notwithstanding the strike."[74] The implication was that, without inquiry into motive, the timeliness of strike action on its own could determine lawfulness and that the statute could stand as a complete code governing the exercise of the right to strike.

Appeal to the Supreme Court of Canada: A Tale of Three Judgments

AFTER A CONTESTED HEARING on 19 March 1962, the Supreme Court granted the CPR leave to appeal.[75] It heard the appeal on 24 April 1962 and the judgment was issued on 25 June 1962.[76]

Before the appeal was heard, the strike ended on 8 April 1962. The settlement called for the recall of almost all of the strikers, in stages, before 30 August 1962. Neither this nor any other settlement term was contingent on the Supreme Court judgment. The outcome in Ottawa mattered only because it would decide the legal issues.

The Supreme Court heard the appeal as a full panel of nine. This in itself demonstrated the case's importance.[77] There were three separate, but essentially concurring opinions. The authors were Justices Locke, John Robert Cartwright, and Wilfred Judson. Chief Justice Patrick Kerwin and Justices Robert Taschereau and Gerald Fauteux signed on with Cartwright. Justices Douglas Abbott, Ronald Martland, and Roland Almon Ritchie signed on with Judson. Locke wrote on his own behalf.

Cartwright accepted, seemingly as the natural order of things, that the Royal York employees had individual contracts of employment at the time they went on strike. In contrast to McRuer, he paid great deference to the authorities submitted by Jackett. "There is the highest authority," Cartwright opined, "for the proposition that a strike which would otherwise be lawful at common law becomes unlawful if the cessation of work is a breach of contract." He worried, however, that the factual basis of the case was deficient in that it did not provide the particulars of the contracts of employment with respect to a notice period or what notice, if any, had been given by the union or individual employees before the strike began. He considered referring the case back to Magistrate Elmore for amplification. In the end, however, he rejected that option. He had come to understand that Jackett's point was not that a contractual condition requiring a stated period of notice had been breached, but that the employees had not terminated their individual contracts at or just before the moment of leaving work. He agreed that this would be a correct statement of an employee's obligation at common law.[78]

But this was as far as Cartwright would travel with Jackett. He endorsed Lewis' position and the judgments of the appellate courts that subsection 1(2) of the *OLRA* had abrogated the common law. He also endorsed Lewis' submission that section 3 conferred the right to strike as a right under the Act. He noted the magistrate's findings of fact documenting the role played by Local 299 in organizing and overseeing the strike. It was, Cartwright said, an activity of the union and a lawful activity of the union. In his opinion, the statute left it to the common law to determine the lawfulness of a strike, but went beyond that to forbid untimely strikes which would otherwise be lawful at common law. This formulation implied that timely strikes might not always be lawful strikes. The Royal York strike was, in his view, "both lawful at common law and not forbidden by the Act." He had no difficulty in finding, on the basis of the MacKinnon letters, that the employer had committed the offences as charged.[79]

In contrast to Cartwright, Judson brought to *C.P.R. Co.* an irreverence for the CPR and its pretensions. He needed only six bristling paragraphs to dismiss the CPR's case, and, in passing, to impale Cartwright. Without directly saying so, he harkened back to the option set out in the Court of Appeal that the statute be considered a complete code. The issue, he said, was "a simple one." The subject of the appeal was alleged offences against the statute. What the common law had to say about unions and strikes and liability for strikes was of no significance because the right to strike was founded within the procedures set out in the statute. What mattered is that the unionists had complied with the statute. The strike therefore was lawful. The statute expressly preserved the employer-employee relationship. Judson had "the greatest difficulty" understanding why Jackett's authorities entered the argument at all. The CPR's argument about terminating contracts made "nonsense" of the legislation. The MacKinnon letters compelled convictions "as a matter of course and . . . nothing else need be considered."[80]

Charles Locke had an independent streak that has made him difficult for historians to classify.[81] His judgment in the Royal York case is consistent with that tendency. He concurred with Cartwright and Judson in the result, but took an original approach on the issue of whether or not the strikers had given notice; differed with Cartwright on the foundation of the right to strike; and went beyond both of his colleagues by seeking to define — and minimize — the extent of the duty imposed on employers by subsection 1(2).

Like Cartwright, Locke understood it to be the natural order of things that the strikers had individual contracts at the time they went on strike. What Locke noted, however, was that, if notice were indeed necessary before the employees walked out, such notice could have been given on their behalf by the union if the union was authorized to do so. Since there had been prolonged negotiations before the strike began, it could not be assumed, Locke said, that management had not received notice from the union of its members' intention to quit work. In the absence of contrary evidence, he proposed to proceed on the assumption that the strike was lawful. Accordingly, pursuant to subsection 1(2) of the *OLRA*, the strikers continued to qualify as employees and were eligible for protection under the statute's unfair practices provisions.

Locke differed from Cartwright, but joined Judson in his route to finding that lawfully striking was a "right under the Act." He objected to the position taken by Lewis, and accepted by Cartwright, that the right to strike was expressly conferred by section 3. Remarking that "no statutory permission is necessary to participate in the *lawful activities* of any organization," Locke dismissed section 3 as mere flourish. Moreover, he agreed with Jackett that striking is an activity of employees, not the union, and therefore was not within the purview of section 3. Having rejected section 3 as the source of a right, he endorsed the alternative position, namely, that the right to strike had its origins in the common law and was recognized, in altered form, in the scheme of the statute. Strikes which conformed to the statutory requirements constituted exercising a right under the Act. On this foundation, and on the grounds that he considered the MacKinnon letters to have been properly construed, he dismissed the appeal.[82]

Then, in statements which he acknowledged as "unnecessary for the disposition of this appeal," Locke set out his views on the limits of the employer's duty not to terminate strikers as employees. In his opinion, employers were "at complete liberty . . . to engage others to fill the places of the strikers" and, when strikes ended, were "not obliged to continue to employ their former employees if they have no work for them to do, due to their positions being filled."[83] The law in Canada, Locke said, was the same as was set out in the United States in the Supreme Court decision in *National Labor Relations Board v. Mackay Radio and Telegraph Co. (Mackay)*.[84] In that case, at the end of a strike, the employer had refused to reinstate certain strikers. The National Labour Relations Board (NLRB) found that the employer had discriminated on the basis of union activities and ordered reinstatement. The Board refrained from deciding whether the continued and preferential employment of strike-breakers constituted forbidden discrimination *per se*. At the Supreme Court, however, the case took on wider dimensions. The *Mackay* Court decided that employers were forbidden from dismissing workers engaged in a legal strike; that employers nonetheless were free to hire other workers to take strikers' jobs; and that the replaced striker, in the words of legal scholars Julius G. Getman and Thomas C. Kohler, "remains an employee, but one who has only a preferential claim to the prior position, if and when it becomes vacant, and only if the former striker has been unable to find comparable work."[85]

Locke's opinion on this issue was, as he himself recognized, *obiter*. His fellow judges avoided commenting on it. We may conclude that *C.P.R. Co.* did not go as far as *Mackay* in sorting out the rights of employees during and after strikes and the duties imposed on employers. The one point the two cases had in common was that employers have the duty to refrain from dismissing workers engaged in a legal strike unless they are able to justify their actions on grounds not tainted by unfair labour practices.

Conviction and Sentencing in Magistrate's Court: A Sideshow

ON 3 JULY 1962, Magistrate Elmore, presiding at City Hall, Toronto, convened proceedings to enter convictions and sentence the CPR. There were only two spectators in the courtroom. The city had turned its attention elsewhere. The focus of interest, in those early days of July, was the Shriners. In the tens of thousands, these Master Masons in Freemasonry and their families had flocked to Toronto for a convention. High jinks — sirens, whistles, klaxon horns, and crazily careening miniature cars — filled the streets below the courtroom, rendering the magistrate barely audible. The huge influx of convention-going guests into the Royal York Hotel had induced Angus MacKinnon to bring back the remaining ex-strikers — ahead of schedule.[86]

David Lewis urged the Court to sentence the CPR so working people would see that the law applied as rigorously to big corporations as to anyone else. The maximum penalty, under the *OLRA*, was $1,000 on each count. Elmore, known by some as "Robin Hood" because he believed that courts, in passing alternative sentences to jail, should consider the social position of accused persons and varying abilities to pay, fined the Canadian Pacific

Railway $500 (apparently $250 on each count, though this is not certain). He further ordered $24 in costs.[87]

The Impact of the Litigation on the Strikers and the CPR

THE COST OF THE litigation was substantial. It was beyond the means of Local 299 alone. Help was sought from the international union, which not only authorized the appeals but heavily contributed to both the litigation costs and the overall strike budget. The international's General Executive Board, meeting in Miami Beach in late November 1961, acceded to Local 299's request for assistance in "meeting obligations, particularly with regard to legal fees" and forwarded partial payment of the bill received by its Toronto affiliate.[88] Awards of costs also helped somewhat with the legal expenses. In his memoirs written many years later, David Lewis recalled his pleasure in preparing a costs bill for service on the CPR for his work in all three appeal courts.[89] But costs levied against the CPR did not pay for everything. Archie Johnstone lobbied the Canadian Labour Congress to help pay a bill that Local 299 had received for its representation at the Supreme Court of Canada of approximately $6,500. The Congress contributed $1,500, which was all it said it could afford.[90]

Financing was not the only strain that the litigation imposed on the unionists. A crucial factor in any strike is morale. Elmore's October 1961 decision discouraged some of the strikers. Some made decisions which changed their lives forever. Some drifted away, perhaps to other jobs, and lost any accumulated seniority.[91] The McRuer decision, conversely, had an uplifting effect. It offered, as an HRE leader recognized, "nothing tangible immediately," but it was "a big lift in morale."[92]

The litigation also may have influenced the parties to reach an agreement when they did. The CPR, for its part, had strong reason to settle the strike regardless of any legal considerations. The company's net earnings in 1961 in its hotels and communications sector had dropped sharply, from roughly $4.4 million in 1960 to $3.7 million in 1961. The company's annual report attributed this mainly to the Royal York strike. Though the company had deep pockets (approximately $32.5 million in net earnings in 1961), the strike was hurting the bottom line and management wanted it to end.[93] Despite the crucial and determining importance of the profit factor, considerations about the litigation probably also figured in management's decision to settle the strike when it did. CPR vice-president Sinclair likely came to realize that his strategy of appealing to the courts to break the picket line after winning at the Supreme

In this Macpherson cartoon, published in the *Toronto Star* on 6 February 1962, unionists Archie Johnstone and Onofrio Zambri advance on CPR executives Angus MacKinnon, Ian Sinclair, and Ronald Mackie. *Library and Archives Canada, 1987-37-84.*

Court of Canada was not a solid bet. As of 13 February 1962 (when the Court of Appeal rendered judgment), the CPR had lost, and lost decisively, at two levels of appeal. In settling when it did, the company probably had a nagging concern that it could not benefit financially by the public relations setback of a Supreme Court of Canada loss while the strike was continuing.

As for the unionists, the predominant sentiment was that they could not win anything better and the strike had lasted long enough.[94] The settlement was the proverbial bitter pill. Nonetheless, it restored almost all the strikers to their jobs, and on a much earlier schedule for return than previously offered. It is consistent with this predominant sentiment, and reasonable to speculate, that the strikers felt they should secure their re-entry into the hotel before, rather than after, the Supreme Court ruled. What if they should suffer an unexpected loss at the Supreme Court? This would have compromised reinstatement and compelled further concessions. Moreover, they had no guarantee management would interpret a union victory in Ottawa as reason to give them their jobs back. It was safest to cut their risk and take the settlement.

It must be acknowledged, however, that the strike may well have played out the same way if the unionists had never taken their fight into the courts. Negotiations occurred from time to time through the many months of the strike. The dismissals were an intimidation tactic. They failed to cause the strike to collapse. Once the CPR saw that the tactic had failed, it continued to negotiate, albeit sporadically. Neither party waited on the courts to decide anything. This, however, is counterfactual history. It is impossible to say whether the strike indeed would have collapsed if the union had *not* responded to the firings by launching the legal proceedings.

The Impact of *C.P.R. Co.* on the Law

THE ONLY IMMEDIATE IMPACT on the law of the Royal York strike litigation was a 1962 amendment to the *OLRA* which inserted an infinitive into one of the unfair practices provisions and thereby addressed the apparent lapse in draftsmanship which Jackett had sought, unsuccessfully, to turn to his client's advantage. This amendment adopted the reading of the provision by McRuer and the Court of Appeal. It came into force before the hearing in the Supreme Court of Canada. Jackett told the Supreme Court he did not agree with the reading in the courts below, but he would not argue against it.[95]

In view of the range of issues at stake, the holding in *C.P.R. Co.* had a narrow reach. The essential holding is that the dismissal of employees on lawful strike, for the sole reason that they are on strike, is forbidden in Ontario.[96] Common law doctrine relating to breach of contract by quitting work without formal termination of the contract was found not to be controlling. This was because of the effect of subsection 1(2) of the *OLRA*. Otherwise expressed, the result was that, through judicial interpretation, a true "right" to strike was recognized. The common law had recognized the freedom of workers to associate, and strike, for better wages and working conditions. But it had not imposed any duty on their employers not to threaten to fire them, nor actually fire them, solely for striking. There was now a right to strike and not be fired solely for having gone on strike. The fact that the collective bargaining statutes in the other Canadian provinces have very similar provisions to those that were at issue in *C.P.R. Co.* has given the case further meaning. The holding as it was found to apply to the Ontario statute is considered to apply to the other statutes. There have not been contrary holdings on the law in those provinces.[97]

Issues concerning strikebreakers and the rights of strikers again came to the fore in Ontario in the mid-1960s. Those issues, as well as heated controversy over an injunction, figured prominently in the Tilco Plastics strike in the south-central Ontario city of Peterborough in 1965–66. Following that strike, the province lured former Supreme Court of Canada justice Ivan Rand out of retirement to conduct an inquiry into issues related to strikes and injunctions.[98] In his 1968 report, Rand urged an interpretation of subsection 1(2) of the *OLRA* which would make strikebreakers provisional employees and confer on striking workers reinstatement rights after a strike ended, unless they had accepted permanent employment with another employer, or the employer's enterprise no longer called for the same number of workers.[99]

In 1970, the Ontario legislature, on the initiative of the Progressive Conservative (PC) government, enacted a reinstatement provision as an amendment to the *OLRA*, but in a more limited form than had been recommended by Rand. The provision required an employee to make an "unconditional" reinstatement application in writing, to the employer, within six months from the start of a strike. The terms of reinstatement were a matter of bargaining by the employer and the individual returnee. Reinstatement also was subject to the condition that the applicant need not be taken back at all if the employer no longer had persons engaged in doing the same or similar work as the returnee had done before the strike.[100] These arrangements were disadvantageous for unions. They undermined collective bargaining, set up a six-month clock on strikes, and forced workers to declare their loyalty either to the union or the employer at the possible expense of their jobs if they did not choose the latter.[101]

The reinstatement amendment of 1970 also had the effect of causing confusion about the rights of strikers in strikes that lasted more than six months. The issue which arose was whether or not strikers had rights to reinstatement in circumstances where an employer discriminated against them after a strike had ended by continuing to employ replacement workers rather than "bump" the replacements in favour of the returnees. In 1983, in *Mini-Skool Ltd. (Mini-Skool)*, the OLRB appeared to make an unqualified statement that, after the expiration of the six-month period from the beginning of a strike, strikers did not have any rights to bump replacements.[102] Three years later, in *Shaw-Almex Industries Ltd.* (*Shaw-Almex*), Board vice-chairman Harry Freedman tried to clarify the issue. He contended that what the Board had in mind in *Mini-Skool* was a situation where there had not been any improper motive on the part of the employer for refusing to displace the employees who had worked during the strike — employees who, in any event, were not actually replacement employees but lesser-seniority employees who had made reinstatement applications and had returned to work. *Shaw-Almex*, continued Freedman, presented different facts. He and the employee representative on the panel were satisfied that the employer had acted with discriminatory motive by refusing to agree to a return-to-work protocol that might cause the displacement of some or all of its replacement employees.[103] The result was a clarification of the fact that in circumstances where strikes continue beyond six months and employers commit unfair labour practices, the Board may craft remedies which include the reinstatement of strikers. However, in the absence of unfair practices, the job security of strikers would continue to depend on their ability to win a settlement. There was no absolute right to reinstatement.

The 1970 reinstatement amendment continued in force through subsequent PC and Liberal governments until 1992. At that time, the New Democratic Party (NDP), which had formed its first and only government in the province in 1990, replaced the 1970 provision by very extensive amendments limiting operations by employers during strikes and mandating reinstatement, as well as the terms of reinstatement, of all employees after a strike ended — unless the parties agreed on alternative reinstatement terms in a settlement.[104] The 1992 amendments also included a new section requiring employers, during strikes and lockouts, to accept payments from unions for the continuation of employment benefits and not to threaten to cancel or cancel the benefits so long as payment was made for their continuation.[105]

In 1995, the election of a PC government resulted in the repeal later that year of the NDP amendments and the re-enactment, word for word, of the 1970 reinstatement provision.[106] This remains the law, not having been repealed or amended by the PC or Liberal governments which have governed the province since then.

In review, therefore, the recognition in 1962 of a right of continued employment status during a lawful strike was followed by the enactment of a brand of reinstatement rights which was unsatisfactory from the perspective of unions. Moreover, to make things worse, the reinstatement rights not only confused matters, they were a step back from the more sweeping and absolute post-strike reinstatement rights that arguably were contemplated, although not actually spelled out, by the statute. This problematic and contradictory development occurred after the previously-mentioned strike at Tilco, in which the strikers, unlike the Royal York strikers, failed to win a settlement and, after almost a year on the picket line, ended up losing their jobs.[107] Although the Royal York case was a victory for workers in that it established a right to strike and not be fired for striking, it did not serve as the platform for clear and unambiguous progress for workers on post-strike reinstatement rights.

It also bears emphasis that the benefits of a right to strike and not be fired for striking were of immediate advantage only to the minority of Canadian workers who were organized in unions. In the early 1960s, the portion of the Canadian non-agricultural workforce which belonged to unions hovered at about 30 percent and was declining.[108] Women and immigrant workers, as well as male and female workers in government jobs, services sector jobs, and small-scale manufacturing, remained, for the most part, outside of unions.[109] It further ought to be noted that reinstatement rights achieved through advances in the law were not of great significance for those unions — usually those with highly-skilled workers or very large bargaining units — which had the strength, regardless of the law, to win full recall of their membership as part of a strike settlement. Recall achieved by way of the law rather than at the bargaining table was potentially most significant where unions were weakest and historically had least penetration — in small-scale manufacturing and in service industries — where it was relatively easy to recruit replacements. Reinstatement rights also assumed greater significance in circumstances where recession and high unemployment enabled employers to recruit replacements even for highly-skilled workers. This was the case, for example, with airline pilots during the Eastern Provincial Airways strike of the early 1980s.[110]

The Royal York Hotel strike and its accompanying litigation brought into focus a long-standing tension within Canadian employment and collective bargaining law: the interplay between the individual employment contract and collectively-organized labour relations. This issue assumed importance even before the era of the compulsory collective bargaining statutes. In that earlier era, it played itself out in cases where courts had to determine whether or not the terms of collective agreements had been incorporated into individual contracts and thereby were enforceable.[111] This tension between the individual and collective forms of workplace organization continued to be important in the compulsory collective bargaining era. In the case of the Royal York strike, we have seen that the CPR negotiated with the union but also repeatedly went behind it and treated the hotel employees as individuals. The company sought to have contract law doctrine relating to serving notice before quitting prevail over the statute. It failed. As a result, the Canadian law on strikes developed along a different line than the British law. The individual contract of employment, although increasingly regulated by statute, remained at the centre of British collective labour law, and lawyers in the UK debated the effect of strike notice on contracts of employment. The Canadian law was able to avoid absorption with this arid and technical discourse.[112]

The tension and interplay between employment law of general application (whether it be common law or statutory law) and collective labour relations law remains a live issue in Canadian workplace regulation. Whereas the result in *C.P.R. Co.* and several other Supreme Court of Canada cases has highlighted the separateness of the world of collective bargaining,[113] the momentum is now swinging in the other direction. In the 2006 case of *Isidore Garon ltée v. Tremblay; Fillion et Frères (1976) inc. v. Syndicat national des employés de garage du Québec inc.*,[114] the Supreme Court upheld, by a majority of only four to three, the long-standing doctrine that individual contracts have no application within a collective bargaining regime, other than at the individual hiring stage. The majority ruled, however, that a labour arbitrator may find that a rule from the general law (whether statutory law or judge-made law) is implicitly included within a collective agreement, and may apply the rule, if it is compatible with the collective labour relations context. Accordingly, the stage is set for ever closer integration of the general law and collective labour law.[115]

This development is convergent, though obviously not intentionally so, with the criticisms levelled at the post-1945 collective bargaining regime by revisionist historians. According to these historians, the much-proclaimed separateness of the world of collective agreements and collective bargaining, and its alleged achievements for workers, are an illusion. According to the revisionists, a preoccupation with the sacredness of the law of contracts lies at the heart of the collective bargaining regime, and at the core of that preoccupation is the repression of rank-and-file initiative and the disciplining of the capitalist workforce by the union bureaucracy.[116] Rather than a great point of departure for workers, the new order has consolidated the old. Supreme Court justices and Marxist or otherwise radical historians have made for strange and unexpected bedfellows.

Notes

1   The subtitle is borrowed from journalist Arnold Bruner, who began an article on the Supreme Court of Canada decision on the Royal York case as follows: "The right of the worker to strike — and not be fired for striking — has become the law of the land." See "Striker's Right to Job Enshrined for First Time in Canadian Law" *Toronto Star* (30 June 1962) 7 [Bruner]. All references to the *Toronto Star* are to the editions of that newspaper preserved in the *Toronto Star Pages of the Past* Micromedia Proquest online database. For 1961–62, this was the "Night Edition" (there was more than one edition daily). References to the *Globe and Mail* (Toronto) are to the editions preserved in the *Canada's Heritage from 1844 — The Globe and Mail* Micromedia Proquest online database. For 1961–62, this was the "Final Edition." References to *Toronto Telegram* are to the editions preserved on microfilm; there is not any online edition. For 1961–62, this was the "Five-Star Night Final" edition. The news clippings on the Royal York Hotel strike preserved in Canada, Department of Labour, Strikes and Lockouts Files, Ottawa: Library and Archives Canada (RG 27, vol. 545, Strike 51, Reel T-3403) appear, in some cases, to have been taken from other editions. As a result, there occasionally are differences in the clippings collection in the titles of articles which otherwise convey the same content. Moreover, in the clippings collection, the same content occasionally appeared in newspapers of other dates (previous day or following day) than in the editions preserved online or on microfilm.

2   I gratefully acknowledge the assistance of the volume editors Judy Fudge and Eric Tucker; the series editor Jim Phillips; the other participants in the "Putting Law to Work: Choices and Context in Key Labour Law Cases" conference at University of Victoria [British Columbia] (19–21 June 2008); an anonymous reviewer; Harry W. Arthurs (for suggestions and reminiscences); Lauretta Davidson, my mother (for research assistance and editorial advice); and Robert B. Sims (for research assistance). I am, of course, wholly responsible for any errors, omissions, or other deficiencies.

3   [1962] S.C.R. 609, 34 D.L.R. (2d) 654, aff'g [1962] O.R. 554, 33 D.L.R. (2d) 30 (Ont. C.A.), aff'g [1962] O.R. 108, 31 D.L.R. (2d) 209, 36 C.R. 355 (Ont. H.C.), rev'g (1961) C.C.H.L.L.R. No. 15, 372 (Mag. Ct.). Onofrio Zambri was the secretary-business agent of Local 299, Hotel and Club Employees, Hotel and Restaurant Employees and Bartenders International Union.

4   Unless otherwise indicated, all references to the *OLRA* are to R.S.O. 1960, c. 202.

5   The strike has been reported and analyzed by Jeremy Milloy, "A Battle Royal: Service Work Activism and the 1961–1962 Royal York Strike" (Fall 2006) 58 Labour/ Le Travail 13 [Milloy]. I have focused on the legal proceedings connected with the strike, rather than on the strike itself.

6   The case initially attracted very little scholarly comment. John D. Neilson, "Labour Relations — Nature of the Employer-Employee Relationship — Effect of a Strike — Right to Strike" (1962) 2 Alta. L. Rev. 138, was written as a comment on the trial judgment, before any appellate judgments had been issued. J. Michael Robinson, "*Canadian Pacific Railway Co. v. Zambri*: How Long Does a Striker Remain an Employee, and What is the Nature of the Employer-Striking Employee Relationship?" (1964) 22 U.T. Fac. L. Rev. 171, included the appellate judgments.

7   On valid reasons for the dismissal of lawfully striking employees, see Harry W. Ar-
    thurs, "The Right to Strike in Ontario and the Common Law Provinces of Canada"
    in *Travaux du quatrième Colloque international de droit comparé/Proceedings of the Fourth
    International Symposium on Comparative Law* (Ottawa: University of Ottawa Press,
    1967) at 194–95 [Arthurs, "Right to Strike"]; R. Ross Dunsmore, "The Employer,
    the Employee and the Legal Strike" (1973–74) 2 Queen's L.J. 3 at 13–15, 17–18, and
    21–22; Geoff England, "Loss of Jobs in Strikes: The Position in England and Canada
    Compared" (1976) 25 I.C.L.Q. 583 at 601–6; and Geoff England, "The Legal Response
    to Striking at the Individual Level in the Common Law Jurisdictions of Canada"
    (1976–77) 3 Dalhousie L.J. 440 at 449–54 and 468 [England, "Legal Response"].

8   For the definition of a "right" as a legal relation carrying with it a correlative "duty,"
    see Wesley Newcomb Hohfeld, "Some Fundamental Legal Conceptions as Applied
    in Judicial Reasoning" (1913–14) 23 Yale L.J. 16 at 28–44. Hohfeld contrasts a "right"
    with a "privilege," the latter meaning a legal relation that does not imply a duty in
    another party not to interfere. Accordingly, what the common law loosely referred
    to as the "right" to strike was actually, in Hohfeldian terms, a "privilege" because
    it did not carry with it a duty on employers not to interfere. I prefer the term "free-
    dom" for this concept because it better conveys the fact that the activity of workers
    in Canada in forming organizations and striking came to be tolerated by the state,
    rather than granted by the state.

9   For criticism of "resort by Canadian courts to English authority" and "uncritical
    adherence to standards of a bygone age," see Harry W. Arthurs, "Tort Liability for
    Strikes in Canada: Some Problems of Judicial Workmanship" (1960) 38 Can. Bar Rev.
    346 at 399–402 [Arthurs, "Tort Liability"].

10 On the "captive court," see Bora Laskin, "The Supreme Court of Canada: A Final
    Court of and for Canadians" (1951) 29 Can. Bar Rev. 1038; Ian Bushnell, *The Cap-
    tive Court: A Study of the Supreme Court of Canada* (Montreal and Kingston: McGill-
    Queens University Press, 1992) [Bushnell]; and Peter McCormick, *Supreme At Last:
    The Evolution of the Supreme Court of Canada* (Toronto: J. Lorimer, 2000) [McCormick].

11 Augustus Bridle, "Like Curtain Raiser in Super-Grand Opera" *Toronto Star* (12
    June 1929) 3; David Macfarlane, "The Royal York" in Barbara Chisholm, ed., *Castles
    of the North: Canada's Grand Hotels* (Toronto: Lynx Images, 2001) at 187–98; Elaine
    Denby, *Grand Hotels: Reality and Illusion. An Architectural and Social History* (London:
    Reaktion Books, 1998) at 171–72; "Royal York Is Largest Hotel," *Toronto Star* (20 Feb-
    ruary 1962) 6. The Royal York was displaced, in 1958, by the newly-opened Queen
    Elizabeth Hotel in Montreal, but regained its supremacy after the completion in 1959
    of a 400-room, seventeen-storey addition.

12 Harry Cude, "Toronto, Canada" (15 June 1929) 38:6 Mixer and Server 34; Cude,
    "Toronto, Ontario, Canada" (December 1929) 38:12 Catering Industry Employee
    34; E. Manfred Roebling, "Toronto, Canada" (March 1930) 39:3 Catering Industry
    Employee 10–11; S.R. Smith, "Toronto, Ont., Canada" (March 1930) 39:3 Catering
    Industry Employee 32; Roebling, untitled report (April 1930) 39:4 Catering Industry
    Employee 11–12; J. Belinfante, "Toronto, Canada" (May 1930) 39:5 Catering Indus-
    try Employee 34; Roebling, untitled report (October 1930) 39:10 Catering Industry

Employee 16; Arthur Guest, "Toronto, Canada, Locals 88, 555, and 608" (November 1930) 39:11 Catering Industry Employee 33; C. Richmond, "Toronto, Ontario, Canada" (June 1934) 43:6 Catering Industry Employee 37; "Flash — Flash — Flash. Largest Hotel in Canadian Dominion Signs Agreement" (August 1941) 50:8 Catering Industry Employee 37 [this was an agreement with an employee committee; the HRE was not recognized, though its staff assisted with negotiations]; Robert Hunt, "Toronto, Canada. Local 7 Reports 'Enthusiasm High'" (August 1941) 50:8 Catering Industry Employee 48; R. Newson, "Toronto, Canada. Local 299 and Local 7 Sign Contract with Royal York Hotel" (July 1945) 54:7 Catering Industry Employee 35; A. R. Johnstone, "Canada. Ontario, Quebec, Nova Scotia" (August 1945) 54:8 Catering Industry Employee 2; H. Parsumi, "Royal York Signs New Contract" (May 1951) 60:5 Catering Industry Employee 20; E. Schofield, "Canadian Workers Demanding Cost-of-Living Pay Hikes" (November 1951) 60:11 Catering Industry Employee 25; "Union Gains New Contract, More Members at Royal York" (August 1952) 61:8 Catering Industry Employee 27; untitled correspondence from Parsumi (April 1953) 62:4 Catering Industry Employee 15–16; "5-Days, 40-Hours Won at Royal York" (December 1954) 63:12 Catering Industry Employee 17–18; "Strike Vote Yields New Gains for 1,300 at Royal York" (September 1956) 65:9 Catering Industry Employee 20; "Rank-and-Filers Credited With Major Share In Toronto Victories" (November 1956) 65:11 Catering Industry Employee 18; Arnold Bruner & Roy Shields, "Last Ditch Battle . . . Then The Walkout" *Toronto Star* (16 January 1962) [Bruner & Shields], 1, 8. Mixer and Server and Catering Industry Employee, which succeeded Mixer and Server in October 1929, were the official monthly journals of the HRE. Both were organs of the international union, as distinguished from any local union of the HRE or any municipal joint board of local unions of the HRE.

13 On Canadian unionists' gains in the 1950s, see Bryan D. Palmer, *Working-Class Experience: The Rise and Reconstitution of Canadian Labour, 1800–1980* (Toronto and Vancouver: Butterworth, 1983) at 231 and 252–53 [Palmer]; and Craig Heron, *The Canadian Labour Movement: A Short History* (Toronto: J. Lorimer, 1989) at 94–101 [Heron]. On the Royal York workers' gains in the 1950s, see the references to Catering Industry Employee dating to the 1950s, and, as well, the reference to Bruner & Shields, above note 12. On Local 299's opinion of its agreements, see "Largest Canadian Local Celebrates" (February 1957) 66:2 Catering Industry Employee 16. The maximum working hours permissible, as of 1954, under the *Hours of Work and Vacations with Pay Act*, R.S.O. 1950, c. 173, as amended, and the accompanying regulations, was eight hours daily and forty-eight hours weekly, but these "maximums" were subject to several exceptions permitting more hours.

14 Robert Bothwell, Ian Drummond, & John English, *Canada Since 1945: Power, Politics, and Provincialism* (Toronto: University of Toronto Press, 1981) at 10–13; Palmer, *ibid.* at 230.

15 David Cruise & Alison Griffiths, *Lords of the Line* (Markham, Ontario: Viking, 1988) at 394–95, 398–99, 405, 412, and 417–20 [Cruise & Griffiths]; and John Lorne McDougall, *Canadian Pacific: A Brief History* (Montreal: McGill University Press, 1968) at 113–22 and 160–65.

16 "Simcoe Hotel Loss Cut" *Toronto Star* (4 May 1961) 9; "New Hotels in City My Doing, Nate Says" *Toronto Star* (10 July 1961) 10; "Plan Hotel Expansion" *Toronto Star* (9
August 1961) 12; "$16 Million More Space to House Metro Visitors" *Toronto Star* (18
August 1961) 12; "Liberal MPP Sides with Hotel Strike" *Toronto Star* (28 August 1961)
25; Ron Haggart, "The Royal York Manager Speaks Up on Hotel Taxes" *Toronto Star*
(14 September 1961) 7; "382 Crowns 'Queen' With Label" (April 1958) 67:4 Catering
Industry Employee 20; Frank Rasky, *Just a Simple Pharmacist: The Story of Murray Kof-
fler Builder of the Shoppers Drug Mart Empire* (Toronto: McClelland & Stewart, 1988) at
206–30; Correspondence of the Assistant Deputy Minister [of Labour], Royal York
[Hotel, Toronto] Strike, Ian D. Sinclair [Vice-President, CPR] to Leslie M. Frost [Pre-
mier] (26 August 1961), Toronto: Archives of Ontario (RG 7-21-0-195).

17 E. F. L. Henry, "Required: More Management Backbone in Labor Relations" (1961)
8:2 Canadian Personnel and Industrial Relations Journal 19 at 20, 21, & 22.

18 Bruner & Shields, above note 12, which refers to the conciliation board members as
Henry, Harry Simon for Local 299, and chair William Dickie.

19 Bruner & Shields, above note 12; Milloy, above note 5 at 19–20. Bruner & Shields
report that the union's wage demand when bargaining opened was for an 8 percent
increase per hour and that the Hotel estimated this would translate into a further
25¢ per hour and $10 per week. If this estimate was correct, the union's eventual
position, by mid-April 1961, of a 10¢ per hour increase would represent a gain of
two-fifths of 8 percent, or 3.2 percent, over the previous agreement. If a copy of the
previous agreement still exists, I have not been able to locate it. Accordingly, I have
not been able to verify the estimate and the calculation derived from it.

20 Local 299, HRE, "Strike at the Royal York. A Study in Deception. How the Strike
Began at the Royal York Hotel," Canadian Labour Congress Papers, Ottawa: Library
and Archives Canada (MG 28-1103, File No. 3, Reel H-118, undated pamphlet).

21 Wilfred List, "Royal York Hotel Staff Strikes" *Globe and Mail* (25 April 1961) 1–2; "Pay
Scales At Our Big Hotels" *Toronto Star* (4 May 1961) 1; Tom Ford, "Neither Side Seek-
ing Peace At Royal York" *Toronto Star* (4 May 1961) 21; Dick Snell, "Toronto's Hotel
Strike — What's At Stake" *Toronto Star* (21 July 1961) 7; "Liberal MPP Sides With Hotel
Strike" *Toronto Star* (28 August 1961) 25; Frank Drea, "The Strike That Split A City"
76:25 *Saturday Night* (9 December 1961) 11 at 13; Bruner & Shields, above note 12.

22 Drea, *ibid.* at 12; Bruner & Shields, *ibid.*

23 Milloy, above note 5 at 20–32.

24 On Hyman Carl Goldenberg (1907–96), see Wilfred List, "Expert Mediator" *Globe
and Mail* (9 April 1962) 7; and *Canadian Who's Who 1996*, Vol 31, ed. Elizabeth Lumley
(Toronto: University of Toronto Press, 1996) at 459–60.

25 "Union Agrees to Terms of Royal York Accord" *Globe and Mail* (9 April 1962) 1–2;
"Walkout Cost $500,000, Hotel Says; Friction Among Workers Expected" *Globe and
Mail* (9 April 1962) 5; "Still Some Loose Ends in Royal York Issue" *Globe and Mail* (9
April 1962) 5; "Strikers at Royal York Back on Pre-Strike Terms" *Toronto Star* (9 April
1962) 1 and 4; "Gaiety Turns Sour As Strikers Get Peace Terms" *Toronto Star* (9 April
1962) 4; "No Winners in Hotel Strike" *Toronto Star* (9 April 1962) 6; "3 Big ??? Remain
At Royal York" *Toronto Star* (9 April 1962) 4; "Pre-Strike Offer Accepted 316-76"

Toronto Telegram (9 April 1962) 1–2. My conclusions on the details of the settlement differ in some respects from Milloy, above note 5 at 32; and Desmond Morton with Terry Copp, *Working People: An Illustrated History of the Canadian Labour Movement*, revised ed. (Ottawa: Deneau Press, 1984) at 240 [Morton with Copp]. Ascertaining the details of the settlement is made more difficult by the fact that there apparently are no surviving copies of the collective agreement.

26 "Ultimatum Ignored Royal York 'Fires' 600" *Toronto Star* (19 July 1961) 8. Both letters (26 June and 18 July) are reproduced in the Magistrate's Court judgment, above note 3. Original copies are apparently no longer extant.

27 On Lewis (1909–81), east European immigrant to Montreal, McGill graduate, Rhodes Scholar, left-wing political party organizer, labour lawyer, and MP and federal New Democratic Party leader, see David Lewis, *The Good Fight: Political Memoirs 1909–1958* (Toronto: MacMillan, 1981), an autobiography [Lewis]; and Cameron Smith, *Unfinished Journey: The Lewis Family* (Toronto: Summerhill, 1989). Co-counsel was Thomas E. "Tim" Armstrong. Mr. Armstrong declined to be interviewed for this project. He noted the passage of time and kindly advised he could offer "no insights that are not apparent from the several judgments."

28 On Jackett (1912–2005), University of Saskatchewan College of Law graduate, Rhodes Scholar, federal Deputy Minister of Justice, CPR general counsel, Exchequer Court judge, and first Chief Justice of the Federal Court of Canada, see Richard W. Pound, *Chief Justice W. R. Jackett: By The Law of the Land* (Montreal and Kingston: McGill-Queen's University Press, 1999) [Pound]; Sabitri Ghosh, "Wilbur Roy Jackett, Jurist 1912–2005" *Globe and Mail* (7 November 2005) S8; and Ian Bushnell, *The Federal Court of Canada: A History, 1875–1992* (Toronto: Published for the Osgoode Society for Canadian Legal History by University of Toronto Press, 1997) at 138–54. Co-counsel was G. P. Miller, Solicitor, CPR Law Department, Toronto.

29 Eric Tucker, "'That Indefinite Area of Toleration': Criminal Conspiracy and Trade Unions in Ontario, 1837–77" (Spring 1991) 27 Labour/Le Travail 15 at 54.

30 Arthurs, "Tort Liability," above note 9 at 349.

31 A yellow-dog contract is "an agreement signed by a worker, as a condition of employment, by which he promises not to join or remain in a union, or to quit his job if he does join a union." See *Dictionary of Labor Law Terms*, 2d ed. (Chicago: Commerce Clearing House, 1953) at 138.

32 Judy Fudge & Eric Tucker, *Labour Before the Law: The Regulation of Workers' Collective Action in Canada, 1900–1948* (Toronto: University of Toronto Press, 2004) at 153–301[Fudge & Tucker]; and Laurel Sefton MacDowell, "The Formation of the Canadian Industrial Relations System During World War Two" (1978) 3 Labour/Le Travailleur 175.

33 The evolution from 1943 through the enactment of the *Labour Relations Act, 1950,* is traced by Frederick David Millar, "Shapes of Power: The Ontario Labour Relations Board, 1944 to 1950" (PhD thesis, York University, 1980). Amendments followed in 1954, 1956, 1957, 1958, 1959, and 1960.

34 Before 1950, the power of consent to institute a prosecution rested with the Minister of Labour.

35 R.S.O. 1960, c. 202. Several categories of workers were excluded from the definition of "employee" and, therefore, from the benefits of the Act: managerial staff, architects, dentists, lawyers, physicians, domestic service workers in homes, agricultural labourers, hunters and trappers, police officers, teachers, and full-time firefighters.

36 See the discussion of Locke's judgment below at 195–97 (especially at 196).

37 The charges as set out in the informations are reproduced in the Ontario High Court judgment, above note 3 at 109 of the O.R. citation. For Lewis' argument as set out in this and the following paragraphs, see Court of Appeal Solicitors' Civil and Criminal Appeal Files, Toronto: Archives of Ontario (RG 22-523, Civil File 26/62) [CASCCAF]; Supreme Court of Canada Fonds, Case Files, Ottawa: Library and Archives Canada (RG 125, vol. 1182, files 9586-1 and 9586-2 [SCCFCF]; "Hear Strike Charges Against Royal York" *Toronto Star* (13 October 1961) 1 and 8; " No Evidence from RY in Firing Charge" *Toronto Telegram* (13 October 1961) 45; "Argue R. York Strike Case 5 Hours" *Toronto Star* (14 October 1961) 1 and 14; "Strike Ruling Held Drastic Weapon" *Globe and Mail* (8 December 1961) 4; "Hotel Ruling is Weapon for Employers — McRuer" *Toronto Star* (8 December 1961) 1 and 4; "Hotel Strike Ruling Basis is Antiquated, Chief Justice Hints" *Globe and Mail* (9 December 1961) 5; "McRuer Disputes Elmore View on Hotel Firings" *Toronto Star* (9 December 1961) 1 and 5; "Labor Act Covers Strike Right –—Judge" *Toronto Star* (12 February 1962) 1; "Firings at Royal York Illegal — Appeal Court" *Toronto Star* (13 February 1962) 1 & 2; "'Right to Fire' Argued in Royal York Appeal" *Toronto Star* (25 April 1962) 12.

38 The two provisions were subsections 50(a) and (c) respectively.

39 For the quotations, see Memorandum of Fact and Law Submitted on Behalf of Respondent, 9, para. 15, CASCCAF, above note 37; and the same words in the correlated, but not precisely duplicative, paragraph in Respondent's Factum, 7, para. 5, SCCFCF, above note 37. The Supreme Court of Canada factum differed in minor ways from the Court of Appeal factum, but the argument remained substantially the same.

40 For Jackett's argument as set out in this and the following paragraphs, see the sources in above note 37.

41 *Denaby and Cadeby Main Collieries, Ltd. v. Yorkshire Miners' Ass'n*, [1906] A.C. 384 (H.L.); *Smithies v. National Association of Operative Plasterers* (1908), [1909] 1 K.B. 310 (C.A.); *Russell v. Amalgamated Society of Carpenters and Joiners*, [1912] A.C. 421 (H.L.).

42 Memorandum of Fact and Law Submitted on Behalf of Respondent, 11, para. 18, CASCCAF, above note 37; and the correlated, but not precisely duplicative Respondent's Factum, 10, para. 10, SCCFCF, above note 37. There is a minor difference of wording in the Supreme Court of Canada factum.

43 This argument might have proceeded on the principles set out in *Syndicat Catholique des Employés de Magasins de Québec inc. v. Paquet Ltée. inc.*, [1959] S.C.R. 206. In that case, the Court had to decide whether a collective agreement term providing for a check-off of union dues qualified as a "condition de travail" under Quebec labour law. The majority found that it did and that it therefore was a valid term. In the course of so deciding, the majority judgment emphasized, at 214, that a collective agreement is "not the equivalent of a bundle of individual contracts between em-

ployer and employee negotiated by the union as agent for the employees" and that the union contracts "as an independent contracting party . . ."

44 Appellant's Memorandum of Facts and of Law, 12, para. 28, CASCCAF, above note 37. The Appellant's factum in the Supreme Court of Canada differed somewhat from the Court of Appeal factum in its approach to this issue. The message remained, however, that the statute had been designed to diminish the right to strike at common law and that the right to strike was not a right under the *OLRA* within the meaning of the unfair practices provisions. See Appellant's Factum, 21–22, para. 30, SCCFCF above note 37.

45 Subsection 50(c) stated that no employer,

> shall seek by threat of dismissal, or by any other kind of threat, or by the imposition of a pecuniary penalty, or by any other means to compel an employee to become or refrain from becoming or to continue to be or to cease to be a member or officer or representative of a trade union or to exercise any other rights under this Act.

Jackett argued that the infinitive "to cease" did not apply to the final words "to exercise any other rights under this Act." The allegation of a breach under this subsection was that the employer had threatened employees to cause them to cease to exercise their right to strike. Jackett's argument on this point was rejected by both Ontario appellate courts. At the Supreme Court, he chose not to challenge those rulings.

46 Compare to George W. Adams, *Canadian Labour Law*, 2d ed. (Aurora, ON.: Canada Law Book, 2007) at 11.80: "Although the right to strike is generally conceded, it seems to have been implied into existence" [Adams].

47 Cruise & Griffiths, above note 15 at 402.

48 Lewis, above note 27 at 398. On Sinclair's tough approach to labour relations, see Cruise & Griffiths, *ibid.* at 408, 419, and 440.

49 Pound, above note 28 at 55 and 139–40; Lewis, *ibid.* at 398–99.

50 See William Kaplan, "The Rand Formula" (essay in this volume) [Kaplan].

51 *Imbleau v. Laskin*, [1962] S.C.R. 338, aff'g [1961] O.R. 438 (C.A.) [sub. nom. *Re Polymer Corp. & O.C.A.W., Local 16-14*], aff'g [1961] O.R. 176 (H.C.). The arbitration awards were reported as *Re O.C.A.W. & Polymer Corp.* (1958), 10 L.A.C. 31 (Laskin, Chair); (1959), 10 L.A.C. 51 (Laskin, Chair).

52 See above note 43.

53 "Should Charge CPR" *Toronto Star* (10 July 1961) 23; "New Party to Ponder Strike" *Toronto Star* (1 August 1961) 23; "Royal York Talks Again on Tuesday" *Toronto Star* (19 August 1961) 9; "O.K. To Sue Royal York Board Says" *Toronto Star* (22 September 1961) 1; *Local 299, Hotel and Club Employees' Union*, O.L.R.B. Mon. Rep., Sept. 1961, 214.

54 "Frost Heeds Hotel Picket Lines" *Globe and Mail* (2 May 1961) 5; "Provincial Ministers Still Use Royal York" *Globe and Mail* (11 July 1961) 5.

55 Bora Laskin, "The Ontario *Labour Relations Amendment Act, 1960*" (1961–62) 14 U.T.L.J. 116 at 120–21; S.O. 1960, c. 54, s. 30 (repeal of, and substitution for, R.S.O. 1950, c. 194, s. 57); R.S.O. 1960, c. 202, s. 65. The amendment came into force on 22 October 1960.

56 Bora Laskin, "Certiorari to Labour Boards: The Apparent Futility of Privative Clauses" (1952) 30 Can. Bar Rev. 986, helps with understanding of the context.

57 *Local 299, Hotel and Club Employees' Union,* O.L.R.B. Mon. Rep., Sept. 1961, 214. The Board file on the application has not been preserved. The report of the endorsement does not record the names of the panel members other than Young. Board practice for successful consent applications was to not issue detailed reasons for fear of prejudicing the trial.

58 Premier John P. Robarts General Correspondence, Toronto: Archives of Ontario (RG 3-26, Box 187, file on "Strikes — Royal York Hotel Nov. 61 — Dec. 65," Memorandum to the Honourable Leslie M. Frost, Q.C., 21 September 1961).

59 The swearing date, the name of the informant, and the employee names are indicated in the "Case Stated by Thomas S. Elmore, Q.C." on appeal: see Appeal Book, 28, para. 1, CASCCAF, above note 37.

60 On Thomas Spaven Elmore (1893–1965), Toronto private practitioner and then magistrate, see "Reluctant Elmore Retires at 70" *Toronto Star* (9 January 1964) 24; "Youngest Graduate, Elmore Retires as Senior Magistrate" *Globe and Mail* (9 January 1964) 21; "Thomas S. Elmore. Former Magistrate Called Robin Hood" *Globe and Mail* (19 July 1965) 2; "Argue Royal York Strike Case 5 Hours" *Toronto Star* (14 October 1961) 1 and 14.

61 The evidence and submissions are reported in "Hear Strike Charges Against Royal York" *Toronto Star* (13 October 1961) 1 and 8; "No Evidence from RY in Firing Charge" *Toronto Telegram* (13 October 1961) 45; and "Argue R. York Strike Case 5 Hours" *Toronto Star* (14 October 1961) 1 and 14. Zambri and Job are identified as two of the three witnesses. The other witness is not identified. It was almost certainly Ireton. As the strike captain, he was a likely witness and, indeed, the logical witness to introduce a picket sign into evidence. The "Case Stated by Thomas Elmore, Q.C." on appeal refers to it having been shown in evidence at trial that Ireton was in charge of assigning picketers: Appeal Book, 30, para. 4, CASCCAF, above note 37.

62 Judgment cited above note 3; quotation at 328.

63 On McRuer (1890–1985), successively Crown Attorney, private practitioner, Ontario Court of Appeal judge, Ontario High Court Chief Justice, and Ontario Royal Commission of Inquiry into Civil Rights chairman, see Patrick Boyer, *A Passion for Justice: The Legacy of James Chalmers McRuer* (Toronto: University of Toronto Press, 1994) [Boyer].

64 On stated case appeals, no longer provided for by the *Criminal Code*, see Austin M. Cooper, "Procedure on Appeals by Stated Case" (1964–65) 7 Crim. L.Q. 155. The Ontario *Summary Convictions Act*, R.S.O. 1960, c. 387, s. 3 incorporated the stated case appeal provisions of the *Criminal Code* except to the extent of any inconsistency.

65 Judgment cited above note 3.

66 Judgment cited above note 3, quotations from O.R. at 115 and 116 respectively.

67 Osgoode Society Oral History Programme — General Programme Interview Files, Interviews with or about J. C. McRuer, Toronto: Archives of Ontario (C 81-1-0-3, File #5, at 444-5).

68 "Hotel Strike Ruling Basis Is Antiquated, Chief Justice Hints" *Globe and Mail* (9 December 1961) 5; "McRuer Disputes Elmore View on Hotel Firings" *Toronto Star* (9 December 1961) 1 and 5.

69 He was defeated as a federal Liberal candidate in Toronto High Park in 1935: Boyer, above note 63 at 108–15.

70 "Allow R. York Appeal Ruling by McRuer" *Toronto Star* (9 January 1962) 1. The panel granting leave consisted of Chief Justice Dana Porter and Justices C. W. G. Gibson and W. F. Schroeder.

71 "Labor Act Covers Strike Right — Judge" *Toronto Star* (12 February 1962) 1; "Firings at Royal York Illegal — Appeal Court" *Toronto Star* (13 February 1962) 1–2.

72 Philip Girard, *Bora Laskin: Bringing Law to Life* (Toronto: Published for the Osgoode Society for Canadian Legal History by University of Toronto Press, 2005) at 338; Kaplan, above note 50.

73 Both judgments as cited above note 3 (Court of Appeal quotation at 554 of O.R.; McRuer quotation at 119 of O.R.).

74 Judgment cited above note 3, quotation at 555 of O.R.

75 The justices hearing the application were Charles Holland Locke, John Robert Cartwright, and Wilfred Judson. See "Royal York Given Right to Appeal" *Toronto Star* (19 March 1962) 39; "Highest Court to Hear Appeal of Royal York" *Globe and Mail* (20 March 1962) 29.

76 Judgment cited above note 3; "Right to Fire Argued in Royal York Appeal" *Toronto Star* (25 April 1962) 12; "Strike Right in Peril If CPR Hotel Claim Is Accepted: Lawyer" *Globe and Mail* (25 April 1962) 15; "Firing Hotel Strikers Illegal, Court Rules" *Toronto Star* (25 June 1962) 2; "Court Orders Royal York Conviction" *Globe and Mail* (26 June 1962) B1; "Orders CPR Be Punished for Firing Hotel Strikers" *Toronto Star* (26 June 1962); Bruner, above note 1.

77 The average size of a panel during the tenure of Patrick Kerwin as Chief Justice (1954–63) was 5.38. See McCormick, above note 10 at 42.

78 Judgment cited above note 3, quotation at 615 of S.C.R.

79 Judgment cited above note 3, quotation at 617 of S.C.R.

80 Judgment cited above note 3, first quotation at 623, second at 623, third at 623, and fourth at 624, of S.C.R.

81 McCormick, above note 10 at 45; Bushnell, above note 10 at 322.

82 Judgment cited above note 3, quotation at 620 of S.C.R. [emphasis in original].

83 Judgment cited above note 3, quotations at 621 of S.C.R.

84 304 U.S. 333 (1938).

85 "The Story of *NLRB v. Mackay Radio & Telegraph Co.*: The High Cost of Solidarity" in Laura J. Cooper & Catherine L. Fisk, eds., *Labor Law Stories* (New York: Foundation Press, 2005) at 13–14.

86 "Fine Royal York $500 for Firing Strikers" *Toronto Star* (4 July 1962) 51; "CPR Fined for Firing Hotel Staff" *Globe and Mail* (4 July 1962) 1; "Hotel Calls All Strikers for Shrine" *Toronto Star* (28 June 1962) 1; "Hotel Clears Decks for Shriners" *Toronto Star* (29 June 1962) 1; "Shrine 1930 Convention Was Wing-Ding, Too" *Toronto Star* (5 July 1962) 28.

87 R.S.O. 1960, c. 202, s. 69(1)(b); "Fine Royal York $500 for Firing Strikers" *Toronto Star* (4 July 1962) 51; "CPR Fined for Firing Hotel Staff" *Globe and Mail* (4 July 1962) 1;

"Thomas S. Elmore. Former Magistrate Called Robin Hood" *Globe and Mail* (19 July 1965) 2.

88 On the funding of the litigation and of the strike generally (rarely were the two differentiated from a funding perspective), see Jack Weinberger, "Notice to Affiliated Local Unions" (August 1961) 70:8 Catering Industry Employee 25; Ed S. Miller, "Royal York Strikers Pledged All-Out Aid" (September 1961) 70:9 Catering Industry Employee 1; "York Ruling Shocks Canadians on Strike Rights" (December 1961) 70:12 Catering Industry Employee 17; "Synopsis of Minutes. Meeting of General Executive Board. Hotel Carillon, Miami Beach, Florida" (January 1962) 71:1 Catering Industry Employee 21 at 26 and 28; "Gaiety Turns Sour As Strikers Get Peace Terms" *Toronto Star* (9 April 1962) 4; and the reports on the "Royal York Solidarity Fund" which appeared in many, if not all, of the monthly editions of the Catering Industry Employee during the strike and continuing through to June 1962.

89 Lewis, above note 27 at 399.

90 Archie R. Johnstone to Claude Jodoin, 28 July 1962; Jodoin to Johnstone, 26 September 1962; Donald MacDonald to Johnstone, 5 March 1963; Johnstone to MacDonald, 9 March 1963, Canadian Labour Congress Papers, Ottawa: Library and Archives Canada (MG 28-1103, File No. 23, Reel H-98).

91 "Orders CPR Be Punished for Firing Hotel Strikers" *Toronto Star* (26 June 1962) 27 (retrospective comments by HRE Canadian vice-president Archie R. Johnstone).

92 "What McRuer Ruling May Mean to Strikers" *Toronto Star* (14 December 1961) 1 (comment by Archie Johnstone).

93 "Royal York Strike Cuts Hotel Revenue" *Toronto Star* (6 April 1962) 14; "Cost of Strike Was Millions, Officials Say" *Globe and Mail* (7 April 1962) 9; "Walkout Cost $500,000, Hotel Says; Friction Among Workers Expected" *Globe and Mail* (9 April 1962) 5.

94 "Gaiety Turns Sour As Strikers Get Peace Terms" *Toronto Star* (9 April 1962) 4; "After 11 Months on Strike, Disillusionment" *Globe and Mail* (9 April 1962) 5.

95 *Labour Relations Amendment Act*, 1961–62, S.O. 1961–62, c. 68, s. 5 (Royal Assent — 18 April 1962); for Jackett's position, see the Cartwright opinion in the Supreme Court of Canada judgment, cited above note 3. See above note 45 for subsection 50(c) before the amendment. The amendment inserted "to cease" before the final words "to exercise any other rights under this Act."

96 Arthurs, "Right to Strike," above note 7 at 192.

97 See generally Adams, above note 46 at 11.80.

98 Joan Sangster, "'We No Longer Respect the Law': The Tilco Strike, Labour Injunctions, and the State" (Spring 2004) 53 Labour/Le Travail 47 [Sangster]; Ontario, *Report of the Royal Commission Inquiry into Labour Disputes* (August 1968) [Rand, Report].

99 Rand, Report, *ibid.* at 22–28.

100 *Labour Relations Amendment Act* (No. 2), S.O. 1970, c. 85, s. 25; R.S.O. 1970, c. 232, s. 64; R.S.O. 1980, c. 228, s. 73; R.S.O. 1990, c. L.2, s. 75.

101 Dunsmore, above note 7 at 23–24; England, "Legal Response," above note 7 at 456–57.

102 [1983] OLRB Rep. Sept. 1514 at 1524.

103 [1986] OLRB Rep. Dec. 1800. Board member J. Kennedy concurred with the Vice-Chairman's disposition of the *Shaw-Almex* strikers' complaints but did not comment

on *Mini-Skool*. The dissent by Board member R. J. Gallivan criticized the majority for, as he saw it, circumventing the intent of the legislature as expressed in the 1970 reinstatement amendment (s 73 of the *OLRA* as it then was). Freedman recognized the controversial nature of his decision in that he took the unusual step of discussing a draft with the Chairman and other Vice-Chairmen of the Board. The employer's application for reconsideration and for a stay of the remedial order is reported in *Shaw-Almex Industries Ltd.*, [1987] OLRB Rep. Feb. 276. The request for reconsideration was dismissed except insofar as the majority responded to criticism of its decision making process by denying error. Gallivan dissented and would have granted the request for reconsideration.

104 *Labour Relations and Employment Statute Law Amendment Act, 1992*, S.O. 1992, v. 1, c. 21, ss. 32–33.

105 *Ibid.*, s. 34.

106 *Labour Relations and Employment Statute Law Amendment Act, 1995*, S.O. 1995, c. 1, s. 1, enacting as Schedule A the *Labour Relations Act, 1995* and repealing virtually all of the 1992 statute, including ss. 32–34. The reinstatement provision, as re-enacted in 1995, constitutes s. 80 of the *Labour Relations Act, 1995*, and remains s. 80 of that statute as of this writing (24 August 2010).

107 Sangster, above note 98 at 53–71.

108 Morton with Copp, above note 25 at 239; Heron, above note 13 at 100 and 109.

109 Morton with Copp, *ibid.* at 275–76; Heron, *ibid.* at 92–93.

110 See *Eastern Provincial Airways Ltd.* and C.A.L.P.A. (1983), 3 Can. L.R.B.R. (N.S.) 75 (C.L.R.B., Lapointe, Chair); C.A.L.P.A. and *Eastern Provincial Airways Ltd. et al.* (1983), 5 Can. L.R.B.R. (N.S.) 368 (C.L.R.B., Jamieson, Chair).

111 C.H. Curtis, *The Development and Enforcement of the Collective Agreement* (Kingston, ON: Industrial Relations Centre, Queen's University, 1966) at 13–41.

112 Paul O'Higgins, "Legal Effect of Strike Notice" (1968) 26 Cambridge L.J. 223; Ken Foster, "Strikes and Employment Contracts" (1971) 34 Mod. L. Rev. 275; Kenneth W. Wedderburn, *The Worker and the Law*, 3d ed. (London: Sweet & Maxwell, 1986) at 190–93 and 576--78. The contemporary British position is summarized by Robert Upex, Richard Benny, & Stephen Hardy, *Labour Law*, 2d ed. (Oxford: Oxford University Press, 2006) at 398: "In most, if not all, strike action, contracts of employment are affected. However, no notice to terminate the contract is given. Even so, strike action amounts to a repudiation of the contract . . . . Consequently, the employer has a choice whether or not to accept the repudiation by the strikers. Such an acceptance results in dismissal."

113 *Syndicat Catholique des Employés de Magasins de Québec Inc. v. Paquet Ltée.*, [1959] S.C.R. 206; *McGavin Toastmaster Ltd. v. Ainscough*, [1976] 1 S.C.R. 718; *St. Anne Nackawic Pulp & Paper v. CPU*, [1986] 1 S.C.R. 704; *Hemond v. Coopérative fédérée du Québec*, [1989] 2 S.C.R. 962; *Weber v. Ontario Hydro*, [1995] 2 S.C.R. 929; *New Brunswick v. O'Leary*, [1995] 2 S.C.R. 967; *Noël v. Société d'énergie de la Baie James*, 2001 SCC 39, [2001] 2 S.C.R. 207.

114 2006 SCC 2, [2006] 1 S.C.R. 27.

115 See Jean Denis Gagnon, "Le contrat individuel de travail et la convention collective. Séparation ou divorce?" (2007) 41 R.J.T. 593; and, for the international context, Michal

Sewerynski, ed., *Collective Agreements and Individual Contracts of Employment* (The Hague: Kluwer Law International, 2003).

116 Among others, see Fudge & Tucker, above note 32 at 300–1; Heron, above note 13 at 91–92; Christopher L. Tomlins, *The State and the Unions: Labor Relations, Law, and the Organized Labor Movement in America, 1880–1960* (Cambridge: Cambridge University Press, 1985) at 317–28; Katherine Van Wezel Stone, "The Post-War Paradigm in American Labor Law" (1981) 90 Yale L.J. 1509 at 1573–80; and Karl E. Klare, "Judicial Deradicalization of the *Wagner Act* and the Origins of Modern Legal Consciousness, 1937–1941" in Piers Beirne & Richard Quinney, eds., *Marxism and Law* (New York: Wiley, 1982) at 138–40 and 167–68. For an opposing viewpoint, see Laurel Sefton MacDowell, *Renegade Lawyer: The Life of J. L. Cohen* (Toronto: Published for the Osgoode Society for Canadian Legal History by University of Toronto Press, 2001) at 294–98.

Hersees of Woodstock Ltd. v. Goldstein: How a Small Town Case Made it Big

Eric Tucker

A CENTRAL PROBLEM FOR any regime of industrial legality is to define the scope for workers' collective action. One characteristic of the post-World War II regime in Canada, commonly known as industrial pluralism, is that it failed to resolve that issue definitively. Most labour relations acts imposed procedural and time constraints on strikes and lockouts, but left the courts to regulate strike activity according to the body of common law they had developed in earlier periods. This produced tension within the regime; clearly legislatures intended that there should be some space for workers' collective action, but, given its historic role as defender of private property and freedom of contract, the judiciary tended to define the boundaries of this space very narrowly.

Although this tension was constant, its salience and visibility varied greatly, depending on the level and scope of industrial conflict. In the period following the post-war strike wave of 1946–47,[1] labour-management conflict settled down throughout most of Canada, as did legal contestation over the rules of the game.[2] By the late 1950s and early 1960s, however, tensions were beginning to rise again. Declining rates of growth, productivity, and profit led some employers to adopt a tougher attitude toward unions, while unions that had achieved a modicum of institutional security were facing stagnating membership growth and threats to existing standards. As a result, not only did the incidence of industrial conflict begin to increase nationally and in Ontario, but so too did its intensity; strikes became more violent and unions renewed the use of some older tactics, like consumer boycotts and picketing, that challenged the boundaries of judicially defined industrial legality.[3]

Harry Arthurs, writing in 1960, colourfully captured one view of the growing sense of crisis produced by this confrontation: "The lusty and forgivable infant that was trade unionism fifteen years ago has developed in public, legislative, and judicial imagery, into a churlish adolescent."[4] The call to make trade unions "responsible" was being revived in a number of influential arenas. From the perspective of trade unionists, however, the imagery was quite different. They perceived employers becoming more antagonistic, governments passing labour legislation hostile to union interests, and judges unfairly granting injunctions against picketing.[5]

Hersees of Woodstock Ltd. v. Goldstein[6] provides an excellent prism through which to view that moment of renewed conflict and understand how and why a tiny labour dispute in small-town Ontario in 1962 created a major precedent that significantly restricted the scope for workers' collective action over the next forty years by holding, in legal parlance, that secondary picketing was *per se* tortious, which means that any picketing at a site other than the struck employer's place of business was unlawful and could be prohibited by law.[7]

Beginning in Belleville

OUR STORY PROPER BEGINS at Deacon Brothers Sportswear Ltd., a men's sportswear manufacturer in Belleville, Ontario, a small regional trading town.[8] Deacon Brothers Sportswear traced its roots to 1897 when William B. Deacon opened a menswear store. In 1903 William B. closed the retail operation to focus on the production of men's shirts. During World War I, the Deacon Shirt Company obtained contracts to manufacture military uniforms. William B.'s brother, Fred S. Deacon, joined the company in 1914. William B.'s oldest son, Fred H. Deacon, joined the business 1923, and his younger brother John followed in 1936. The company expanded its business after the war to include men's leisure wear, and changed its name to Deacon Brothers Ltd. During World War II the company produced shirts and outerwear for the military and in 1941 it constructed a new plant, where it remained until it closed in 1990. After the war, the company's business expanded as it moved into outdoor wear, which it marketed chiefly through independent menswear stores across Canada.[9] Following the deaths of William B. and Fred S.

Deacon in the 1940s, the firm was operated by William B.'s sons; John was primarily responsible for production, and Fred. H. for sales.

Up to this point, the company's employees had never been unionized, despite the strong presence of the Amalgamated Clothing Workers (ACW) in the men's clothing industry. The ACW was founded in 1913 by a group of secessionists from the United Garment Workers (UGW) who were dissatisfied with the leadership's focus on organizing native-born workers in small towns. The ACW, in contrast, concentrated its efforts on the urban immigrant workforce in the men's clothing industry, which it successfully organized in Toronto, Montreal, and Winnipeg.[10] In 1960 it had forty locals and 15,000 members. The UGW survived as a minor player in the garment industry; in 1960 it had twelve locals scattered across the country and 2,000 members.[11]

What led the ACW to Belleville in the late 1950s? According to Stanley Clair, then the Ontario director of the ACW union-label department and president of the Canadian Labour Congress trade union label department, Deacon Brothers was the only major clothing manufacturer not under union contract and their wage scale was 25 percent lower than the ACW's, a claim that Fred B. disputed.[12] In 1959 the ACW commenced an organizing drive at Deacon Brothers among the largely female, Canadian-born workforce of about ninety full-time production employees. Under Ontario labour law at the time, the union could be certified either by signing up 55 percent or more of the bargaining unit employees as members, or by winning an election, which would be held if the union could demonstrate that at least 45 percent of the employees were members.[13] The union signed up enough employees to get an election, but not enough to be certified on the basis of membership evidence alone. The ACW lost the October 1959 election thirty-four to forty-three,[14] but continued the organizing drive. Presumably as part of a union avoidance strategy, Deacon Brothers participated in the creation of the Belle-Tex Association, which applied for certification in May 1960.[15] The ACW intervened and the application was dismissed by the Ontario Labour Relations Board (OLRB) on the ground of employer involvement.[16]

Notwithstanding this finding, Deacon Brothers entered into a collective agreement with Belle-Tex Association, dated 7 July 1960. This action proved futile. The ACW subsequently signed up more than 55 percent of Deacon Brothers employees and was certified without a vote in August 1960 for a unit consisting of seventy-two production employees. The OLRB dismissed the argument of the Belle-Tex Association that the existence of a collective agreement between it and Deacon Brothers made the ACW's application untimely: because of the employer involvement, the 7 July agreement was found not to be a collective agreement within the meaning of the *Labour Relations Act (LRA)*.[17]

Some bargaining between the ACW and Deacon Brothers followed, but no agreement was reached. An unsuccessful conciliation process was completed on 19 January 1961, putting the union in a legal strike position, yet for reasons about which we can only speculate, no strike was called. The most likely explanation is that although the union enjoyed majority support, it lacked the solidarity needed to win a strike. It is also possible that the union supporters, lacking any previous union experience, were uncomfortable with the idea of strikes and picketing. Finally, the ACW itself had developed a harmonious relationship with most employers in the men's clothing industry based upon industrial standards legislation passed in the 1930s and third-party arbitration to resolve most disputes.[18] According to Stanley Clair, the "Amalgamated Clothing Workers of America has a policy of avoiding strikes whenever possible . . ."[19] Indeed, it had not conducted a strike in Canada in the thirty-five years before 1962.[20]

Meanwhile, changes were also taking place at Deacon Brothers. Fred H. died in 1958 and his son, Fred B. (hereinafter referred to as Fred), took his place in the fall of 1959 after graduating from the Ivey School of Business Administration at the University of Western Ontario. Within a short time, disagreements with his uncle John over the future of the company resulted in Fred buying out John and reorganizing the firm as Deacon Brothers Sportswear Ltd. in December 1961. Fred did not recall having any dealings with the union prior to, or at the time of taking over the company.[21]

This changed in the summer of 1962 when, according to Fred, he received a phone call from ACW representatives in New York who wished to meet with him. Fred contacted his lawyer, Hugh Gibson, in Kingston, Ontario, who advised that he should agree to meet since Deacon Brothers Sportswear Ltd. was the successor to Deacon Brothers and so the union remained the certified bargaining agent. Based on subsequent statements made by Fred in the press, however, it also seems he did not believe that the union enjoyed majority support.[22] Not surprisingly, the subsequent meeting did not go well. According to Fred, the union representatives arrived at his office and demanded that he sign a collective agreement they had prepared in advance. The talks ended quickly. Then, according to Fred, the union representatives subsequently met with the employees. He does not know what transpired at the meeting, but we can assume the union decided that a strike by Deacon Brothers Sportswear employees was not a viable option.[23]

Later that summer, Fred received a phone call from William Hersee, the manager of Hersee's Men's Wear in Woodstock, Ontario, advising him that he had been requested to stop doing business with Deacon Brothers Sportswear. How and why did the locus and subject of the dispute shift from stalled negotiations with a Belleville manufacturer to a retail store in Woodstock, more than 300 kilometres away? There is no direct evidence of the chain of communication, but we can surmise that the ACW officials who failed to obtain a collective agreement at Deacon Brothers Sportswear requested the assistance of both the ACW and the Canadian Labour Congress (CLC) union label departments to promote a boycott of Deacon Brothers Sportswear clothing in order to pressure the company to sign a collective agreement. At the time, both were headed by Stanley Clair.[24] It is not clear whether Clair was acting in his CLC or his ACW capacity, or both, but this response went beyond the CLC union label department's normal work of promoting the purchase of clothing with the union label through displays at fairs and trade union events, or the distribution of promotional material at shopping plazas.[25] Instead, on 22 August, Stanley Clair traveled from his home in Windsor to Hersee's Men's Wear in Woodstock.

Hersee's was a family-owned men's and boy's clothing retail business that was started in about 1920 by William F. and L. Beverley Hersee. The Hersee family had deep roots in Woodstock, a community that was home to a number of industrial establishments, including the Gardner-Denver Co., a heavy equipment manufacturer, and York Knit, the manufacturer of Harvey Woods underwear.[26] There is no indication why Clair selected Woodstock or Hersee's, but what followed is fairly clear, notwithstanding some dispute over the details. Clair approached William Hersee, the proprietor of the store, identifying himself either as the CLC or the ACW union label department director.[27] He was accompanied by Charles E. Carson, secretary-treasurer of the local labour council. Clair asked Hersee if his store did business with Deacon Brothers Sportswear. Upon receiving a positive response, Clair asked Hersee to write or telephone Deacon Brothers Sportswear letting it know that he had been called upon by local labour representatives asking him to protest the fact that its goods were not union-made. Clair also allegedly asked Hersee to cancel outstanding orders but, in any event, according to William Hersee, there were no outstanding orders at the time. Hersee let Clair know that he had no intention of complying with his request.

Presumably it was after this first encounter that Hersee called Fred Deacon. In a newspaper interview, Hersee reported that he received a letter from Fred Deacon on 24 August stating that, in his view, the union only represented a minority of the employees and that the company would only discuss a contract with the union when it could prove to management it enjoyed majority support. Deacon's letter also stated his opinion that, if the union did represent the majority, it would close the plant by simply walking off the job.[28] In short, Fred dared the union to strike.

Clair and Carson returned the following day to ask Hersee whether he had given their request further thought. When Hersee again indicated he had no intention of acceding to their demands, Clair advised that he was planning an educational program to be carried out by picketing and the distribution of leaflets at the premises of some retailers for the purpose of advising members of the public that Deacon Brothers Sportswear's goods were not union-made.[29] Hersee told them that if that was their attitude they should go ahead. They did; on Tuesday, 28 August 1962, Clair and Peter Goldstein, a representative of the ACW, appeared outside of Hersee's dressed in suits and carrying placards advising shoppers that Deacon Brothers Sportswear, made by non-union labour, was being sold at Hersee's.

This was not the first time the ACW had picketed a retail store or been taken to court over such tactics,[30] but the legal consequences of this action were to have far-reaching implications for the Canadian labour movement.

Mobilizing Working-Class Purchasing Power: "The Secret Weapon Of Trade Unionism"[31]

WHILE HISTORICALLY THE LABOUR movement primarily gained bargaining leverage by withdrawing labour at the point of production, these events indicate that it also resorted to strategies that aimed to discourage suppliers, distributors, and customers from doing business with employers who failed to pay union wages or sign collective agreements. Our focus here is on consumer boycotts and the tactics used to make them effective. One of the earliest was the union label campaign, which encouraged workers and their families to purchase union-made goods by identifying them with a label that unionized manufacturers were authorized or required to put on their products. This tactic originated in the United States in the 1870s, and was used by white, unionized cigar makers to discourage consumers from buying cigars produced by Chinese immigrants. During the 1880s, the Knights of Labor and

Stanley Clair and Peter Goldstein, outside Hersee's Men's Wear
Daily Sentinel Review [Woodstock] (28 August 1962) 1

craft unionists associated with the American Federation of Labor adapted the tactic to mark consumer products made by their members. In the first decades of the twentieth century, both the International Ladies Garment Workers and the UGW relied heavily on the union label as an alternative to the use of strikes.[32]

The tactic also gained popularity among Canadian unions. In 1895 the Toronto Trades and Labour Council organized the Union Label League, and shortly thereafter it published a directory which included pages from the Journeymen Tailors' Union and the United Garment Workers promoting their labels.[33]

The Trades and Labour Congress of Canada (TLC) also became actively involved in promoting the union label at this time, incorporating a demand into its 1898 *Platform of Principles* that the union label be placed on all manufactured goods where practicable and on all government and municipal

UNITED
GARMENT • WORKERS
OF AMERICA.

THE only guarantee you have when purchasing Ready-made Clothing, Shirts, Overalls, Rubber Clothing that they are not the product of prison, sweat shop or child labor, is when the article bears the above Label.

TAKE NO OTHER

And do your share towards Abolishing the Sweating System.

Union Label, United Garment Workers of America, Toronto Trades and Labour Council Directory (c. 1895)

supplies.[34] Although local unions and their councils continued to promote the union label, interest seems to have tailed off in the period between the world wars, but revived in the 1950s, perhaps in response to the growth of consumer spending.[35] The TLC re-created a union label department in 1952, which continued as a department of the (CLC) after its founding in 1956. Stanley Clair, president of the Windsor union label council and the ACW's Ontario union label director, became its president.[36]

The mobilization of consumer spending "as the secret weapon of trade unionism" was not limited to labelling products and encouraging consumers to buy union. Unions also resorted to so-called negative boycotts that involved efforts to actively discourage vendors from carrying "unfair" products and purchasers from buying them. Tactics ranged from maintaining "we don't patronize" lists to more active measures, including the ones that occurred at Hersee's in Woodstock. These kinds of measures were adopted in both the United States and Canada beginning in the 1880s but their legality was challenged in the courts.[37]

By The Time We Got to Woodstock: Legal Regulation of Labour Boycotts And Picketing

THE FUNDAMENTAL LEGAL QUESTION in *Hersees* was whether and in what circumstances individuals could be held liable for intentionally inflicting economic harm on another. Although the English courts rejected the general proposition that the intentional infliction of economic harm was an unlawful act in and of itself (tortious), they were nevertheless prepared to impose liability in some circumstances and developed a number of specific torts, including inducing breach of contract and civil conspiracy to injure, for this purpose.[38]

When picketing was added to the mix of tactics, legal issues became more complicated. At the time, the law was concerned with three aspects of picketing: its form; its purpose; and its result. In general, peaceful picketing that aimed to provide information or persuade individuals to engage in actions they were lawfully entitled to pursue was lawful. Picketing became illegal because of its form if it involved criminal behaviour or the commission of nominate torts such as trespass, nuisance, intimidation, and defamation, and it became illegal in its purpose or result when it aimed to or persuaded people to commit unlawful acts including breaches of statute, civil conspiracies, or breaches of contract. This meant that the legality of picketing was in part determined by what courts considered to be an inducement of a breach of contract or a civil conspiracy to injure.[39]

A final legal consideration was the procedure governing the availability of injunctions to stop picketing. As a general matter, injunctions are an equitable remedy available to a party in a civil action on both a permanent and an interlocutory (before there has been a final determination of the merits) basis. The controversial area was with respect to the latter. In principle, interlocutory injunctions are available on the basis of three factors: the relative strength of the cases; irreparable harm; and the balance of convenience. By 1962, courts had adopted the practice of readily granting interlocutory injunctions to halt labour picketing, often doing so initially on an *ex parte* application, meaning that the union did not even get notice of the proceeding.[40]

While the question of the legality of union labels, union-led consumer boycotts, and picketing in support of boycotts was formally resolved by the application of English common law, as described above, it would be a mistake to proceed on the assumption that judges were sticklers for the formal rules they themselves constructed. Rather, as we shall see, the outcome of cases depended at least as much on the attitudes of the judiciary toward workers' collective action, on the broader environment in which they operated.

The legality of having union labels attached to union-made products was not challenged in Canada or the United States.[41] Indeed, Canadian courts upheld legal actions against individuals for fraudulent use of the union label and, in 1927, after nearly thirty years of trying, the TLC succeeding in getting trademark legislation amended to allow registration of union labels. The TLC promptly registered its own label the following year.[42] As well, the legality of unions positively encouraging their members and the public to buy products bearing the union label or to patronize unionized businesses was not questioned.

The law became less clear when labour unions initiated negative campaigns, for example, urging consumers not to purchase goods of a particular producer or not to patronize listed businesses. The first challenge occurred in the United States in the 1880s when bakers in New York City were convicted of a criminal conspiracy for calling upon consumers to boycott Mrs. Gray's bakery. Criminal prosecutions followed in other states and American judges also began to adapt the common law to hold that labour boycotts were civil conspiracies. Judges also crafted effective remedies, providing injunctive relief and holding trade union officials *and* members personally liable for damages.[43]

Some Canadian employers were inspired by these US developments, but were not nearly as successful. As a general matter, Canadian courts relying on English precedent rejected the view that a union-led consumer boycott targeting the employer with which it was having a dispute was tortious.[44] Similarly, picketing that was otherwise lawful did not become tortious because the picketers called for a primary boycott.[45] The situation began to change, however, when secondary action was involved. Prior to 1962, secondary action was not a legal term of art; its usage in Canada seems to have originated in a 1956 study by Alfred W.R. Carrothers, a labour law professor, where he used the label, "secondary" (initially in quotation marks), to identify one of a series of factual situations in which courts were likely to find picketing unlawful because of its objects.[46] After examining a series of cases which fit this category, Carrothers concluded:

> [W]here picketing occurs in a location where there is no labour dispute the picketing is not necessarily unlawful, but the further the picketing is removed from a labour dispute the more likely it will be interpreted as intimidation, as a conspiracy to injure or to induce an illegal strike, or as intended to induce a breach of contract. And the propensity of secondary picketing for illegality is increased where the picketing does not reach the public.[47]

The essential feature of secondary picketing was that it occurred at a location where there was no active labour dispute, most typically at a location other than the struck employer's place of business. By the early 1960s, the issue of the legality of secondary picketing in support of a consumer boycott had been considered in several more cases. Although some judges had expressed the view that such activity was *per se* wrongful, other illegalities were also present in those cases, and so their outcome did not depend on that view.[48] Carrothers was attentive to these developments and in 1962 published an article entitled "Secondary Picketing" in which he reviewed the English and American law on the subject and then turned to Canada, where he found surprisingly little attention had been paid to secondary picketing. Nevertheless, on the basis of a small, but growing body of cases, Carrothers concluded that Canadian judges were deciding the cases based on evaluation "as to whether the interests prejudiced by the picketing should prevail over the interests which the picketing is calculated to advance" but that this was being disguised by "invocation of the common law relating to civil conspiracy, inducing breach of contract and interference with favourable trade relationships, by the attribution of motive stemming from the invocation of pejorative adjectives, and from inferences based on tortious elements in the manner in which the picketing is carried out."[49]

The growing judicial hostility to secondary action was not isolated. Legislatures too were under pressure from employers to enact restrictive legislation. In British Columbia, employer lobbying yielded legislation in 1954 and 1959 that aimed to deter unlawful strikes and make unions more liable for illegal activities. The 1959 amendment specifically prohibited secondary action.[50] In Ontario, the government appointed a select legislative committee in 1957 to conduct a review of the operation of the *LRA*.[51] In its report, issued in 1958, the committee endorsed the principles of industrial voluntarism in its broad terms, while seeking to refine its implementation.[52] The labour movement viewed it otherwise, seeing its recommendation as tilted heavily in favour of employers who had argued that unions needed to be subject to great legal discipline to make them more responsible.[53] One controversial recommendation was to prohibit picketing an employer who was not a party to a labour dispute.[54] Following a provincial election in 1959 that returned another Progressive Conservative government, and after some behind-the-scenes maneuvering, in 1960 the government amended the *LRA*. Although the government did not implement the recommendations that trade unionists found most objectionable, it did seek to better deter unlawful strike activity by prohibiting persons from doing any act that as a reasonable consequence might cause an unlawful strike or act. The effect of this law would be to prohibit secondary picketing that aimed to induce the employees at the secondary site to strike unlawfully. It did not, however, go as far a the committee had recommended and prohibit secondary picketing in support of a consumer boycott.[55]

Events after 1960 intensified the debate over the legal regulation of workers' collective action. Residential construction strikes in metropolitan Toronto in 1960 and 1961, and a Teamsters' strike in the spring of 1962 were conducted in violation of the *LRA* and were accompanied by violence.[56] The Ontario Attorney General, Kelso Roberts, issued a statement on 20 June 1961 calling for all citizens, and especially those involved in the construction dispute, to obey the law and warned that instructions to enforce the law had been issued to Ontario Provincial Police, who would be assisting local police.[57] Also during the summer of 1962, inter-union conflicts on the Great Lakes were accompanied by violence and disrupted shipping.[58] The editorial writers at the *Globe and Mail* denounced the irresponsibility of union leaders and called for more stringent enforcement of the law as well as legislation to make labour leaders legally liable for the unlawful actions of their members. These editorialists also expressed alarm at the spread of disputes beyond the immediate parties. For example, in response to the secondary picketing that occurred during the construction strikes, the *Globe and Mail* warned: "What happens here in the next few years will determine whether Canada can devise an orderly and sensible system of labour relations or whether the law of the jungle is to continue until it involves the whole nation-labor, management and the public alike."[59] Finally, in late July 1962, editorialists at both the *Globe and Mail* and the more labour-friendly *Toronto Star* denounced the tactics of the Amalgamated Meat Cutters during a strike against a tannery: the strikers picketed the homes of men who continued to work, the factories that used the leather to manufacture shoes, and retail establishments where the shoes were sold.[60]

A Small Town Case Makes it Big: From Woodstock to Toronto

THE PICKETING IN FRONT of Hersee's continued on the 29th and 30th of August. Fred Deacon sent a letter to the *Woodstock Sentinel Review* in support of William Hersee and denounced the ACW's actions. To further demonstrate how distant Hersee was from the dispute, Deacon wrote that the store did not have any orders with his firm. He also provided his side of the dispute with the ACW and condemned the union's tactics in language that resonated with that of the *Globe and Mail* editorialists. "The union has intimidated retail stores throughout the province. They have demanded that retailers cancel orders with this company or face the embarrassment of having their stores picketed. This is an affront to our democratic way of life."[61]

William Hersee clearly had Fred Deacon's moral support, but Deacon insists that was all — and that he did not help finance the litigation.[62] In any event, Hersee was angry and upset about the picketing and on 30 August his lawyer, William E.G. Young,[63] filed for and obtained an *ex parte* injunction, based entirely on an affidavit by Hersee.[64] There was nothing exceptional about this; in Ontario *ex parte* injunctions were routinely being granted, even after the minor amendments to the *Judicature Act* in 1960.[65] One indication of just how normal the practice had become is that the county court judge who issued the injunction, Eric W. Cross, was also a well-regarded labour arbitrator who heard numerous cases coming out of the large unionized industrial plants in southern Ontario.[66]

After the injunction was issued, the picketing was called off, but for reasons that are not apparent, Hersee sought to have the injunction continued. An application needed to be made in the Supreme Court of Ontario and so Young called upon his firm's Toronto agent, Kimber and Dubin. The firm, and its principal lawyer, Charles Dubin, had acted in the past for both organized labour and management. Horace Krever, a member of the firm who graduated from Osgoode Hall Law School and was called to the bar in 1956, took the brief.[67]

Unlike in the original application, the defendants got notice of the motion and retained John Osler to represent them. Osler was born into an upper-middle class family in Winnipeg in 1915 but was radicalized in his university years and became an active socialist and member of the Co-operative Commonwealth Federation (CCF). He graduated from Osgoode Hall Law School and was called to the bar in 1940. Following military service during World War II, Osler returned to Toronto where he joined up with fellow CCFers Ted Joliffe and Bert Carson to start what was to become the leading union-side labour law practice in Ontario.[68] For the purpose of defending the motion, Osler filed an affidavit sworn by Stanley Clair.

The motion was argued on 14 September 1962 before Mr. Justice J.C. McRuer, the Chief Justice of the High Court of Ontario. This might have seemed like a good draw for the plaintiff; although McRuer was not unsympathetic to workers, and recognized that they enjoyed a right to engage in peaceful picketing, even in support of an unlawful strike, he had expressed strong doubts about the legality of secondary action in a 1951 decision, *General Dry Batteries*:

> I am not at all convinced that, in what one may call the guise of advancing their interest in a labour dispute, employees are entitled to bring external pressure to bear on others who are doing business with a particular person for the purpose of injuring the business of their employer so that he may capitulate in the dispute. It is one thing to exercise all the lawful rights to strike and the lawful rights to picket; that is a freedom that should be preserved and its preservation has advanced the interests of the labouring man and

the community as a whole to an untold degree over the last half-century. But it is another thing to recognize a conspiracy to injure so that benefits to any particular person or class may be realized. Further, if what any person or group of persons does amounts to a common nuisance to another what is being done may be restrained by an injunction.[69]

McRuer reiterated this concern about secondary action in a 1958 case involving picketing at a construction site for which there was no operative collective agreement, but, as in the previous case, he ultimately based his judgment on the ground that the picket line was inducing breaches of contract.[70] This approach was reflective of McRuer's preference to stay within, and strictly apply, well-established tort principles, rather than to stray too deeply into a field that he regarded as being "not too well settled as yet."[71]

No written submissions were made to McRuer and there is no record of the oral arguments, so we cannot know the strategies adopted by counsel. McRuer reserved judgment, presumably to give him time to review the evidence and reflect on the law.

While McRuer was considering the case, Stanley Clair decided to continue the Union Label Department's campaign against Deacon Brothers Sportswear. On 20 September, Clair appeared in front of Shaw's Men's Clothing Store in Belleville, the home of Deacon Brothers Sportswear, and later moved across the street to Meagher's, another men's clothing store. Clair, however, had learned something from his experience in Woodstock. At no point did he speak directly to the owner of either store and at the bottom of the picket sign, printed in smaller lettering, it was stated that the picketing was not directed against the merchants. In an interview with the local reporter, Clair emphasized that he was not asking people to boycott the stores or asking the merchants being picketed to boycott Deacon Brothers Sportswear. Rather, he said, the pickets were "just to educate the consumer." Fred Deacon was not pleased. He told the reporter that the situation was "serious" and again denied that the union really represented his workers, evidenced by the fact that it did not call a strike. He also stated that there was nothing Deacon Brothers Sportswear could do to stop the picketing, although he noted that merchants in Woodstock had succeeded in obtaining a judgment. Belleville police stated they would not intervene as long as the picketing was peaceful and did not obstruct traffic.[72] As far as can be determined, the picketing lasted for one day. There is also one report of picketing in Trenton, Ontario but the day and target have not been identified.[73]

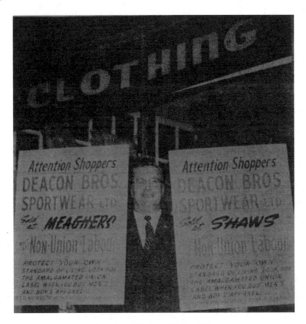

Stanley Clair in Belleville
Belleville Intelligencer (21 September 1962) 11

By this time it was clear that the ACW was losing support among the employees at Deacon Brothers Sportswear. Sometime in September or October, an application for decertification was made to the OLRB, although it was dismissed because the board was not satisfied there was no employer involvement in the petition. Around the same time, perhaps out of desperation, the ACW sought the OLRB's consent to prosecute Deacon Brothers Sportswear, apparently for violating its duty to bargain in good faith, but the application was withdrawn.[74]

McRuer issued his judgment on 23 October. Whatever temptation he may have felt to give effect to his concerns about secondary action and hold it *per se* tortious, he clearly resisted it. Rather, he took the position that for there to be liability, it was necessary to find that the secondary action involved the commission of a nominate tort previously recognized by the courts. Moreover, McRuer was scrupulous in applying the law to the facts disclosed in the affidavits of William Hersee and Stanley Clair.[75] There was no suggestion of a trespass; picketing was not *per se* a nuisance and there was no evidence of a nuisance on the facts of this case; there was no conspiracy to bring about a breach of contract since the affidavit evidence of Hersee made it clear that there was no contract between Hersee's and Deacon Brothers Sportswear at the time of the picketing; and, finally, there was no civil conspiracy to injure because the evidence did not establish an intention to injure the plaintiff distinct from the main intention of benefiting the union.[76]

One week later the plaintiff filed a notice of appeal and Krever subsequently submitted a written memorandum of fact and law that set out the case to be argued. Krever adopted a two-pronged strategy. On the one hand, he argued that the picketing did fit within one of the existing nominate torts, notably civil conspiracy to injure and inducing breach of contract. With regard to the civil conspiracy claim, Krever argued that the affidavit evidence established that this was not merely "an educational campaign" but rather a concerted effort to harm Hersee's because of the store's refusal to comply with the defendants' demands. In support of this argument, Krever urged the court to take notice that, given the development of trade unionism and the ethic that "it was almost a treasonous act for one to cross a picket line," a picket line's purpose was never merely to communicate information, but to cause economic loss to the business whose premises are being picketed.[77] Krever also argued that the picketing was illegal (and implied it was also criminal) insofar as it attempted to require a person not to do something that he had a legal right to do.[78] Later in the memorandum, Krever also argued that quite apart from conspiracy, the picketing was in violation of a new tort, recently recognized by the Supreme Court of Canada in the *Therien* case — interference with the right to trade by unlawful means — and that there was a conspiracy to induce a breach of contract.[79]

The second prong of Krever's strategy built on the observations made by Carrothers, discussed earlier, that the courts were operating on the underlying, unspoken principle that the right to trade should take precedence over the freedom to engage in secondary picketing. Thus, following his discussion of the elements of conspiracy, Krever directly addressed the secondary character of the action. He argued that it was never in the contemplation of the courts that members of a union could legitimately inflict harm on an innocent person who had dealings with the employer. He went on to urge that it was the function of the law to strike a proper balance between competing rights and that courts had wisely allowed workers to work together to advance their interest by interfering with a person with whom they had a direct conflict, but that the law of conspiracy did not permit interference with the right to trade of persons who were far removed from that dispute. Finally, he argued that the right to free speech was properly limited to prevent one party from causing unnecessary harm to another who is some 200 miles away from the scene of the real dispute.[80]

Although these arguments were made in support of the claim that the picketing was wrongful as a civil conspiracy to injure, one paragraph later the memorandum offered the courts another alternative:

> [I]t is submitted that secondary picketing, in the circumstances of this case, is illegal. Except for the Judgment appealed from, in all cases in which Canadian Courts have considered secondary picketing, whether directly or obiter dictum, judicial opinion has been that secondary picketing is illegal.[81]

In support of that proposition, Krever cited a number of cases, including of course, McRuer's own observations in *General Dry Batteries*, as well as four other cases in which secondary boycotts had been held to be civil conspiracies to injure.[82]

In short, the brief not only provided the Ontario Court of Appeal with several legal pegs on which it could hang its judgment — including the option of doing directly what courts had been doing indirectly and holding secondary picketing to be *per se* tortious — but also invoked broad legal principles that could be used to give support for the growing sentiment among many judges and opinion leaders like the *Globe and Mail* that workers' collective action needed to be curtailed in order to limit the ability of unions to disrupt the economy and interfere with trade.

The defendants' brief, prepared by Osler, was, well, briefer. It emphasized that the manner in which the picketing was conducted was lawful and that the defendants had every right to advise members of the public that some of the clothing being sold at Hersee's was manufactured at a firm where union standards were not met. Osler also argued that the defendants had a right to persuade members of the public to prefer union-made goods and that the defendants were not limited to picketing at premises where there was an employer-employee relationship between the picketers and the proprietor of the premises. Finally, he argued there could not be liability for inducing a breach of contract because no contracts were in existence. In short, Osler's strategy was to follow McRuer and argue that the defendants' actions did not fall afoul of any nominate tort, while giving short shrift to the secondary action issue. This proved to be a mistake.

Oral argument was heard on 10 December in Toronto before Justices John Aylesworth, Frederick MacKay, and George McGillivray. Neither Justices MacKay nor McGillivray practiced labour law before their appointment to the bench and, while on the bench, neither had ruled on a labour injunction case.[83] Aylesworth, the most senior of the three, was an experienced management-side labour lawyer in Windsor, who had represented major automobile companies and other heavy manufacturers prior to his appointment to the bench in 1946. As discussed in William Kaplan's chapter in this collection, in 1943 Aylesworth appeared before the Select Committee of the Ontario Legislative Assembly holding hearings into proposed collective bargaining legislation, where he recommended that if compulsory collective bargaining legislation was to be adopted then it was necessary to ensure that it would promote improved industrial relations and impose greater responsibility on the part of "bargaining agencies."[84] He also represented Ford during the 1945 strike that produced the Rand Formula.[85] Despite his long tenure on the bench, prior to this case Aylesworth had only participated in one reported labour injunction case, in which he concurred with his two colleagues who wrote lengthy judgments.[86]

There is no report of the oral argument, and the court reserved judgment. In the meantime, another decertification application was made at Deacon Brothers Sportswear and this time the OLRB ordered that a vote be held on 17 December. The union lost by a vote of thirty-seven to thirty, and on 7 January 1963 the OLRB formally terminated the ACW's bargaining rights.[87]

Later that month there was one other event that contributed to the growing concern among certain circles that organized labour was out of control. A wildcat strike of 3,500 lumber and sawmill workers began on 14 January outside the northern Ontario town of Kapuskasing. Picketers targeted independent operators who continued to supply the struck mill with logs. Violent confrontations between the two groups climaxed tragically on 11 February when independent loggers fired into a large crowd of striking workers who were advancing toward their stockpile of logs at Reesor Siding. Three strikers were killed and many more were wounded.[88] The *Globe and Mail* editorialists were quick to condemn the government for not providing enough police to stop the violence earlier and called for stronger laws to penalize irresponsible trade unionists who were blamed for inciting labour violence.[89]

The Court of Appeal issued its judgment on 27 February 1963, ruling in favour of Hersee's.[90] Aylesworth wrote the main opinion, with which both MacKay and McGillivray concurred, while MacKay provided additional reasons for allowing the appeal. Aylesworth's and MacKay's application of existing common law principles was, as Harry Arthurs' later scathing case comment abundantly demonstrated,[91] sloppy to say the least. Aylesworth held that, contrary to McRuer, the picketing was tortious because it induced a breach of contract. To support this result, Aylesworth first had to find that there was a contract between Hersee's and Deacon Brothers Sportswear, notwithstanding that William Hersee's affidavit expressly stated that at the time Clair approached him, there were no orders. To do this, Aylesworth pointed to a statement in Clair's affidavit that Hersee showed him an invoice for an order already placed, but Aylesworth ignored the rest of Clair's statement in which he stated that Hersee also told him that he had not placed an order for the fall. Moreover, he seemingly preferred Clair's ambiguous statement to Hersee's unequivocal statement that he had no outstanding orders with Deacon Brothers Sportswear, despite the fact that Hersee was in the best position to know.[92] Moreover, Aylesworth never noticed that the wrong plaintiff had brought the inducing breach of contract action since it was the innocent victim of the breach who was entitled to sue, not the person who allowed himself to be induced. From there his judgment rambled. Aylesworth noted, "In this day and age the power of organized labour is very far indeed from negligible." He then took judicial notice of the power of a peaceful picket line to deter both union members and "members of the general public in a community where . . . there is widespread organization of labour" from doing business at picketed premises. Moreover, he found that the content of the picket signs was likely to confuse the public, making them think that Hersee's was in a dispute with organized labour. What any of this had to do with the tort of inducing breach of contract was never made clear, and Aylesworth concluded his analysis of this branch of the case by stating, without any analysis, that the picketing was also criminal watching and besetting.[93]

MacKay's analysis of civil conspiracy to injure was equally problematic. Not only did he find it difficult to see how the unionized employees of Deacon Brothers Sportswear could possibly gain economic leverage from the promotion of a consumer boycott of their employer's products in Woodstock, but he also refused to accept there was a legitimate business justification for the union's action because the harm being inflicted on Hersee's outweighed the "negligible" benefit it would gain. Apart from his willful blindness, MacKay's turn to interest balancing departed from earlier precedent which refused to give weight to the quantum of damages being inflicted once a legitimate purpose was established.[94]

To this point, Aylesworth's and MacKay's judgments were perfectly consistent with the observation made earlier by Carrothers that "the characterization of secondary picketing as being unlawful on the basis of common-law principles as they stand at present presents a colourful confusion of fact, inference, assumption, law and policy that would be kaleidoscopic in quality had it the saving grace of internal order."[95] The significance of the case, however, did not lie in its incremental contribution to the large pool of poorly crafted judgments in the tort law of picketing. Rather, what made the case precedent-setting was the court's decision to take up the invitation in Krever's brief and hold that secondary picketing was *per se* tortious and no longer had to be squeezed into the requirements of an existing tort. To justify this result, Aylesworth's judgment relied in part on a sweeping assertion that the right to trade is "far more fundamental and of far greater importance" than the right ("if there be such a right") to engage in secondary picketing, the former being for the benefit of the community, the latter for the benefit of a particular class.[96] In reaching this conclusion, he never adverted to the fact that earlier in his judgment he took judicial notice of the fact that members of the public, particularly in working-class communities, are likely to choose not to cross a picket line to do business with a merchant selling goods made by workers not being paid union wages. Secondly, he also pointed to a line of cases in which courts had expressed their antipathy to secondary action, but admitted that in all those cases the picketing had been enjoined because of its illegality. Nevertheless, he chose to "view them as declaring secondary picketing to be illegal *per se*,"[97] implying that his judgment was merely giving effect to existing precedent, when clearly it was not.

The defendants' lawyer sought leave to appeal to the Supreme Court of Canada, but the motion was denied on 22 April 1963, in part because the ACW had been decertified as bargaining agent for Deacon Brothers Sportswear, although that hardly made the issue moot.

And the Rest Is History

So HOW DID A small town case make it big? There really is no surprise here. It was a matter of the right case, at the right time, with the right people. The case was right because a court would have had to stretch to find any illegality based on the existing common law torts of nuisance, inducing breach of contract, or conspiracy to injure. It was also at the right time in the sense that among certain elites there was a growing sense that organized labour was out of control and needed to be made more responsible both for the violence that sometimes accompanied industrial disputes and for economic disruption caused by secondary action. Finally, there were the right people. Horace

Krever authored a brief that squarely invited the court to hold secondary action *per se* illegal and provided them with broad legal principles, if not precedents, that supported this step, and John Aylesworth, who while in practice sought to make unions more legally responsible, now had the opportunity to do so as a judge by narrowing the scope for workers' collective action.

But there is one other dimension to this case's importance that this paper has not yet explored, and that is its widespread impact and durability. The decision was, after all, a judgment of the Ontario Court of Appeal, and so was not binding in other provinces. Moreover, it could have been overturned by the Supreme Court of Canada (SCC) or by legislation. Yet, the tort of secondary picketing came to be accepted in most jurisdictions, was not legislatively reversed, and was not overruled by the SCC until 2002.

The judgment did not attract much attention immediately after it was released. Yes, the *Woodstock Sentinel-Review* endorsed the court's decision, but there were no editorials in the *Globe and Mail* or the *Star*.[98] As mentioned, Harry Arthurs published a withering case comment in the *Canadian Bar Review* in late 1963 that condemned the court's flawed legal reasoning, including its failure to notice that the tort was brought by the wrong plaintiff, and its sweeping policy pronouncements, while leaving open the possibility that a legislature might legitimately restrict secondary action.[99] Excerpts of Arthurs' comment subsequently made their way into the *Globe and Mail* when Wilfred List, the paper's labour reporter, chose to write up Arthurs' criticism in an article provocatively entitled, "Picketing and the Law: Judge vs. Professor." List focused more on Arthurs' criticism of the court's policy pronouncements than on its legal reasoning, reproducing a passage in which Arthurs condemned the court's assertion that individual and group interests should yield to the interests of the community as "an affirmation of totalitarian philosophy quite inconsistent with constitutional government."[100]

Whatever consternation these words may have stirred in the legal community, Arthurs' critiques of *Hersees* gained little traction. The industrial relations community, informed as it was by the industrial pluralist perspective, would have agreed with his critique of the judiciary as reflexively hostile to collective action that interfered with private property rights. Therefore, they were poor judicial craftsmen and improperly manipulated the common law to achieve their desired results, and yet, they would have also shared the judiciary's concern that industrial conflict needed to be contained within narrow limits. While the legislature and not the judiciary should have made the decision about where to draw the line, the substantive result did not deeply offend the industrial pluralist view of the limits of industrial legality.

Indeed, even the labour movement did little to challenge the result in *Hersees*. Rather, its focus was almost exclusively on the easy availability of *ex parte* and interlocutory injunctions, a matter that was of concern before the *Hersees* judgment, but that grew in importance afterwards as a result of growing labour militancy that challenged the bounds of industrial legality.[101] In 1965 the Ontario Federation of Labour (OFL) published a report on injunctions prepared by John Osler, the union counsel in *Hersees*, which focused on the unfairness of the procedures, but did not say a word about secondary action.[102] The following year, the OFL made a special submission to the government on injunctions in labour disputes, in part as a result of their use in the Tilco strike.[103] Again, the focus was on the use of injunctions, not the tort law of secondary picketing. In June 1966, the Ontario Minister of Labour commissioned a study on the role of labour injunctions in Ontario directed by Carrothers. Seven studies were produced, one of which was a study of the law of injunctions by Horace Krever, who had become a professor of law at the University of Toronto in 1964. Although his focus was on procedure, not substantive law, Krever was critical of the courts' unwillingness to give the interests of labour the same weight as the interests of employers, and, ironically, cited the Court of Appeal's judgment in *Hersees* as an example.[104] Carrothers' report made no formal recommendations and no action was taken, but before the study was released, the Ontario government appointed former Supreme Court of Canada Justice Ivan Rand to head a commission of inquiry into labour disputes.[105] As well, late in 1966 the federal government established the Task Force on Labour Relations, one of whose members was Carrothers.

The OFL's submissions to the Rand commission contained short sections defending the right to strike and picket, and a much longer section advocating prohibition of the use of injunctions in labour matters, but no mention was made of secondary picketing.[106] Employer submissions, however, called specifically for picketing to be limited to the struck employer's place of business.[107] The Rand Report, published in 1968, contained sweeping recommendations for labour law reform, including a prohibition on secondary picketing and boycotts except in cases where the target had become an ally of the struck employer.[108] The report was heavily criticized by the OFL, which for the first time specifically defended secondary action, calling for legislation to permit it.[109] The OFL's position was largely accepted by the federal

Task Force report, which recommended that secondary picketing in support of consumer boycotts be permitted.[110]

Political support to overturn *Hersees*, however, did not materialize. In 1970 a majority conservative Ontario government implemented some of Rand's recommendations in amendments to the *Labour Relations Act*.[111] The government also amended the *Judicature Act* to limit generally the availability of injunctions in labour disputes, and specifically to restrict the use of *ex parte* injunctions.[112] Although these measures were extensively debated, the question of secondary picketing or boycotts was never raised.[113]

In the period after 1970, courts in much of Canada continued to rely heavily on *Hersees* and the sharp distinction that it drew between primary and secondary picketing. Indeed, this distinction was applied to the interpretation of the *Judicature Act* amendments, holding that its restrictions on granting injunctions in labour disputes did not apply to secondary picketing, since this was not picketing in a labour dispute.[114] Given its significance, much litigation focused on the boundary between primary and secondary picketing which, in turn, produced another round of critical academic commentary, leading David Beatty to write "so much has already been written of this area generally by Canadian labour law teachers who have been attracted to the topic with a child-like and absorbing pre-occupation" before he proceeded to make his own contribution.[115]

The reconfiguration of the line between primary and secondary picketing provided one avenue of retreat from *Hersees*, but in general movement was slow.[116] Legislation in Manitoba in 1970 more severely restricted the availability of injunctions than in Ontario and it was interpreted by the Manitoba Court of Appeal as permitting secondary picketing that was otherwise lawful[117] but, for the most part, there remained a high level of judicial hostility to secondary action in labour disputes and little political support for legislative action to reverse it. Indeed, in 1971 New Brunswick joined British Columbia and Newfoundland in limiting secondary action.[118] Its eventual undoing by the Supreme Court of Canada in the *Pepsi* case is a story for another day. It is, however, fair to speculate that the change was partly contingent on a shift in the judicial imagery of organized labour from the "churlish adolescent" that Harry Arthurs described in 1960 to that of a senior citizen who no longer poses a threat to others and is losing her capacity to cope in an increasingly hostile environment.[119] Now that's a labour movement the courts can trust to deliver autonomy, equality, and democracy to Canadian workers.[120]

Postscript

THE WORKERS OF DEACON Brothers Sportswear were subsequently organized by the UGW, the more conservative historic rival of the ACW, in 1979. Ironically, the union organizer was Andre Bekerman, a self-described revolutionary socialist.[121] After lengthy negotiations, the parties reached a collective agreement which was renewed several times until the company went out of business in 1991.[122] Fred became a school trustee and conducted labour negotiations on the school board's behalf. This turned into a career as a school board negotiator after Deacon Brothers Sportswear closed its doors. William Hersee continued to operate his clothing store in Woodstock until the early 1990s. He passed away in 2000.[123] Hugh Gibson was appointed to the Exchequer court in 1964; John Osler was appointed to the High Court of Ontario in 1968; and Horace Krever followed him there in 1975. Krever went to the Court of Appeal in 1986 but is best known for his work leading several commissions, including the 1993 Commission of Inquiry on the Blood System of Canada.

Notes

1   See Kaplan (this volume).

2   British Columbia was the exception. See Alfred W.R. Carrothers, *The Labour Injunction in British Columbia* (Toronto: CCH Canadian Limited, 1956) [Carrothers, "Labour Injunction"]. For a view of Ontario that emphasizes the extent of the ongoing conflict, particularly around issues of union security, see Charles W. Smith, "The Politics of the *Ontario Labour Relations Act*: Business, Labour, and Government in the Consolidation of Post-War Industrial Relations, 1949–1961" (2008) 62 Labour/Le Travail 109 at 115–28 [Smith].

3   On the incidence of strikes, see Canada Department of Labour, Economics and Research Branch, *Strikes and Lockouts in Canada* (various years); Research Branch, Ontario Department of Labour, "Industrial Conflict in Ontario: 1958–1965," in Alfred W. R. Carrothers, *Report of a Study on the Labour Injunction in Ontario* (October 1966) at 227 [Carrothers, *Report*]; Stuart Marshall Jamieson, *Times of Trouble: Labour Unrest and Industrial Conflict in Canada, 1900–66* (Ottawa: Task Force on Labour Relations, Study No. 22, 1968) at 344–73 [Jamieson].

4   Harry W. Arthurs, "Tort Liability for Strikes in Canada: Some Problems of Judicial Workmanship" (1960) 38 Can. Bar Rev. 346 [Arthurs, "Tort Law"].

5   For expressions of concern that employers were becoming more hostile, see Lab. Gazette (1958), 1372 and 1375. On hostile labour legislation, see Lab. Gaz. (1960), 1281; (1961), 134 and 449–50. On injunctions, see Lab. Gaz. [1958] 348; Lab. Gaz. [1962] 1356; Lab. Gaz. [1963] 32.

6   *Hersees of Woodstock Ltd. v. Goldstein* (1963), 38 D.L.R. (2d) 449 (Ont. C.A.) [*Hersees* C.A.] rev'g 35 D.L.R. (2d) 616 (Ont. H.C.J.) [*Hersees* H.C.].

7   *Hersees* was overruled by the Supreme Court of Canada in *R.W.D.S.U., Local 558 v. Pepsi-Cola Canada Beverages (West) Ltd.*, [2002] 1 S.C.R. 156.

8   Nick Mika & Helma Mika, *Belleville, Friendly City* (Belleville: Mika, 1973) at 85–127.

9   Fred B. Deacon, Speaking Notes [unpublished, n.d.]; Interview of Fred B. Deacon (3 July 2007) [Deacon interview].

10   On the history of the ACW, see Steven Fraser, *Labor Will Rule* (New York: Free Press, 1991). In Canada, see Ruth A. Frager, *Sweatshop Strife* (Toronto: University of Toronto Press, 1992); Mercedes Steedman, *Angels of the Workplace* (Toronto: Oxford University Press, 1997) [Steedman].

11   Canada, Department of Labour, Economic and Research Branch, *Labour Organization in Canada* (Ottawa: Queen's Printer, 1960).

12   *Daily Sentinel Review* [Woodstock] (28 August 1962) 9; Fred B. Deacon (25 September 2008) [Letter to the author].

13   See S.O. 1950, c. 34, s. 7. On post-war certification procedures, see John Logan, "How 'Anti-Union' Laws Saved Canadian Labour: Certification and Striker Replacements in Post-War Industrial Relations" (2002) 57 Relations Industrielles 129.

14   Ontario Labour Relations Board, *O.L.R.B. Report* (October 1959) at 251.

15   Fred B. Deacon speculates that his uncle John may have been getting advice on union avoidance techniques from a relative, Deacon interview, above note 9.

16 Ontario Labour Relations Board, *O.L.R.B. Report* (May 1960) at 64 (H.F. Irwin dissenting). The *OLRA* prohibited the board from certifying a union "if any employer or employers' organization has participated in its formation or administration or has contributed financial or other support to it . . . ." *OLRA*, S.O. 1950, c. 34, s. 9 (now s. 15).

17 Ontario Labour Relations Board, *O.L.R.B. Report* (August 1960) at 176.

18 For a discussion of these developments, see Steedman, above note 10 at 190–253; Michael Brecher, "Pattern of Accommodation in the Men's Garment Industry of Quebec 1914–1959" in H.D. Woods, ed., *Patterns of Industrial Dispute Settlement in Five Canadian Industries* (Montreal: Industrial Relations Centre, McGill University, 1958) at 89–186.

19 *Hersees* (Affidavit of Stanley Clair, 5 September 1962, at para. 5), Toronto, Archives of Ontario, Court File (RG 22-523, B214344. File 442/1962) [Court File].

20 *Daily Sentinel Review* [Woodstock] (28 August 1962) 9.

21 Deacon interview, above note 9.

22 *Ibid.*

23 *Ibid.*

24 A union label is, as its name implies, a label placed on a product to indicate that it was produced by union labour. The labour movement actively promoted its use. For further discussion of the union label and Stanley Clair, see below text accompanying notes 30 to 36.

25 For example, see typescript report of Stanley Clair to the Third Convention of the Department, CLC (April 8, 1962) in CLC, Union Label Trades Department files, Ottawa, National Archives of Canada (R5699-96-X-E, Microfilm reel H-234).

26 Hersee Family, Woodstock, Woodstock Public Library (Vertical Files); Art Williams and Edward Baker, *Woodstock Bits and Pieces* (Erin, ON: Boston Mills Press, 1967); *Vernon's City of Woodstock Directory* (Hamilton, ON: Henry Vernon & Son, 1920).

27 William Hersee states that Clair identified himself as the president of the CLC Union Label Department while Clair identifies himself as the Ontario Union Label Director for the ACW. Court File, above note 19 at paras. 1 and 3.

28 *Daily Sentinel Review* [Woodstock] (28 August 1962) 9.

29 *Ibid*; Court File, above note 19.

30 There is no discussion of this strategy in the Union Label Trades Department files (NA, R5699-96-X-E), or in their Convention reports. In Quebec in 1958, the ACW picketed a retail store selling suits manufactured by an employer the union was seeking to organize. The store owner obtained an interlocutory injunction. See *Sauve Frères v. Amalgamated Clothing Workers of America* [1959] C.S. 341 (Que. S.C.) [*Sauve Frères*].

31 Jacob Clayman, (then the director of organization and union label for the ACW, speech to the founding convention of the union label department) Lab. Gaz. [June 1956] 659.

32 Dana Frank, *Purchasing Power* (New York: Cambridge University Press, 1994) at 193–211; Daniel Bensman, *The Practice of Solidarity* (Urbana: University of Illinois Press, 1985) at 151–67 and 185–211; Harry W. Laidler, *Boycotts and the Labor Struggle*, rev. ed. (1913; repr., New York: Russell & Russell, 1968) [Laidler].

33 Toronto Trades and Labour Council *Toronto Labor Directory and Union Label Handbook* [unpublished, n.d]; Steedman, above note 10 at 61 and 107–8.

34 Trades and Labor Congress of Canada, *Proceedings* (1898) at 31.

35 For discussions of consumer spending and consumer advocacy, see Joy Parr, *Domestic Goods* (Toronto: University of Toronto Press, 1999); Julie Guard, "Canadian Citizens or Dangerous Foreign Women? Canada's Radical Consumer Movement, 1947–1950" in Marlene Epp, Franca Iacovetta, & Frances Swyripa, eds., *Sisters or Strangers* (Toronto: University of Toronto Press, 2004) at 161–89.

36 (September 1952) Lab. Gaz. 1189; (June 1956) Lab. Gaz. 659.

37 On the history of boycotting in the US, see Laidler, above note 32; Gary Minda, *Boycott in America* (Carbondale, IL: Southern Illinois University Press, 1999). There is a paucity of writing on Canadian consumer boycotts in the labour context. I discuss some early efforts in "The Faces of Coercion: The Legal Regulation of Labor Conflict in Ontario, 1880–1889" (Fall 1994) 12 Law and History Rev. 308.

38 Douglas Brodie, *A History of British Labour Law 1867–1945* (Oxford: Hart, 2003) at 27–38; Carrothers, "Labour Injunction," above note 2 at 38–98; Arthurs, "Tort Law," above note 4 at 362–88; Innis M. Christie, *The Liability of Strikers in the Law of Tort* (Kingston, ON: Industrial Relations Centre, Queen's University, 1967) at 61–130 [Christie, *Liability of Strikers*].

39 Carrothers, above note 2, c. 3.

40 *Ibid.* at 3–10 and 192–215.

41 Laidler, above note 32 at 169 (" . . . boycotts, prosecuted primarily by means of the union label, are unquestionably legal."). The legality of municipal bylaws requiring the city to purchase products bearing the union label, however, has been contested. For example, in 1903 the City of Toronto passed a bylaw requiring the union label on all clothing bought by the city. The bylaw was struck down by the court as beyond the powers of the city. Lab. Gaz. (December 1903) 598.

42 The first attempt to get union label legislation in 1898 passed the Commons but failed in the Senate. Subsequent efforts met a similar fate until 1927 (S.C. 1926-27, c. 71). See, CLC, Union Label Trades Department, Circulars, Correspondence, Relevant legislation (Code 2-L) (NA, R5699-96-X-E, Microfilm reel H-425). Even prior to this legislation, fraudulent use of the union label was unlawful and, in one case, David Pearlstein was sentenced to one day in jail for violating an injunction prohibiting him from placing union labels on boxes of cigars he was selling to tobacconists. Lab. Gaz. (November 1907) 618.

43 The literature is vast. Daniel R. Ernst, *Lawyers Against Labor* (Urbana and Chicago: University of Illinois Press, 1995); William E. Forbath, *Law and the Shaping of the American Labor Movement* (Cambridge: Harvard University Press, 1991) at 79–95; Haggai Hurvitz, "American Labor Law and the Doctrine of Entrepreneurial Property Rights: Boycotts, Courts, and the Judicial Reorientation of 1886–1895" (1986) 8 Indus. Rel. L.J. 307; Michael A. Gordon, "The Labor Boycott in New York City, 1880–1886" (1975) 16 Lab. His. 184.

44 For some early exceptions, see Judy Fudge & Eric Tucker, "Forging Responsible Unions: Metal Workers and the Rise of the Labour Injunction in Canada" (Spring 1996) 37 Labour/Le Travail 107.

45 BC was exceptional. See *Hollywood Theatres v. Tenney*, [1940] 1 D.L.R. 452.

46 Carrothers, "Labour Injunction" above note 2 at 47. The primary/secondary distinction had been identified much earlier in American writing on the subject. For example, see Laidler above note 32 at 64.

47 *Ibid.* at 65.

48 Quebec cases include *Verdun Printing and Publishing Inc. v. Union internationale des clicheurs et électrotypeurs de Montréal, local 33*, [1957] C.S. 204 [*Verdun Printing*]; *Sauve Frères*, above note 30; *Noe Bourassa Ltée. v. United Packinghouse Workers*, [1961] C.S. 604 (QC). *Verdun Printing* was commented upon favourably in Marie-Louis Beaulieu, "Critique des arrest" (1958) 18 Revue du Bareau 161. See also *Dusessoy's Supermarkets St. James Ltd. v. Retail Clerks Union, Local 832, et al.* (1961), 30 D.L.R. (2d) 51 (Man. QB).

49 Alfred W.R. Carrothers, "Secondary Picketing" (1962) Can. Bar. Rev. 57 at 66 [Carrothers, "Secondary Picketing"].

50 *Labour Relations Act*, S.B.C. 1954, c. 17 [*Labour Relations Act*]; *Trade-unions Act*, S.B.C. 1959, c. 90, s. 3(2). Jamieson, above note 3 at 374–86.

51 The impetus for the appointment came from the Ontario Federation of Labour (OFL) which conducted hearings around the province in 1956 and submitted a brief to the legislature that was highly critical of the administration of the *Labour Relations Act*. Some submissions to the OFL condemned *ex parte* injunctions, but they were not a primary concern. Both the CCF and the Liberals supported the appointment of a select legislative committee. See Lab. Gaz. (1956) 972; Ontario, *Legislative Debates* (1957) at 1040–45, 1487, and 1672–76. For an extended discussion of these developments, see Smith, above note 2 at 128–34.

52 Ontario, Legislative Assembly, *Report of the Select Committee on Labour Relations* (1958) at 6.

53 Smith, above note 2 at 134.

54 Above note 52, recommendations 34, 36, and 41.

55 *Ontario Labour Relations Amendment Act*, S.O. 1960, c. 54. See also Monroe Johnson, "Illegal Picketing Wasn't Mentioned but Section 27 Covers It" *Toronto Star* (9 March 1960) 7 ("Many people will be interested in knowing whether Section 27 is intended as an instrument against illegal picketing and secondary boycotts."); "The Labor Law-and the Law," Editorial, *Globe and Mail* (26 February 1960) (failure of amendment to deal with picket line violence and dissatisfaction with provincial authorities for not enforcing the criminal law). More generally, see Bora Laskin, "The *Ontario Labour Relations Amendment Act, 1960*" (1961) 14 Can. Bar Rev. 117 [Laskin] and Smith, above note 2 at 134–40.

56 The construction strike is discussed in Jamieson, above note 3 at 408–9.

57 W.M. McIntyre, Secretary of the Cabinet, to A. Kelso Roberts, 19 June 1961; A. Kelso Roberts, Press Release, OA, RG4-2, File 159.9 (20 June 1961).

58 William Kaplan, *Everything That Floats* (Toronto: University of Toronto Press, 1987) at 101–12.

59 "Time for a Stand," Editorial, *Globe and Mail* (9 June 1961). A sample of additional *Globe and Mail* editorials includes: "Labour Anarchy," Editorial, *Globe and Mail* (16 June 1961); "Labor and the Law," Editorial, *Globe and Mail* (20 June 1961); "Surrender to Violence," Editorial, *Globe and Mail* (30 April 1962); "Dealing with the Team-

sters," Editorial, *Globe and Mail* (25 June 1962); "The Nation's Shame," Editorial, *Globe and Mail* (2 July 1962); "Action to End Violence," Editorial, *Globe and Mail* (7 July 1962).

60 "No Place for Pickets," Editorial, *Toronto Star* (1 August 1962); "Intimidation by Pickets," Editorial, *Globe and Mail* (2 August 1962). Two picketers were subsequently convicted of criminal watching and besetting. Warren K. Winkler, "Picketing of Private Homes: The Anomalous Peaceful Picketing Clause" (1963) 2 Osgoode Hall L.J. 437

61 Fred Deacon, "Store Picketing Continues in Clothing Company Issue," Letter to the Editor, *Daily Sentinel Review* [Woodstock] (30 August 1962) 13.

62 Fred B. Deacon said that his lawyer, Hugh Gibson, advised him not to become involved. Deacon interview, above note 9.

63 Young was a partner in a small local firm, Young and Hutchinson. In 1963 he ran unsuccessfully for the Liberals against Wallace Nesbitt, the long-serving Progressive-Conservative member of Federal parliament for Oxford.

64 Court File, above note 19; *Daily Sentinel Review* [Woodstock] (31 August 1962) 1.

65 E.E. Palmer, "The Labour Injunction in Ontario: Juridical Data 1958–1966" in Carrothers, *Report*, above note 3 at 87; *Judicature Act*, S.O. 1960, c. 52, s. 1. On the *Judicature Act* amendment, see Laskin, above note 55.

66 Eric W. Cross, Papers, Toronto, Archives of Ontario (F 1025). His arbitration work began in the early 1950s and continued until his death in 1965. He lived in Woodstock and would have known the Hersee's store. Prior to his judicial appointment, Cross was a Liberal member of the legislative assembly and minister in Hepburn's cabinet.

67 Interview of Horace Krever (15 October 2007).

68 Interview of John H. Osler (27 June 2001), Toronto, Archives of Ontario (Osgoode Society Fonds, C-81); David Lewis, *The Good Fight* (Toronto: Macmillan, 1981) at 373 and 389.

69 *General Dry Batteries of Canada Unlimited v. Brigenshaw et al.*, [1951] O.R. 522 at para. 15. Charles Dubin represented the union in this case.

70 *Wilson Court Apts. v. Jenovese et al.*, [1958] O.W.N. 302. For a more general and favourable discussion of McRuer's labour law decisions, and a full biography, see Patrick Boyer, *A Passion for Justice* (Toronto: Osgoode Society, 1994) especially at 258–68 [Boyer].

71 *Dewar et al. v. Dwan et al.*, [1957] O.R. 546 at para. 4. In that case McRuer also observed (at para. 28) that the *Rights of Labour Act*, which gave trade unions protection against civil conspiracies to injure, had not been judicially applied or interpreted and that he too would refrain from doing so since it was not necessary to decide the case.

72 *Belleville Intelligencer* (21 September 1962) 11.

73 *Belleville Intelligencer* (18 December 1962).

74 Ontario Labour Relations Board, *O.L.R.B. Reports* [1962–63] at 227 and 229. A spokesperson for Deacon Brothers told the *Belleville Intelligencer* (18 December 1962) that the board had ruled on the ACW's application, holding "that the Union was the author

of its own misfortune in this matter, and the refusal of the company to continue to bargain, in the circumstances of this case, was not unreasonable or in bad faith."

75 Indeed, McRuer was critical of Hersee's lawyer for including reference to a newspaper report of the picketing, which was inadmissible as hearsay. *Hersees* H.C., above note 6 at 617.

76 *Hersees* H.C., *ibid*. As in previous cases, the *Rights of Labour Act* was ignored.

77 *Ibid.*, Plainitff's Memorandum at para. 8.

78 *Ibid.* at para. 9. The implication of its criminality arose from the citation of the *Criminal Code* to support the claim made that the picketing was illegal.

79 *Ibid.* at paras. 13 and 15. *International Brotherhood of Teamsters v. Therien*, [1960] S.C.R. 265.

80 *Ibid.* at paras. 10–12.

81 *Ibid.* at para. 14.

82 *Ibid.*

83 I have not found biographical material on either. Krever recalls that MacKay was a small town lawyer in Owen Sound, while McGillivray was general counsel to the TTC prior to their appointments to the bench. A Quicklaw search found no labour injunctions cases in which either was involved. This is not surprising; the Ontario Court of Appeal heard very few such cases in the decade prior to *Hersees*.

84 Ontario, Journals of the Legislative Assembly, *Report and Proceedings of the Select Committee of the Legislative Assembly Appointed to Inquire into Collective Bargaining between Employers and Employees* vol. 77 (1943), Part Two, Appendix No. 2, 1214; Kaplan, this volume.

85 Herb Colling, *Ninety-Nine Days* (Toronto: NC Press, 1995) at 63 and 175; Kaplan, this volume.

86 *Fokhul v. Raymond et al.*, [1949] 4 D.L.R. 145 (injunction based on wrongful interference with contractual relations).

87 OLRB Reports (1963) at 413; Letter from A.M. Brunskill to Messrs. Kimber & Dubin (17 April 1963) in Court File, Affidavit of H. Lorne Morphy (18 April 1963); *Belleville Intelligencer* (18 December 1962).

88 Jamieson, above note 3 at 412–14.

89 "Threat Made Good," Editorial, *Globe and Mail* (12 February 1963); "Crime and Punishment," Editorial, *Globe and Mail* (14 February 1963). Twenty independent loggers who shot into the crowd of strikers were subsequently arrested and charged with murder. The charges were dismissed by the local grand jury. Three of the loggers were subsequently convicted of illegal possession of firearms and were fined $100 each. Two-hundred and twenty three strikers were charged with rioting and were convicted on the lesser offence of unlawful assembly and fined $200 each. Chief Justice McRuer presided over these trials. Jamieson, above note 3 at 412–14; Boyer, above note 70 at 259–61.

90 *Hersees* C.A., above note 6.

91 Harry W. Arthurs, "Comment," (1963) 41 Can. Bar Rev. 573 [Arthurs, "Comment"].

92 *Hersees* H.C., above note 6, Affidavit of Stanley Clair, para. 8. The phrase "garment order already placed" is underlined in the court file and in the margin is written "a contract."

93 *Hersees* C.A., above note 6 at 454. Arthurs, "Comment," above note 91 at 575–76, was also critical of Ayleworth's failure to notice that it was the party that had been induced to breach the contract that was the plaintiff, rather than the third party would had been injured by the inducement. The too was a complete departure from precedent.

94 *Ibid.* at 457–58; Arthurs, "Comment," above note 91 at 578–79.

95 Carrothers, "Secondary Picketing," above note 49 at 74.

96 *Hersees* C.A., above note 6 at 454–55.

97 *Ibid.* at 456.

98 *Daily Sentinel Review* [Woodstock] (2 March 1963) 4.

99 Arthurs, "Comment," above note 91 at 584–85.

100 Wilfred List, "Picketing and the Law: Judge vs. Professor" *Globe and Mail* (20 December 1963) 7. Arthurs was not pleased with List's account and wrote a letter to the editor pointing to two "embarrassing distortions": *Globe and Mail* (27 December 1963) 6. At least two other academic criticisms of *Hersees* were published in the 1960s. See Alfred W.R. Carrothers, "Labour Law: Doctrine, Dogma, Fiction and Myth" (1964) 14 U.N.B.L.J. 12; and Christie, *Liability of Strikers*, above note 38 at 184–87.

101 For a discussion of the 1964–66 period that focuses on wildcat strikes, see Bryan D. Palmer, *Canada's 1960s: The Ironies of Identity in a Rebellious Era* (Toronto: University of Toronto Press, 2009) at 211–41.

102 John H. Osler, *Report on Injunctions* (Toronto: Ontario Federation of Labour, 1965).

103 Ontario Federation of Labour, *Submission to the Ontario Government on Matter of Injunctions* (Toronto: Ontario Federation of Labour, 1965) at 5–6 [OFL, *Submission*]; Joan Sangster, "'We No Longer Respect the'Law': The Tilco Strike, Labour Injunctions, and the State" (Spring 2004) 53 Labour/Le Travail 47.

104 Horace Krever, "The Labour Injunction in Ontario: Procedure and Practice" in Carrothers, *Report*, above note 3 at 26.

105 For a discussion of Rand's work on the commission, see William Kaplan, *Canadian Maverick: The Life of Ivan C. Rand* (Toronto: Osgoode Society, 2009) at 391–421.

106 OFL, *Submission*, above note 103 at 14–27.

107 See, for example, Canadian Electrical Manufacturers Association, *Submission to the Royal Commission of Inquiry into Labour Disputes* (January 1967) at 13; Automotive Transport Association of Ontario, *Submission to the Royal Commission Inquiry into Labour Disputes* (March 1967) at 17.

108 *Report of the Royal Commission Inquiry into Labour Disputes* (Toronto: Queen's Printer, 1968) at 33 and 77.

109 Ontario Federation of Labour, *Submission to Honourable Dalton Bales, Q.C., Minister of Labour, Ontario in regards to the Report of the Royal Commission Inquiry into Labour Disputes* (January 1969) at 11–12.

110 Task Force on Labour Relations, *Canadian Industrial Relations* (Ottawa: Privy Council Office, 1968) at para. 628.

111 *Labour Relations Amendment Act, 1970 (No. 2)*, S.O. 1970, c. 85.

112 *Judicature Amendment Act, 1970 (No. 2)*, S.O. 1970, c. 91.

113 Ontario, *Debates of the Legislative Assembly* (1970).

114 *Darrigo's Grape Juice Ltd. v. Masterson* (1971), 21 D.L.R. (3d) 660. For a discussion of this case and on the post-*Hersees* caselaw generally, see Susan A. Tacon, *Tort Liability in a Collective Bargaining Regime* (Toronto: Butterworths, 1980).

115 David M. Beatty, "Secondary Boycotts: A Functional Analysis" (1974) 52 Can. Bar Rev. 388. Also see Paul Weiler, "The 'Slippery Slope' of Judicial Intervention" (1971) 9 Osgoode Hall L.J. 47 (describing *Hersees* as "the worst example of the deficiencies of abstract doctrinal analysis which is unrelated to the realities of labour relations policies"); J. Craig Patterson, "Union Secondary Conduct: A Comparative Study of the American and Ontario Positions" (1973) 8 U.B.C.L. Rev. 77.

116 For a discussion, see Alfred W.R. Carrothers, E.E. Palmer, & W.B. Rayner, *Collective Bargaining Law in Canada*, 2d ed. (Toronto: Butterworths, 1986) at 676–720.

117 S.M. 1970, c. 79, s. 2; *Channel Seven Television Ltd. v. National Association of Broadcast Employees & Technicians AFL-CIO-CLC* (1971), 21 D.L.R. (3d) 424 (Man. C.A.).

118 S.N.B. 1971, c. 9, s. 105. British Columbia and Newfoundland had limited secondary action prior to the *Hersees* decision.

119 Even the *Globe and Mail* welcomed the decision, characterizing the *Hersees* decision as an "overstatement." See "Where pickets may legally protest," *Globe and Mail* (26 January 2002).

120 *Health Services and Support — Facilities Subsector Bargaining Assn. v. British Columbia*, [2007] 2 S.C.R. 391 at paras. 81–86.

121 Gord Doctorow, "André Bekerman 1943–1999[:] Revolutionary Youth and Labour Cadre" Socialist Action (Fall 1999), online: www.socialisthistory.ca/Remember/Profiles/Bekerman.htm.

122 "Board to Rule on Union Issue" *Belleville Intelligencer* (6 July 1979); "City Clothing Firm Seeks Conciliation to Settle Dispute" *Belleville Intelligencer* (25 October 1979); "Firm, Union Reach Accord" *Belleville Intelligencer* (20 December 1979); Deacon interview, above note 9.

123 Interview of Gail Hersee (23 August 2007).

A Certain "Mallaise": *Harrison v. Carswell*, Shopping Centre Picketing, and the Limits of the Post-war Settlement

*Philip Girard and Jim Phillips**

Introduction

IN *HARRISON V. CARSWELL* six judges of the Supreme Court of Canada held, in a judgment written by future-Chief Justice Dickson, that a private property owner could eject any person for any or no reason.[1] They did so despite the fact that the property in question was a shopping mall and the owner had extended an invitation to all members of the public to enter, and despite the fact that the trespassers who were ejected were members of a union picketing on a mall-owned sidewalk in front of their struck employer's grocery store. For the majority judges, the case was simply one about private property rights, and those rights must always prevail at common law no matter what the context. Any diminution of them must come from the legislature. To the three dissenting judges, led by Laskin C.J.C., the case was more about labour rights, and its resolution required a balance between those rights and the claims of property. It would be hard to find a better example of the commonplace observation that in the common law, categorization of the issue is often decisive.

Categorization, of course, is not a neutral act, and in failing or refusing to see the case as one about the rights of labour, Dickson J. and his five colleagues reflected a long-standing judicial antipathy to labour organizations in general and to picketing in particular.[2] As A.W.R. Carrothers observed in his 1965 treatise on collective bargaining law, "an effective system of collective bargaining requires that [employees] be free to engage in three kinds of activity: to form themselves into associations, to engage employers in collective bargaining with the associations, and to invoke meaningful economic sanctions in support of the bargaining."[3] Yet while Canadian courts in the post-war period applied the legislation conferring these first two rights in a generally faithful manner, they were much less willing to go beyond its strict limits to extend labour rights in strike-related areas such as picketing so as to diminish the property rights of employers and third parties. In elevating the common law right of property to a kind of quasi-constitutional status by insisting that it could only be altered by specific legislative amendment, Dickson's judgment was faithful to mainstream understandings of the post-war settlement even as Laskin sought to reshape it in a direction more congenial to labour.

In what follows, we provide an account of *Harrison v. Carswell* which analyzes the various arguments and judgments around this theme of whether property or labour should be the controlling paradigm. Two judgments, those of Freedman C.J.M. at the Manitoba Court of Appeal, and Laskin's in the Supreme Court, saw the post-war collective bargaining legislation as a kind of bill of rights for labour, one that necessarily implied a new way of looking at property rights. The other judgments failed to do so, and the Supreme Court majority consequently bequeathed us an impoverished approach to disputes between property and other rights. As we discuss later, there has only been one other occasion since 1975 when a Canadian court has taken the broader view by seeing a reduction in the absolute nature of property rights as necessary to give vitality to the general rights of labour. That, significantly, was in the context of an organizing drive and not a strike, and thus involved a limited intrusion in which individuals were approached about joining the union and not the more substantial and visible activities associated with picketing. The most recent word on the relationship between picketing and private property has confirmed that *Harrison v. Carswell* is very much alive and well.

Polo Park

THE SITE ON WINNIPEG'S Portage Avenue West eventually occupied by the Polo Park Shopping Centre epitomized the values and practices of the pre-war world. In the early-twentieth century, John David Eaton rented part of it to provide an athletic ground for the use of the T. Eaton Company staff. In 1925, R. James Speers constructed the racetrack that gave the area its name, although it was for the steeplechase, not polo. Speers created an atmosphere of serene civility: a large grove of trees shaded part of the property, a white fence was erected around the perimeter with broad gates facing Portage Avenue, and swans floated on a pond in the centre of the racetrack oval. Parimutuel betting was allowed but racing occurred only twenty-eight days per year: two weeks in the spring and two in the fall. In between, the site was used for other events such as the Highland Games on 1 July, while a golf course constructed on adjoining lands in 1931 attracted many during the spring and summer. In the winter the golf course maintained a well-iced slide open to the public, and provided toboggans at a nominal charge. The streetcar stopped right outside the grounds of Polo Park, ensuring the site's accessibility to all. Activities available only to the relatively wealthy, such as racing, were balanced with those such as tobogganing — open at virtually no cost, even to the labouring poor — and with mass entertainment events.[4]

Rising land values in the post-war period sealed the fate of the racetrack and the golf course, both of which closed in 1956, just as the automobile sealed the fate of Winnipeg's streetcar. Polo Park Centre Ltd., controlled by the Bronfman family through the Fairview Corporation, selected the property to be the site of Manitoba's first modern shopping centre.[5] The well-known gates were demolished and, in spite of local protests, so were the many trees that graced the site. On 20 August 1959, Mayor Stephen Juba cut the ribbon and declared the 400,000-square foot centre officially open for business.[6] A year later, the *Winnipeg Tribune* declared the project had done "exceptionally well" in "selling Greater Winnipeg shoppers on the principle of the 'family' approach to buying."[7] Initially built as an open shopping centre, Polo Park enclosed its centre mall in 1963, and Eaton's joined the original anchor tenant Simpson-Sears in 1968.[8] Until the late 1970s, when several more shopping malls opened to provide serious competition, Polo Park reigned supreme in Winnipeg.

The growth of shopping centres posed many challenges for labour, from the difficulty of organizing the largely part-time and short-term staff at mall stores, to the picketing problem exposed in *Harrison v. Carswell*. Social justice groups, too, found their ability to communicate with the public increasingly constrained by the transformation of publicly accessible downtown spaces to privatized mall spaces. As one US judge observed, mall owners had "taken [the] old downtown away from its former home and moved all of it, except free speech, to the suburbs."[9] Even as the shopping centre "sought . . . to legitimize itself as a true community center[,] [it tried] to define that community in exclusionary socioeconomic and racial terms" and tried to eliminate any activity that might "distract" shoppers from their mission of consumption.[10] Labour picketing, with its reminder that real people worked in mall stores under sometimes less than ideal conditions, was high on the list of such "distractions." Whether mall owners would succeed in their quest to ban such activities ultimately depended on the legal characterization of those mall spaces open to the public, and invested *Harrison v. Carswell* with a significance far beyond the $40 fine levied against Sophie Carswell at first instance for her acts of "trespass."

The Strike

THE YEAR 1973 WAS a transitional one between the optimism and economic growth of the 1960s, and the pessimism and stagflation of the 1970s. Wages had risen by 6.7 percent over 1972, but they were subject to erosion by rapidly rising prices.[11] The women who made up most of the supermarket clerk staff at Winnipeg's grocery stores were undoubtedly uneasy about their wages' shrinking purchasing power as they rang in those prices at their cash registers every day. But when Dominion Stores employees went on strike on 11 May 1973, pensions, not wages, were the main issue. The Retail Store Employees Union (Local 832) which represented employees at all the grocery chains was trying to get all the stores to agree to jointly-run, company-paid pension plans. Some agreed, but Dominion held out, arguing that its own plan was superior.[12]

The strike was not popular with Dominion Store employees. A week after it began, the company gleefully reported that three of its nine stores were fully staffed by union members, while about 70 percent of staff were reporting for work at other stores.[13] This may explain why the president of the local, Bernard Christophe, was anxious to broadcast the union's message as widely as possible, and to test the limits of the law regarding picketing at Polo Park. Elsewhere, workers could picket on public sidewalks adjacent to the store. At Polo Park, however, the Dominion Store was far from the sidewalks bordering Portage Avenue and St. James Street, moated by large parking lots owned by the Fairview Corporation. Thus, when Sophie Carswell took a small step on the sidewalk outside the Polo Park Dominion Store, she took a large step into legal immortality.

Sophie Carswell was a checkout clerk at the Polo Park Dominion Store and Friday 18 May was the first day of her picket duty. She and eleven co-workers gathered in the early afternoon on the city sidewalk bordering the parking lot at one of the entrances to the shopping centre property. They did not attempt to stop any cars, but if a car stopped, they gave the driver a pamphlet about the strike. After a few hours of this, Carswell went home from four to six o'clock to make dinner for her family. When she returned, Bernard Christophe was there, and he urged the picketers to move their picket to the sidewalk immediately outside the Dominion Store premises. According to Christophe, Alvin McGregor (the union's solicitor), had advised that the law was unclear as to whether such picketing was allowed; Chrisophe added that the police "would not arrest us, that their concern was that the pickets be peaceful, that the police would not take sides . . . but were there to keep the peace."[14] Carswell and her co-workers duly moved their picket as requested.

Within minutes, the manager of Polo Park, Peter Harrison, arrived with the police. Both spoke with Carswell, and the manager told her that picketing was illegal on private property and that she could be charged if she did not leave. Harrison did not demand that she leave immediately, however, and the group remained at their new picket station until about nine thirty that evening. On three subsequent dates — 24 May, 26 May, and 7 June — Carswell's presence on the same sidewalk generated the same ritual. After the first picket, Peter Harrison swore an information in Magistrate's Court on 22 May, followed by others on the subsequent dates, alleging that Carswell had breached the *Petty Trespasses Act*. These were genuine private prosecutions, carried forward with Harrison's name in the style of cause as informant, though Fairview Corporation was the real instigator. Carswell appeared in court on 1 June and pleaded not guilty, and the case was remanded to 22 June.

We have little direct information as to why Sophie Carswell was willing to step forward, except that she was a faithful union member and felt strongly that she was in the right.[15] She was around forty years old, with two of her three sons still living at home. Born Sophie Drabik in Winnipeg Beach, she came from a family of Ukrainian descent. Her husband had a union job, and the household could afford to forego Sophie's usual income during the seven-week strike. Probably even more important than this relative security, however, was her state of mind. Family members remember her as "feisty — she liked a good fight."[16] Carswell was not intimidated by the prospect of being charged with trespass, or possibly being escorted off the premises by the police or private security. Counsel for the union would defend her without charge, but her actions still required courage.

The strike ended just two days after the hearing, on Sunday 24 June, and the next day Carswell and her co-workers returned to work. The union lost the pension plan battle, but won a virtually costless drug plan that none of the other grocery chains offered, and slightly higher wage increases compared to the other stores. Clerks such as Carswell would get $3.60 per hour, rising to $4.01 in January 1975.[17] Two days later, Carswell received more good news: Judge Michael Baryluk dismissed all charges against the alleged trespassers. The day after that, Ed Schreyer's New Democratic Party (NDP) government was returned to power with an enhanced majority.[18] Carswell's victory proved to be short-lived, however; it was only the first skirmish in a court battle that would conclude in the Supreme Court of Canada.

Legislative Background

THE LEGISLATIVE CONTEXT WAS shaped by major controversies in Manitoba in the 1960s over the use of the labour injunction.[19] After the NDP came to power in 1969, the government attempted to limit its use and clarify what kinds of striker conduct would be protected. In the summer of 1970 it amended the *Queen's Bench Act*[20] so as to forbid the granting of any injunction "that requires a person to work for or perform personal services for his employer" (in section 60.1(1)), while section 60.1(2) prohibited the grant of an injunction that "restrains a person in the exercise of his right to freedom of speech." Section 60.2(2) as amended tried to define the parameters of that right:

> 60.2(2) For the purposes of this section the communication by a person on a public thoroughfare of information by true statements, either orally or through printed material or through any other means, shall be deemed to be the exercise of the right of that person to freedom of speech.

No definition of "public thoroughfare" was provided in the legislation, suggesting the possibility of an expansive interpretation. However, section 60.2(3) seemed to undercut the right just recognized by stating that the section was not to affect the enforcement in criminal, quasi-criminal, or civil proceedings of any law passed by any level of government relating to the use of public thoroughfares or conduct in public places.[21]

Read literally, the section suggested that the *Petty Trespasses Act* could still be enforced even if the phrase "public thoroughfare" was given an expansive interpretation so as to include quasi-public areas of shopping centres. At the very least, however, the amendment suggested that enhanced protection for freedom of speech was now a matter of public policy in Manitoba.

During a lengthy debate on the amendment, triggered by a hostile editorial in the *Winnipeg Free Press*, an opposition member raised exactly the issue that would come up in *Harrison v. Carswell*: "Just what do we mean by a 'public thoroughfare'?" asked Jake Froese. "Does this mean, for instance, that [at] the shopping centre in Polo Park that people can picket before any of the stores?"[22] Attorney General Alvin Mackling answered "that public thoroughfare will be given its common sense meaning and surely it's a place to which the public has access by right, it's something that's owned jointly by the people and it's somewhere where you can come and go . . . . It's only where there's some ambiguity that there would be any difficulty. But — (Interjection) — Not private property, no. It doesn't say anything about that . . ."[23] Mackling did not answer the question about Polo Park directly but the tenor of his answer suggested that "public thoroughfare" was meant to include traditionally public areas such as streets and parks, but not necessarily privately held land opened to the public by general invitation.

Some provisions of the *Labour Relations Act*[24] were also relevant. A new version of the Act providing enhanced protection for labour had just been passed and had come into force on 1 January 1973. Section 23(1) stated that "Nothing in this Act deprives any person of his freedom to express his views if he does not use intimidation, coercion, threats, or undue influence," but section 24 specifically addressed the issue of trespass: "Nothing in this Act curtails, abridges, or affects, the right of an employer who is in lawful possession of land or premises to recover damages from, or to any other remedy against, a trespasser."[25] Clearly no right to picket on the employer's own premises was being recognized. In *Harrison v. Carswell*, it was not the employer, but the shopping centre which was the plaintiff, however, with the result that the relevance, if any, of section 24 depended on interpretation.

The absence of specific provisions dealing with labour picketing in Manitoba was not accidental. Sidney Green, a labour lawyer who was a member of cabinet during both Schreyer administrations, held strongly to the view that "unions receive equal treatment rather than special treatment."[26] He supported the right of strikers to picket peacefully but was adamant that such a right did not belong exclusively to labour and was merely an example of a more general public right to convey information peacefully through picketing. Green was thus instrumental in placing the anti-injunction provisions in the *Court of Queen's Bench Act* rather than the *Labour Relations Act.*[27] Manitoba was by no means alone, however, in providing little express legislative support for picketing in its labour relations legislation. As of 1973, only British Columbia had done so, as will be discussed below. The seeming void about picketing in the *Labour Relations Act*, and its preservation of the employer's trespass remedy, would come to play a crucial role when *Harrison v. Carswell* reached the Supreme Court of Canada.

The Existing Law

WHEN ALVIN MCGREGOR ADVISED Bernard Christophe that the status of picketing on shopping centre sidewalks was unclear, he was correct. In fact there were two conflicting provincial Court of Appeal decisions arguably on point, from Saskatchewan and Ontario, and another from British Columbia that was relevant, if not exactly on point. The latter, *Zeller's (Western) Ltd. v. Retail Food & Drug Store Clerks Union, Local 1518,* held that peaceful picketing of Zeller's on a sidewalk outside the Zeller's store over which Zeller's had an easement could not be actionable at the suit of the employer (Zeller's) unless the conduct amounted to a nuisance at common law.[28] *Zeller's* was thus distinguishable from *Harrison*, most importantly on the ground that the plaintiff was the tenant-employer, not the shopping centre owner, and thus the issue of possession of the sidewalk did not arise. The case did, however, support the proposition that picketing on shopping centre premises was legal under some circumstances.

By the time the issue came up again, this time in Saskatchewan, counsel for shopping centres and tenant retailers had learned their lesson. In *Grosvenor Park Shopping Centre Ltd. v. Waloshin*, the landlord sought an injunction against strikers who were picketing their employer, Loblaw's, in the parking area of the shopping centre and on sidewalks adjacent to the store premises. This time the mall owner's case was pleaded in trespass, and it succeeded at trial before Bence C.J.Q.B.[29] Chief Justice Bence held that all property was either private or public for the purposes of the law of trespass, and no category of "quasi-public" property was known to the law. The Court of Appeal reversed, with Chief Justice Culliton writing for a unanimous bench of five. He found that the mall owner did not have actual possession of the premises in question because it had "extended an unrestricted invitation to the public to enter upon the premises." In the Court's view, "the respondent exercises control over the premises but does not exercise that control to the exclusion of other persons." If the picketers were unduly interfering with the passage of shoppers, they could be restrained via an action properly framed in nuisance. As the labour dispute had ended, however, there was no point in amending the pleadings, and the injunction was set aside.[30]

Grosvenor Park appeared to be a very strong precedent in favour of the union interest, but in focusing only on the issue of trespass and possession, it in effect took the case out of the realm of labour law entirely. By using property law as the exclusive analytical lens, it left labour with little to rely on if another court should take a different view of the ever-flexible concept of possession. That is exactly what happened in *R. v. Peters*, a decision of the Ontario Court of Appeal upheld in the Supreme Court of Canada.[31] Mr. Peters, the president of the Brampton Labour Council, was charged under the *Petty Trespass Act* for circulating peacefully with seven other people on the sidewalk in front of the Safeway Store in Shoppers World Plaza, Brampton, with placards containing the words "Local 1285 U.A.W. requests that you don't shop at Safeway because they sell California Grapes." When Mr. Peters was asked to leave by an agent of the owner of the premises, he politely declined. His counsel naturally relied heavily on *Grosvenor Park*, but the Court of Appeal declined to follow it. Chief Justice Gale observed that the owner of premises does not lose possession by inviting the public thereon, provided it retains the right to control the entry of the public or portions of it. Nothing was made of the fact that *Grosvenor Park* involved a labour dispute, while *Peters* did not — or at least, not a labour dispute with Safeway.[32]

What *Zeller's*, *Grosvenor Park*, and *Peters* all had in common was their method: all approached the issue in terms of pure property law doctrine, without identifying explicitly the competing interests involved. They all assumed that correctly identifying the type and degree of possession of the mall owner over particular pieces of sidewalk or parking lot would resolve the dispute. The interests of the picketers were thereby rendered irrelevant; it mattered not whether they were on strike, urging a boycott of a particular product, or declaring that judgment day was nigh. Even in their analysis of possession and property rights, the courts did not really come to grips with the new type of social space represented by the shopping centre. They scrutinized lease terms and spoke of easements and licences rather than attempting to understand the functions of shopping centre spaces.[33]

The Canadian decisions presented a rather stark contrast with the emergent US jurisprudence on this topic. In a 1968 decision called *Logan Valley Plaza*,[34] a majority of the US Supreme Court analogized the common areas of shopping centres to the commercial precincts of company towns, which had been held to be spaces amenable to the exercise of constitutional rights in *Marsh v. Alabama* (1946).[35] Justice Thurgood Marshall was also sensitive to the need to establish a level playing field between "downtown" businesses and those located in shopping centres: "Business enterprises located in downtown areas would be subject to on-the-spot criticism for their practices, but businesses situated in the suburbs could largely immunize themselves from similar criticism by creating a *cordon sanitaire* of parking lots around their stores."[36] In an earlier decision, *Schwartz-Torrance Investment Corp. v. Bakery and Confectionery Workers' Union, Local No. 31*, the California Supreme Court had given the conflicting interests of the parties a poetic twist: "The interest of the union thus rests upon the solid substance of public policy and constitutional right; the interest of the plaintiff lies in the shadow cast by a property right worn thin by public usage."[37] It was a sign of important shifts in Canadian legal thought that these US authorities and their more openly policy-oriented analysis would play an important role as *Harrison v. Carswell* ascended the judicial hierarchy, even though arguments based on them would not ultimately succeed.

The Litigation

COUNSEL FOR THE PROSECUTION was Derek A. Booth. Called to the bar in 1966, he was an associate at Winnipeg's premier law firm — and Brian Dickson's old firm — Aikins, Macaulay & Thorvaldson. Counsel for the defence was Alvin R. McGregor of Gallagher, Chapman, Greenberg, McGregor & Sheps. McGregor had just been called to the bar in 1968, but his mentor Roy Gallagher was a very well-known senior lawyer. The firm did a lot of labour law, representing the Retail Store Employees Union, the Teamsters, and other unions, but they also worked for management on occasion, and did both civil and criminal litigation. Booth and McGregor would stick with the case all the way to the Supreme Court of Canada.[38]

Although Peter Harrison, as the informant, was the named plaintiff, Booth took his instructions from Fairview Corporation. Likewise, McGregor took his instructions from the union president, Bernard Christophe. Christophe had an unusual background for a prairie labour leader. Born and raised in Paris, he lived briefly in England before coming to Canada in 1956. President of the Retail Store Employees Union by 1964, he saw it grow from 700 to 16,000 members by the time he retired in 2002.[39] Christophe's instructions to McGregor were clear: win the case, and take it as far as you need to do so. The union was affiliated with the Retail Store Employees International Union, whose legal staff provided considerable assistance to McGregor as he prepared his case.

The man before whom Booth and McGregor first crossed swords was one of the earliest ethnic appointments to the bench in Canada. Michael Baryluk was born in Brandon to a pioneering Ukrainian couple. The war brought him first to Thunder Bay, where he served as shop steward for the local union in an aircraft factory, then to England with the Royal Canadian Air Force. Upon his return home he took up the law and practiced mostly in small firms with fellow lawyers of Ukrainian descent. In 1968 he was appointed by the Progressive Conservative government of Walter Weir to the Provincial Court (Criminal Division), where his duties included presiding at the Winnipeg Magistrate's Court from time to time.[40]

The trial proceeded in a straightforward fashion.[41] An agreed statement of facts was produced and both sides called further evidence. Booth called Peter Harrison and George Fleming, a security guard who had had some dealings with Carswell on dates after the initial 18 May picket. McGregor called Sophie Carswell and Bernard Christophe. The argument boiled down to two main points: whether Fairview had the degree of possession required to support a conviction under the *Petty Trespasses Act*; and whether Sophie Carswell could raise the defence mentioned in section 2 of the Act, which excused anyone who "acted under a fair and reasonable supposition that he had a right to do the act of which complaint is made." The first issue would remain a live one all the way to the Supreme Court of Canada, while the second disappeared as a distinct issue at the Manitoba Court of Appeal.

Judge Baryluk found for Carswell on both issues, although his brief reasons were opaquely expressed and not terribly persuasive. Fairview appealed from the acquittal to the county court, where the procedure required a trial *de novo*. Clarence Irving Keith, the presiding judge, came from a much more traditional background than Judge Baryluk. He practiced primarily as a corporate solicitor with the law firm of his father, Clarence Garfield Keith, until named senior county court judge (analogous to chief judge) of the Eastern Judicial District in 1964. Keith *père* had been promoted to the county court bench in 1949, and the third member of the firm, Ralph Maybank, joined the Manitoba Court of Queen's Bench in 1951 after long service as a Liberal MP. Irving Keith had a variety of interests outside the law: a faithful Liberal Party worker who had served on the national executive of the party, he also founded the Winnipeg Light Opera Company and was an amateur Egyptologist and Biblical scholar.[42]

While McGregor continued to argue alone, Derek Booth was joined by a senior partner in the firm, William Steward Arnold Martin, Q.C. (hereinafter referred to as Stu). Stu Martin was a well-known labour lawyer who moved easily amongst the legal and business elites of Winnipeg, and rounded out his career with the vigorous pursuit of literary, historical, and philanthropic interests.[43] The Aikins firm was clearly taking no chances in its efforts to nip its client's problem in the bud.

At the appeal on 16 November 1973 the trial transcript was taken as evidence and the witnesses were not recalled.[44] When Alvin McGregor started to make an argument about the relevance of the *Labour Relations Act*, Judge Keith showed little interest: "I regret that under the circumstances, I don't feel that it is a field that I would care to enter into in this particular instance. Maybe I am wrong. Maybe the Court of Appeal will disagree with me."[45] At the end of the argument, the judge said he would be ready to give judgment after a five-minute recess. McGregor was not terribly surprised when he heard of his client's conviction, as Judge Keith was reputed not to be enamoured of unions.[46] His reasons are not available, but it is clear that he judged Fairview to have sufficient possession to support a trespass charge, and found no facts sufficient to support a section 2 defence on the part of Sophie Carswell. The sole notation on the file is "Appeal allowed. Fine $10 each on 4 charges, total $40, no costs." Stu Martin had made a show of not asking for costs, observing magnanimously that "we have no fight against the Union or the complainant. It's just for right of protecting private ground."[47]

Alvin McGregor applied to the Manitoba Court of Appeal for leave to appeal, which was granted by Guy J.A. Given the *Peters* decision, upon which Booth relied heavily in his factum, McGregor had the more challenging task in constructing his arguments.[48] He of course tried to distinguish *Peters* as a case involving a member of the public at large rather than a striking worker. But he also tried to flesh out the argument in *Grosvenor Park* (regarding the landlord's lack of possession, relied on the 1970 amendment to the *Queen's Bench Act* that recognized a right to communicate true statements on a "public thoroughfare," and adopted the balancing approach found in the US caselaw, as advocated by Harry Arthurs in his 1965 comment on the *Zeller's* and *Grosvenor Park* cases.[49]

McGregor tried to show that the landlord's possession had indeed been "worn thin by public usage." He noted the presence of various public services at Polo Park to which members of the public had a right of access, including Manitoba Liquor Commission and Canada Post outlets, and also observed that the *Highway Traffic Act* treated parking lots as if they were public highways for various purposes. These examples were used to buttress McGregor's conclusion that the doctrine that there were only two types of property, public and private, was "badly out of date." Some property should be recognized as "quasi-public," and such sites were outside the purview of the *Petty Trespasses Act*. McGregor further argued that Sophie Carswell's actions could not be said to have been "unlawful" as required by that Act because she was exercising her right to freedom of speech as guaranteed by the *Court of Queen's Bench Act*. He did not provide any explicit discussion of why the sidewalk outside the Dominion Store should be considered a "public thoroughfare," although implicitly his arguments about why the landlord should not be considered in possession of the public areas of the premises would have served here.

Neither of these two arguments had much to do with labour law or the position of striking workers as such. However, McGregor's third argument did: in asserting that the court had the power to balance the property rights of the landlord against the union's interest in peaceful picketing, he provided the court with a way around the *Peters* case. In that case the Supreme Court had dealt with the picketing rights of an "officious bystander" in a distant dispute, not those of an employee of a tenant of the shopping centre. The former might well be accorded less weight than the latter because the informational message was not as closely tied to the picketing site as the message sought to be conveyed by striking workers. Significantly, however, McGregor did not tie this argument to any specific provisions of the *Labour Relations Act*. This suggests that contemporary understanding of the Act did not see it as providing any effective protection for picketing.

Booth, for his part, aimed to maintain the bright line between private and public property that McGregor tried to blur, and also sought to downplay the labour aspects of the dispute. According to Booth, the Saskatchewan Court of Appeal in *Grosvenor Park* had not overturned Bence C.J.Q.B.'s proposition that all property was either private or public; it had merely found that whatever the quality of the space, the shopping centre did not have sufficient possession of it. And, "the Informant was not trying to stop the Accused from communicating information or picketing but was merely stopping the Accused from an activity on its private property . . . . [I]t would not have mattered what activity the Accused was engaged in, the mere fact remains that the Informant did not want the activity to continue." The factum also raised section 24 of the Manitoba *Labour Relations Act*, which, as noted above, preserved the right of an employer to sue for trespass. The employer was not in possession in this case, but the section did suggest an absence of legislative intent to alter the law of trespass merely because of the presence of a labour dispute.

The appeal was heard on 11 February 1974 and the decision came down on 19 March. Chief Justice Samuel Freedman wrote the majority judgment allowing the appeal, in which Matas J.A. concurred, while Guy J.A. dissented. The majority judgment went off on a completely different tack compared to previous discussions of shopping centre picketing in Canada. Instead of the landlord's possession, the nature of the union's interest in the issue was highlighted. *Peters* involved an "entirely gratuitous, even if well motivated" intervention by the picketer, leaving the issue open for decision where a picketer on a legal strike was concerned. Freedman C.J.M. constructed the issue as a pure conflict of common law rights, and invoked functionalism and US authority to resolve it. There is an almost Platonic quality to the reasoning: the *Petty Trespasses Act* is mentioned only incidentally, while neither the *Labour Relations Act* nor the *Court of Queen's Bench Act* is mentioned at all. Under the majority's analysis, the common law property right of the shopping centre owner collided with the common law right of a worker on a legal strike to picket peacefully, and "public policy and good sense" required the former to give way to the latter. Freedman C.J.M.'s discussion of the landlord's property right was more a matter of sociological observation than legal analysis: "In weighing the property right one cannot consider naked title alone, divorced from the reality of its setting in a shopping centre. The continuing invitation which the landlord-owner has extended to the public to come there for proper purposes has already resulted in inroads upon that property right and qualified its exercise to some degree."[50] Justice Tobriner's statement about "a property right worn thin by public usage" was quoted and accepted at face value.

Chief Justice Freedman was much more expansive when discussing the right of striking employees to picket peacefully. To deny such an employee access to the sidewalk in question, he observed, was "to prevent the exercise of picketing at the one point where it can really be effective."[51] Perimeter picketing was possible but much less effective: many more picketers would be required, and the identity of the targeted store would be much more difficult to establish to passersby, possibly leading to an unfair advantage to the struck store and unfairness to other stores. With Laskinian verve, Freedman concluded: "Peaceful picketing deserves better than this."[52] He then segued into a discussion of the *Schwartz-Torrance* and *Logan Valley* cases, adopting their reasoning as applicable in Canada with only the substitution of the phrase "common law right" where "constitutional right" appeared in the originals. Chief Justice Freedman also found attractive Thurgood Marshall's observation about the need to create a level playing field between downtown businesses and those in the suburbs, and concluded with a bare reference to "the helpful article by Professor (now Dean) H.W. Arthurs on 'Labour Law — Picketing on Shopping Centres.'"[53] Justice of Appeal Guy, for his part, was not convinced by the majority's attempt to distinguish *Peters*, and held himself bound to follow it; in any case, he preferred the balance traditionally struck between labour picketing and private property in Canadian law to that arrived at in the US.

A panel of Justices Martland, Ritchie, and Dickson heard Fairview Corporation's motion for leave to appeal on 17 June and granted leave; the case was argued before the full court on 3 and 4 February 1975. Stu Martin and Derek Booth again appeared for the informant, while Alvin McGregor was joined by a junior, F.E. Bortoluzzi. Ken Lysyk appeared for the intervenant, the Attorney General of Saskatchewan, to defend the constitutional validity of the *Petty Trespasses Act.*[54] In his factum, Booth vigorously denied that any property rights of mall owners had been "worn thin by public usage"; he charged the Court of Appeal with misidentifying the issue, which in his view was trespass, not picketing; and he argued that there was no common law right to picket on private property, although he admitted there was a statutory right to picket on "public thoroughfares" as guaranteed by the *Court of Queen's Bench Act.*[55]

Booth also hammered away at the weakest part of the Court of Appeal's reasons — the failure to address the *Petty Trespasses Act*. Even if there were a common law right to picket under some circumstances, how could it trump the statutory trespass claim seemingly available to Fairview? As Booth summed up,

> There is a danger in allowing the concern for the inconvenience to Union members to override and extinguish property owners' rights with respect to trespass reserved in the existing laws. If public policy dictates that the cause of peaceful picketing required furtherance, the proper way to do this would seem to be to change the law to assist the ends of peaceful picketing and not to disregard the existing law contained in the *Petty Trespasses Act.*[56]

As it turned out, the characterization of the union's interest as involving mere "inconvenience," coupled with the appeal to curial deference, was a master stroke, one that carried a strong majority of the Supreme Court.

The Supreme Court split 6:3 in allowing the appeal. Chief Justice Laskin, predictably, dissented, joined by Wishart Spence and Jean Beetz. Chief Justice Laskin began by saying he would have been content to adopt the reasons of Freedman C.J.M. "if I did not feel compelled . . . to add some observations bearing on the decision of this Court in *Peters v. The Queen*."[57] In fact, Laskin's reasons were quite different from Freedman's, which represented a kind of poisoned chalice. Laskin agreed wholeheartedly with Freedman's result, but would have immediately seen the weakness in framing the issue as one involving a pure conflict of common law rights. In such a contest, property would always win. The issues, as Laskin saw them, related first to the role of *stare decisis* at the Supreme Court, and second, "whether this Court has a balancing role to play, without yielding place to the Legislature, where an ancient doctrine, in this case trespass, is invoked in a new setting to suppress a lawful activity *supported both by legislation and by a well-understood legislative policy*."[58]

Laskin knew that there would have to be some legislative basis for the union's asserted right if it were to have a fighting chance of success, but was confronted with the somewhat contradictory provisions of the Manitoba *Labour Relations Act*, as well as the whole post-war jurisprudence which was highly reluctant to read such statutes as protecting picketing. The most he could say was that Carswell had "an interest, sanctioned by the law, in pursuing legitimate claims against her employer through the peaceful picketing in furtherance of a lawful strike" but he did not specify the source of that right or elaborate on its extent.[59] If Laskin really wished to argue that the *Labour Relations Act* should be read as supporting Carrothers's third desideratum for an effective collective bargaining law — the ability "to invoke meaningful economic sanctions in support of the bargaining"[60] — he should have offered an extended analysis of how this could be done. This was a tall order in view of the existing jurisprudence, and Laskin may have felt that *Harrison* was not the ideal setting in which to make it. In any case, he went off on a rather different tack, relying more on private law than public law in support of his position.

After distinguishing the Supreme Court's decision in *Peters*, which he interpreted narrowly as answering only the question of whether a shopping centre owner could ever have sufficient possession of a sidewalk to support a charge under the *Petty Trespass Act*, Laskin went on to consider trespass in some detail.[61] The present case involved "a search for an appropriate legal framework for new social facts which show up the inaptness of an old doctrine developed upon a completely different social foundation" — a familiar refrain from Laskin's functionalist repertoire.[62] He invoked the US cases only in passing for the proposition that "in light of the interests involved there can be no solution to their reconciliation by positing a flat all or nothing approach."[63] Laskin proposed two alternate solutions. The first was to "read down" the tort of trespass, whether common law or statutory, in cases involving quasi-public areas such as those in shopping malls. In cases involving such areas, the court would balance the mall owner's reason for exclusion against the interloper's justification for entry. If the latter was found more compelling, the plaintiff would in effect be non-suited, or at least this is a reasonable inference from Laskin's train of thought. The second proposed solution was "to recognize a continuing privilege in using the areas of the shopping centre provided for public passage subject to limitations arising out of the nature of the activity thereon and to the object pursued thereby."[64] This approach departed from earlier precedents such as *Grosvenor Park* which had focused on the nature of the landlord's possession. In fact it cleverly finessed the issue: Laskin could concede that the landlord might have possession of the premises in question (and thus be entitled to bring a trespass action) but allow the "picketer's privilege" to trump it.

One of the curiosities of Laskin's dissent is that he did not adopt the rather bolder approach to this question that he had advanced as a scholar and arbitrator. As early as 1937 he had lamented that the courts seemed disposed to rule "that any picketing which is likely to be effective must be prohibited."[65] And although he did not directly address the issue of picketing on private property in that scholarship, he did propose a way of dealing with such conflicts: sounding like Chief Justice Freedman, he had urged that judges "take cognizance of the trend in social forces and treat . . . statute[s] as a means to the realization of a social end."[66] Later, as a labour arbitrator, Laskin employed this approach in deciding a grievance against Canadian General Electric in 1951. The company had disciplined an employee who had distributed union material to employees who spent their dinner hour on company premises. Laskin dismissed the grievance because he found the grievor had disturbed working employees, but in an elaborate obiter he asserted that if she had not disturbed them, the employer should not be able to object to the activity even though it happened on company premises. In a related case he noted that "statutory provisions for collective bargaining in force in Ontario require property owners who are employers to accommodate their rights of property to the statutory policy . . . [T]his means only that abstract rights of property ought not to be put forward as barriers to communication between the Union and its members."[67] It is true that this argument was put forth in the context of the "core" right of the union to organize, but its logic can be extended plausibly to the picketing situation.

Perhaps the curiosity is resolved by recalling that Laskin was a long-time teacher and scholar of property law as well as labour and constitutional law. His rhetorical abuse of "abstract property rights" was by no means a rejection of property rights in general; "functional" property rights were still welcome in Laskin's universe. Thus any balancing of interests that might disadvantage the property owner in an individual case should still be done in a way that did not threaten property in general. Laskin thought he had found the necessary reconciliation in his concept of "privilege," which he drew from Prosser's *Handbook of the Law of Torts*. Sophie Carswell, by engaging in an activity within a penumbra of statutory protection, should be able to assert her "privilege" to do so as a defence to the trespass claim. At one level, this may be interpreted as a conservative turn in Laskin's thought on this question, but at another level it may be viewed as a refinement of his earlier thought rather than a rejection of it. It also had the advantage of appearing more "legal," and less overtly policy-oriented, in a court where "policy" was still not an altogether respectable word.

Nonetheless, in conceding the limits of his proposed resolution, Laskin virtually gave away the store to the majority. He agreed that

> it does not follow that because unrestricted access is given to members of the public to certain areas of the shopping centre during business hours, those areas are available at all times during those hours and in all circumstances to any kind of peaceful activity by members of the public, regardless of the interest being promoted by that activity and regardless of the numbers of members of the public who are involved. The Court will draw lines here as it does in other branches of the law as may be appropriate in the light of the legal principle and particular facts.[68]

In failing to provide any criteria by which such "lines" could be drawn, Laskin more or less invited the kind of curial deference argument that would characterize Dickson's majority judgment.[69]

As his biographers reveal, Brian Dickson initially wanted to allow the appeal purely on the basis that the *Peters* case ruled: he thought it "difficult to make a meaningful distinction between a picketer who tells people not to go to Safeway because of a labour dispute in California and a picketer who tells people not to go to Dominion Stores because she and her fellow employees are on strike."[70] In his decision, Dickson described *Peters* and *Harrison* as coming before the court "on much the same facts, picketing within a shopping centre in connection with a labour dispute."[71] In his initial memo, Dickson had stated that it did "not seem to [him] that there is any need for [him] to get into the policy aspect."[72] Laskin's draft, which decried curial tendencies to "be simply mechanistic about previous decisions,"[73] and urged his colleagues to depart from previous decisions where necessary, provided a "strong intellectual challenge" to which Dickson felt compelled to respond.[74]

His response invoked the doctrine of curial deference, relying on jurists such as Benjamin Cardozo and Oliver Wendell Holmes — ironically, Laskin's heroes — for support. Dickson noted that section 24 of the Manitoba *Labour Relations Act* specifically preserved remedies against trespassers, while BC's 1973 *Labour Code* created a legislative privilege insulating picketers from trespass suits regarding real property to which a member of the public ordinarily had access. The *Schwartz-Torrance* case also indirectly supported this approach because the legislature had "specifically subordinated the rights of the property owner to those of persons engaged in lawful labour activities."[75] Balancing "the respective values to society of the right to property and the right to picket" raised important issues "the resolution of which must, by their very nature, be arbitrary and embody personal economic and social beliefs."[76]

On the surface, Dickson's judgment looked, and still looks, powerful. In fact, Dickson's framing of the case as simply a matter of property law, one that therefore pitted an "owner" against a "trespasser," prevented him from addressing the impact of this perspective on the underlying conflict, that of employer against employee. As a result, he failed to consider to what extent the actions of a third party — even assuming that in this case Fairview Corporation was acting solely in its own interest — should be allowed to interfere with a union's exercise of its *statutory* right to exert economic pressure against an employer. To what extent can a third party rely on other statutory rights, such as those contained in the *Petty Trespasses Act*, to curtail the rights recognized under the *Labour Relations Act*? Dickson was correct to note the absence of an unambiguous statutory provision in Manitoba permitting strikers to picket with impunity on private property. But that was to frame the issue too narrowly. Picketing is only a means to an end, the end being the application of economic pressure against the employer. Union members had a statutory right to exert economic pressure against their employers, and one way of doing so was through picketing. There was arguably a balancing to be done here, but of statutory rights, not, as Chief Justice Freedman had said, of common law rights. Framed this way, the deference argument disappears, and Laskin's abuse of rights argument, derived from Quebec civil law but with some analogue in the common law, becomes more powerful.[77] Why should the court sanction the use by a shopping mall owner of the *Petty Trespasses Act* in this context when the primary goal of the action was to reduce the scope and effectiveness of the economic pressure being exerted by the union against the tenant-employer?

McGregor's factum focused more on tearing down property than building up labour's right to exert economic pressure on the employer, while Laskin's dissent did not articulate clearly enough the statutory basis of the right asserted by Carswell. Even if they had made their arguments more fully, however, it is unlikely that the majority would have been persuaded. For the judges of the majority who had, as lawyers, spent their entire careers protecting the property rights of corporations and individuals, Carswell's argument was simply, viscerally, wrong. It was not one of those grey areas where reasonable people could differ. The only way property could be trumped was by the clearest legislative direction, as in the BC *Labour Code*.

Of the three dissenting judges, Laskin and Beetz had been full-time academics, while Spence had spent a key part of his career in the public sector, running the Toronto rental tribunal set up under the Wartime Prices and Trade Board in the 1940s. For them, it was not heretical to consider balancing property rights against the rights labour had gained through collective bargaining legislation. And there was indeed a big difference between "a picketer who tells people not to go to Safeway because of a labour dispute in California and a picketer who tells people not to go to Dominion Stores because she and her fellow employees are on strike." The latter had a variety of rights conferred by positive law, the former only a general right to freedom of expression not yet elevated to constitutional status.

After their victory, Stu Martin and Derek Booth discussed billing the Fairview Corporation for their services. Martin rejected the first draft of the bill as too high. The NDP government was likely to change the law, he thought, so it would be unfair to charge the client top dollar for a short-lived victory.[78] Martin was exactly right. The Supreme Court decision came down on 26 June 1975, and a year later the Manitoba government presented a bill to amend the *Petty Trespasses Act* to permit informational picketing of all kinds on "any walk, driveway, roadway, square or parking area provided outdoors at the site of or in conjunction with the premises in which any business or undertaking is operated and to which the public is normally admitted without fee or charge."[79] There was a fairly brief debate but the outcome was never in doubt.[80] The decision to amend the *Petty Trespasses Act* rather than the *Labour Relations Act*, however, meant that an opportunity to clarify the existence of a right to picket in conjunction with a legal strike was carefully avoided.

Harrison v. Carswell in the Courts

HARRISON HAS BEEN CITED in over thirty subsequent cases, the vast majority of times for the proposition that a property owner has an unrestricted right to invoke trespass against a person she wishes to exclude.[81] Indeed, on only four occasions has the majority judgment been distinguished, and two of those will be discussed below.[82] *Harrison* has been cited by Dickson C.J.C. himself, although ironically for his statement in the majority judgment that "a public interest is served by permitting union members to bring economic pressure to bear upon their respective employers through peaceful picketing."[83] Space constraints prevent any discussion of the vast majority of these cases, and we will limit ourselves to those involving a conflict between private property rights and union activity of various kinds.

R. v. Layton[84] concerned union organizing and private property. The future leader of the federal NDP, Jack Layton, was charged with trespass for refusing to leave the Eaton Centre in Toronto when requested to do so, the basis for his ejection being that he was handing out leaflets supporting a union's attempt to organize workers at Eaton's. In fact, this was in connection with the same organizing drive that gave rise to the very significant judgment of the Court of Appeal in the *Cadillac Fairview* case, discussed below. Provincial Court Judge Scott based his decision on the *Charter*'s guarantee of freedom of expression, which he decided had elevated expressive rights over property. This argument has been made in a number of cases, but has not otherwise been successful when dealing with private property.[85] Judge Scott thought it "self-evident" that freedom of expression covered "the distribution of informational literature, union or otherwise," and he found that the *Trespass to Property Act* was the government action which infringed on the section 2(b) right. Ironically, he was able to conclude that expression was infringed simply because *Peters* and

Harrison had made it clear that the statute "must be interpreted as permitting the occupier to exclude" a person from "the common areas of the mall." And while *Harrison* had affirmed the broad right to exclude, the persons involved in that pre-1982 case were, unlike Layton, "persons whose rights and freedoms were not guaranteed by the *Charter*." In dealing with the section 1 test he quoted extensively from that part of Laskin's dissent in *Harrison* which argued that the element of protection of privacy, a core purpose of trespass law, was inapplicable in a mall.

By far the most significant post-1975 case is the Ontario Court of Appeal's decision in *Cadillac Fairview Corp v. R.W.D.S.U.*.[86] The union was trying to organize the workers in Eaton's department store, which was wholly located within the Eaton Centre mall in Toronto, owned by Cadillac Fairview. None of the access points to the Eaton's store were accessible from public property; they were all within the mall itself. The union leafleted at the store entrances inside the mall and Cadillac Fairview ordered them to stop. The union challenged this action as an unfair labour practice and succeeded.

On a judicial review, the Court of Appeal upheld the Labour Relations Board and rejected Cadillac Fairview's argument that *Harrison* required that its property rights to exclude were to be treated as absolute. Crucially, Robins J.A. for the court agreed with the Board that Cadillac Fairview had acted on behalf of the employer Eaton's, and then analyzed the issue according to the statutory labour relations scheme. In holding that Cadillac Fairview had committed an unfair labour practice, it gave a broad interpretation to section 3 of the *Labour Relations Act*, which guaranteed that "every person is free to join a Trade Union of his own choice and participate in its lawful activities." Robins argued that if the legislature had conferred these rights, it could be "assumed to have intended" that employees "be permitted to make a free and reasoned choice." In turn such a choice "necessarily implies that employees have access to Union information free from restrictions," and a further extension of that proposition was that "[t]he legislature can also be assumed to have recognized that the organizational rights guaranteed by s. 3 may come into conflict with traditional property . . . rights." In deciding whether the mall owner had committed an unfair labour practice, the Board "was not obliged as a matter of law to treat Cadillac Fairview's property rights as absolute." Rather, "its responsibility was to apply the general prohibitory language of s. 64 [unfair labour practices] to the circumstances." What conduct constituted an unfair practice was not specified in the Act, and decisions about whether certain actions by an employer did so were made in the particular context of each case. But the focus needed to be unfair practice; neither property rights nor any other consideration could be treated as absolute and determinative.

The court distinguished *Harrison* specifically, on the ground that the Supreme Court had not had to deal with "a ruling by a labour relations board determining whether particular conduct contravened the provisions of [a] labour relations statute," and the court had therefore not been asked "to resolve . . . a conflict between private property rights and statutorily protected organizational rights." They key phrase here, of course, is "statutorily protected"; Robins J.A. argued that the provincial legislation made it possible to overrule common law rules, including the common law rule upheld by Dickson J. As he put it, "the conduct of the persons found to be trespassers in those cases [*Peters* and *Harrison*] was sought to be justified on common-law grounds and was not, as in this case, sanctioned by statute."

One can argue both that the Cadillac Fairview decision represents a substantial limit on the ambit of the majority judgment in Harrison, and that it does not do so because its context is so different. That is, here we have an imaginative use of the provincial labour relations scheme to reduce the property rights of third parties when they were being invoked at the employer's behest; presumably the same principles would, in appropriate circumstances, also persuade the court to reduce an employer's property rights. The Court of Appeal's approach was similar to Laskin J.'s dissent, but went well beyond it in detailing specifically what an employee's rights are and why their source —provincial statutes — matters. But where Laskin referred only in very general terms to Carswell's actions as being "supported both by legislation and by a well-understood legislative policy," Robins J.A. was able to be much more precise about the statutory provisions in play because of the nature of the proceeding.

Moreover, Robins J.A., like Laskin C.J.C., balanced rights, but not simply two different common law rights. Statutory rights trumped the common law. The decision, including the innovative use of unfair labour practices to reduce property rights, supports the first of Carrothers's three requirements for an effective system of collective bargaining, a requirement specifically included in legislative provisions which themselves have generally been liberally interpreted by courts. It is worth noting in this regard that the Manitoba *Labour Relations Act* in the 1970s contained provisions on organization and participation rights and on unfair labour practices very similar to those relied on by Robins J.A.[87] Laskin could not employ them directly as Robins J.A. did, largely because there had been no complaint of an unfair labour practice in *Harrison*. As we have indicated above, no such complaint had been made because counsel for the union shared the consensus view that the Act provided no effective protection for picketing. But it is still noteworthy that Laskin failed to use even the very limited ammunition available to him to flesh out what he meant by Carswell's interests being supported by legislative policy.

A 1992 amendment to Ontario's *Labour Relations Act* illustrates the general reluctance of legislatures to extend Cadillac Fairview to the strike/picketing context. Section 11.1 provided that union members "have the right to be present" on "premises to which the public normally has access" even if the property is private, for the purposes of either "attempting to persuade employees to join a trade union" or of picketing in connection with a lockout or strike. The private property in question had to be "at or near but outside the entrances and exits to the employees' workplace."[88] One might see this as a refutation of *Harrison v. Carswell*. It is better, we think, to see it as narrowing the potential of *Cadillac Fairview*. The amendment effectively put the *Cadillac Fairview* result into legislative form. In the future, courts would have little discretion to decide if intrusions on private property were justified; if such intrusions qualify under the statutory language, they would be permitted, if they did not the courts likely could not extend union rights to, for example, private property to which the public does not "normally have access" or property that is not "at or near" entrances and exits to and from the workplace.. The British Columbia courts have taken this position with regard to a provision in that province's *Labour Relations Code* that is very similar to section 11.1.[89] As it happens, section 11.1 was repealed in 1995 by the Ontario legislature, a measure introduced by the government of Mike Harris.[90]

Conclusion

JUSTICE DICKSON'S MAJORITY JUDGMENT has stood the test of time and remains a potent precedent, both in the labour context and more generally. Property rights are a powerful trope, and invariably win the day over other societal values, even though property remains formally outside the *Charter*. More than fifty years ago John Willis referred to the sacrosanct nature of property rights as part of the "common law bill of rights," and his observation remains true today.[91] One result is that labour's ability to "invoke meaningful economic sanctions" in support of collective bargaining — Carrothers's third criterion for an effective labour law — is reduced. Some might see a harbinger of change in this position in the Supreme Court's recent decision to extend constitutional protection to collective bargaining rights.[92] Such change is far from guaranteed, however. The BC health workers' case does not specifically address picketing, and its very lack of protection historically means that it not amenable to the kind of analysis undertaken by the Supreme Court in that decision.

To illustrate this point, and the continued potency and breadth of the ideology of private property, we end with perhaps the most unusual case that has applied *Harrison* to union activity. *Michelin & Cie v. C.A.W.*[93] involved a campaign to organize workers at Michelin plants in Nova Scotia. Part of the campaign included the union distributing pictures of the "Michelin Man" with a foot raised to crush a Michelin worker. The court first decided that Michelin had copyright in the Michelin Man and then, having rejected a constitutional defence based on freedom of expression, used *Harrison* as support for the principle that "private property [in this case a copyrighted image] cannot be used as a location or forum for expression." The traditional injunction to "keep off my sidewalk" has now, in the new age of intellectual property, become "don't picket on my picture."

Notes

* We thank Lisa Helps, Dianne Pothier, and Eric Tucker, as well as the symposium participants, for comments received on an earlier draft of this paper. Our title is offered with apologies to W.S. Kowinski, *The Malling of America: An Inside Look at the Great Consumer Paradise* (NY: W. Morrow, 1985).

1   [1976] 2 S.C.R. 200 [*Harrison*].

2   The Supreme Court of Canada had at last decided in *Williams et al. v. Aristocratic Restaurants (1947) Ltd.*, [1951] S.C.R. 762 that peaceful picketing on public property was lawful at common law. However, lower courts continued to allow the economic torts to be invoked by the employer to restrict and even negate this supposed right and to enjoin all secondary picketing. See Earl E. Palmer, "The Short, Unhappy Life of the 'Aristocratic' Doctrine" (1960) 13 U.T.L.J. 166 and Eric Tucker in this volume. For a useful overview of the law of picketing as it existed in the late 1960s, see Innis M. Christie, *The Liability of Strikers in the Law of Tort: A Comparative Study of the Law in England and Canada* (Kingston, ON: Queen's University Industrial Relations Centre, 1967).

3   Alfred W.R. Carrothers, *Collective Bargaining Law in Canada* (Toronto: Butterworths, 1965) at 415 [Carrothers].

4   *Winnipeg Real Estate News* (28 April 1989) 5.

5   The assets of Polo Park Centre were purchased by the Bronfman's better-known real estate arm, Fairview Corporation, in 1970, and in 1974 Fairview merged with another Bronfman company to form the Cadillac Fairview Corporation. See www.cadillacfairview.com.

6   *Winnipeg Tribune* (20 August 1959).

7   *Winnipeg Tribune* (29 August 1960).

8   *Winnipeg Tribune* (3 May 1968).

9   Per Chief Justice Robert N. Wilentz of the New Jersey Supreme Court, in *New Jersey Coalition Against War in the Middle East v. J.M.B. Realty Corp.*, 650 A2d 757 (1994), as cited in Lizabeth Cohen, *A Consumers' Republic: The Politics of Mass Consumption in Postwar America* (New York: Knopf, 2003) at 276 [Cohen]. We thank Lisa Helps for this reference.

10   Cohen, *ibid.* at 265.

11   Manitoba Department of Labour, *Annual Report 1973* (Winnipeg, 1974).

12   *Winnipeg Free Press*, 18, 19 May, 25 June 1973. For additional context on union organization in the retail food sector, see Jan Kainer, *Cashing in on Pay Equity? Supermarket Restructuring and Gender Equality* (Toronto: Sumach Press, 2002).

13   *Winnipeg Free Press* (18 May 1973). The union confirmed that about two-thirds of the staff at the Polo Park Dominion store were crossing the picket line.

14   Book of Evidence and Proceedings filed in the Manitoba Court of Appeal sub nom. *Carswell v. Harrison*, p. 109, Manitoba Archives, Court of Appeal fonds, ATG 0001/ GR595/B-3-6-6/file 275/73 [Book of Evidence]; *Winnipeg Tribune* (19 May 1973).

15   We do know, however, that the union's counsel chose Carswell as the named defendant because she was the only one who worked at the Polo Park store, whereas her co-picketers came from other locations; counsel wanted to ensure that the de-

fendant had the status of employee and not mere interloper: telephone interview of Alvin R. McGregor, Q.C. (17 July 2007).

16 Personal information is derived from a telephone interview of Sophie Carswell's son Barron Carswell (9 March 2008), and from her obituary in the *Winnipeg Free Press* (9 March 2000). After some years of work at Dominion Stores, Carswell went on — somewhat ironically, given her role in *Harrison* — to a career as a real estate agent.

17 *Winnipeg Tribune* and *Winnipeg Free Press* (25 June 1973).

18 The first Schreyer government, elected in 1969, was one seat short of a majority, but one Liberal member indicated his intention to sit as a "Liberal Democrat" and vote with the government, enabling Schreyer to govern as if he had a majority.

19 A particularly bitter battle was fought all the way to the Supreme Court of Canada: *International Brotherhood of Electrical Workers, Local 2085 v. Winnipeg Builders' Exchange*, [1967] S.C.R. 628, in which an injunction directed certain employees to cease taking part in an illegal strike. In spite of arguments that the effect of the injunction was to direct the specific performance of a contract for personal service — traditionally prohibited in common law jurisdictions — the injunction was upheld in the Supreme Court.

20 R.S.M. 1970, c. C280.

21 *Petty Trespasses Act*, S.M. 1970, c. 79.

22 Manitoba, *Debates and Proceedings — Legislative Assembly of Manitoba* (30 June 1970) at 3502 (Jake Froese). The entire debate is at 3480-3506.

23 *Ibid.* at 3504 (Hon. Alvin Mackling).

24 S.M. 1972, c. 75.

25 *Ibid.*

26 Sidney Green, *Rise and Fall of a Political Animal: A Memoir* (Winnipeg: Great Plains Publications, 2003) at 119 [Green].

27 Green was the principal speaker on the government side during the debate, even though he was Minister of Mines at the time. He had been counsel for the union in the *Winnipeg Builders' Exchange* case.

28 (1963), 42 D.L.R. (2d) 582. The Court held that s. 3(1) of the *Trade-unions Act*, R.S.B.C. 1960, c. 384, in allowing members of a trade union on a legal strike to "persuade . . . anyone not to enter the employer's place of business . . . or do business with the employer" provided they did so "without acts that are otherwise unlawful," meant that peaceful picketing in itself was rendered lawful. See also the earlier decision in the same dispute, where the B.C.C.A. first established the nuisance test, at (1962), 36 D.L.R. (2d) 581.

29 (1963), 40 D.L.R. (2d) 1006 (Sask. Q.B.) [*Grosvenor Park*]. Common law trespass was invoked, as Saskatchewan did not have a *Petty Trespass Act*. It should be noted that an easement is a non-possessory interest in land; hence a trespass action is not available to an easement holder.

30 (1964), 46 D.L.R. (2d) 750 (Sask. C.A.).

31 [1971] O.R. 597 (C.A.), aff'd 17 D.L.R. (3d) 128n (S.C.C.). The Supreme Court dismissed the appeal without reasons.

32 In the late 1960s, the United Farm Workers Association urged North American consumers to boycott California grapes in order to force the industry to provide better wages and working conditions for its Mexican and Filipino workers.

33 In a case comment entitled "Labour Law — Picketing on Shopping Centres" (1965), 43 Can. Bar Rev. 357, Harry Arthurs critiqued the courts' exclusive recourse to property law to decide these disputes, even though he generally agreed with the result in *Grosvenor Park*.

34 *Amalgamated Food Employees Union Local 590 et al. v. Logan Valley Plaza, Inc, et al.*, 391 U.S. 308 [*Amalgamated Food Employees*].

35 326 U.S. 501.

36 *Amalgamated Food Employees*, above note 34 at 324–25.

37 *Schwartz-Torrance Investment Corporation v. Bakery and Confectionery Workers' Union, Local No. 31*, 61 Cal. 2d 766 (1964).

38 A year later, Booth would briefly join the Gallagher firm before creating his own firm, known today as Booth Dennehy LLP. Interview of D. Booth (7 April 2008).

39 *Winnipeg Free Press* (11 July 1987); *Winnipeg Free Press* (20 Sept. 2002). The union is now called the Manitoba Food and Commercial Workers Union Local 832.

40 *Winnipeg Free Press* (14 September 1968) (feted by Ukrainian community on appointment); *Winnipeg Free Press* (11 December 1998) (obituary).

41 Book of Evidence, above note 14.

42 *Winnipeg Free Press* (13 October 1964); *Winnipeg Free Press* (15 November 1989).

43 *Winnipeg Free Press* (12 January 1996) (obituary). Martin is perhaps better known to Canadian legal history as the appellant in *Martin v. Gray*, [1990] 3 S.C.R. 1235, a leading case on conflicts of interest in law firms. We thank Derek Booth for drawing this to our attention.

44 Manitoba Archives, County Court of Winnipeg, ATG 0004A/GR4913/Q005818, file 2590/73.

45 Book of Evidence, above note 14 at 144.

46 Interview of Alvin R. McGregor, Q.C. (17 July 2007).

47 *Ibid.* at 145.

48 The facta filed in the Court of Appeal can be found in Book of Evidence, above note 14.

49 Above note 33.

50 *Harrison v. Carswell* (1974), 48 D.L.R. (3d) 137 at para. 8 (Man. C.A.).

51 *Ibid.* at para. 9.

52 *Ibid.*

53 *Ibid.* at para. 19. In fact, much of his analysis repeated that of Arthurs.

54 In fact, Lysyk's role really seemed to be defending the honour of the Saskatchewan Court of Appeal in *Grosvenor Park*, which is what his factum centred on. However, this was arguably outside the parameters of his permission to intervene. As Saskatchewan had no *Petty Trespasses Act*, it was ironic that it was the only province to intervene to uphold the validity of such legislation.

55 We refer to the factum as Booth's because only he signed it. Martin joined him for oral argument. The facta are available from the Supreme Court of Canada, and we thank Lee Seshagiri for his assistance in obtaining them.

56 Appellant's factum at 13.

57 *Harrison,* above note 1 at 202.

58 *Ibid.* [emphasis added].

59 *Ibid.* at 209.

60 Carrothers, above note 3.

61 Laskin had been part of the Court in *Peters*; in retrospect, he probably regretted not having given reasons in the case.

62 *Harrison,* above note 1. at 209. On the role of functionalism in Laskin's legal thought, see Philip Girard, *Bora Laskin: Bringing Law to Life* (Toronto: University of Toronto Press for the Osgoode Society, 2005) [Girard].

63 *Harrison,* above note 1 at 210. It is worth noting that the US caselaw has not stood still since the *Logan Valley* and *Schwartz-Torrance* cases. In fact, it abruptly changed direction when the Burger Court succeeded the Warren Court in the 1970s. In *Hudgens v. National Labour Relations Board*, 424 U.S. 507 (1976), the Court overruled *Logan Valley,* denying First Amendment protection to an employee picketing in front of an employer's store in a private shopping centre. Cohen, above note 9, contains an excellent review of the caselaw at 274–78. She notes that the US Supreme Court has essentially left the issue to be decided under state constitutions, and in only "six states — California, Colorado, Massachusetts, New Jersey, Oregon, and Washington — have state supreme courts protected citizens' right of free speech in privately owned shopping centers" (at 275).

64 *Harrison,* above note 1 at 210.

65 "Picketing: A Comparison of Certain Canadian and American Doctrines" (1937) 15 Can. Bar Rev. 10 at 19.

66 "The Protection of Interests by Statute and the Problem of 'Contracting Out'" (1938) 16 Can. Bar Rev. 669 at 689.

67 Cited in Girard, above note 62 at 235.

68 *Harrison,* above note 1 at 212.

69 Even Paul Weiler, a labour law scholar normally found in the Laskin camp, confessed that he found the deference argument convincing in this instance. See his essay, "Of Judges and Scholars: Reflections in a Centennial Year" (1975) 53 Can. Bar Rev. 563.

70 Robert Sharpe & Kent Roach, *Brian Dickson: A Judge's Journey* (Toronto: University of Toronto Press for the Osgoode Society 2003) at 148–49 [Sharpe & Roach].

71 *Harrison,* above note 1 at 213.

72 Sharpe & Roach, above note 70 at 149.

73 *Harrison,* above note 1 at 204.

74 Sharpe & Roach, above note 70 at 150.

75 *Harrison,* above note 1 at 217.

76 *Ibid.* at 218. Dickson also quoted from Harry Arthurs' earlier case comment which contained his summary of the reasons supporting the mall owner's position without noting that Arthurs himself ultimately rejected such arguments in favour of limited picketing rights for strikers, and that Arthurs' "bottom line" supported Laskin's position.

77 See *Pugliese v. National Capital Commission* (1979), 25 N.R. 498 (S.C.C.).

78 Telephone interview of Derek Booth (7 April 2008).

79 S.M. 1976, c. 71; see now C.C.S.M., c. P50, s. 4. The *Court of Queen's Bench Act* was amended at the same time to provide a definition of "public thoroughfare" on all fours with the amended *Petty Trespasses Act*.

80 Manitoba, *Debates and Proceedings— Legislative Assembly of Manitoba* (10 June 1976) 4813–17.

81 These include *Russo v. Ontario Jockey Club* (1987), 62 O.R. (2d) 731 (H.C.J.), in which Russo argued that she could not be excluded from parimutuel betting facilities otherwise open to the public. The Jockey Club had banned her because she was a very skilled bettor and won too much. Boland J. simply followed *Harrison*, noting that if the Supreme Court refused to balance private property rights with picketing, there was even less of a case to be made for balancing property against a "right to bet." It is nonetheless at least arguable that Dickson's implicit qualification of the absolutism of the owner's rights contained in his "caprice, whimsy or *mala fides*" statement could have been used here. Barring a person from facilities otherwise open to the public for betting because they won too often is certainly capricious and could well amount to bad faith.

82 The other two are *Wildwood Mall Ltd. v. Stevens*, [1980] 2 W.W.R. 638 (Sask. Q.B.) and *R. v. M. (E.B.)*, [1988] Carswell Ont 2810 (Fam. Ct.). In the former, the Saskatchewan Court of Queen's Bench held somewhat dubiously that *Harrison* was not the law in that province because it was predicated on Manitoba having a provincial statute making trespass a petty offence. Since Saskatchewan had no such statute, the Court of Appeal decision in *Grosvenor Park* was the controlling authority. This was clearly not a valid ground of distinction, given that *Harrison* involved trespass generally, not the statute specifically, but the decision was not appealed, presumably because it was an application for an interim injunction to restrain picketing during the Christmas season. In the latter case, the court rejected the argument of the Toronto Transit Authority that it had an unfettered right to invoke trespass against any person. In what was a rather bold refutation of the Supreme Court, the court expressed a preference for the Laskin dissent's approach to functionally public space and held that *Harrison* "should be strictly interpreted and not extended any further into the public domain," and noted that "[t]he public nature of the transit authority business is even more extensive than the public aspects of shopping malls." Agencies such as the Transit Authority should use trespass law to deal with specific prohibited activities, "rather then relying on the ancient doctrine which gives a land owner the unfettered right to evict invitees without cause."

83 *B.C.G.E.U. v. British Columbia (Attorney-General)*, [1988] 2 S.C.R. 214 at 230. *Harrison* was cited for the same point by other judges in *UFCW, Local 1518 v. KMart Canada Ltd*, [1999] 2 S.C.R. 1083 at 1111, and *Maple Leaf Foods Inc. v. Thorne* (1997), 41 C.L.R.B.R. (2d) 268 at 283 (Ont. G.D.).

84 (1986), 33 C.C.C. (3d) 550 (Ont. Prov. Ct.).

85 The most germane of these for our purposes is *281856 British Columbia Ltd. v. Kamloops, Revelstoke, Okanagan Building Trades Union* (1986), 37 C.C.L.T. 262 (B.C.C.A.),

which involved picketing. The Court noted that while the Supreme Court of Canada might reach a different conclusion in light of the *Charter of Rights*, that was a decision for that court itself. See also for the same conclusion *R. v. Marcocchio* (2002), 213 N.S.R. (2d) 86 (S.C.), and *R. v. Asante-Mensah*, [2001] O.J. No. 3819 (C.A.).

86 (1989), 71 O.R. (2d) 206 (C.A.) at 217–18, 219, 220, & 221 [*Cadillac Fairview*]. For a detailed discussion of this case and the *Layton* case discussed above, see Eric Tucker, "The Malling of Labour Law? The Toronto Eaton Centre Cases, 1984–1987 and the Right to Exclude," in James Muir, Eric Tucker, & Bruce Ziff, eds., *Canadian Property Law Stories* (Toronto: Irwin Law, forthcoming 2012).

87 Section 5 of the Manitoba *Labour Relations Act*, S.M. 1972, c. 75, states: "Every employee has the right (a) to be a member of a union; (b) to participate in the activities of a union."

88 R.S.O. 1990, c. L.2, as amended by S.O. 1992, c. 21, s. 12. In *Queen's University at Kingston v. C.U.P.E. Local 229*, [1994] O.J. No. 2910 (C.A.), Weiler J.A. said that the amendment discussed here followed from *Harrison*, and the Divisional Court said the same thing in *Great Atlantic and Pacific Company of Canada v. UFCW Locals 175 & 633* (1995), 24 O.R. (3d) 809 (Div. Ct.), but given the timing and the content of the amendment that is surely wrong.

89 See in this regard *RMH Teleservices International Inc. v. B.C.G.E.U.* (2003), 223 D.L.R. (4th) 750 (B.C.S.C.). A union was seeking to organize a workplace, and used the parking lot of the employer's premises to do so. The case turned on whether the parking lot was within an exemption to the *Harrison* principle created by s. 66 of the BC *Labour Relations Code*, R.S.B.C. 1996, c. 224. Section 66 provides that no action would lie for trespass "to land to which a member of the public ordinarily has access" if such a "trespass" arose out of a strike, lockout, or picketing that was permitted by the *Code*, or from "attempts to persuade employees to join a trade union made at or near but outside entrances and exits and exits to an employer's workplace." The court held that the parking lot in question was not a place to which the public "ordinarily has access," and having done so reaffirmed that *Harrison* provided the applicable principle for all cases of trespass not covered by the statutory exemption. It found *Cadillac Fairview* inapplicable, principally because it was based on the unfair labour practices section of the Ontario Act and not on legislation dealing with picketing on private property. British Columbia had legislated on the point, leaving no room for broad use of unfair labour practices, and outside of s. 66, the common law, as enunciated in *Harrison*, prevailed. Any further incursion into the absolutism of the Supreme Court's judgment must come from the legislature.

90 *Labour Relations and Employment Statute Law Amendment Act*, S.O. 1995, c. 1, s. 1(4). The issue of the right to exclude from publicly-used private property attracted attention in the 1980s in a different, non-union, context. In 1980 the Ontario legislature amended the old *Petty Trespasses Act*, replacing it with the *Trespass to Property Act*, R.S.O. 1980, c. 511. The new legislation included in the definition of trespasser, any person "who does not leave the premises immediately after he is directed to do so by the occupier of the premises or a person authorized by the occupier" (s. 2 (1)(b)). This new provision effectively put into legislative form a broad reading of Dickson

J's judgment in *Harrison*. Following complaints that this power was being used in a discriminatory fashion against youth and minorities, the Ontario government (Attorney General Ian Scott) appointed well-known Toronto human rights lawyer Raj Anand in 1986 as a task force to investigate whether discriminatory enforcement had been practiced or whether the Act had the potential to encourage it. Malls were one of the locations specifically mentioned. Anand concluded that there was evidence of discrimination and recommended, *inter alia*, a requirement of cause to be written into the Act — there should be "misconduct" and misconduct needed to be defined. In doing so he quoted extensively from Laskin C.J.C.'s dissent in *Harrison*. See Task Force on the Law Concerning Trespass to Publicly Used Property as it Affects Youth and Minorities (Toronto: Ministry of the Attorney-General, 1987). The Peterson government accepted the principal recommendation of a need for cause for removal, and in 1990 introduced a short amending bill that was lost when an election was called. Rather surprisingly, the successor NDP government of Bob Rae did not carry through with the measure. (We thank Raj Anand for his recollections about this.) The ironic result was that when s. 11.1 of the *Labour Relations Act* was passed, only union members, in the circumstances outlined above, had the same rights on functionally public private property as they did on public property itself. All other members of society were subject to the absolutist regime laid down in *Harrison*.

91 J. Willis, "Statute Interpretation in a Nutshell" (1938) 16 Can. Bar Rev. 1. We respectfully disagree with Kevin Gray & Susan Francis Gray, "Private Property and Public Propriety" in Janet McLean, ed., *Property and the Constitution* (Oxford & Portland, OR: Hart, 1999) at 26, who assert that a shift in the common law paradigm of trespass, derived from Laskin's dissent in *Harrison*, has "give[n] way to a rather different rule under which the private owner of quasi-public premises may exclude members of the public only on grounds which are objectively and communicably reasonable."

92 *Health Services and Support — Facilities Subsector Bargaining Assn. v. British Columbia*, [2007] 2 S.C.R. 391.

93 [1997] 2 F.C. 306 (T.D.). For a critique of the decision, see Graham Reynolds, "A Step in the Wrong Direction: The Impact of the Legislative Protection of Technological Protection Measures on Fair Dealing and Freedom of Expression" (2006) 5 C.J.L.T. 179.

PART FOUR

Human Rights Norms at Work

Debating Maternity Rights: Pacific Western Airlines and Flight Attendants' Struggle to "Fly Pregnant" in the 1970s

Joan Sangster

Introduction

IN CANADA, THE 1970s witnessed an unprecedented number of feminist court challenges on equality issues,[1] some of which reflected problems that had been percolating within the workforce over the entire post-World War II period. As the labour participation rate of married women[2] increased significantly, transforming the face of the workforce, maternity leave became one such issue that could not be ignored. The changing demography, importance, and nature of female wage labour produced fissures in the male breadwinner ideal, and as more women with families worked for pay, they began to articulate a different sense of what was both possible and socially permissible during pregnancy and immediately after giving birth. Workplace struggles over pregnancy and maternity issues were shaped by class and race; women with better-paying, more secure jobs were obviously more privileged than marginal workers who lacked job security and thus could barely imagine something as luxurious as a maternity leave.[3] Fewer economic choices, however, did not necessarily produce workplace apathy, for working-class women with unions to back them up became some of the most assertive opponents of both marriage and pregnancy prohibitions in the workplace. They felt they should be able to determine whether and when they worked while pregnant, based on their families' economic needs and their own judgments about their physical capabilities. Although the post-war settlement — through which unions secured collective bargaining rights, and capital achieved more labour peace and stability — has been correctly characterized as a limited "bargain" for labour,[4] for those women who *were* unionized, it offered new avenues to challenge the law, labour contracts, and workplace custom concerning pregnancy. Moreover, even when they did not win their legal battles, workers might be accruing points in a longer-term ideological struggle to redefine the "normal" and acceptable working woman.

This paper explores unionized women's efforts to use the courts to secure new maternity rights, focusing on one specific legal battle: the attempt by the Canadian Airline Flight Attendants Association (CALFAA) to secure women's legal right to "fly pregnant" rather than be forced into early, and thus unpaid, maternity leaves. The CALFAA case bore some resemblance to the significant Supreme Court of Canada *Bliss* case[5] in that flight attendants were challenging the notion that women did not "belong in the public sphere in the period around childbirth";[6] however, the CALFAA court battle focused more intensely on the pregnant body, since the airlines claimed that pregnant workers, after their fourth month, were unsafe workers in the air.[7] CALFAA remained convinced that the airlines' ban on pregnant flight attendants was an appearance issue, a perception that was inevitably acute in a union that had increasingly criticized the marketing of its workers as sex symbols in the 1960s and 1970s. Flight attendants rejected what they called the "bunny club"[8] philosophy of their employers, and asserted their right to judge their own physical capabilities during pregnancy. Finally, they also came to argue for their right to choose whichever legal protection they preferred: the *Canada Labour Code* (*Labour Code*)[9] or their own collective agreement.

CALFAA court battles reflected debates and tensions within feminist discourses at the time concerning perceived choices between "equality versus difference": the former suggesting feminists should strive for the same or identical treatment with men, the latter suggesting women's distinct needs and interests (such as their reproductive roles) had to be recognized to secure equality.[10] While these political strategies became increasingly less dichotomous in feminist discourse, at the time, there were concerns that conceding to female "difference" might take the struggle for equality backwards. CALFAA primarily used a language of individual and equal rights as their guide, downplaying the need for extra, or "special" health protection for pregnant women, apprehensive that an emphasis on bodily difference would lend weight to the airlines' claim to be protecting women's health, as well as that of the fetus and the travelling public. In the context of the times, this approach was completely understandable, though in the long run, it made advocacy for flight attendants' specific health needs as pregnant female workers more difficult to advance. Like other women workers, they also discovered that a focus on strict equality in legal terms rather than more "substantive" and thorough-going social and economic equality[11] for all women meant that the gains of the 1970s were fragile indeed in the face of privatization and retrenchment. Advances in maternity rights, while certainly important, were also partial and class specific; some unionized and better-paid women, and more recently men, have gained enhanced parental rights, particularly if they conform to a specific nuclear family form. However, more marginal women workers and their families remain largely outside the benefits of a maternity/parental leave program that is tied so tightly to regular labour force participation, and that is not accompanied by other crucial social supports such as child care.[12]

Post-World War II Pressures for Maternity Rights

CALFAA's COURT BATTLE MUST be placed within two overlapping contexts: changing views on maternity rights,[13] and labour relations in the airline industry. Women's efforts to secure better maternity rights in the post-World War II period ranged from subterfuge to the use of grievance systems, and from individual complaints to pressure on the state as women lobbied for legislative change. In the latter case, women could point to Canada's embarrassing failure to live up to the principles of the International Labour Organization (ILO), which had called for maternity leave with monetary benefits for working mothers in 1919, a convention the ILO substantially expanded in 1952. This ILO convention on maternity leave was never ratified by the Canadian government, leaving the government free to ignore the principles involved.[14]

Employers' rules concerning the employment of married women, pregnant women, and women with family responsibilities varied across occupations, workplaces, and provincial legal regimes. Those employing women in lower-paid and part-time jobs rarely worried about their marital status, and the same was increasingly true for some feminized white collar jobs, like telephone operating, where capital's search for a flexible labour force necessitated relaxing the marriage bar. Better remunerated blue collar jobs in industry, imagined as the "standard employment relation,"[15] were more likely to be seen as "off limits" to married women, and certainly women with children. If married working women upset the dominant image of a male breadwinner, a pregnant woman was even more problematic, her swelling body a visible reminder of the prospect of working mothers. Still, mass production unions like the United Auto Workers felt duty bound (and were sometimes forced) to take up women's grievances over marriage bars when the contract was clearly violated,[16] and female union members were also pressing their leaders to take up their pregnancy discrimination cases.

By the time the federal government legislated a limited system of maternity leave benefits through the Unemployment Insurance (UI) system in 1971, maternity *leave* itself was far from a radical issue.[17] For one thing, women had been rebelling for some time, simply staying on the job, unlike their mothers before them. Ann Porter has documented the way in which pregnant women tried to argue for their rightful access to "regular" benefits under the UI system, though it was decidedly stacked against the interests of pregnant, out-of-work women. Evidence gathered from union grievance files, as well as from a survey of twenty years of Labour Arbitration Cases (LAC) also supports the importance of this "rebellion from below."[18] Although reported arbitrations represent only the "tip of the arbitral iceberg,"[19] it is revealing that the largest number of women's discharge cases cited as new and noteworthy in the LAC from 1948 to 1968 were fought over issues of marriage and pregnancy. Women were attempting to secure new rights, literally from the shop floor upwards, as the union leadership rarely took a proactive role on these issues.

While few unions put maternity leave at the top of their bargaining list, the main problem most working women faced was management's insistence that it was its prerogative to make the rules about how long a pregnant woman could work, and whether she could return to the same job. Even those employers who offered maternity leaves usually saw them as "privileges not rights."[20] The view that it was management's prerogative to shape pregnancy policies was shared by many provincial and federal officials as well, at least until the late 1960s.[21] Some employers expressed the rather improbable fear that maternity leave rights would lead to a state of "perpetual pregnancy,"[22] that is, all their employees would be reproducing so quickly that production would be disrupted. "An employee could only work a few months of the year between pregnancies and maintain full seniority rights," worried one such employer.[23] One has to question whether all women in this manufacturing plant were interested in giving birth every year.

Management's stated concerns about both pregnant working women and maternity leaves related to safety, efficiency, absenteeism, and the expense and trouble of providing replacements. Without maternity leaves with guaranteed seniority, women would have to be re-hired after a pregnancy, starting at the bottom of the pay scale, thus providing employers with a flexible, cheap labour force. However, more than money was at stake: the moralism that pervaded some employers' rationales and arbitrators' decisions revealed an ideological antipathy to having visibly pregnant women on the job, and to their return to work as new mothers, as their place was supposedly at home, taking care of their "household duties."[24] Concerns about the physical display of pregnant bodies varied with the class designation of the job. In one survey, private sector employers in Ontario admitted that the length of leave given *before* birth depended on the job "setting and product," with employers taking factors such as whether the woman "meets the public" into account. If her body was on view to the public, they preferred her to leave between the fourth and sixth month.[25] In the midst of a baby boom, women were presumably encouraged to reproduce — but only in private.

By the time the federally-appointed Royal Commission on the Status of Women (RCSW) held cross-country hearings in 1968, legislated maternity leave had become such a "motherhood" issue that even the Jaycettes were on board.[26] The question of benefits was somewhat more contested, with unions the most adamant advocates of benefits paid by the state, though other groups — like the Anglican Church — were also quick to point out that Canada had yet to catch up with the 1919 ILO principle of paid state benefits.[27] Briefs to the Commission from women's organizations and clubs, as well as unions, often cited maternity leave and benefits policies as reforms past their due. One nurse writing from BC criticized the "shocking maternity policies" that existed in most workplaces, with women pressured to leave in their "third month . . . so she doesn't shock away the customers with her stomach."[28] Even some of the private letters to the RCSW claiming married women's place was in the home admitted that maternity leaves should be provided for those (unfortunate) women who *had* to work.

These pressures from below were buttressed by other political efforts that gave visibility and legitimacy to the concept of maternity leave: between 1968 and 1970 Grace MacInnis, a New Democratic Party (NDP) member of parliament, put forward no less than three private member bills for legislated maternity leave for federally regulated women workers,[29] and the federal government's own Women's Bureau was openly supportive as well. By the late 1960s maternity leave legislation seemed almost inevitable: the only question was what form the law would take. Both a 1967 Women's Bureau study of Maternity Leave in Canada and an internal government "working group" on maternity leave were careful to consult expert medical opinion — a voice of significant influence in the CALFAA case — as part of the policy process, particularly on the question of whether leaves should be mandatory. Some doctors, revealing a class-based and moralistic view, saw a woman's physiological capabilities in light of her social role: they emphasized a "traditional" family in which "a mother should retire from the labour force when her first baby is born and devote herself entirely to her family."[30] There was a strong disposition to trust these medical experts on women's health issues, an inclination that could itself veer toward protective paternalism. If a woman wanted to return to work early, the Women's Bureau suggested both a doctor's certificate *and* an interview with the employer, assuming that they would have the "best interests" of the mother and child at heart.[31] There may be a difference between nineteenth-century notions of protecting "fragile" bodies and twentieth-century guarantees to protect women's health and "reproductive function,"[32] but the line could become blurred in practice, precisely the reason that equal rights feminists opposed protective legislation.[33]

Revisions to the *Canada Labour Code* in 1970 generally followed the Royal Commission's recommendations on maternity leave, including prohibitions on employers dismissing pregnant employees, though the RCSW recommended wording was slightly more rigorous.[34] Benefits came under UI legislation, an example of "faulty policy design"[35] according to some political scientists. Yet placing benefits under UI did have a capitalist economic logic in terms of the work ethic, an actuarial impulse to keep UI pay outs limited, and an aversion to any universal system of maternity benefits. Just as maternity benefits were contingent on regular attachment to the labour force, the prohibitions in the *Labour Code* against dismissing pregnant workers turned out to be contingent as well, for they offered the airlines a legal loophole: employers could not lay off women "solely" because of pregnancy. What "solely" meant became the object of legal debate for CALFAA and the courts.

Setting the Scene: Airline Labour Relations

THE CALFAA COURT BATTLE also needs to be understood in the context of airline labour relations in the post-World War II years. This era was, without a doubt, a period of new employment opportunity for flight attendants, as the industry was rapidly expanding. While Trans Canada Airlines (TCA) had sought out nurses as attendants in the interwar years, this qualification was increasingly abandoned in the post-war years, with airlines favouring applicants who had the poise, character, and the ability to play the role of reassuring hostess in the air. Discrimination in favour of white, better educated, and, of course, young women, was taken for granted as an employer right until these forms of discrimination were challenged by workers in the 1960s.

Even in the 1940s, flight attendants were quite aware that the airlines used them as a means of "promoting an appealing image of air travel,"[36] while simultaneously ignoring their working conditions. "Safe and decent"[37] transportation to and from the airport, along with wages and uniforms paid for by the employer, were the motivating factors behind the organization of a union in 1946, initially named an "association" as the word "union" was an anathema to some of the members. Although male airline pursers organized separately from female flight attendants, their arguments for two separate unions failed to convince the War Labour Board, which ruled that they must remain together in CALFAA, though separate wage scales and seniority lists were taken for granted at the time.[38]

CALFAA was certified for TCA attendants in 1947; in 1951, Canadian Pacific (CP) attendants joined, and in 1958, the small staff of Pacific Western Airlines (PWA) attendants organized secretly, fearful that they would be immediately fired if management discovered their plans. In its first ten years, the union was loosely structured and ran largely on volunteer labour, drawing its executive from the area where the head office was located in Montreal. Despite these drawbacks, they were able to negotiate some of the first agreements in North America.[39] By 1954, however, their lack of experience and time for bargaining led some locals to consider merging with a larger union, while others sought outside bargaining advice. CALFAA did affiliate with the Canadian Labour Congress (CLC) in 1958, and the Vancouver-based CP attendants began to use the services of a Canadian Brotherhood of Railway Employees (CBRE) member, Bob Smeal, who advised them until 1959, when he was hired as the first CALFAA business agent. With a new CALFAA office based in the West, Smeal professionalized the union, and under his guidance, improvements in contracts were secured, often by using Air Canada (the former TCA) as an industry-setting precedent in bargaining. As a Crown corporation, Air Canada was subject to political scrutiny that other airlines were not, undoubtedly one reason women often made gains with them first.

"COFFEE, TEA OR HOMEMADE MUFFINS?"

CALFAA presented a brief to the RCSW which protested the airlines'
"bunny club" attitude toward flight attendants.
Source: London Free Press, 9 December 1970. Reprinted courtesy of Merle Tingley.

Labour relations were not entirely smooth flying. In 1963, the first strike
of airline attendants occurred at PWA, in unison with a walkout of the Pacific
Western Airlines Traffic Employees Association (TEA). PWA was founded by
a bush pilot and self-made man of the BC frontier, Russ Baker, who had taken
one plane and parlayed it into a profitable western regional carrier. Aided especially by contracts relating to northern development, and arguably also by
the federal regulation of the industry, PWA cornered routes between and within Alberta, BC, and the Northwest Territories, then began to push eastwards.[40]

Striking PWA flight attendants demanded better wages (parity with CP),
a set number of attendants on each flight, and pay for delays, a sore spot
when the women could be on duty as long as fourteen hours, but paid only
for four flying hours.[41] Under the federal *Industrial Relations Dispute Investigation Act*,[42] a Board of Conciliation and Investigation had to be convened,
but it was unable to head off the strike. The company and government representatives issued a majority report that diverged widely from the union

representative's minority report.⁴³ The fifteen attendants who walked off the job were aided not only by the more powerful TEA, but also by some pilots, veterans of the RCAF, who refused to cross the picket line. The pilots were swiftly disciplined with loss of pay and demerit points, and threatened with dismissal. Women strikers were also punitively targeted. Nine of ten women picketers were accused of yelling at the "scabs" crossing the picket line; PWA sent them letters of dismissal, citing their failure to "maintain dignified deportment" and their use of "insulting language" while in uniform.⁴⁴ Three more strikers were charged with "watching and besetting" a strikebreaker's home, and the PWA was able to secure an *ex parte* injunction severely limiting the number of pickets. However, with the aid of the BC Federation of Labour, including a loggers' boycott of PWA, CALFAA won the strike after six months, with one of the most difficult sticking points being the reinstatement of those women who were fired. PWA also tried to encourage a company union made up of strikebreakers; as a result, CALFAA was almost decertified, and was saved only by a sympathetic Labour Board decision.⁴⁵

The strike could only reinforce PWA's image as an anti-union employer (not the least because it locked its northern TEA grounds employees out of their company homes in the middle of the wilderness)⁴⁶ and it set an adversarial tone for future labour relations. This was a company with ideological resolve, and no hesitation about using the courts to defeat its unions. It also believed in the power of positive public relations: a company executive proudly claimed PWA won the strike "by attrition," a rather skewed reading of the facts.⁴⁷ Labour relations did not change markedly when PWA ownership was taken over by the Alberta government in 1974 for almost a decade.⁴⁸

Emboldened by the support it received for the strike, CALFAA intensified its political lobbying in other areas, such as the need for legislated safety regulations and prohibitions on gender discrimination in the industry. In order to maintain the image of the young, attractive flight attendant, most airlines fired stewardesses at thirty-two years of age, and a firm marriage bar existed. These forms of discrimination were first on CALFAA's list of injustices, and in 1965 they filed a grievance against PWA when Deanne Konderat (née Rivey) was fired upon her marriage. Even though CALFAA lost this grievance, it set a pattern for the future: the union used either labour relations machinery or the courts to challenge discrimination, and even when it lost, it followed up with political pressure that might lead to contract changes.

As Konderat's arbitration made clear, gendered assumptions about the breadwinner ethic and domesticated maternity were still firmly set in the minds of many federal labour board arbitrators. While one question was whether dismissal upon marriage was an accepted term of her employment, the other was whether such a term was "void and unenforceable as being contrary to public policy."[49] The company had a stronger case on the first question, since its policy on qualifications (though these were not in the collective agreement) stated women should not be married or divorced, and since the return to work agreement after the strike conceded that women married during the strike would not be re-hired. The second question was more revealing. Rejecting the union's citation of European cases in its favour, the labour board drew on American cases justifying the marriage bar. Quoting a 1964 Southern Airways case, it related the problem of marriage to the "danger" of pregnancy: "[T]he duties required of a stewardess are such that, if she should become pregnant, she might endanger herself and her unborn child, as well as the passengers under her care." This decision also stressed that the married stewardess' proper social role was really at "home with her husband," and thus she might be called away from work at short notice, or required to move when he did, otherwise her marriage might be "jeopardized." Finding that the matrimonial bar was a "reasonable restraint," not a policy "repugnant" to the "public conscience," the board ruled against Konderat.[50]

Trade union opposition to the decision was immediate. Bob Smeal involved the BC Federation of Labour, wrote to the Human Rights Department at the CLC,[51] and lobbied the Minister of Transportation, while Vancouver CCF MP Ernie Winch decried the airlines' shameful practice of discrimination in the House of Commons.[52] PWA's marriage bar and refusal to hire divorced women were ridiculed by the union,[53] which pointed out that airline policy favoured women "living in sin" over married women, and that no other women, save for nuns, were forced to comply with similar rules.[54] The campaign won results. The next year, the industry leader, Air Canada, relaxed its marriage bar; other airlines followed suit within a couple of years. The age bar was conquered soon afterwards. By 1972, Air Canada estimated that 30 percent of its stewardesses were married, and some had children.[55]

In the context of industry affluence, an ongoing demand for labour, and stability in the union, this strategy of legal engagement followed by public pressure was politically astute. It was bolstered too by union members' increasing confidence in challenging airline discrimination and by Smeal's strong support for equity issues. Unfortunately, the latter also became a cause for dissent within the union. Problems had been brewing for some time, relating to eastern resentment at "western" control, and Smeal's inordinate influence over decisions. An opposition group coalesced in the largely male executive in 1974–75, and according to Smeal and others, the "revolt" had much to do with the recent thwarting of male privilege. The integration of men's and women's seniority lists in 1973 challenged men's "preferential treatment," leading to an attempt to secure a court injunction to reassert "male super seniority" in the contract.[56] Another opposition complaint was Smeal's support for funding a "pregnancy committee" set up to deal with pregnancy discrimination.

The CLC representative charged with investigating the divisions concluded that the executive had overstepped their bounds and had "besmirched" Smeal's name with false charges. He also claimed they had allowed their Winnipeg lawyer, Israel Asper, to assume "an extraordinary influence" on the union "[seemingly] in violation of the letter, spirit and intent of the Constitution." The new executive had been "advised at an exorbitant cost by law firms whose advice had succeeded in raiding the union treasury of CALFAA funds built up by good management." It was a damning picture.[57] By 1976, the union was trying to rebuild with a new female president but shortly after his name was cleared, Smeal died of a heart attack. That the union could gear up for and sustain the next difficult legal battle was testament to the strong resolve on the part of the new executive to deal with the pregnancy issue.

Pregnancy in Flight

BEFORE SMEAL'S DEATH, A challenge to the pregnancy bar in PWA had already been launched. At PWA, as with most airlines, women had to inform the employer in writing when they knew they were pregnant, no later than their fourth month, and then were required to stop working. Their collective agreement allowed them a longer maternity leave than the federal *Canada Labour Code* provisions and they could accrue seniority when on leave, but they were not entitled to any more than fifteen weeks of UI benefits. The prohibition against working while pregnant was absolute: whatever women believed their physical capabilities to be, whatever they saw as socially acceptable, the company was to judge their bodily capabilities and limitations. Why, they asked, were they not protected by the stipulation in the *Canada Labour Code* that said women could not be dismissed when pregnant?

The pregnancy court case must also be framed by the union's growing opposition to the industry's efforts to promote a more eroticized flight attendant image. Flight attendants, as other scholars have documented, were part of the product sold to customers.[58] Initially, women were to be attractive hostesses but also caring, polite, and nurturing, especially to those afraid of flying. Despite such "maternal instincts," they were only mothers-to-be: the job was promoted as a way for young women to see the world before finding the ideal husband. In the popular culture of the Harlequin romance, the stewardess sees Paris and New York, then finds love in the arms of the older, experienced, handsome pilot. With female readers in mind, however, the Harlequin stewardess is portrayed as intelligent and independent: in one plot she courageously helps the flight engineer repair the landing gear from inside the baggage hatch, thus averting a crash.[59] In contrast, the airlines, with the male businessman as their imagined consumer, increasingly marketed the stewardess not as the perfect wife, but as the jet-age sex object. The flight attendant's work thus encompassed forms of both emotional and aesthetic labour,[60] the former requiring her to suppress her own feelings and "act out" emotionally for others, the latter requiring her to spend considerable time making her body appropriately attractive — indeed, attendants claimed that makeup lessons were as crucial (if not more so) than first aid lessons in their training. This gendered "body work," contend contemporary sociologists, is a key reason that flight attendant work was, and still is, devalued.[61]

While the Canadian union argued persuasively that this sexualization was far more pervasive in the US,[62] there were nonetheless parallels, from the promotion of beauty contests at TCA to the airlines' open acknowledgment that they only recruited women of "good appearance" with height and weight requirements, and no "eyeglasses."[63] While some flight attendants may have welcomed the emphasis on a fashionable rather than military-like uniforms in this period, there was growing antipathy to the "fly me" style advertising campaigns that were used in the US. In CALFAA's brief to the RCSW in 1968, for instance, the airlines' age and maternity bars were characterized as "cheap and degrading" forms of discrimination, reflecting the airlines' "bunny club" philosophy. Dismissing the airlines attitudes as "Victorian," and stressing the similarity of men and women's physical abilities, they urged an "equal rights" approach to job issues.[64] This did not stop the press from commenting on the "young, attractive"[65] women delivering the brief.

PWA attendants, perhaps more than others, were convinced their employer intended to use their bodies as a marketing lure for leering customers, since they had already fought a grievance over "sexualization" issues. In 1971, two BC-based PWA attendants refused to wear the Stampeder cowboy costume which the airline had already introduced on its Vancouver to

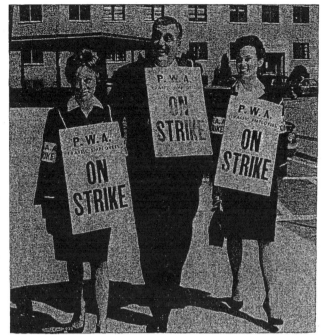

During a recent visit to Vancouver, CLC President Claude Jodoin walked the picket line with two members of the Canadian Air Line Flight Attendants' Association, on strike against Pacific Western Airlines for several months. From left: Jean Wheatley, Jodoin, and Bev. Dame.

Canadian Labour, July–August 1963 at 37

Calgary run. With a very short, fringed skirt and prominent red bloomers underneath, they argued it simply invited male groping. When an attendant was "grabbed and pawed" on a flight to the BC Interior, she refused to don the "red panties," resulting in charges of insubordination, her suspension, and a threat of dismissal. A grievance ensued which the union won on the basis that this was not the "standard uniform" noted in the attendants' job description. What is revealing about the grievance process is the strong feminist language union members used to make their case, and the Board's majority concurrence with their sentiments. One of the two grievors sent a letter to the Board, arguing the uniform was "degrading," and intended to send a clear message: "make a pass at me. I'm easy and will take on anybody. Putting women on display like this," she wrote, "negates the purpose of the Emergency demonstration" since attention is focused on their bodies, not on the procedures. The majority Board decision agreed the uniform was "demeaning" and reflected the "undue exploitation of the sex of the wearer," language that was quite different from earlier arbitrations endorsing the gender status quo.[66] This "red panty" grievance was the only well publicized one analogous to the "fly me" case in the US, but it reinforced PWA attendants' conviction that their employer was primarily concerned with selling their appearance.

This was at the core of CALFAA's argument in the 1975 pregnancy case. Because women were "laid off" when four months pregnant, the union persuaded the Crown to prosecute the PWA (a fairly rare occurrence) for violating the *Canada Labour Code* which prohibited dismissal for pregnancy or if the employee requested a maternity leave. This prohibition stood "notwithstanding any other law or any custom, contract or arrangement,"[67] but if contract provisions were more favourable, the *Labour Code* did not negate them.

CALFAA's test case involved Gail Anderson and Janet Asselstine, both with good work records and substantial service. Anderson claimed to have initially consulted the company doctor, who said her concerns about flying while pregnant were "groundless," though when testifying for the company, he later denied this statement. Justice Reed, the Provincial Court Judge, began by asking the women to assess their own physical and mental capabilities. Anderson admitted to some initial morning sickness but claimed she now had more "energy and stamina" than ever before, and both women insisted they could physically perform their jobs, including all emergency procedures, with Asselstine wryly adding that their "brainwashing" about these procedures would assume precedence in any crisis.[68] Stressing the "normalcy" of her condition, Asselstine told the Judge she had helped her husband build their carport, surely an indication that pregnancy had not rendered her fragile and weak. The Judge was also interested in their mental state of mind; indeed, many witnesses were asked if they thought a woman's emotional concern for the "unborn child" might result in her placing passengers' safety behind her own.

Other witnesses from the company and union then provided contradictory testimony over the terms of the contract and the *Labour Code*. The union contract chairman, Mrs. James, believed that the *Labour Code* provisions trumped the contract, which stipulated that women were required to go on "leave of absence without pay" after their fourth month. She also attempted to reinforce Anderson and Asselstine's testimony by arguing she herself could have safely flown while pregnant and that the question of "to fly or not to fly," should be an "individual choice."[69] The company manager, in contrast, insisted that women were not "laid off" but "got a leave of absence," though he conceded no federal aviation regulation prohibited pregnant flight attendants from working — and in fact, women pilots could fly while pregnant.

The Crown's case rested not only on women's physical and mental ability to work, but also on whether the *Labour Code* took precedence over the contract. The Crown lawyer was on showing that the company's claim to be concerned with safety actually disguised the fact that it was really preoccupied with women's appearance. Dr. Korn, an obstetrician and gynaecologist, and the Crown's only medical expert, described pregnancy as a "normal physiological state" that would not affect flight attendants' work capabilities. However, with only one expert witness in its corner, the Crown had considerable difficulty proving its appearance theory, particularly because company personnel knew better than to talk openly in court about the beauty imperative attached to the flight attendant's job. Still, one PWA manager's offhand comment to a reporter caught up with him in court: "as a young man" he asked the reporter (who then testified for the Crown), do you really want to be "waited on by an obviously pregnant attendant?" The Crown was able to push a couple of PWA executives to admit that "appearance and personality" were important to the job — but not to the pregnancy issue. The company doctor, when pressed, pointed out that in flight "service" might be hurt as men might be reluctant to "ask for help"[70] from a visibly pregnant attendant (presumably in a chivalrous attempt to not tax her). PWA executives stuck to their story about safety, despite the Crown's best efforts to reveal different motives.

PWA put considerable resources into the trial, calling a long parade of expert witnesses. If a courtroom observer had not been afraid of flying before the trial, she surely would have been after hearing the PWA case, which was built largely on safety issues, though secondarily on their rules constituting a valid "leave of absence." Medical and aviation experts testified for PWA as well as former stewardesses involved in major accidents. In the latter case, the company generously argued the "expert" designation should not be "confined to professional men," but extended to these women since they had valuable work experience. In an attempt to validate some women's knowledge, however, other women's knowledge — that of Anderson and Asselstine — was downplayed. The judge heard long descriptions of two horrific crashes from the survivor attendants, one in which only fifteen survivors made it out of the tail section of a burning plane, aided by the attendant who had to slip under her seat belt to get out, and another in which a dismembered plane landed upside down on treetops. Both former attendants unequivocally stated they would have been "physically and emotionally impeded" by pregnancy in these emergencies. Assessing all possibilities of movement in a plane during a crisis, the judge tried to imagine two attendants, both eight months pregnant, attempting to get by each other in a narrow aisle.[71] This image may have unsettled him, but supporters of the flight attendants later argued that some very large men would create the same problem.[72]

Under cross examination, these flight attendants who testified for PWA admitted that they held to "traditional" views on married working women, whom they believed should preferably be at home caring for their children. The Crown presented their views as proof of their ideological bias, but this argument was hardly enough to overcome the impressive number, variety, and prestige of those on the defence witness list. As well as doctors, the PWA produced aviation experts and pilots, including the head of the Canadian Airline Pilots Association (speaking for himself and the Association, a powerful voice), all of whom supported PWA's safety argument. Given the patriarchal organization of the airplane as workspace, pilots' sense of being justifiably "in charge" of their domain was clearly affronted by the PWA attendants' campaign to fly pregnant.[73] Another pilot, with the authoritative name Captain Cook, indicated he would not even take off if he had a flight crew member over four months pregnant; moreover, more than one pilot at the trial described incidents in which a pregnant flight attendant became "hysterical" during a flight emergency problem. They offered up dramatic portrayals of emergency problems in the air, including potentially fatal shear turbulence that could throw a plane up or down thousands of feet ("you almost lose control of the aircraft"), tear chairs out of their sockets, and throw flight attendants against the walls so hard that they were rendered "unconscious."[74]

As if this scare testimony was not enough, PWA produced a number of doctors, including their own company expert on health and aviation, all of whom confirmed that pregnant flight attendants were safety risks because of their girth, the possibility of miscarriage, the extra dangers of jet lag effect and fatigue, their inability to get immunizations for foreign travel, vein problems, swollen legs, and their emotional state of mind. This medical testimony was an eerie *déjà vu* of many earlier investigations of women's work which devolved into assessments of vulnerable bodies.[75] The flight attendants' physical inability to help passengers out of a disabled plan in an emergency weighed heavily in the defence case; the choice seemed to be between death in a fiery crash with pregnant attendants, or a chance at life with nonpregnant attendants. Who could possibly argue for the former? Even after the Crown had shown that job training involved a lot of time preparing cocktails and not nearly as much as PWA claimed on safety, this evidence could not counteract the powerful effect of this "dramatic"[76] safety evidence.

In finding for PWA, the judge reasoned that it had negotiated a contract "in good faith," and that it was not trying to sidestep the *Canada Labour Code*, but rather protect itself and its clientele by paying attention to safety issues.[77] Moreover, laying off women during pregnancy was not "tantamount to dismissal" but rather was "a conditional cessation of work." Since seniority was accrued and one was hired back in the same position after the birth, PWA had been able to argue this point persuasively. Nor did the judge accept the argument that PWA rules were shaped primarily by appearance issues (though he conceded attractive appearance was part of the job description). Perhaps most importantly, he rejected the view that the *Canada Labour Code* provided absolute protection against dismissal. Great emphasis was placed on the fact that women could not be dismissed "solely" for being pregnant. A long rumination on the legal meaning of the word "solely" ensued: if it denotes "determining cause" or "principal reason," as in other judgments, he reasoned, then the Crown had not proven its case.[78] Anderson and Asselstine were not "laid off" because they were pregnant, but because of "conditions which existed prior to the *Labour Code* and are composed of the peculiarities of air transportation which seem to be incompatible to a considerable extent with the physical and emotional problem of human reproduction."[79] It was a circular argument: they were not laid off only because they were pregnant, but because they were a safety problem, and they were a safety problem because they were pregnant.

It is hard to imagine that the judge was not subtly influenced by two things: disaster stories and scientific expert advice. Even someone who did not fear flying would have been scared after the terrifying disaster stories told and the immense influence of expert, scientific claims made by doctors and pilots must have been quite powerful. The latter buttressed long-standing perceptions of pregnancy as an "unnatural" condition that weakened women and destabilized their emotions: in the judge's words, reproduction was a *"problem"* for women.[80] Press reports also zeroed in on safety, repeating Judge Reed's fear that in an emergency there was "no evidence how a pregnant woman would react."[81] This unpredictability, in other words, might jeopardize the passengers' safety. The safety issue was so convincing that it had supporters in the government,[82] and labour rights advocates also gave it credence. The CLC's Shirley Carr wanted the Minister of Labour to consider a remedial solution since this judgement went against "the spirit" of the *Labour Code* protections. Women should be assured "security of income ... taking into account the substantive considerations of safety to the mother, the unborn child and the traveling public."[83] In other words, assuming safety *was* an issue, attendants should be allowed a longer paid benefit period. Within the bureaucracy, the Department of Labour convened an interdepartmental working group in 1975 to consider solutions to health-related maternity leave issues such as the "grounding of airline stewardesses," again relying on a medical expert to shape the new policy. Although solutions such as alternative employment or extra benefits were mentioned, the committee did not follow through.[84]

CALFAA was nothing if not persistent. In 1976, when the PWA case was ongoing, it had tried another tactic, using the BC *Human Rights Code* (the *Code*) to challenge the dismissal of a pregnant Canadian Pacific flight attendant in *Culley*.[85] The BC case was not even heard, however, since the company argued successfully that her employment was regulated by federal law.[86] In the PWA case, the Crown appealed by way of "trial *de novo*" before Catliff J., who after eleven days, also acquitted PWA. The contract and *Code* provisions exist "side by side" Judge Catliff said, providing "alternative benefits"[87] to pregnant women. Flight attendants clearly did not see the "alternative" benefits that many weeks without pay provided. According to one left-wing publication, this "out of touch" Surrey judge even "expressed his surprise that pregnant women were allowed UIC benefits!"[88] This decision did widen CALFAA's political support, as the Canadian Advisory Council on the Status of Women now voiced their support for CALFAA.[89]

The Crown's appeal of Judge Catliff's decision conceded that their case did not involve dismissal in the conventional use of the term, but the "mandatory nature" of the leaves made them "the same as layoffs."[90] The BC Court of Appeal disagreed. The three judges employed a somewhat different rationale, but nonetheless ended up with the same conclusion as the trial judge. One simply gave a rather vague post-modern comment about "layoffs" having "different meanings in different contexts," but the more substantial reasoning came from Judge Taggart, a ten-year veteran on the Appeal Court.[91] He emphasized that legislators had meant to draw a distinction between "layoff" or "dismiss" and "absence of leave for maternity" or "maternity leave," and that the *Code*'s reference to maternity leave corresponded to the word "leave" in the collective agreement. Ergo, there was no dismissal or layoff, simply a leave. Discussing the second issue, section 28 of the *Code*, dealing with "more favourable" choices, Taggart J. seconded Catliff J., who had conceded that the *Code* might well be more favourable than the contractual benefits, but did not then grant workers the right to choose between the two. Even if the *Code* is more favourable, he concluded, "it does not follow" that the contractual terms are "void."[92] This seemed to press against the spirit of the *Code*, which was liberally offering women "the better" of two options. Not so, according to Catliff J. and the other appeal judges.[93]

However, based on Judge Catliff's use of the term "alternative" options, another legal tactic was then employed: an appeal for declaratory relief, heard by the Supreme Court of BC in 1979.[94] Explaining this new strategy to the press, the union's lawyer never mentioned the appearance/safety debate and he took the heat off the company, claiming there was no desire to "penalize" PWA.[95] Rather, CALFAA's counsel sought declarations from the court that flight attendants were entitled to use *either* the *Labour Code* or contract provisions, whichever they preferred, and that pregnant flight attendants were entitled under the *Labour Code* to continue working up until the date of their confinement should they choose, *not withstanding* other agreements. Judge Locke rejected the union argument that a woman should be able to choose the more favourable "alternative," as well as the corollary that to deny this choice contravened the *Code*. Although he acknowledged the ingenious argument, he also noted that it was simply a way to circumvent the appeal decision, so he denied the request for declaratory relief.[96]

Both of these decisions suggest a narrow reading of workers' rights that could be particularly harmful for more marginalized workers, or those bargaining in bad economic times. If a union could establish the right to choose the more favourable terms laid out in either a statute or a contract, they might be able to stave off the erosion of contracts or secure slightly better working conditions. The relationship between statutes and arbitration, and whether arbitrators had the authority to interpret statutes, was already a source of legal contention, but even if the courts had the upper hand in interpreting statutes, this did not mean that workers would benefit.[97]

CALFAA made one last attempt to appeal the denial of declaratory relief. The crux of this final appeal rested on how restrictive or flexible the *Labour Code* was. Did the *Code* entitle women *only* to a leave of absence, or did it, more expansively, provide an entitlement to continue working if this was the woman's choice? At the Court of Appeal, Judge Seaton's answer was emphatically "only the former." The term "more *favourable*," he said, does not mean "that which is *preferred* by the worker."[98] (Who then, was to decide what was favourable?). While granting the worker could not be forced to take any leave at all dictated by the employer, limitations could be decided "in the collective agreement,"[99] which of course was a limiting factor for the flight attendants. His reasoning came down even more decisively on the side of employer privileges, as he did not see the *Code* as limiting "the employer's right to enforce a leave of absence." Safety was no longer the central issue in this case: it was now used more as an example of why various employers had the right to limit workers' choices. The second judge, Carrothers J.A., rubber stamped Judge Seaton's view, while Judge Hutcheon went back to points made in the very first case. While he agreed that there were some "limitations" on employers' rights to enforce leaves, he went on to emphasize employers' entitlement to make decisions about women's health. When a woman could not do her job because of a pregnancy, the employer could "enforce a leave."[100] Apparently, it was the employer who decided when she could perform properly, unless the contract offered an alternative.[101]

This BC Court of Appeal ruling came down in 1981 and by that time a new contract with PWA had been signed that included advances on the pregnancy issue. There was still some measure of mandatory maternity leave, but women were allowed to work longer provided they produced a doctor's note every two weeks to ascertain they could perform their jobs — a provision that CALFAA had earlier fought as an invasion of privacy and a contract violation.[102] The company could place them on leave at any time, but it was then required to provide some monetary aid until the employee qualified for UI. Within a few years, other legal reforms further transformed the situation. In the wake of pressures from below, including feminist mobilizations, the *Canadian Human Rights Code* was amended in 1985 to prohibit discrimination based on pregnancy; this, along with changes to the *Labour Code* in 1985 finally gave attendants the right to mount effective challenges to "no fly" policies for pregnant attendants. [103] The shift in the social and legal climate was articulated a few years later in *Brooks v. Canada Safeway*,[104] the significant Supreme Court decision that overturned *Bliss*. Not only did the court categorically reject the Supreme Court's earlier claim in *Bliss* that pregnant women were limited "not by legislation but by nature,"[105] but it asserted clearly that pregnancy discrimination was a example of sex discrimination, and it stressed the social benefit of childbearing to society, with the corollary need to protect the equality of pregnant working women by preventing them from being penalized by discrimination.

If the airlines truly believed flight attendants were a serious risk to everyone's safety, they might have responded to these new events and rulings by providing full maternity benefits over a longer period of time, but they did not. It is possible they too had come to change their minds, but their apparent abandonment of the safety issue simply confirmed the flight attendants' conviction that the pregnancy case always had more to do with their appearance than with women's inability to fly pregnant and keep the passengers safe.

Discussion

AS MORE MARRIED WOMEN participated in the labour force in the post-war period, they began to employ multiple tactics, both formal and informal, to expand their maternity rights. Despite the apathy or opposition voiced by some male union members, unionized women pressed their leadership to use labour law and the courts to secure women's right not to be discriminated against because of pregnancy, to determine their own physical abilities relating to work and childbirth, and to gain full access to state-provided maternity benefits. CALFAA's strategy of simultaneously pursuing political-legal mobilization and contract changes produced some concrete and ideological benefits for these women workers, but this is not to say that this strategy is successful by its very nature: the historical and social context mattered a great deal. Indeed, Chief Justice Brian Dickson justified the path-breaking *Brooks*[106] decision by stating that changing social and economic circumstances — such as increasing numbers of women combining paid work and motherhood — must be met with new legal perspectives and court decisions. Another reason for changes in the prevailing legal discourse was surely the circulation of new feminist ideas about women's paid work. CALFAA's struggle to abolish pregnancy discrimination reflected, and was encouraged by, an upsurge in union organizing in the service sector, in part inspired by feminist ideas[107] and a reinvigorated women's movement in the 1960s and 1970s.[108]

In order to secure new maternity rights for women, the union employed an equal rights discourse, challenging prevailing views of an innately "unpredictable" female body and confronting an ideology of feminine physical incapacity, both of which feminists believed were grounded in socialization, not nature. In the 1950s and 1960s, biological, naturalized notions of femaleness and motherhood were still quite powerful, and they were linked to the remnants of a much older, "separate spheres" ideology that equated pregnancy and maternity with the "private" and domestic familial sphere. It was precisely these antiquated ideas, many women's organizations and unions told the RCSW, that had to be challenged. In order to gain access to occupations long denied to them so as to deconstruct an ideology of physical and emotional fragility, feminists focused on de-emphasizing bodily difference and stressing their equal, indeed, same physical capabilities as men.

Stressing women's right to know and control their own bodies also challenged the expert medical opinion that had long prevailed in discussions about maternity leave and which was so important in the 1975 case. Feminists were developing a critique of medicine that questioned its absolute objectivity and stressed instead the social, historical, and gendered construction of women's bodies in medical discourses. The variability of airlines' medical objections to pregnant attendants could only reinforce this critique: across North America, airlines came up with different "danger zones" of pregnancy, some claiming women could not possibly work in the first trimester, some in the last trimester, some pointing to nausea, others to unstable minds, and so on. No wonder the expert testimony presented by PWA at the CALFAA trial seemed like an *ex-post facto* justification for very different motives, namely the marketing of women's single, sexy, slim, and available bodies — especially when the union had already been fighting precisely this problem within PWA.

Women's objections to the claim that they could not judge their ability to "fly safe" was inseparable from their protests about the objectification and sexualization of their bodies. It is certainly possible that pilots and airlines genuinely believed the safety argument — even some attendants endorsed the notion that they could not cope with emergencies while they were pregnant. But "aesthetic concerns and moral qualms" were also involved. As Lucinda Finley suggests, society was uneasy and ambivalent about the pregnant body, symbolizing as it did one form of sexuality, but also eliciting "fear, discomfort, protective impulses, even disgust" from others who had not experienced pregnancy.[109] The problem, one way or the other, was primarily in the eye of the beholder. The flight attendants behind this battle were also well aware that in challenging ideas about an essential, natural female body, they were challenging the broader ideology that placed married women and mothers in their "proper" sphere, the home.[110] The idea that all women can easily become, by virtue of conception, unpredictable workers, not only sustains pregnancy prohibitions, it also creates much broader restrictions on women's wage work. As long as pregnancy was seen as both enfeebling and as women's primary social role, the notion that women must choose between motherhood and work remained strong. This modern version of separate spheres ideology justified and encouraged a male breadwinner hierarchy of wages, separate seniority lists, and fewer opportunities for women's advancement, because these were ultimately seen as contradictions to their natural maternal/childbearing roles. No wonder then, that some feminists were so wary of protective legislation, seeing the only political strategy possible as one equating men and women's health protections as similar, if not identical.

Understanding why a certain political strategy is assumed at one time, however, does not mean we should not critically assess the long-term implications. The approach of CALFAA in the 1970s was one which stressed equality over difference, equating the latter with the pernicious past of state and employer protectionism. However, women could not so easily deconstruct the dichotomy between the two, since the realities (or limitations) of labour law and legal strategies often pressed women into difficult choices, neither of which offered ideal solutions to the actual health hazards some encountered. As Judy Fudge argues, both sides of the coin — difference and equality, or protectionism versus human rights approaches — had limitations; there was no easy way to reconcile the choices women and unions had to make.[111] The pregnant body has been, and remains, a difficult dilemma for feminist legal discourse. Equality for pregnant women, some feminists continue to argue, will not emerge from stressing sameness with men, from comparing pregnancy with either disability or male health problems.[112] It is a "unique condition"[113] that might be better recognized as such within an equality framework. The problem is not simply with "difference" *per se*, but who controls its definition, how, and why, is a question linked directly to structural and ideological power.[114] For others, the key has become women's absolute control, *contra* the state, over their pregnant bodies.[115] Of course, it is difficult to combine a commitment to women's full equality and to their "unique" health needs unless we are situated in a somewhat ideal nation with social, welfare, and health regimes that stress the benefit of childbearing for society as a whole, that offer universal benefits and rights to pregnant women, and that do not denigrate child care and parenting. Most of us don't live there.

CALFAA's challenge to employer-controlled, sexualized constructions of their bodies was a success story of the 1970s and 1980s: women were offered an opportunity to dispel images of the weakened pregnant body and their ability to continue working until they collected UI enhanced their economic choices. Whether these court battles encouraged a critique of the economic imperatives of capitalism, as one writer has suggested, is more doubtful.[116]

As the CALFAA case wound its way through the courts, the safety/body argument of the employer faded from view, and new arguments concerning workers' rights to the best possible protection — state legislation or negotiated contract — came to the fore. The court decisions that did not allow workers to choose the better alternative not only affected flight attendants: they potentially narrowed all workers' rights. This trade-off — of better maternity rights for women but weaker worker protection in general — might be seen as highly symbolic of the 1980s. During this period, better educated, more privileged women workers were making some economic gains, but this was not true of all women workers and the gains of some women were visible in part because the wages of working-class males were falling behind. In other words, the gains of feminism were differentially enjoyed according to class. Lending weight to this argument are recent feminist critiques of the supposedly egalitarian reform of parental leave, introduced in the 1990s. Parental leave, these critics argue, has benefited some families, but left other women, based on their occupation, class, and family form, even further down the economic ladder, raising the question of how "feminist" these reforms really were. Economic deregulation, job losses, and an assault on trade union freedoms also created a new labour relations context in the airline industry by the late 1980s. Attendants could "fly pregnant" but they now had to worry about keeping their jobs and not becoming another example of contingent labour. This is not to say that CALFAA's earlier strategy of legal mobilization to secure both enhanced contract and human rights protections was not a necessary and useful endeavour. It is, however, a reminder that such incremental gains are not the final antidote to women workers' subordination in the workforce.

Notes

1   Ann Porter, *Gendered States: Women, Unemployment Insurance, and the Political Economy of the Welfare State in Canada, 1945–97* (Toronto: University of Toronto Press, 2003) at 136 [Porter].

2   There are technically problems with this term, as it leaves out women who were divorced, widowed, common law, etc. Since it was used at the time as a marker of women who were not single and sometimes had dependents, I employ it as well, on the understanding that it encompasses these other categories of women.

3   Undoubtedly, the public debate was also framed by class and race: women who were poor, racialized, and new immigrants historically had high labour force participation rates but new attention was focused on the issue when white working-class and middle-class women increasingly worked for pay as well.

4   On the post-war settlement, sometimes also referred to as the Fordist accord, see Peter McInnis, *Harnessing Labour Confrontation: Shaping the Postwar Settlement in Canada* (Toronto: University of Toronto Press, 1998).

5   *Bliss v. Attorney General of Canada*, [1979] 1 SCR 183. For the argument about public pressure, see Leslie Pal & F.L. Morton, "*Bliss v. Attorney General of Canada*: From Legal Defeat to Political Victory" (1986) 24:1 Osgoode Hall L.J. 141.

6   Porter, above note 1.

7   It also differs from many other labour cases involving reproductive health issues as these focused on the effect of chemicals, etc. on women and the fetus. Labour Canada, *The Selective Protection of Canadian Women* (Ottawa, 1989) at 43.

8   National Archives Canada (NAC), Royal Commission on the Status of Women RG 33-89 (RCSW), vol. 18, CALFAA brief 441.

9   *Canada Labour Code*, R.S.C. 1970, c. L-1.

10 For an early discussion of the term, see Ruth Milkman, "Women's History and the *Sears* Case" (Summer 1986) 12 Feminist Studies 375–400. Later writings downplayed dichotomies; see, for example, Gisela Bock, ed., *Beyond Equality and Difference: Citizenship, Feminist Politics, and Female Subjectivity* (New York: Routledge, 1992). For discussions of the maternity rights issue in the US, see Karen Maschke, *Litigation, Courts, and Women Workers* (New York: Praeger, 1989); Lise Vogel, *Mothers on the Job: Maternity Policy in the U.S. Workplace* (New Brunswick, NJ: Rutgers University Press, 1993); Nadine Taub & Wendy Willams, "Will Equality Require More Than Assimilation, Accommodation or Separation From The Existing Social Structure?" (1984–85) 37:4 Rutgers L. Rev. 825–44; Mark Evan Edwards, "Pregnancy Discrimination Litigation: Legal Erosion of Capitalist Ideology Under Equal Employment Opportunity Law" (September 1996) 75:1 Social Forces 247–69; and on flight attendant cases, Pamela Whiteside, "Flight Attendant Weight Policies: a Title VII Wrong Without a Remedy" (1990) 64 S. Cal. L. Rev. 1–50. For Canadian discussion, see Judy Fudge, "Rungs on the Labour Law Ladder: Using Gender to Challenge Hierarchy" (1996) 60 Sask. L. Rev. 237–63. On the earlier period, Ulla Wikander, Alice Kessler-Harris, & Jane Lewis, eds., *Protecting Women: Labor Legislation in Europe, the US and Australia, 1880–1920* (Urbana: University of Illinois, 1995).

11 Judy Fudge, "From Segregation to Privatization: Equality, the Law, and Women Public Servants, 1908–2000" in Brenda Cossman & Judy Fudge, eds., *Privatization, Law and the Challenge to Feminism* (Toronto: University of Toronto Press, 2002) at 86–127.

12 Nitya Iyer, "Some Mothers are Better Than Others: A Re-examination of Maternity Benefits," in Susan B. Boyd, ed., *Challenging the Public Private Divide: Feminism, Law and Public Policy* (Toronto: University of Toronto Press, 1997) at 168–94; Lene Madsen, "Citizen, Workers, Mother: Canadian Women's Claims to Parental Leave and Childcare" (2002) 19 Can. J. Fam. L. 11–74; Gillian Calder, "Recent Changes to the Maternity and Parental Leave Benefits Regime, A Case Study: The Impact of Globalization on the Delivery of Social Programs in Canada" (2003) 15:2 C.J.W.L. 342–66.

13 By maternity rights, I mean the broad array of policies regarding leaves, benefits, seniority rights, and so on relating to both the pregnancy and postnatal leaves.

14 G.A. Johnson, *The International Labour Organization: Its Work for Social and Economic Progress* (London: Europa Publications, 1970) at 93. Conventions were "obligation-creating instruments" while recommendations only provided "guidance." But conventions had to be ratified by the home government in order to be binding.

15 Leah Vosko, *Temporary Work: The Gendered Rise of a Precarious Employment Relationship* (Toronto: University of Toronto Press, 2000) at 14–15.

16 Pamela Sugiman, *Labour's Dilemma: The Gender Politics of Auto Workers in Canada, 1937–79* (Toronto: University of Toronto Press, 1994) at 128–34.

17 *Unemployment Insurance Act*, S.C. 1970–71 c. 48. In fact, Gallup polls in 1970s found the majority supported legislated maternity leaves. Women's Bureau, Department of Labour, *Canadian Attitudes Towards Women: Thirty Years of Change* (Ottawa, 1984) Table 6 and 51.

18 Porter, above note 1. These findings suggest that maternity leave was far from a state-sponsored reform. For discussion on grievance files see Joan Sangster, *Transforming Labour: Women and Work in the Post-World War II Period* (Toronto: University of Toronto Press, 2010), and for some oral history evidence see Joan Sangster, "Doing Two Jobs: The Wage-Earning Mother, 1945–70," in Joy Parr, ed., *A Diversity of Women: Ontario, 1945–80* (Toronto: University of Toronto Press, 1995) at 98–134. The LAC was compiled by the Central Ontario Industrial Relations Institute, an employer group. Some later cases had employer "footnotes" that betrayed this bias, but most of these cases simply repeated the legal judgement. I looked at all discharge cases in vol. 1 to 20 (about 1948 to 1969) to ascertain the nature of women's discharge grievances. Just over half were cases dealing with maternity and pregnancy.

19 Granted, the arbitration system only served unionized women, who arguably had a firmer sense of their workplace rights, and arbitrated grievances were a very small proportion of grievances fought. But key decisions had an ideological "trickle down" effect on the workplace.

20 Archives of Ontario (AO), Dept of Labour RG 7, Women's Bureau (WB), Series VIII, Box 1, Maternity Leave file, "What is Maternity Leave?" 10.

21 AO, RG 7, WB, Series VIII, Box 1, "Maternity Leave" file, Deputy Minister of Labour in Ontario to Deputy Minister of Labour in Ottawa, 4 November 1964. Even in the

federal Women's Bureau, it was initially suggested that issues such as seniority, in relation to maternity, were management prerogatives.

22 Lucinda Finley, "Transcending Equality Theory: A Way Out of the Maternity and the Workplace Debate" (1986) 86:6 Colum. L. Rev. 1118 at 1131.

23 *UAW and Essco Stamping Products Ltd*, (1957) LAC 8, 26.

24 *Ibid.*

25 AO, above note 20 at 7. Similarly, in the 1950s, Ann Porter found women's UI claims depended on whether they were too pregnant in appearance to be hired by an employer, especially if they were visible to the public. In UI cases, this began to change in the 1960s.

26 NAC, RCSW, vol. 11, Brief 27, Saskatchewan Jaycettes. On the Royal Commission's efforts to explore and report on means of enhancing gender equality, see Jane Arscott, "Twenty-Five Years and Sixty-Five Minutes after The Royal Commission on the Status of Women" (Spring 1995) 11 International Review of Canadian Studies 35–58; Annis May Timpson, "Royal Commissions As Sites of Resistance: Women's Challenges on Child Care in the Royal Commission on the Status of Women" (Fall 1999) 20 International Review of Canadian Studies 1–24; Caroline Andrew & Sheila Rogers, eds., *Women and the Canadian State* (Montreal: McGill Queens University Press, 1997).

27 NAC, RCSW, Vol. 11, Brief 52, Anglican Church of Canada.

28 NAC, RCSW, Vol. 14, Brief 240, Mrs Raya Lonquist.

29 Porter, above note 1 at 83.

30 Canada, Department of Labour, WB, *Maternity Leave in Canada* (Ottawa, 1967). See also NAC, RG 27, WB, vol. 1904, 38-11-3-4 C "Maternity Leave Survey" and vol. 4159, file 722-4-2, pts 1-3 for Working Committee on Maternity Leave.

31 NAC, WB, Int. Box 16, file 38-11-6-3.

32 Alena Heitlinger, *Women's Equality, Demography and Public Policies* (London: St. Martin's Press, 1993) at 175.

33 In fact, the new head of the WB, Sylva Gelber, was worried about maternity benefits that did not come out of a fund for "disability" that both men and women could draw on. See also Porter, above note 1 at 87.

34 The RCSW suggested legislation preventing dismissal of an "employee on any grounds during the maternity leave to which she is entitled." RCSW, *The Status of Women in Canada* (Ottawa, 1970) at 86–87.

35 Leslie Pal, "Maternity Benefits and Unemployment Insurance: A Question of Faulty Policy Design" (1985) XI Canadian Public Policy 551–60.

36 N. Jill Newby, *The Sky's the Limit: the Story of the Canadian Air Line Flight Attendants Association* (Vancouver: CAFAA, 1986) at 10.

37 *Ibid.* at 11.

38 The Board decision rejected two units on the basis that "they were not the appropriate ones for collective bargaining" and recommended the appropriate unit would include all of "flight attendants, purer-stewards, flight steward and air line stewardesses." *Labour Gazette* (March 1948) at 173.

39 Newby, above note 36. This is Newby's claim, but the difference with the US was minor since US flight attendants essentially organized at the same time. See Geor-

gina Nielsen, *From Sky Girl to Flight Attendant: Women and the Making of Union* (Ithaca: Cornell University Press, 1982).

40 John Condit, *Wings Over the West: Russ Baker and the Rise of Pacific Western Airlines* (Vancouver: Harbour Publishing, 1984) at 4.

41 NAC, RG 27, Dept of Labour file 760-856-62, clipping, "Girls Unpaid for Delays," *Vancouver Sun* (n.d).

42 *Industrial Relations Investigation Act*, S.C. 1948, c. 54. This Act essentially carried on the spirit of the *Industrial Disputes Investigation Act*, first passed in 1907, which required a public investigation of labour disputes under federal jurisdiction by a third party.

43 NAC, RG 27, file 760–856-62, Department of Labour Memo re Pacific Western Airlines Ltd. from G. R. Currie, 25 Feb 1963, and telegram to Bernard Wilson, Director of Industrial Relations in the Department. See also "Report of Board in Dispute between Pacific Western Airlines and Canadian Air Lines Flight Attendants' Association" (March 1963) *Labour Gazette* 229–30.

44 "PWA Fires Stewardesses in Walkout" *Vancouver Sun* (1 March 1963); "Strike at PWA Involves Three Unions" *Globe and Mail* (21 November 1963).

45 "The federal Labour Board's only comment was that the Pacific Western Airlines Flight Attendants Association was not, at the time of its application, an operating trade union within the meaning of the Act" (December 1963) *Labour Gazette* 1109.

46 "3 Striking PWA Agents Evicted" *Vancouver Sun* (4 March 1963).

47 Condit, above note 40 at 4.

48 It was returned to the private sector in 1983. The Conservative government wanted to use the airline to ensure the province's northern development. This foray into state ownership by politicians committed to the "free" market did not go uncriticized.

49 NAC, Canadian Labour Congress Papers (CLC) MG 28 I103, Reel H238, In the Matter of an Arbitration between Pacific Western Airlines Ltd. and Canadian Air Line Flight Attendants Association and Deanne Konderat, 2.

50 *Ibid.* at 7–8.

51 NAC, CLC Papers, Bob Smeal to Hon. Alan J. MacEachen, 16 June, 1965; B.C. Federation of Labour to Claude Jodoin, 17 June, 1965; News from B.C. Federation of Labour, 16 June, 1966.

52 Canada, *Hansard*, Ernie Winch, 18 June, 1965, 2601 and Alan MacEachen, 28 June, 1965, 2932-33.

53 CP Air also admitted it did not hire "divorced or widowed" women, though Air Canada did. "Travel-Log: Next Year You Could be a Stewardess?" *Chatelaine* (October 1972) at 24–25. The ban on divorcees can only be seen as intensely moralistic, an attempt to prop up the desired image of the single, sexually available young woman.

54 NAC, CLC Papers, reel H 284, News from the BC Federation, 16 June, 1966.

55 *Chatelaine*, above note 53 at 24–25.

56 "Smeal was suspended after sixteen years with the union, he says because of the issue of equal rights for women, doing away with separate seniority lists": NAC, CLC, vol. 435, file 17-3, Ed Johnston to Joe Morris, Pres. CLC, 3 Feb. 1976.

57 NAC, CLC, Ed Johnston, "Report on the Manner in which Executive Officers of CALFA suspended Bob Smeal and Relevant Documentation," 8 Sept. 1976, 1, 5.

58 Kathleen Barry, *Femininity in Flight: A History of Flight Attendants* (Durham: Duke University Press, 2007). See also Eileen Boris, "Desirable Dress: Rosies, Sky Girls and the Politics of Appearance," (Spring 2006) 69 International Labor and Working Class History 123–42; Dorothy Sue Cobble, "A Spontaneous Loss of Enthusiasm: Workplace Feminism and the Transformation of Women's Service Industry Jobs in the 1970s," (Fall 1999) 56 International Labor and Working Class History 23–44.

59 For this rather unlikely plot, see Betty Beaty, *Maiden Flight* (Winnipeg: Harlequin Books, 1963), and on the theme of independence, Jane Blackmore, *Flight Into Love* (New York: Paperback Library, 1964).

60 Arlie Hochschild coined the term emotional labour in *The Managed Heart: Commercialization of Human Feeling* (Berkeley: University of California Press, 1983). On aesthetic labour, see Anne Witz, Chris Wsarhurst, & Dennis Nickson, "The Labour of Aesthetics and the Aesthetics of Organization" (2003) 10:1 Organization 33–54. This term refers less to emotional alienation than to the performance of femininity and the creation of a particular physical "look." See also Lisa Adkins & Celia Lury, "The Labour of Identity: Performing Identities, Performing Economies" (November 1999) 28:4 Economy and Society 598–614.

61 The literature is quite extensive. Two examples are Melissa Tyler & P. Abbott, "Chocs Away: Weight Watching in the Contemporary Airline Industry" (August 1998) 32:3 Sociology 433–50, and S. Taylor & Melissa Tyler, "Emotional Labour and Sexual Difference in the Airline Industry" (1998) 14:1 Employment and Society 77–95.

62 There were some differences in airline strategies based on the owner, the nation involved, competition issues, and history. In the immediate post-war period, for instance, Albert Mills argues that the role was "de-sexualized" in Britain, and even in the 1960s, sexualization was more apparent in US airlines: Albert Mills, *Sex, Strategy and the Stratosphere: Airlines and the Gendering of Organizational Culture* (London: Palgrave, 2006) at 133. One reason why sexualization may have been more prevalent in the US was the greater number of airlines competing for business, with the attendants part of the "product" being sold.

63 *Chatelaine*, above note 53 at 24–25.

64 NAC, RCSW, Submission to the RCSW by the CALFAA, c 4882.

65 NAC, RCSW, vol. 43, clipping, *Southeasterner Times* (9 October 1968).

66 *Vancouver Sun* (18 December 1971). There seems to be no official record of the arbitration. It is discussed in Newby, above note 36, and author Jill Newby only cites who was on the Board. It is interesting that both the union history and the papers at the time spoke of harassment by miners and loggers who were the clientele on this flight. One suspects that the image of the "rough" blue collar male worker was being invoked, though there is no evidence that men in suits were any less prone to harass.

67 *Canada Labour Code*, R.S.C. 1970, c. L-1, ss. 59.4 and 28(1) quoted in *R. v. Pacific Western Ltd.*, [1975] B.C. J. No. 58 at 2 [*Pacific Western*].

68 *Pacific Western, ibid.* at 4.

69　*Ibid.*

70　*Ibid.* at 11.

71　*Ibid.* at 10.

72　*Canadian Dimension* mocked this concern with women's bodies by pointing out that overweight pilots were not seen as threats to safety, and that the average seven-month pregnant stewardess was equal in girth to an average forty-four year old man. "Stewardesses Fight Sexism" *Canadian Dimension* (September 1977) 10.

73　Mills, above note 62.

74　*Pacific Western*, above note 67 at 15.

75　Joan Sangster, "The Bell Telephone Strike of 1907: Organizing Women Workers" 3 (1978) Labour/Le Travailleur 109–30.

76　*Pacific Western*, above note 67 at 7. They were dramatic by Reed J.'s own admission.

77　*Ibid.* Justice Reed did not, however, place significant emphasis on the safety of the fetus outweighing other safety considerations.

78　*Ibid.* at 20.

79　*Ibid.*

80　*Ibid.* [emphasis added.]. Note that this judge and others for the defence claimed the physical effects of pregnancy became "more pronounced" — some said far more difficult — after the fourth month. Since morning sickness and risk of miscarriage were more likely in the first three months, it does lead one to believe CALFAA's claim that it was a woman's pregnant figure that was a problem or PWA.

81　"PWA Didn't Violate Federal Labour Code by Dropping Pregnant Stewardesses: Judge" *Globe and Mail* (10 July 1975) 9.

82　In response to pressure from the employers, a high-ranking Transport Canada bureaucrat proposed a new federal "air regulation" which would prohibit attendants from flying after thirteen weeks. Public pressure led to its withdrawal. Above note 36 at 62; see also "Need for Vigilance Cited" *Toronto Star* (1 February 1975) 15.

83　NAC, CLC papers, vol. 435, file 17-5, Shirley Carr and Don Lee to Joe Morris, 1 August 1975.

84　NAC, RG 27, WB, Working Party on Maternity Leave, file 722-4-11. The file ended in 1976 with no clear resolution.

85　*Culley (Re) In The Matter of the Human Rights Code of British Columbia,* [1976] B.C.J. No. 46.

86　*Ibid.*

87　*C.A.L.F.A.A. v. Pacific Western Airlines Ltd.* (1979), 105 D.L.R. (3d) 477 at para 12.

88　*Canadian Dimension*, above note 72.

89　*Ibid.*

90　*R. v. Pacific Western Airlines Ltd.,* [1977] B.C.J. No. 800, 4.

91　*Ibid.*, Taggart J. at para 11. John Taggart was described as a "solid counsel but a born judge" in his obituary. *The Advocate* (January 2004) 129. He was part of the majority judgment in the appeal of *Delgamuukw* (1993). Dara Culhane, *The Pleasure of the Crown: Anthropology, Law and First Nations* (Vancouver: Talonbooks, 1998) at 328–29.

92　*Ibid.* at para 15.

93 *Ibid.* Justice Catliff had implicitly acknowledged the leaves were "involuntary" for the women yet this did not result in him accepting the Crown's argument they were "mandatory" and therefore akin to dismissals.

94 Under the *Federal Courts Act* R.S.C. 1970 (2nd Supp.), c. 10, as a means of an "extraordinary" remedy one could ask a federal court to provide declaratory relief from the decision of a commission or tribunal.

95 Declaratory relief was first mentioned when the case was lost in 1977. "Appeal Planned to High Court on Stewardesses" *Globe and Mail* (4 November 1977) 13.

96 Quoted in *Canadian Airline Flight Attendants' Association v. Pacific Western Airlines* (1979), 105 DLR (3d) 479.

97 For example, see discussion of who can interpret a statute in Supreme Court of Canada in *McLeod et al. v. Egan et al.*, [1975] 1 SCR 517.

98 *Canadian Air Line Flight Attendants' Association v. Pacific Western Airline Ltd.* (1981), 124 DLR (3d) 688.

99 *Ibid.* at 5–6.

100 *Ibid.* at 10.

101 *Ibid.* He rightfully pointed out that the new contract offered some guidance (the doctor's certificates) on this issue.

102 *Canadian Dimension*, above note 72.

103 Canadian flight attendants did not have the same state machinery, namely Title VII, that American unions could draw on, but the Canadian strategy of using the courts to challenge airlines' marriage and pregnancy prohibitions was similar to some US battles. However, the different organization of the industry, state welfare and health regimes, and labour law meant these struggles took on a distinct form south of the 49th parallel. For a review of US cases see Whiteside, above note 10.

104 *Brooks v. Canada Safeway Ltd.*, [1989] 1 SCR 1219.

105 *Ibid.* at 1247.

106 *Brooks*, above note 104.

107 On the US see Cobble, above note 58. An excellent example in Canada is the Service, Office and Retail Workers Union of Canada (SORWUC). See also Bank Book Collective, *An Account to Settle: The Story of the United Bank Workers (SORWUC)* (Vancouver: Press Gang, 1979).

108 Some service organizations like SORWUC were influenced by socialist feminist ideas. On the latter, see Nancy Adamson, Linda Briskin, & Margaret McPhail, *Feminist Organizing for Change: The Contemporary Women's Movement in Canada* (Toronto: Oxford University Press, 1988).

109 Finley, above note 22 at 1134.

110 *Ibid.* at 1120.

111 Fudge, above note 10 at 237.

112 Ellen E. Hodgson, "Pregnancy as a Disability" (1993) 1 Health Law Journal 119–45.

113 Wendy Chavkin, "Walking a Tightrope: Pregnancy, Parenting and Work" in Wendy Chavkin, ed., *Double Exposure: Women's Health Hazards on the Job and at Home* (New York: Monthly Review Press, 1984) 196 at 202.

114 Ava Baron, "Feminist Legal Strategies: the Power of Difference" in Myra Marx Ferree & Beth Hess, eds., *Analyzing Gender: Perspectives from the Social Sciences* (Beverly Hills: Sage, 1987) at 474–503.

115 Of course, more recent writing is concerned with debates that have emerged about protection of the fetus. See Julie Hanigsberg, "Power and Procreation: State Interference in Pregnancy" (1991) 23:1 Ottawa L. Rev. 35.

116 Edwards, above note 10.

Challenging Norms and Creating Precedents: The Tale of a Woman Firefighter in the Forests of British Columbia

Judy Fudge and Hester Lessard[1]

ON 9 SEPTEMBER 1999, the Supreme Court of Canada rendered its decision in *British Columbia v. BCGSEU (Meiorin)*.[2] The case arose out of the dismissal of Tawney Meiorin from a British Columbia forest firefighting crew on the grounds of her repeated failure of the running component of a physical fitness test imposed as a job qualification by her employer. The Court found unanimously, in a decision by Justice Beverley McLachlin, who later was to become the first woman appointed as Chief Justice of the Supreme Court of Canada, that the test Meiorin had failed discriminated against her on the basis of sex. The Supreme Court of Canada's decision was regarded as groundbreaking for several reasons. It was heralded as an important sex equality victory, especially for women working in male-dominated occupations. As Meiorin commented at the time of the decision, "I did a dance right on the spot. My twenty-pound chainsaw felt like two pounds."[3] The case also radically revised the doctrinal structure of human rights law in a manner that aspired to extend the reach of human rights protections for workers. More generally, it was viewed as the Court's most emphatic and clear endorsement of a substantive approach to discrimination and equality cases that recognizes that equality is more than treating like cases alike (formal equality) and, thus, requires attention to how social norms, social practices, and institutions create and reinforce advantage and disadvantage. Finally, the Court's aim of providing more effective legal protection from discrimination resulted in real gains for workers, particularly for those with disabilities.

Tawney Meiorin was certainly not the first woman to find herself dismissed from work because of her inability to meet ostensibly neutral job requirements in occupations historically performed by men. What lay behind her victory at this particular moment? The prior caselaw was complex and uncertain. However, the need to simplify and to rationalize the caselaw alone does not explain the strong language McLachlin J. used to reject established human rights jurisprudence, namely that it "may serve to entrench the male norm as the 'mainstream' into which women must integrate."[4] A closer examination of the case not only illuminates the complexity of the converging factors that propelled the *Meiorin* litigation forward but also offers a more qualified understanding of the decision's importance as a precedent.

This paper is divided into four main parts. In the first part, we trace the nature of the British Columbia government's involvement in wildland firefighting and its investment in establishing its right as an employer to impose physical fitness tests on employees in the sector. In the second part, we turn to Tawney Meiorin's story. Here we delve into the history of her involvement in this area of work and the events leading to her termination. The third part focuses on the litigation, starting with Meiorin's grievance under the collective agreement and following with the expansion of the legal action to include intervenors and the case's increasing prominence as it worked its way toward the Supreme Court of Canada. The fourth part places the Supreme Court's decision in the broader context of its equality and discrimination jurisprudence.

Wildland Fires and Physical Fitness Tests

NINETY PERCENT OF THE forests in British Columbia are on Crown land. Since the late 1970s, the British Columbia Forest Service, which is part of the provincial Ministry of Forests, has operated an extensive fire suppression program, which provides training for firefighters. In addition to directly hiring employees to fight fires, the BC Forest Service hires private contractors to provide forest firefighting crews. As of 1978, the major objective of the fire control program of the BC Forest Service is "to minimize the total costs plus damage through the operational objectives of controlling all fires prior to 10 AM on the day following discovery."[5] Remote sensing coupled with the use of technology, especially helicopters, and an emphasis on quick detection and initial attack has resulted in the majority of fires being suppressed within twenty-four hours of discovery.

The Initial Attack Crews are the forest firefighting elite. Each crew has three members, who are transported by helicopter into remote and inaccessible terrain to suppress or contain forest fires. Larger (typically twenty-person) district and Native crews are deployed if the initial attack crew is unable to suppress the fire or to fight larger-scale fires. The work of the Initial Attack Crews involves carrying heavy and cumbersome water pumps and hoses, felling trees, moving logs, digging trenches, and shovelling soil in order to locate and destroy hotspots. These tasks are onerous, the conditions in which they are performed are demanding, and the hours are long. Forest firefighting has long been a man's job; in the early 1990s fewer than 10 percent of the government's forest firefighters were women.[6]

In 1988, the British Columbia Forest Service introduced a compulsory physical fitness requirement for Initial Attack Crew members. This test was a variation of the US Forest Service Smokejumpers test, which was developed by Dr. Brian Sharkey, an expert in physical fitness. It consisted of four components: twenty-four push-ups in less than one minute, twenty-four sit-ups in less than one minute, seven pull-ups (chin-ups) in less than one minute, with a maximum five-minute rest between each, which, after a rest of between fifteen and thirty minutes, was to be followed by a two-and-a-half-kilometre run to be completed in eleven minutes or less.[7] However, the Forest Service was organized on a district basis, and the physical fitness test was not uniformly applied across districts.[8]

Two events that occurred in 1991 proved to be crucial for the development of a new mandatory province-wide physical fitness test for forest firefighters. While the first event confirmed the government's right (acting in its capacity as the employer) to impose the Smokejumpers fitness test, the second prompted it to revise the physical fitness standard for initial attack forest firefighters.

In 1989, the Fire Service official in charge of the Cariboo Forest Region decided that the successful completion of the Smokejumper's test would be made a mandatory condition of employment. Three men on Initial Attack crews failed the running component and, as a consequence, were not recalled to work. Represented by the British Columbia Government Employees' Union (B.C.G.E.U.), they lodged grievances claiming lost overtime pay and wages. The grievance raised the issue of "the Employer's right to have auxiliary employees pass a physical fitness test as part of a determination of qualifications for recall."[9]

The grievance hearing took place on 24 April 1991. On 7 June, Hugh C. Ladner, a senior and well-established arbitrator, issued his award, which became known as the *Bouchard* grievance.[10] He began by recognizing the right of an employer to unilaterally impose job qualifications upon employees, referring to the evidence of Dr. Brian J. Sharkey, the expert called by the employer, that a high level of physical fitness "is important, if not essential, to a firefighter to help protect against that stress and fatigue and that it directly impacts upon productivity and safety."[11] Ladner also noted that the union's lay counsel, Colleen Fitzpatrick, did not challenge Dr. Sharkey's evidence, although she argued that past performance in the job by an employee with seniority and recall rights is more significant than the physical fitness test. For Ladner, job performance was not at issue. Rather, the key question was whether the job qualification was reasonable. In dismissing the grievance, he stated:

> It would not, one would think, be reasonable to expect a firefighter to pass a
> typing test. But Dr. Sharkey's evidence makes it abundantly clear that there is
> a relationship between fitness and the work performance of a . . . firefighter,
> and that the particular test imposed by the Employer is a reasonable one.[12]

This grievance award provided a key element in the legal context that shaped Tawney Meiorin's case. First, it involved male rather than female members of Initial Attack crews. Thus, the human rights dimension of a physical fitness test in a traditionally male-dominated job was not readily apparent, and the union's representative did not question Dr. Sharkey's remark that the standard was "well within the reach of motivated men and women interested in this strenuous form of employment."[13] Second, since the grievors subsequently passed the running component of the test, the grievance did not involve dismissal, but simply lost wages. Thus, the union did not allocate much time or money to the case, refraining, for example, from hiring its own expert witnesses. By contrast, the government had an incentive to devote some of its considerable resources to defending its prerogative to impose job-related requirements. Third, Arbitrator Ladner imposed a very low standard of relevance between the physical standard imposed and job performance in situations in which an employee's job was not in question. Fourth, Ladner's award established a precedent that allowed the government unilaterally to impose a physical fitness test as a job requirement on incumbent forest firefighters.

The second event that triggered the new fitness standard was tragic. On 1 August 1991, Ernest Gordon Kingston, a logger, was killed while attempting to suppress a fire that was ignited by logging equipment. The loggers were initially dispatched to fight the fire and after a few hours they were pulled out when water bombers were sent to the area. Later that day, after the Forest Service Officer deemed the area to be safe, together with five other loggers, Kingston was sent by his supervisor down a steep grade with a fire hose to put out a fire. However, once the workers were down the slope, the wind changed, causing the fire beneath the crew to flare up. The loggers raced up the steep slope; however, the fire overtook Kingston, who was the farthest down the slope, fifteen feet from the road where the other loggers had retreated to safety.[14]

On 29 November 1991, Coroner D.A. Devlin released his report into Kingston's death. He noted the confusion with respect to who was in charge of the suppression activities: the company supervisor or a Forest Service officer at the site.[15] He also emphasized the qualifications and characteristics of the man who died. Although Kingston was an experienced logger, not only had he limited experience with fighting fires, he had received no formal firefighting training. He was heavy-set, weighing 250 pounds, and he had been off work due to back injuries, returning only a month before his death.[16]

Coroner Devlin made ten recommendations. The first nine dealt with the obligations of logging companies regarding forest protection, the training of supervisors and employees in fire suppression, and the relationship between the logging companies and the Forest Service when it came to fighting forest fires. The final recommendation dealt with the physical condition of forest firefighters; the Coroner recommended that "[r]egardless of previous firefighting training, only workers who are physically fit and familiar with working in heavy brush conditions should be assigned front-line firefighting tasks."[17] This recommendation had direct impact on Tawney Meiorin. It led the government to evaluate its physical fitness standard for forest firefighters, to develop a new physical fitness test to reflect the standard, and to impose this requirement as a condition of employment as a forest firefighter.

The BC Forest Services contracted with the University of Victoria to determine the appropriate level of physical fitness needed by front-line forest firefighters and to develop a physical fitness test that would assess the fitness of both incumbent and applicant forest firefighters. Part of the researchers' mandate was "to ensure that procedures for establishing 'fitness for duty' are not discriminatory against a person or class in any manner prohibited by the B.C. *Human Rights Act* or *Canadian Human Rights Act*."[18] The research team began by identifying the main physical components of the job. The team then conducted laboratory work to analyze whether heart rate data could be used to assess the metabolic costs of firefighting. Ten physically active University of Victoria students, six women and four men dressed in full fire-fighting gear, were put through simulated firefighting tasks and their oxygen consumption was measured using a gas analysis system. The next step was to determine the relationship of selected fitness tests to wildland firefighting performance. Data was collected on thirty-one male BC Forest Service Unit Trainees and fifteen physically active female students at the University of Victoria, who completed the test battery over a four-day period.[19]

Forest firefighting requires aerobic fitness, namely the ability of the heart and lungs to take in and transport oxygen in energy production measured by the metabolic cost from oxygen consumption (VO_2 max). The aerobic capacity tests — the shuttle and the two-and-a-half-kilometre runs — were the most controversial because crew members could not readily see the relevance of their capacity to run to the activities involved in firefighting. In addition, the researchers selected an aerobic capacity of $VO_2$50 max on the ground that firefighters who achieved this aerobic standard could work at lower percentages of maximum output, thereby reducing cumulative fatigue over several days and enhancing safety. This standard dictated the time threshold for both the shuttle run, which required the candidate to run between two marks twenty metres apart at a progressively faster pace, and the two-and-a-half-kilometre run, and became the focus of Tawney Meiorin's grievance that she was unjustly dismissed.

In their 1992 report, the University of Victoria researchers recommended a new fitness test for wildland forest firefighters, optimistically called the *Bona Fide* Occupational (BFO) Fitness Test. Instead of consulting legal academics or human rights lawyers, the physical education researchers referred to federal human rights commission policy on *bona fide* occupational requirements in relation to the *Canadian Human Rights Act*.[20] They also noted a Supreme Court of Canada "test" case that suggested two criteria must be considered: there must be an objective basis for the job requirement and the requirement must be reasonable, such that varying or modifying it would cause undue hardship.[21]

The Forest Service adopted the BFO test in February 1993 but did not make passing the new test a job requirement until 1994, two years after the Forest Service hired Tawney Meiorin.[22] The University of Victoria research team did a 1994 follow-up study of the performance of seventy-seven forest firefighters (only one of whom was a woman), recommending, among other things, that the impact of the BFO tests on women recruits and forest firefighters should be examined.[23] The government, however, never commissioned a study of female forest firefighters.

Tawney Meiorin: Wildland Firefighter

WHEN TAWNEY MEIORIN BEGAN working on contract firefighting crews in 1989 there were few women firefighters in the districts in which she worked, and she was one of the very few women amongst a couple hundred men at fire suppression camps. According to her,

> When I took the basic firefighting course the instructor said if somebody had their first aid ticket they'd be hired for sure. So I got my Industrial First Aid certificate and I got on a contract firefighting crew. After three years, one of the government's Initial Attack Crew members suggested that I apply for a job with a government crew. Then I was told by the Castlegar Forest District that I needed chainsaw experience. So I bought a chainsaw and I got hired for thinning and spacing. I had applied everywhere in the Kootenays for an Initial Attack Crew and I was told there was a physical fitness test. On my return from a course in Alberta, I applied in Golden to be a member of an initial attack crew. I didn't go through an interview or anything, they basically phoned and asked if I wanted the job.[24]

Meiorin applied for the Initial Attack Crew because she could rely on full-time employment during the summer and earn almost twice as much as she did working for a contractor.

On 25 May 1992 she was offered a job as an Auxiliary Forest Technician 1-2 Initial Attack Crew person in the Golden Forest District starting on 15 June 1992. Her employment letter set out the terms and conditions of her job, including the requirement that she pass the modified Smokejumpers test.[25] However, Meiorin was never asked to take the test, and she successfully completed the fire season in September. Her immediate crew boss, Darcy Dahlin, characterized her performance as ranging from satisfactory to outstanding, although he thought she needed more experience to cope with stress and pressure. According to him, Tawney Meiorin was "eager and willing to learn and apply fireline knowledge. [She] compensates for lack of strength by seeking alternative methods."[26] The following March, she received an offer of employment for the same job stipulating again that she pass a fitness test.[27] But, once again, the test was never imposed, and Meiorin successfully completed a second fire season on an Initial Attack crew.

However, by the 1994 fire season, the Fire Service had been centralized and the discretion of district officials to waive fitness tests removed. The BFO tests, devised by the University of Victoria, were now mandatory and the new "Minimum Physical Fitness Standards" were set out in the Forest Service Protection Manual.[28]

On 19 January 1994, Meiorin received a letter from Rob Beugeling, a Resource Officer with the Protection Branch of the Nelson Forest Region, informing her that the BFO tests were the provincial/regional standard for all initial attack personnel beginning in the 1994 fire season.[29] He also advised her that the standards outlined in the letter and accompanying "Fit for Duty" brochure would be a condition of employment for the 1994 season. Not only would she be required to pass the test, she would be retested a minimum of two additional times during the term of her employment. A second letter, dated 13 April 1994 followed, offering Meiorin employment and setting out the terms and conditions, including the requirement that she pass the BFO tests.[30] In short, the government took a great deal of care to ensure that the test was properly imposed as a job requirement.

A few days after receiving her offer of employment, Meiorin informed Beugeling that the shuttle run instructions indicated that it was not advised for people who had knee injuries and that she had previously had knee surgery. Beugeling informed her that, as a recalled employee, she was entitled to take the run component of the old test, the two-and-a-half-kilometre run that was to be performed in less than eleven minutes.[31] On 4 May 1994, Meiorin took the BFO test — passing the upright row and pump hose components, but failing the two-and-a-half-kilometre run, which took her eleven minutes and eight seconds to complete. Beugeling gave her a pass conditional upon her successful completion of the run at the next re-test. On 8 June, after she ran the course in eleven minutes and thirty seconds, Meiorin was informed she had one last chance, in a week's time, to pass the test. At the re-test on 15 June 1994, she was told that the old track was forty metres too short. She ran the new course in eleven minutes and forty-nine seconds.[32] On 15 June, Darci Hamilton, the Manager of the Forest Service, wrote her that she was suspended from duty, and that she was recommending to the Deputy Minister that Meiorin's employment be terminated.[33]

After consulting with her union steward, Meiorin submitted a grievance on 20 June, challenging her termination. In it, she outlined her employment history with the Forest Service, the fact that no fitness test was imposed until the 1994 fire season, and how her failure to pass the running component led to her suspension. She complained that

> [t]he test is not reasonable, nor is it applied to all firefighters. In addition it is not related to firefighting duties and it is an arbitrary standard. The rule making it a condition of employment was introduced but never enforced in the Golden District until 1994. My work in the past has been satisfactory. I feel that I have been wrongfully suspended.[34]

Meiorin felt the *bona fide* test was unreasonable since it did not measure "fire smarts." She did not frame her grievance in terms of sex discrimination. According to her, it was her union representative in Cranbrook and officials with the B.C.G.E.U. who persuaded her that "unjust termination really didn't have that much power behind it whereas going after a gender issue had a lot more power."[35] She found it "really hard" to complain that the running test was sex discriminatory. As she elaborated,

> I've always been an equal firefighting, logging, whatever. I don't say I need special treatment because I'm a female . . . . It's hard and I've been verbally attacked until I got somebody . . . to sit down and listen to the whole story of what happened. But to just say that it was a legal case for discrimination against females, I mean that wasn't my goal. My goal was unjust termination, but if that was the buying power to win and get my job back then it was go for it. But I did put up with a lot of flack over that.[36]

The flack came from male co-workers who claimed that while she wanted to do a man's job, she wanted special treatment in order to do it. But, Meiorin was consistently clear that the problem that she had with the running test was that it did not measure firefighting skills. She was concerned also for the experienced men who left forest firefighting out of fear of failing the physical fitness test.[37]

After she was laid off, Meiorin became a logger. She decided to fight the case because she was angry that she had been replaced by someone with no forest firefighting experience.[38] She had already started "digging into the fitness test and who designed it and how many people they used."[39] Meiorin talked to Paula McFayden, one of the University of Victoria researchers involved in designing the BFO test. She recounted that McFayden's pet peeve was the chin-ups in the Smokejumpers test because it was a lot harder for women than for men to do chin-ups, and that McFayden "did apparently tell the government right off the bat on that new test that they should have been using more females."[40] Once the government found out Meiorin was talking to the researchers, they were banned from discussing the tests with her.[41]

In light of Arbitrator Ladner's ruling in the *Bouchard* grievance upholding the modified Smokejumpers test, it would have been well nigh impossible for the union successfully to challenge the running component of the fitness test as unreasonable. Ken Curry, the B.C.G.E.U. lawyer who represented Meiorin throughout the five years of legal proceedings, characterized her position as "I can do the job, and I just can't run two and half kilometres in 11 minutes and that is unfair."[42] Without having yet obtained an expert to explain why women's aerobic capacity tends to be lower than men's aerobic capacity, he believed the two-and-a-half-kilometre running test to be unfair to women; "look at world class athletes — men and women don't race together, right? And that's common knowledge."[43]

The Litigation

A Tortuous Legal Terrain

WHILE THE *BOUCHARD* GRIEVANCE made the construction of Meiorin's claim as a sex equality claim imperative, her legal arguments were also shaped by the confused state of human rights law. The confusion was rooted in an unresolved tension between formal and substantive equality that manifested itself in a series of inconsistent Supreme Court of Canada decisions. The Court alternated between a rhetorical commitment to generous human rights protections and a set of doctrinal directives that undermined any such possibility. The legal tale begins with the *O'Malley*[44] and *Bhinder*[45] cases, decided together by the Court in 1985.

The *O'Malley* decision represents the substantive equality approach. *O'Malley* concerned a complaint of religious discrimination arising from the adverse effects of an employment schedule that conflicted with an employee's religious observance obligations. The Supreme Court of Canada affirmed that the first step of any claim imposes a relatively light burden on claimants to establish a *prima facie* case of discrimination, namely that they have been disadvantaged, in relation to a human rights ground. The Court elaborated that discrimination may take the form of indirect or adverse effects, as well as direct actions, thus widening the scope of protection significantly to extend to the *O'Malley* situation.[46] The Court then articulated a duty on employers to take positive steps to accommodate, to the point of undue hardship, persons vulnerable to indirect effects discrimination.[47] It did so despite the absence of any explicit statutory language setting out protection from indirect discrimination, a duty to accommodate, or any kind of employer defence.

However, *O'Malley*'s substantive approach was severely undercut in the companion case of *Bhinder*. At issue in *Bhinder* were the indirect effects of an employment rule requiring employees to wear hard hats on an employee whose religious beliefs obliged him to wear a turban. Unlike the Ontario statute which applied in *O'Malley*, there was a provision in the federal regime at play in *Bhinder* explicitly stipulating a *bona fide* occupational requirement defence (known as the BFOR defence). The BFOR defence consists of a two-part test. Employers have to show good faith by demonstrating that the rule was imposed for business reasons (the subjective test), and that the rule was reasonably necessary for the efficient, economic, and safe performance of the employment (the objective test).[48] The *Bhinder* majority found that the employer's hard hat rule met this two-pronged BFOR test and that the employer did not have a further obligation to provide any form of individualized accommodation. The complainant lost.

Five years later, *Bhinder* was partially overruled in *Dairy Pool*,[49] a case concerning the adverse effects of an employment schedule on a worker's religious observance obligations. Although *Dairy Pool* presented the Court with the same combination found in *Bhinder* of indirect discrimination and a statutory BFOR defence for employers, the complainant won. Writing for the majority, Wilson J. established a bifurcated approach to resolving complaints of discrimination. In cases of direct discrimination, *Bhinder* remained good law; an employer could successfully defend against a *prima facie* case of discrimination by meeting the two-part statutory BFOR test, with no further duty to accommodate the individual employee. However, Wilson J. overturned *Bhinder* in cases of indirect or adverse effects discrimination. Here, relying on *O'Malley*, she replaced the two-part statutory BFOR test and its relatively stringent inquiry into the rule's necessity, with a "rational relation to the performance of the job" test for the rule, and an obligation on the employer to accommodate individuals to the point of undue hardship.[50] Thus the focus of indirect discrimination analysis is on individual accommodation while leaving the blanket rule in place.

The *Large* decision,[51] handed down roughly a year after Meiorin was dismissed, confirmed the bifurcated approach. *Large* overruled creative efforts of some advocates to integrate a duty to accommodate into the BFOR defence. *Large* concerned an allegation of direct discrimination, specifically, a challenge by a police officer to an age-based mandatory retirement policy, in which a statutory BFOR defence was available to the employer. The court conceded that with respect to an age-based retirement rule, the employer must explore whether it is reasonably feasible to assess, on an individual basis, the ability of persons who have reached retirement age to continue to perform the job. However, anything more than this "individual testing" alternative, in particular, any obligation to instead change job requirements to accommodate a worker's specific, human rights-based concerns and needs, was firmly ruled out.

Critics were quick to point out the absurdities of the bifurcated approach. It inflexibly tied the type of remedy available to the type of discrimination alleged. In direct discrimination cases, the rule can be struck down but no individual accommodation is available; in indirect discrimination cases, individual accommodation to the point of undue hardship is available but the rule remains in place so long as it meets the minimal scrutiny of the "rational relation" test. Commentators argued this meant that complainants of direct discrimination would often be worse off than complainants of indirect discrimination.[52] Although most concern was directed at the lack of any accommodation remedy where a directly discriminatory rule can be defended under the BFOR test, some also pointed to the fact that the inability to meaningfully challenge the rule itself in the context of indirect discrimination would mean that courts and tribunals are often precluded from providing systemic remedies for systemic inequalities.[53] After all, ostensibly neutral rules are exactly what ensure that systemic inequalities — manifested by their "effects" on individuals — remain in place. As well, it was observed that the path marked out by the cases invited "highly technical and time-consuming" arguments, turning on often unclear distinctions between direct and indirect discrimination.[54]

By the time *Dairy Pool* and *Large* were decided in the early 1990s, the Court had rendered its first equality rights decision under the *Charter* — *Andrews* — which was decided in 1989.[55] The *Andrews* case was heralded as a groundbreaking decision setting out a strong commitment to substantive equality because of its explicit commitment to protection against effects-based, as well as direct violations of rights, its rejection of formal equality's same treatment standard, and the central focus on broad patterns of disadvantage in Wilson J.'s concurring reasons. The constitutional, rather than human rights, provenance of the Court's equality statements, plus the fact that it was the Court's first section 15 decision, gave *Andrews* not only much more stature than human rights cases but also the aura of introducing something "new." Tellingly, the majority in *Andrews,* when looking for jurisprudential support for its foundational assertions of a commitment to substantive equality, relied explicitly on *O'Malley,* not *Bhinder.*[56] Equality activists and scholars, not surprisingly then, drew on *Andrews* to push back at *Bhinder* and its legacy.[57]

However, *Andrews* contained something "old" — the substantive versus formal equality tension found in the pairing of *O'Malley* with its companion, *Bhinder.* Justice McIntyre's majority reasons in *Andrews* provided as their doctrinal centrepiece a notion of discrimination that lacked a substantive focus on inequalities entrenched in social and historical practices, norms and attitudes in favour of an individualized and decontextualized focus on the distinction between individual merit and capacities, on the one hand, and, on the other, irrelevant stereotypes. As we will see, this ambivalence at the heart of *Andrews* was put to good use by the government's counsel in the *Meiorin* litigation. In the next sections, we trace the strategies and factors, including the troublesome bifurcated approach, that propelled the *Meiorin* litigation forward, from the arbitration stage, to the BC Court of Appeal, and finally to the Supreme Court of Canada.

Tawney Meiorin's Grievance

MEIORIN'S COUNSEL, KEN CURRY, and her union were committed to her case.[58] Unions rarely refuse to take a grievance forward in dismissal cases. However, where a woman challenges, on the basis of sex discrimination, requirements in a male-dominated job, frequently there is conflict between employees along gender lines, a conflict that unions, which are majority-based institutions, find difficult to resolve.[59] But, in Meiorin's case, although the specific job and the particular unit of the union was male-dominated, the B.C.G.E.U. is a broad-based public sector union with a membership that comprised (and continues to comprise) a very large number of women and had an active women's committee.[60] Moreover, fitness tests also had a disproportionately negative impact on older men, who were well represented within the union. Union support for the grievance was crucial. It meant that the union was willing to put resources into fighting Meiorin's dismissal and the fitness standard that led to her termination.

As the arbitration hearing approached, the lawyers identified their key objectives and hurdles. Curry, in the face of the *Bouchard* grievance, saw Meiorin's claim as an uphill battle for the union from the start: "A huge hurdle was a prior arbitration decision that says it is okay for the employer to impose these tests."[61] Curry's argument was crafted to get around the *Bouchard* grievance by casting it as a case about the reasonableness of the relationship between the standard and the job. Thus *Bouchard* could be analogized to human rights cases dealing with direct discrimination in which the focal point is the reasonableness of directly discriminatory, but ostensibly *bona fide*, occupational requirements. Meiorin's claim, Curry argued, was that the fitness standard was an example of indirect discrimination in which the key issue is not the reasonableness of the standard itself but whether the employer has accommodated the employee to the point of undue hardship. He pointed out that women have less aerobic capacity than men and that even with training they will have difficulty in attaining the required level of fitness. Although the test did not discriminate on its face against women, overall fewer women can successfully complete the two-and-a-half-kilometre run in the time required. Moreover, Curry asserted that Meiorin's successful performance of her job for two fire seasons was evidence that accommodation would not cause her employer undue hardship. In short, Curry's strategy was to cleave closely to the Supreme Court's bifurcated approach and its rigidly maintained distinction between direct and indirect discrimination. As the BC human rights regime had no provisions regarding indirect discrimination, a BFOR defence, or a duty to accommodate, the Supreme Court's jurisprudence was determinative.

The government's counsel, Peter Gall, recollects that the case "really . . . had little if nothing to do with Ms. Meiorin other than she happened to be the first female to . . . fail the test . . . . [F]rom the government's perspective, what was at issue was the integrity of their test."[62] His instructions were to argue vigorously that whatever fitness standard the government imposed, so long as the standard was proven to be valid and necessary, "couldn't be reduced for anybody regardless of your age, your sex or disability."[63] Gall's strategy contrasted with Curry's on a number of points. He emphasized the continuing significance of the finding in *Bouchard* that the fitness standard was reasonable. He also argued, expanding on *Large*, that a reasonable standard applied through individual testing, rather than as a blanket rule, could not constitute discrimination.

Gall's argument had three parts. First, he claimed that the fitness standard was not discriminatory. It did not directly discriminate because the evidence established that 35 percent of the women who took it passed the two-and-a-half-kilometre run.[64] Nor was it indirectly discriminatory, even though the test was harder for women than for men, because both the test and standard were reasonable, and the employer had engaged in individual testing rather than relying on stereotypes.[65] He suggested that the definition of discrimination developed by the Supreme Court of Canada in *Andrews* in relation to the *Charter* equality guarantee should be imported into human rights law.[66] However, he emphasized the formal equality dimension of the *Andrews* approach, in particular its individualized and decontextualized distinction between merit or capacities and irrelevant stereotypes. Thus, he argued that the union had failed to meet the first requirement of any human rights claim, proof of a *prima facie* case of discrimination. Second, Gall argued, that even if the fitness standard was indirectly discriminatory, the arbitrator should not be bound by the bifurcated approach since it was too rigid and not appropriate in the instant case.[67] The employer had established that the standard was rationally connected to the job and had put in place a system of individual testing and, according to Gall, these actions should constitute a *bona fide* occupational defence against a claim of discrimination even in a case of indirect discrimination. Third, he argued that lowering a standard shown to be reasonably necessary for the safe performance of the job would cause undue hardship.[68] He also downplayed the absence of any evidence that Tawney Meiorin could not safely perform her job.

The grievance proceedings also involved a battle of the experts. Curry relied upon Stephen Brown, a laboratory instructor at Simon Fraser University with a Master's degree in kinesiology. Importantly, his report detailed the different aerobic capacities of men and women.[69] Peter Gall relied on Dr. Howard A. Wenger as his expert, along with Wendy Pethick.[70] Both Wenger and Pethick had been part of the University of Victoria team that developed the BFO test and endorsed $VO_2 50$ max as the appropriate fitness standard. Wenger, a PhD in physical education, was asked to provide an expert opinion about whether the BFO tests were gender biased. He asserted, "if gender bias (adverse impact) exists, then according to the *Canadian Human Rights Act* (1985), it is acceptable if based on a *Bona Fide* Occupational Requirement."[71] In addition to offering a legal conclusion, Wenger claimed that the aerobic standard "is certainly attainable with proper training by members of either sex. As such that standard is also reasonable."[72] However, he did not provide any evidence that with the proper training women could achieve the fitness standard.

Mervin Chertkow, an experienced arbitrator who was assigned the case because he was on the government and union's list of arbitrators, released his decision on 17 September 1996. He accepted the government's key factual claims: that the aerobic standard was reasonably related to firefighting and that the run was an accurate measure and fairly administered. When Chertkow turned to the law, he ignored Gall's invitation to deviate from the bifurcated approach, and classified the case as involving indirect discrimination because it was a neutral rule that applied to all equally but which has "a discriminatory effect on women because women are less able to do aerobic work than are men. That is because of different physiological characteristics when women are compared to men."[73] Combined with the higher failure rates of women, Brown's report and testimony provided the evidentiary basis for Chertkow's conclusion. Moreover, he rejected Wenger's evidence that most women can meet the standard with training as "anecdotal and not based on scientific evidence."[74] He also rejected the availability of a BFOR defence in a case of indirect discrimination as "[t]o hold otherwise would not be in harmony with the pronouncements of the Supreme Court of Canada."[75] With respect to accommodation and undue hardship, the only defence available to the employer, Chertkow stated, "the employer has presented no cogent evidence ... to support its position that it cannot accommodate Ms. Meiorin."[76] "Simply put," Chertkow was "not persuaded that the inability of Ms. Meiorin to run two-and-a-half kilomoetres in less than 11 minutes and 49 seconds would pose a serious safety risk to herself, fellow employees, or the public at large."[77] He ordered the government to reinstate Ms. Meiorin and to compensate her for her loss of income during her wrongful termination and he told the union and the government to work out the issue of accommodation. Significantly, Chertkow did not order the government to revise the test, although he had the jurisdiction to do so. Individualized remedies such as this are typical in the arbitration arena because arbitrators, appointed by consent of the parties, tend to refrain from orders that radically reconfigure the status quo.

The British Columbia Court of Appeal: Waving the Red Flag of Reverse Discrimination

INSTEAD OF REINSTATING TAWNEY Meiorin and revising the test, the government appealed the arbitration decision to the British Columbia Court of Appeal.[78] Here Peter Gall, joined by Lindsay Lyster, continued to challenge the bifurcated approach. The government's factum began:

The issue in this case can be put quite simply: does the imposition of a physical fitness standard that is found to be reasonably required for the safe and
efficient performance of forest fire fighting constitute illegal discrimination
under the B.C. *Human Rights Act* because women are, on average, physiologic-
ally less able to meet this standard than are men[?].[79]

It continued that since Chertkow held that the test was discriminatory, the
standard would have to be lowered for Ms. Meiorin and possibly other
women and older and disabled people, "despite the risk that this will pose
to the safe performance of this very dangerous work."[80] Thus, in addition to
making legal arguments, the government's lawyers challenged Cherkow's
finding that there was no relationship between the fitness standard and safety.[81] The essence of the government's argument was that

it simply cannot be the case that an employer which has instituted a necessary workplace fitness standard and testing regime would neither be permitted to establish the absence of a *prima facie* case of discrimination on the basis
of having made appropriate individual assessments nor be able to rebut a
prima facie case of discrimination on the basis of the reasonable necessity of
the fitness standard and testing regime imposed.[82]

In contrast, the union's factum, written by Ken Curry and Michelle J. Alman, another staff lawyer from the union, emphasized that Chertkow had
found neither that the fitness standard was reasonably necessary for the safe
and efficient performance of the work, only that it was reasonably related to
the work,[83] nor that it would have to be lowered for older or disabled people.
The union's position was that "simply naming a test 'the *Bona Fide* Occupational Test' does not negate its discriminatory effect on protected groups."[84]
Curry and Alman also continued to insist on the Supreme Court of Canada's
bifurcated approach. They urged the Court of Appeal to *"resist the employer's
invitations to bring the BFOR defense into adverse discrimination cases . . ."*[85]

The hearing before Justices Cumming, Hollinrake, and Braidwood was
on 13 June 1997. According to Curry, the respondent union "had a terrible
hearing" and it was clear that "anyone in the courtroom would know things
weren't going well."[86] In particular, Justice Braidwood "was pretty aggressive
and pretty indignant" and he indicated his support for the government's
submissions, when he suggested that changing the fitness standard for Tawney Meiorin would be reverse discrimination.[87]

The Court of Appeal released a short (twenty-one paragraphs) collective decision granting the appeal less than a month later. Gall had read the Court correctly. The Court in essence agreed with Gall's argument regarding individual testing:

> The significance of this case is the principle that in a case such as *Large,* an employer seeking to establish a *bona fide* occupational requirement must demonstrate that individual assessment is impracticable and therefore a general rule is necessary. The appellant submits that the necessary corollary to this principle must be that if individual testing is carried out, there is no discrimination. We agree.[88]

Thus, the Court concluded, "the *Bona Fide* Occupational Fitness Test does not discriminate on the basis of sex and that being so the appellant has not discriminated against Ms. Meiorin."[89]

The Court did not let the matter rest there. In the penultimate paragraph of the decision, it gave Justice Braidwood's indignation over the implications of Meiorin's claim for male workers the gloss of legal authority. The Court commented that if the employer lowered the fitness test requirements for women to ensure that roughly equal percentages of women and men meet the requirements, then there would be a group of men that would fail the men's test, some of whom could pass, or even surpass, the women's test. The Court observed

> that would serve, it seems to us, to introduce a new concept which could be labeled "reserve/adverse effect discrimination." . . . [M]ales in that group would, in turn, be denied admission because, and only because, of their maleness, and thus be subject to the very type of discrimination that would constitute a breach of their guaranteed human rights.[90]

This statement was a "red flag," not only ensuring that the union would appeal, but also that "[the Women's Legal Education and Action Fund] LEAF and everybody else would join in."[91] It also virtually guaranteed that the Supreme Court of Canada would grant leave to appeal, which it did on 12 February 1998. The case was now a *cause célèbre.* It was not simply about the complexities of the bifurcated approach, an issue that only legal insiders and activists understood; it had been transformed from a case challenging male-dominated workplaces into a case about the threat posed by such claims to men's "guaranteed human rights." The Court of Appeal decision also forced both parties to change course at the Supreme Court. The union would need to consider arguments that did not rely on the bifurcated approach. The government would have to distance itself from a decision that, although in its favour, was attracting attention, some of it negative, in the media and the legal community.

Changing Strategy

IN THE FACE OF the pending appeal on what was now a significant human rights case, Ken Curry invited John Brewin, an experienced union lawyer, and Gwen Brodsky, a well-known human rights advocate and equality litigator, to join the union's legal team.[92] Brodsky understood the significance of the case as an opportunity to challenge the Supreme Court's bifurcated approach to human rights law.[93] Together with Shelagh Day, she had published an influential article that focused on the indirect discrimination prong of the bifurcated approach.[94] Brodsky and Day argued that in the indirect discrimination arena it was often not sufficient simply to accommodate individuals, and that sometimes it was necessary to challenge the rule itself. In particular, they identified situations involving sex, race, and disability discrimination in which simply accommodating the individual would leave sexist, racist, and ableist norms in place.[95] At the Supreme Court of Canada the union dropped its insistence on the bifurcated approach and advocated a unified approach to human rights complaints that required employers to consider changing workplace norms regardless of whether the discrimination alleged was direct or indirect.[96]

Not only did Brodsky help to shape the union's legal argument, she also helped to coordinate the legal strategy taken by a coalition of intervenors made up of the Canadian Labour Congress (CLC), the Disabled Women's Network (DAWN), and the Women's Legal Education and Action Fund (LEAF) (the Coalition).[97] The common submission of these three groups was unprecedented, and it illustrated how significant the Meiorin case had become to equality jurisprudence. Moreover, the unified position of three of its traditional allies placed the NDP government, which had been in power from the initial grievance and continued to defend the test, in a difficult political position.

In their factum, Brodsky and Curry emphasized the novel nature of Meiorin's indirect discrimination claim: that it was not being raised in the context of religious minorities, but rather in the context of the systemic barriers faced by women seeking to enter male-dominated occupations.[98] In this situation, they argued that individual adjustment in the form of accommodation was not sufficient:

> Rather, where a discriminatory standard affects women generally the issue is not an individual adjustment, but rather the adjustment of the standard. The inquiry must necessarily be focused on modification of the rule itself in order to accommodate the group as a whole.[99]

Pursuing a unified approach, they argued that the standard of justification must be the same for both direct and indirect discrimination. In Meiorin's case, this meant that the government must show that adequate job performance can only be assured by the imposition of this particular standard (rather than that there is simply a rational relation between the two), *and* that there had been accommodation to the point of undue hardship. They submitted that the government had done neither of these things. In particular, it had not examined the impact of the standard on women, investigated the possible ways in which the discriminatory effects on women could be eliminated, nor proven that departing from the standard would constitute an undue hardship. The researchers did not test women firefighters who did poorly on the test in light of their actual performance, a point that Chertkow had found had been conceded by Wenger.[100] In addition to asking the Court to reinstate Tawney Meiorin with full back pay, they asked it to order the government to revise the standard and to adopt a new rule that excluded women as little as possible from employment as wildland firefighters.[101]

The government also changed its legal strategy between the Court of Appeal and the Supreme Court of Canada. First, it tried to introduce new evidence about two studies conducted by the University of Victoria after Meiorin's dismissal. Both studies focused on women's ability to pass the BFO tests. Justice L'Heureux-Dubé refused to admit the evidence.[102] When challenged during the hearing about the government's failure to do studies that tested women, Gall referred to the rejected motion.[103] However, neither of the studies addressed the factual issue in dispute — that experienced women firefighters who failed the shuttle run created a safety hazard. Also, by the time of the hearing, the government was not concerned about the particular test.[104] Rather, the government was

> concerned about fitness standards being entirely invalidated as discriminatory . . . . What they were bothered by was the possibility that the court might accept some of the academic writing that suggested that height and weight

and fitness and all of those kinds of things were inherently discriminatory and just couldn't be used at all. So they really wanted a statement by the court that it was okay to impose physical fitness tests as long as they were properly designed.[105]

The government's lawyers also found they "were having to run against the Court of Appeal's reasoning."[106] In their factum, although Gall and Lyster argued that the Court of Appeal was correct in finding that the physical fitness standard was not discriminatory, they offered three other approaches to the case, all of which supported the Court of Appeal's conclusion.[107] The first was a unified approach to the issue of discrimination. The second was a more limited approach that preserved the distinction between direct and indirect discrimination and distinguished between situations where the work rule or standard is merely reasonable from a business standpoint and those where the standard is objectively necessary to the safe performance of work. And the third kept the undue hardship defence of indirect discrimination, but placed the burden upon the complainant to show that the employer can accommodate without undue hardship.

All of the parties and intervenors urged the Supreme Court of Canada to replace the bifurcated approach with a unified one. The key question dividing them was what such a unified approach should look like. According to the government, a unified approach could be achieved by getting rid of the accommodation requirement altogether, and ending the inquiry once the "essential question" of the standard's reasonableness with respect to "the safe and efficient performance of the job" is settled.[108]

In her intervention for the BC Human Rights Commission, Deirdre Rice countered that the government's analysis absolved itself and other employers of any responsibility to develop standards that are more inclusive.[109] In addition, Rice was particularly concerned to address the government's position, endorsed at the Court of Appeal, that individual testing is inherently non-discriminatory. Instead, she submitted that individual testing may itself be the agent of discrimination where the test excludes protected groups.[110]

The Coalition's factum, submitted by Melina Buckley and Kate Hughes, most clearly described the problem with the bifurcated approach in substantive equality terms. The influence of their factum on the ultimate decision is apparent. They argued that systemic discrimination can only be addressed by scrutinizing "underlying norms,"[111] and that pre-employment or job testing was a barrier faced by women seeking to enter into traditionally male-dominated jobs. Meiorin's case was a prime example of ostensibly neutral testing standards masking requirements based on male physical characteristics and abilities:

> The respondent has commissioned studies to assess the fitness standards, but each was biased in favour of experienced male fire fighters. The aerobic capacity standard was developed primarily on the basis of a male population of firefighters and then applied to women.[112]

Under a revised unified approach, the Coalition argued, accommodation should also include changing the norm or standard and not be limited simply to accommodating the individual.[113]

The Supreme Court of Canada Hearing

MEIORIN ATTENDED THE HEARING at the Supreme Court of Canada on 23 February 1999. But she cannot be seen in the official video of the hearing, which focuses on the nine members of the Court who heard the case and the swarm of lawyers appearing before them.[114] Nor does the video show the large number of media representatives in the audience. An 11 February 1999 newspaper story, which reflected how the case was generally portrayed, began:

> Tawney Meiroin can buck logs with the best of them. She likes to climb steep mountain slopes in her skis and roar down them from the top. She could probably leap tall buildings at a single bound. But she can't run 2.5 kilometres in less than 11 minutes. In 1994 that made her too slow for the British Columbia fitness standard and cost her a good job fighting forest fires.[115]

The story quoted Shelagh Day describing the case as the most significant sex discrimination case the Supreme Court of Canada had faced in a decade.

It was clear from the beginning of the hearing that the members of the Court were concerned primarily with factual questions. Curry was thrown off his argument almost immediately by a question from Justice Major about whether there was anything in the record that established the need for the specific aerobic capacity selected as the fitness standard.[116] With a few exceptions, all of the questions that followed returned to the issue of whether the government had shown that the aerobic capacity the government had established as its fitness standard was necessary for the job.

Despite their much briefer presentations, Rice and Hughes were able to address the broader legal questions. Hughes noted that while the outcome in the instant case was simple because the fitness standard was not reasonably necessary for the job, she urged the Court to take the opportunity to revisit the law.[117] She focused on the duty to accommodate and emphasized the difference between the Coalition's unified approach to the question of discrimination and that advocated by the government.

Gall began on a conciliatory note, stating that the government agreed fully with the proposition that its standard should not unnecessarily exclude anyone.[118] He also minimized the difference between the Coalition's and the government's unified approach to discrimination. However, as with Curry, members of the Court quickly jumped in to pepper him with factual questions. In response to Justice L'Heureux-Dubé's questions, Gall admitted that the government had never examined whether men and women could satisfy the aerobic fitness standard in different ways.[119] Justice Major noted that it was "curious" that although Ms. Meiorin could not meet the standard she had done the job for two years, which called into question whether or not the standard was necessary.[120] The problem with the fitness standard, according to Justice Binnie, was that it described the characteristics of the male firefighters, but it did not actually prescribe a fitness standard for the requirements of the job.[121]

The focus of the last stage of the hearing was whether the case should be remitted to the arbitrator. In his initial reply, Curry emphasized the need to reinstate Tawney Meiorin and to compensate her for her loss of wages and benefits for the five years that elapsed since she was dismissed. Although Gall did not take a position on reinstatement and back pay, he was concerned that the government not be left without a standard or with a lower standard.[122] However, Curry noted that since the fitness standard was discriminatory, it should not be allowed to stand.

In the aftermath of the case, media coverage varied in tone. One intervention showed a photograph of a jubilant Meiorin leaving the hearing and quoted Gall to the effect that the British Columbia government would consider changing the fitness standard; "the government never approached this as [if] this test was cast in stone."[123] For the first time in the five years of legal wrangling over the fitness test, through its lawyer, the government announced it was "quite prepared to revisit it and to work with the union and work with everybody who has an interest in this matter to ensure that these are the appropriate minimum standards."[124] But this last-ditch attempt to be conciliatory proved to be too little too late; for far too long the government had put too much store in the physical education experts.[125]

Tawney Meiorin leaving the Supreme Court with lawyer John Brewin after her hearing.
Source: Canadian Press

Other reporting was less supportive of Meiorin's claim. One story began:

> Tawney Meiroin may have been getting ready to dust off her firefighting boots after a sympathetic hearing on Monday at the Supreme Court of Canada, but many say she should put her training shoes back on and learn to run faster.[126]

The article went on to quote Debra Owen, a government witness who had run the recruitment program aimed at women and who was herself a wild-land firefighter. She had failed the running portion of the fitness test on her first attempt, considered it a matter of personal responsibility to pass the test, and was willing to train all year for it as a cost of qualifying for the job. She believed that it would be a mistake to lower the standard because passing the same test as the men was a "starting point for respect on the fire line."[127] She also noted "already male firefighters are asking her if in the future blazes will be designated as 'guy' fires or 'girl' fires."[128] The article also recounted comments by physical fitness experts who developed the test. They were adamant that, not only was the fitness standard relevant, there should be only one standard for men and women. For example, Dr. Wenger stated that the job of forest firefighting "isn't just going to the office. This isn't just a walk in the woods."[129] Norm Gledhill, who developed a similar test for firefighters in Ontario, asserted that "if it is a *bona fide* occupational requirement and has been validated as such, then it should make no difference what the person is — man or women, black or white."[130] But, what the physical fitness experts did not appreciate was the fact that the US Forest Service Step Test, which applied to all personnel hired for District Unit Crews prior to 1994, set different heights for men (15.75 inches) and for women (13 inches) of the benches used in the test.[131] However, it was possible to impose rigorous fitness standards because forest firefighting was an extremely competitive job; in 1999 in British Columbia, 1600 people, including 300 women, applied for sixty jobs. Of the province's 774 forest firefighters, only forty-five, about 6 percent, were women.[132]

The Supreme Court of Canada's Decision: Challenging the Male Employment Norm

ALTHOUGH NONE OF THE lawyers were surprised that the Supreme Court of Canada upheld the appeal and decided for the union, they were astonished that the Court went well beyond what the parties asked for in developing a unified approach to discrimination.[133] Justice McLachlin, writing for the majority, drew heavily on the Coalition's factum and critical commentary in the academic literature. She pointed to the absurdity of pairing individual accommodation remedies with indirect discrimination complaints, as well as the importance of making such remedies available in direct discrimination complaints. She described Meiorin's case as a "good example of how the conventional [bifurcated] analysis prevents the Court from rigorously assessing a standard which, in the course of regulating entry to a male dominated occupation, adversely affects women as a group."[134] Equality rights, she observed, are

> reduced to a question of whether the "mainstream" can afford to confer proper treatment on those adversely affected, within the confines of its existing formal standard. If it cannot, the edifice of systemic discrimination receives the law's approval. This cannot be right.[135]

Justice McLachlin set out a "reformed" approach applicable to all types of discrimination that consisted of three steps. The first two steps, reflecting the objective and subjective prongs of the previous BFOR defence, ask the employer to show that the standard was adopted for a purpose rationally connected to job performance and that it was adopted in the honest and good faith belief that it is necessary to that purpose. The third step heightens the scrutiny on the employer and is the crux of the newly integrated analysis. It asks the employer to show that the relation between the standard and the work related purpose is one of "reasonable necessity." In addition, it stipulates that to do so, the employer must demonstrate that "it is impossible to accommodate individual employees sharing the characteristics of the claimant without imposing undue hardship upon the employer."[136] Justice McLachlin elaborated on the nature of the inquiry at this stage in terms that heighten the responsibility on employers through a stringent scrutiny of workplace practices and rules:

> Employers designing workplace standards owe an obligation to be aware of both the differences between individuals, and differences that characterize groups of individuals. They must build conceptions of equality into workplace standards . . . . The standard *itself* is required to provide for individual accommodation, if reasonably possible.[137]

Applying the reformed approach to the case on appeal, Justice McLachlin found that despite the government's reliance on experts to develop the test, "the resulting aerobic standard has not been shown to be reasonably necessary to the safe and efficient performance of the work a forest firefighter."[138] She buttressed her position by pointing to the descriptive character of the research team's methodology and its failure — contrary to its own recommendations — to test men and women subjects. Dr. Wenger's defence of the team's decision to not separately analyze the aerobic performance of men and women, both experienced and inexperienced, was also criticized.[139] Significantly, she noted the absence of any evidence that the government embarked upon a study of the discriminatory effects of the standard when the issue was raised by Ms. Meiorin.[140]

Justice McLachlin also found that the government failed to show it would experience undue hardship if a different standard were used. Here she referred to the Arbitrator's finding that the government presented no cogent evidence that Ms. Meiorin presented a safety risk. She dismissed the government's concerns that accommodating Ms. Meiorin would undermine the morale of Initial Attack crews as not only unsupported by evidence but illegitimate in any event.[141]

Finally, she expressed her disagreement with the Court of Appeal. She rejected her former court's suggestion "that accommodating women by permitting them to meet a lower aerobic standard than men would constitute 'reverse discrimination'" on the ground that "true equality requires differences to be accommodated."[142] She also rejected the appeal court's suggestion that individualized testing immunized the government from discrimination, stating that "the individual must be tested against a realistic standard that reflects his or her capacities and potential contributions."[143]

Given the breadth of Justice McLachlin's reasons, her remedy was disappointing. She ordered the government to reinstate Ms. Meiorin in her former position and compensate her for lost wages, and awarded costs to the union.[144] In light of the fact that the appellants had asked the court to order the government to revise the standard and adopt a new rule that did not exclude women from employment as wildland firefighters, it is surprising that she said nothing about the fitness standard.

The newspaper stories and editorials about the decision were generally favourable, applauding the Supreme Court of Canada for exercising "common sense" in ordering Tawney Meiorin's reinstatement.[145] However, it was the lawyers who understood just how path breaking it was for human rights law.[146] Although the case arose in the context of fitness tests developed in male-dominated occupations, the Supreme Court's decision would have its greatest impact for people with physical disabilities.[147]

The impact of the Supreme Court of Canada's decision on physical fitness standards for firefighting was immediate in British Columbia, but it took a longer time to change practices for developing fitness standards in the rest of Canada. In British Columbia, the union and the government worked out a different fitness standard, one that did not require firefighters to attain an aerobic capacity of $VO_2 50$ max.[148] The percentage of women hired as forest firefighters continued to increase in British Columbia, and today the Forest Services website is replete with pictures of women forest firefighters and recruits.[149] Ontario continues to include a shuttle run as part of its fitness test. However, the standard for the test is based on a lower aerobic capacity.[150]

Despite the Supreme Court of Canada's ruling that fitness standards that ignore differences in men's and women's physiology will be found to indirectly discriminate against women, employers in physically demanding occupations continue to assume that external hazards such as forest fires authorize them to ignore human rights considerations in setting such standards. For example, after *Meiorin*, the Department of National Defence introduced a fitness test for firefighters that imposed, according to the arbitrator who struck down the fitness standard in a 2006 grievance award, a uniform aerobic stan-

Wildfire Management Branch, New Recruit Bootcamp, 2004, chainsaw instruction class.
Photo courtesy of the BC Ministry of Labour and Citizens' Services

dard for firefighters that used "a younger male norm in place of a fair-minded gender and age neutral job analysis."[151] In addition, in the post-*Meiorin* context, employers who can legitimately be characterized as concerned with public safety are highly unlikely to apply the more transformative aspects of the *Meiorin* ruling that require the redesign of workplaces and workplace methods to ensure that women can safely work in these occupations and are much more likely simply to adjust the fitness testing standards.[152]

The *Meiorin* decision has, however, had a discernible impact on the practices of exercise physiologists who tend to dominate the field of employment-related fitness standards. A year after the decision was rendered, a forum on "Establishing *BONA FIDE* Requirements For Physically Demanding Occupations" was convened at which scientists, lawyers, and employer representatives aimed to clarify the implications of *Meiorin* on employment-related physical fitness testing. The proceedings set out a framework for developing fitness screening tests that is considered by those who were involved to be the baseline for any work in this area.[153] The approaches contained in the proceedings have been criticized for their reliance on exercise physiology and fitness testing to the exclusion of consideration of ergonomics and more contextual factors encompassing the diverse ways in which workers interact with tasks, equipment, and work environments.[154] However, it is clear that *Meiorin* has altered the methodologies employed by exercise physiologists when developing employee fitness tests. Dr. David Docherty, who worked on the test put in place for wildland firefighters in BC after the Smokejumpers test, observes that he now does things "quite differently," particularly at the initial stage of task analysis.[155] As he put it, after he has done the initial task analysis, he often goes back to the employer with concerns about gender and persons of small stature and asks, "Okay, that's the way you're doing it now, could you do that any other way?" He also recounts one instance where, out of concern for human rights implications, he urged employers to use the test as an educational tool rather than "to demote somebody and promote them based on how they do on the test." In workplaces in which women are entirely absent or too few to provide a good sample, he endeavours to compensate for this in a transparent way and to think through concerns about systemic bias.[156] Thus, in this one field, the ruling in *Meiorin* has resulted in much greater attention to and knowledge of human rights standards, along with significantly reshaping practices on the ground.

Although she was delighted that the Supreme Court vindicated her claim, Tawney Meiorin never worked again as a BC Forest Service forest firefighter. By the time she won the case, five years had elapsed, she was thirty-three years old, and earned better money as a logger, largely because there was a longer season. In fact, in 2000 she was offered her old position on condition that she passed the fitness test that the Supreme Court of Canada had found to be discriminatory since the government had yet to change the test. Thus, her victory was bittersweet, tainted by the fact that she had to endure a seven-year struggle with the government. Moreover, she continued to have to fight the government for over a year after the Supreme Court's decision in order to obtain her back pay.[157] What she learned was

> that number one, you should never take anything for granted. I don't think I've ever found a job that I was so positive about yet. I really loved my job and moved to Golden (and didn't know a single soul in Golden when I moved there), just because I wanted that job so badly, and how hard I had trained to pass that test. People probably have no idea, a lot of females can hardly even do chin-ups, to pump out seven of them in a row and to have marathon runners that say that they can't even run [two-and-a-half kilometres in under eleven minutes].[158]

Conclusion

THE STORY OF TAWNEY Meiorin's litigation reveals the range of factors that drive forward claims that become leading precedents. In retrospect, Meiorin's dismissal went to arbitration at a particularly auspicious moment from the perspective of the legal trends. Human rights law had been set on a path — the bifurcated approach — that not only seemed destined to become increasingly complex and contradictory, but, even more importantly, foreclosed any serious engagement with systemic inequalities. Human rights and anti-discrimination academics and activists were uniformly critical of the jurisprudence. Early *Charter* equality decisions such as *Andrews*, which were viewed as staking out a substantive approach to equality and questions of discrimination, seemed to offer a contrast and thus an added incentive to revise unwieldy and formalistic human rights doctrine.[159]

However, as significant as these legal and doctrinal dimensions were, other factors converged to give momentum to Meiorin's dispute with her employer. First, several features of the case's broader legal context help to account for its trajectory. In particular, the nature and direction of the various arguments and decisions spurred the litigation onward. For example, the bid for leave to appeal to the Supreme Court of Canada was certainly strengthened by the fact that the Court of Appeal decision framed its distaste for Meiorin's argument in broadly gendered terms as "reverse discrimination against men." In addition, the remarkable agreement of all of the parties and intervenors that the bifurcated approach should be replaced by a unified approach no doubt made it easier for the Supreme Court of Canada to take the rare step of overruling its previous caselaw, despite that law's recent vintage. Furthermore, many of the lawyers involved saw the case not just as a way to serve a particular client's immediate interests but also as an opportunity to shape the broader contours of anti-discrimination law.

For instance, from the very beginning of the process, Peter Gall pursued a strategy of circumventing the bifurcated approach, if not directly asking for its rejection. He also promoted raising the burden on the complainant at the first step in any human rights claim, namely, proving *prima facie* discrimination. Although the judicial reasons in the *Meiorin* case and the arguments of the other counsel ended up focusing exclusively on the second step, namely, the justifications available to the employer, Gall's strategy with respect to altering the first step to favour the employer foreshadowed developments in the recent case of *McGill University Health Centre v. Syndicat des Employés de L'Hopital Général de Montréal.*[160] Brodsky also immediately saw the significance of the case for human rights law more generally. In particular, more than many other specialists in the area, she understood, and had already articulated in her incisive article with Day, the ways in which the duty to accommodate often simply meant accommodating systemic discrimination. Moreover, the intervenors (the Coalition) understood the broader implications of the case and of Gall's argument that individual testing combined with a rational standard precluded any finding of discrimination.

These law-related factors, however, do not fully explain why this case became a leading precedent on the nature of substantive equality and human rights protections. There are a number of non-legal factors that played a crucial role. First, Tawney Meiorin was a credible and charismatic complainant who inspired her lawyers, worked indefatigably at uncovering the provenance of the problematic fitness test, was a good media subject, and never gave up. Second, the financial and political support of her union and the fact that the general membership was sympathetic to the gender equality dimension of her claim, were both crucial to her claim's success. Third, Meiorin launched her claim after the second wave of the women's movement had crested.[161] Although women, especially women in the unionized public sector, had fought for equality at work since the 1970s, Meiorin and a handful of other brave women lodged equality complaints in the heartland of male privilege at work — firefighting and policing. Finally, in the end, Meiorin's claim was "easy"— not for her, but for the Court — because of the methodological failures in the development of the test, in particular the failure to develop a standard that reflected the safe and effective performance of the job by experienced female wildland firefighters. The inspiring language in McLachlin J.'s reasons about challenging the inequalities that arise from workplaces organized around dominant male norms was sparked by what is probably an exceptional situation. At base, once you dig down through the processes and studies that generated the "neutral" fitness test, the case is one of direct discrimination. Women firefighters were left out of the design of the test. Dominant norms, be they gendered, racial, ableist or heterosexist, are not often so easily traced to clearly and directly exclusionary practices. In addition, Meiorin's case was facilitated by the fact that there actually was a handful of experienced female wildland forest fighters, like herself, who had successfully performed the job in the days when the requirement to pass a physical fitness test was inconsistently applied.

Finally, it is important to place the *Meiorin* decision in the larger context of equality and discrimination law. On the positive side, it swept away the bifurcated approach, and more importantly, did so in the name of sub-stantive equality and a meaningful engagement with systemic discrimina-tion. However, it was followed by the Court's decision, also unanimous, in *Nancy Law*, which, although it contained similar language endorsing substantive equality, reinvigorated formal equality analysis in the Court's *Charter* jurisprudence through doctrinal requirements that emphasize a decontextualized focus on harms to individual dignity and similar treat-ment.[162] Recently, in *R. v. Kapp*, the Court has acknowledged the failures in the post-*Nancy Law* cases and, without rejecting *Nancy Law*, has recommit-ted itself to the substantive equality standard associated with *Andrews*.[163] However, as we have seen, *Andrews'* emphasis on prejudice and stereotyp-ing undermines a meaningful substantive equality analysis, such as the Court embarked on in *Meiorin*, which engages with systemic and struc-tural obstacles to equality at work. Thus, the larger legacy of *O'Malley* and *Bhinder* in terms of the abiding tension between formal and substantive equality continues to cast its shadow over equality jurisprudence. *Meiorin*, by taking a more stringent and substantive approach to employer justifica-tions for human rights violations, signals the possibility of a human rights jurisprudence that acknowledges rather than ignores the significant dis-parities in power, resources, social capital, and normative legitimacy that skew workplace disputes between complainant employees and respondent employers, and hold deeply embedded social inequalities in place. How-ever, post-*Meiorin* developments suggest a more skeptical assessment of the Court's commitment to that larger project.[164]

Notes

1   We would like to thank Jessica Derynck for her excellent research assistance, all of the people who generously gave of their time for interviews, especially Tawney Meiorin, and the Faculty of Law at the University of Victoria for financial and institutional support. Judy Fudge would also like to thank the SSHRC for funding the research upon which this study was based.

2   [1999] 3 S.C.R. 3 [*Meiorin* SCC].

3   Kirk Makin, "Top Court Restores Woman's Dream of Becoming a Forest-fire Fighter" *Globe and Mail* (10 September 1991) A1.

4   *Meiorin* SCC, above note 2 at para. 36.

5   John Vye Parminter, *An Historical Review of Forest Fire Management in British Columbia* (Master of Forestry Thesis, University of British Columbia, 1978) at 94 and 101–2, online: British Columbia Ministry of Forests and Range www.for.gov.bc.ca/HFD/LIBRARY/documents/bib32984.pdf.

6   *Meiorin* SCC, above note 2 (Respondent's New Evidence Motion Book at Supreme Court of Canada, 29 September 1998; Affidavit of James Dunlop, 28 September 1998; Lynneth Wolski, Kirstin Lane, & Catherine Gaul, The Efficacy of the "Fit for Duty" Training Program for Preparing Women for the B.C. Forest Fitness Test, EXHIBIT C, Numbers of applicants, male and female; numbers hired, and total number of female firefighters).

7   *British Columbia (Public Service Employee Relations Commission) v. B.C.G.E.U.* (1996), 58 L.A.C. (4th) 159 at para. 52 (B.C. Arb. Bd.) [*Meiorin* arbitration]. The length of the run in the Smokejumpers test, which was 1.5 miles, was 86 metres shorter than the length of the run in the BC test, which was 2.5 kilometres.

8   *Ibid.* at para. 79.

9   *British Columbia v. B.C.G.E.U. (Bouchard Grievance)*, [1991] B.C.C.A. No. 146 at para. 1 [*Bouchard*].

10 *Ibid.*

11 *Ibid.* at para. 16.

12 *Ibid.* at para. 19.

13 *Ibid.* at para. 16.

14 D.A. Devlin, BC Coroners Service, *Circumstances as a Result of the Inquiry Into The Death Of Kingston, Ernest Gordon* (Gibsons, BC: Ministry of Solicitor General, 29 November 1991) at 1 [Devlin]; *British Columbia (Public Service Employee Relations Commission) v. B.C.G.E.U.* (1997), 149 D.L.R. (4th) 261 (B.C.C.A.) [*Meiorin* BCCA] (Appeal Book of the Appellant at 2 [ABA]).

15 Devlin, *ibid.* at 1. ABA, *ibid.* at 2.

16 Devlin, *ibid.* at 2. ABA, *ibid.* at 1.

17 Devlin, *ibid.* at 3. ABA, *ibid.* at 3.

18 ABA, *ibid.* at 35 (*Bona Fide* Occupational Fitness Tests and Standards for B.C. Forest Service Wildland Firefighters, prepared by David Docherty, Paul McFadyen, & Gordon G. Seivert, Department of Physical Education, University of Victoria, August 1992).

19 *Ibid.* at 65–78.

20 *Ibid.* at 49; *Canadian Human Rights Act*, R.S.C. 1985, c. H-6.

21 ABA, *ibid.* at 49. Although the Report referred to a case, it provided neither the case name nor citation.

22 ABA, above note 14 at 201; British Columbia Forest Service, *Protection Manual — Volume I — Interim Manual Amendment* (17 February 1993) s 7.8.5 [Protection Manual Amendment].

23 *Meiorin* SCC, above note 2 (Appellant's Record at 75). Paula McFadyen *et al.*, *Psychological Cost of Wildland Firefighting and Bona Fide Occupational Fitness Requirements* (University of Victoria Department of Physical Education, 1994) at 4.

24 Interview of Tawney Meiorin (18 December 2007) [Meiorin interview].

25 ABA, above note 14 at 20–21; Letter from Darci Hamilton to Tawney Meiorin (26 May 1992).

26 ABA, *ibid.* at 175; Performance rating of Tawney Meiorin by Fireline Supervisor Darcy Dahlin (21 September 1994).

27 ABA, *ibid.* at 22–23; Letter from Darci Hamilton to Tawney Meiorin (26 March 1993).

28 ABA, *ibid.* at 201–6; Protection Manual Amendment, above note 22.

29 ABA, *ibid.* at 24; Letter from Rob Beugeling to Tawney Meiorin (18 January 1994).

30 ABA, *ibid.* at 28; Letter from Darci Hamilton to Tawney Meiorin (13 April 1994).

31 *Meiorin* Arbitration, above note 7 at para. 15.

32 *Ibid.* at paras. 16 and 18.

33 ABA, above note 14 at 31–32; Letter from Darci Hamilton to Tawney Meiorin (15 June 1994).

34 ABA, *ibid.* at 207–8; Grievance form completed by Tawney Meiorin (20 June 1994).

35 Meiorin interview, above note 24.

36 *Ibid.*

37 *Ibid.*

38 *Ibid.*

39 *Ibid.*

40 *Ibid.*

41 *Ibid.*

42 Interview of Ken Curry with B.C.G.E.U. (27 September 2007) [Curry interview].

43 *Ibid.*

44 *Ontario (Human Rights Commission) v. Simpsons Sears Ltd.*, [1985] 2 S.C.R. 536 [*O'Malley*].

45 *Bhinder v. Canadian National Railway Co.*, [1985] 2 SCR 561 [*Bhinder*].

46 *O'Malley*, above note 44 at para. 18.

47 *Ibid.* at para 23.

48 This test was set out in the earlier case, *Ontario (Human Rights Commission) v. Borough of Etobicoke*, [1982] 1 S.C.R. 202 at 208.

49 *Central Alberta Dairy Pool v. Alberta (Human Rights Commission)*, [1990] 2 S.C.R. 489 [*Dairy Pool*].

50 *Ibid.* at paras. 51 and 58.

51 *Large v. Stratford (City)*, [1995] 3 S.C.R. 733 [*Large*].

52   M.C. Crane, "Human Rights, *Bona Fide* Occupational Requirements and the Duty to Accommodate: Semantics or Substance" (1996) 4 C.L.E.L.J. 228 [Crane]; Anne Molloy, "Disability and the Duty to Accommodate" (1993) 1 Canadian Labour Law Journal 36 [Molloy].

53   Gwen Brodsky & Shelagh Day, "The Duty to Accommodate: Who Benefits?" (1995) 75 Can. Bar Rev. 469 [Brodsky & Day].

54   Crane, above note 52 at 228.

55   *Law Society of British Columbia v. Andrews*, [1989] 1 S.C.R. 143 [*Andrews*].

56   *Ibid.* at para. 37.

57   Molloy, above note 52 at 25.

58   Meiorin interview, above note 24; Curry interview, above note 42.

59   Anne Forrest, "Securing the Male Breadwinner: A Feminist Interpretation of PC 1003" in Cy Gonick, *et al.* eds., *Labour Gains, Labour* (Halifax: Society for Socialist Studies/ Fernwood, 1995); Gillian Creese, *Contracting Masculinity: Gender, Class and Race in a White-Collar Union, 1944–1994* (Don Mills, ON: Oxford University Press, 1999); Pamela Sugiman, *Labour's Dilemma: The Gender Politics of Auto Workers in Canada, 1937–1979* (Toronto: University of Toronto Press, 1994).

60   Forest firefighters are part of Component 20 of the BCGEU, which includes Environmental, Technical and Operational Employees. The union is composed of eleven components, some of which, like the Hospital and Allied Services, are female dominated, while others, such as Component 20, are male dominated. BC Government and Service Employees' Union, *Components*, online: Components — BCGEU www.bcgeu.ca/structure_components.

61   Curry interview, above note 42.

62   Interview of Peter Gall (7 January 2008) [Gall interview]. Peter Gall was (and continues to be) a lawyer with Heenan Blaikie, a well known firm that represents employers. Notably, the BC government contracts out its employment-related litigation rather than having its own lawyers conduct it.

63   *Ibid.*

64   *Meiorin* arbitration, above note 7 at paras. 111 and 128.

65   *Ibid.* at para. 112.

66   *Ibid.* at para. 127.

67   *Ibid.* at para. 137.

68   *Ibid.* at para. 143.

69   ABA, above note 14 at 213; *Meiorin* BCCA, above note 14 (Stephen Brown's report, *Aerobic Fitness and Ministry of Forest Physical Fitness Tests*, report, 21 February 1996).

70   ABA, *ibid.* at 106 and 112.

71   ABA, *ibid.* at 106 (Howard A. Wenger, Report on *Bona Fide* Fitness Test) [Wenger]; ABA, *ibid.* at 112 (report of Ms. W. Pethick and Dr. H.A. Wenger in response to the "Brown Report").

72   Wenger, *ibid.* at 110.

73   *Ibid.* at para. 172.

74   *Ibid.* at para. 173.

75   *Ibid.* at para. 174.

76 *Ibid.* at para. 180.

77 *Ibid.* at para. 181.

78 Under the BC *Labour Relations Code*, R.S.B.C. 1996, c. 244, parties can apply directly to the Court of Appeal if the basis of the decision or award is a matter or issue of the general law.

79 *Meiorin* BCCA, above note 14 (Factum of the Appellant at para. 1 [FOA]).

80 FOA, *ibid.* at para. 2.

81 *Ibid.* at para. 3.

82 *Ibid.* at para. 89.

83 *Meiorin* BCCA, above note 14 (Factum of the Respondent at paras. 52 & 53 [FOR]).

84 FOR, *ibid.* at para. 57.

85 *Ibid.* at para. 21 [emphasis in the original].

86 Curry interview, above note 42; Gall interview, above note 62.

87 Gall interview, *ibid.*

88 *Meiorin* BCCA, above note 14 at para. 18.

89 *Ibid.* at para. 20.

90 *Ibid.* at para. 19.

91 Gall interview, above note 62.

92 Curry interview, above note 42.

93 Interview of Gwen Brodsky (28 September 2007) [Brodsky interview].

94 Brodsky & Day, above note 53.

95 *Ibid.* at 468–71.

96 *Meiorin* SCC, above note 2 (Factum of Appellants at para. 117 [Appellant's Factum SCC]).

97 Brodsky interview, above note 93.

98 Appellant's Factum SCC, above 96 at paras. 110–16.

99 *Ibid.* at para. 116.

100 *Ibid.* at para. 160.

101 *Ibid.* at para. 159.

102 *British Columbia v. BCGSEU (Meiorin)* (10 January 1998), 26274, (S.C.C.).

103 *Ibid.* (Transcript at 51 [Transcript]).

104 Gall interview, above note 62.

105 *Ibid.*

106 Interview of Lindsay Lyster (28 September 2007) [Lyster interview].

107 *Meiorin* SCC, above note 2 (Respondent's Factum, Peter Gall and Lindsay Lyster at para. 58 [Respondent's Factum SCC]).

108 *Ibid.* at para. 83.

109 According to the Commission, the key issue was whether the employer could have adopted a non-discriminatory standard in order to achieve its legitimate safety objective. *Meiorin* SCC, above note 2 (Factum of the Intervenor the BC Human Rights Commission, Deirdre A. Rice, filed 29 October 1998, at para. 40).

110 *Ibid.*

111 *Meiorin* SCC, above note 2 (Factum of Interveners Women's Legal Education and Action Fund (LEAF), The Disabled Women's Network (DAWN), and the Canadian

Labour Congress (CLC) (Kate A. Hughes and Melina Buckley) at the Supreme Court of Canada, Filed 29 October 1998, at para. 15).

112 *Ibid.* at para. 49.

113 *Ibid.* at paras. 24 and 73.

114 The courtroom was packed with lawyers; there were four on the union's team, (Curry and Alman who were joined by Brewin and Brodsky), three on the government's team (Gall, Lyster, and Janine Benedet who joined at the last stage), two lawyers for the Coalition (Buckley and Hughes), and one lawyer for the BC Human Rights Commission (Deirdre Rice).

115 Rod Mickleburg, "A Fitness Ruling's Supreme Challenge" *Globe and Mail* (11 February 1999) A1.

116 Transcript, above note 103 at 2.

117 *Ibid.* at 42.

118 *Ibid.* at 50.

119 *Ibid.* at 55–56.

120 *Ibid.* at 58.

121 *Ibid.* at 67–68.

122 *Ibid.* at 76–77.

123 Nahlam Ayed, "B.C. Fitness Standards for Firefighters Eyed" *Globe and Mail* (23 February 1999) A4.

124 *Ibid.*

125 Lyster interview, above note 106.

126 Janet Rae Brooks, "Must a Firefighter be Fleet Footed?" *Globe and Mail* (27 February 1999) D2.

127 *Ibid.*

128 *Ibid.*

129 *Ibid.*

130 *Ibid.*

131 Province of British Columbia, Ministry of Forests, Protection Manual — Volume I, Interim Manual Amendment, 94/04/06, Chapter 7, Section 7.8.5., pp 1–2.

132 *Ibid.*

133 Interview of Janine Benedet (26 September 2008) [Benedet interview]; Lyster interview, above note 106.

134 *Meiorin* SCC, above note 2 at para. 42.

135 *Ibid.* at para. 42.

136 *Ibid.* at para. 54.

137 *Ibid.* at para. 68.

138 *Ibid.* at para. 73.

139 *Ibid.* at paras. 74–76.

140 *Ibid.* at para. 77. Note that the 1997 study commissioned by the government on the effect of training on female subjects would have partly addressed these concerns if the Court had allowed it to be admitted as evidence. See discussion above at note 102.

141 *Meiorin* SCC, above note 2 at para. 80.

142 *Ibid.* at para. 81.

143 *Ibid.* at para. 82.

144 *Ibid.* at para. 84.

145 "Judging Common Sense," Editorial, *Globe and Mail* (11 September 1999) D10.

146 Benedet interview, above note 133; Lyster interview, above note 106.

147 Michael Lynk, "Disability and Work: The Transformation of the Legal Status of Employees with Disabilities in Canada" in The Law Society of Upper Canada, *Special Lectures 2007: Employment Law* (Toronto: Irwin Law, 2007).

148 The current pump and hose test is the only one component of the three-part University of Victoria *Bona Fide* Occupational Test that is still used. In addition to the pump and hose test, the current test used by the BC fire service includes a pack test, which is a job-specific test in which participants must carry a 45-pound pack over a measured level 3-mile course in less than forty-five minutes. British Columbia Forest Service, Protection Branch, *Fitness*, online: Fitness — Protection Branch — Ministry of Forests and Range — Province of British Columbia bcwildfire.ca/Employment/FireFighter/fitness.htm.

149 In 2007, roughly 30 percent of the Unit and Initial Attack crews (950 employees) were women. Communication with Ralph Mohrmann, Superintendent, Staff Development and Safety, Fire Operations Section (19 September 2007).

150 Howard Dupuis, "An Overview of the Development and Implementation of Ontario Ministry of Natural Resources Physical Readiness Evaluation for Initial Attack Forest Fire Fighters (PRE-FIT)" (Paper presented at the Proceedings of the 2001 Wildfire Safety Summit, University of Montana) (6–8 November 2001) at 4, online: Wildfire Safety Summit 2001 www.iawfonline.org/summit/2001%20Presentations/proceedings.htm. See also Ontario, Ministry of Natural Resources, *Physical Readiness Evaluation for Initial Attack Forest Firefighters*, online: Physical Readiness Evaluation for Initial Attack Forest Firefighters www.mnr.gov.on.ca/en/Business/AFFM/2ColumSubPage/STEL02_165700.html.

151 *Barr and Flannery v. Treasury Board (Department of National Defence)*, grievance under the Public Service Staff Relations Act, 7 July 2006 (Guy Giguère, adjudicator).

152 Rachel Cox & Karen Messing, "Legal and Biological Perspectives on Employment Testing for Physical Abilities: A Post-*Meiorin* Review" (2006) 24 Windsor Y.B. Access Just. 23–53, 41.

153 N. Gledhill, V. Jamnik, & J. Shaw, "Establishing a *Bona Fide* Occupational Requirement for Physically Demanding Occupations," in N. Gledhill, J. Bonneau, & A. Salmon, eds., *Bona Fide Occupational Requirements: Proceedings of the Consensus Forum on Establishing BONA FIDE Requirements for Physically Demanding Occupations* (Toronto: 2000).

154 Above note 153, 34 and 41.

155 Interview of Dr. David Docherty (15 January 2009). Dr. Docherty was a member of the physical education department at the University of Victoria at the time of the *Meiorin* litigation. He was part of the team that was commissioned by BC to develop a replacement for the Smokejumper's test.

156 *Ibid.*

157 Meiorin recollects having to threaten to go to the media to obtain her cheque. Meiorin interview, above note 24. The problem was setting a date for the hearing to determine her back pay.

158 *Ibid.*

159 Equality advocates, however, failed to attend to the extent to which *Andrews* required that the plaintiff establish that the treatment complained of embodied or reinforced stereotypes. Judy Fudge, "The Supreme Court of Canada, Substantive Equality, and Inequality at Work" in Ockert Dupper and Christoph Garbers, eds., *Equality in the Workplace* (South Africa, Juta Legal Publisher, 2009).

160 [2007] 1 S.C.R. 161 [*McGill University Health Centre*]. In this case, Abella J. wrote concurring reasons, with McLachlin C.J. and Bastarache J. in agreement, which increase the burden on claimants with respect to the first step in any claim, namely establishing a *prima facie* case of discrimination. See paras. 44–49.

161 Judy Fudge, "From Segregation to Privatization: Equality, Law and Women Public Servants, 1908–2000" in B. Cossman & Judy Fudge, eds., *Privatization, Law and the Challenge to Feminism* (Toronto: University of Toronto Press, 2002) 86–127; Jacquetta Newman & Linda A. White, *Women, Politics, and Public Policy: The Political Struggles of Canadian Women* (Don Mills, ON: Oxford University Press, 2006).

162 *Law v. Canada (Minister of Employment and Immigration),* [1999] 1 S.C.R. 497.

163 2008 SCC 41.

164 It appears that *Kapp* signals a return to the two-step test set out in *Andrews*. See *Ermineskin Indian Band and Nation v. Canada,* 2009 SCC 9 at para. 188.

PART FIVE

Changing Common Law Norms

The Micropolitics of *Wallace v. United Grain Growers Ltd.*

Daphne G. Taras

WALLACE V. UNITED GRAIN GROWERS (1997) has become a mainstay of employment law.[1] It speaks to the manner in which the employment relationship is severed. In *Wallace*, the Supreme Court signalled that the point of dismissal is a time of particular vulnerability to employees, and, if employers are harsh and derisory when firing employees without cause, they must pay for their behaviour by increasing the period of reasonable notice for which they would be required to pay the employees' wages. This increase in reasonable notice damages has come to be known as the *Wallace* "extension," "bump," or "damages."[2]

This paper examines the micropolitics of the *Wallace* case,[3] paying particular attention to the impact on the lives of the people involved in the litigation.[4] When fifty-nine-year-old star salesman Jack Wallace was abruptly fired by United Grain Growers' Public Press division (UGG) on 22 August 1986, he engaged in eleven years of almost constant litigation, a period during which he was bankrupt, unemployed, and in a near-suicidal state. Three questions that were not answered in the legal reports — why the company fired its top salesman, how a bankrupt employee who was not unionized had the resources to sustain a complex legal battle, and why UGG pursued the defense of the wrongful dismissal action — will be answered in this chapter.

The conventional story is that UGG recruited Wallace, capriciously fired him, made baseless accusations against him, and then continued to pursue litigation to the Supreme Court, where Wallace won and was vindicated.[5] However, the backstory is quite different. Though UGG surely engaged in hardball tactics, it was Wallace's side that drove the case to the Supreme Court. Though the case is widely interpreted as a "win" for Wallace, his legal team actually failed to convince any level of court to adopt a new tort, [6] articulate a new form of damage, or develop a modern doctrine about employment. The team did, however, do a remarkable job of having unconditional faith in a client who had been wronged, and in persevering in a difficult fight to make employers pay for the use of unjust hardball litigation. The case was a gamble against long odds, fully consistent with Wallace's thoroughbred racing proclivities. Indeed, Wallace's 2005 obituary announced that a gathering to celebrate his life was held at the Assiniboine Downs Race Track.[7] This case reveals something about the odds of an ordinary person — with all the requisite foibles and inadequacies — litigating an employment case to the Supreme Court.

The Legal Terrain Underpinning the *Wallace* Litigation

WALLACE WAS ARGUED AT the crossroad between the traditional contract-based interpretation of employment, and a rapidly-developing pressure to treat labour as more than a commodity engaged in an exchange relationship.[8] The battle in *Wallace* was whether there ought to be an implied common law duty of good faith in employment imposed upon employers and expected by employees, particularly during the termination process.[9] Wallace's counsel argued for a good faith duty, and also urged the courts to create a new tort of bad faith discharge. The practical struggle in *Wallace* is exactly how the courts — finally sympathetic to the plight of unfairly discharged servants in the master-servant relationship — might craft some additional recompense for an employee the justices believe has been metaphorically kicked while being ushered out the door of the master's home.

The Supreme Court grappled in *Wallace* with the precedent first set in *Addis v. Gramophone* (1909).[10] *Addis* expressly foreclosed damages for "the manner in which the wrongful dismissal took place, for injured feelings or for any loss he [the employee] may sustain from the fact of his having been dismissed of itself makes it more difficult for him to obtain fresh employment."[11] This approach was affirmed in Canada in *Peso Silver Mines* (1966).[12] But there seemed something distasteful about not providing some measure of relief for blameless employees who were treated terribly while being fired. Beginning especially in the 1980s, lower courts began finding ways of softening, blurring, and working around the edges of *Addis* and *Peso*. For example, if the terminated employee's acute distress was reasonably foresee-able, and the employer's actions needlessly created harm, then damages for the distress could be based upon a tort of reckless or intentional inflection of emotional distress. Further, some judges simply exercised their discretion to lengthen the notice period in order to compensate for the effects of joblessness and paralysis due to mental anguish, while avoiding any overt legal characterization. The key for the judiciary was to avoid tackling *Addis* and *Peso* head on, and, instead, to maintain the substantial room for judicial discretion in devising notice period remedies.[13]

The 1989 case of *Vorvis*[14] opened a window for the Supreme Court to re-assess *Addis* and *Peso*, but the majority decision disappointed those anticipating a departure from the contract approach to employment. *Vorvis* was criticized for its insensitivity to the long-term nature of the employment contract, which requires elements of ongoing cooperation, trust, and reciprocal relationship-building.[15] While the majority decision, written by Justice McIntyre, explicitly upheld the rule that the only damage that can arise from common law employment is from a failure to give notice, the decision contained a whiff of hope for the future:

> I would not wish to be taken as saying that aggravated [emotional distress] damages could never be awarded in a case of wrongful dismissal, particularly where the acts complained of are also independently actionable, a factor not present here.[16]

In other words, perhaps different facts might lead to a substantial doctrinal revision.

While *Vorvis* seemed to confirm the judiciary's traditional approach to the employment relationship, Chief Justice Dickson's oft-quoted dissent in *Reference Alberta* (1987) affirmed the importance of employment in modern life.[17] He stated:

> Work is one of the most fundamental aspects in a person's life, providing the individual with a means of financial support and, as importantly, a contributory role in society. A person's employment is an essential component of his or her sense of identity, self-worth and emotional well-being.

Lawyers and legal scholars hoped that *Wallace* might be the vehicle through which the Supreme Court could affirm Dickson's holistic appreciation of the employee, the role of work in attaching the person to society and community, and place an obligation on employers to treat their employees decently.

If the Supreme Court continued to embrace the reasoning in *Addis*, then the only issue in *Wallace* was the amount of compensation owed to the employee for wages during the period of reasonable notice. In a 1960 case, *Bardal v. The Globe and Mail*,[18] the Ontario High Court calculated the notice period (or severance in lieu of) on the basis of employee attributes such as age, experience, training and qualifications, and the nature of the employment, including the seniority held by the employee. *Bardal* factors were developed to estimate the impact of termination on the ability of an employee to acquire alternative employment. *Bardal* simply did not include any consideration of the employer's behaviour, and whether that behaviour was considerate or egregious. That was to change in the *Wallace* case.

Jack Wallace[19]

UNTIL HIS FIRING, JACK Wallace had been a man of great vigour. During most of his working life, from 1947 to 1972, he worked for Lawson Graphics. With a grade ten education, he entered the printing industry at a menial level. At age thirty-three, he went into sales, developing business accounts with clients who needed printed products such as advertisements and brochures. He flourished, becoming his employer's top salesman, an honour he held until he left the company.

Wallace was not "induced" to leave Lawson; instead, he became amenable to leaving because he had serious disputes with his employer. Lawson twice only paid him a finder's fee for a Bulova Watch account and not the larger commission to which he was entitled, and then, due to a restructuring, planned to remove all his Toronto customers. He also felt that Lawson Graphics had unjustly dismissed an employee half a year earlier.

At the same time, a minor player in the printing industry had a major business decision to make. Public Press was a wholly-owned subsidiary of UGG. The commercial printing operation at Public Press was on the brink of disappearing. Commercial printing only accounted for 2 percent of the company's production, and the printing plant was obsolete. In 1972, Public Press authorized a complete overhaul of the business to make it more profitable. Don Logan was given the task of taking a printing division with a value of only $200,000 and increasing its value to $3 million. Part of the urgency was to recoup the cost of purchasing an expensive "web" press. He started with a sales staff of two, and continued recruiting. He needed someone with a stellar sales record in a specific type of equipment and with certain kinds of customers. In short, and in his own words, "We wanted someone like Jack Wallace so bad we could taste it."[20]

Wallace initiated the contact with Logan by telephone and then the men met, secretly, at the duck pond in Winnipeg's City Park. Wallace did not want his current employer to know he was looking, and he wanted explicit assurances from Logan that Public Press would provide the strongest possible job security. He told Logan that he was making good money and had a pension and excellent benefits. He worried that Public Press offered only salaries, while he preferred a commission plan. He was fearful that his lucrative accounts might be taken away from him and redistributed to Public Press sales staff. He also confessed that his life was in turmoil, as he had separated from his first wife and was with a younger woman who later became his second wife. Logan testified that he said to Wallace:

> Jack, there is no earthly reason why you can't have a job for the rest of your days. If you perform like you say you're going to perform and like I believe you're going to perform . . . . And I might add like he did perform . . . that he could be assured that he had a job. There was no way Public Press of UGG would release a man with no cause when he was performing properly.[21]

Logan offered a better benefit package, assurance that Wallace could retain his accounts, and fair treatment on commission rates; he also promised that other matters would be ironed out over time, smoothed out over the foundation of a trusting relationship between the two men.

When Wallace moved to Public Press, 90 percent of his clients followed. By 1976, Public Press achieved its turnaround. Wallace received praise and accolades. There is no doubt that Wallace and his loyal client base were instrumental to the success of his employer. Even after Logan left Public Press in 1975, Wallace prospered.

Wallace's downfall commenced with the arrival of new management. In early 1986, Public Press hired Sales Manager Leonard Domerecki, and General Manager Jim Kirch. Within days of assuming their duties, they spearheaded a change in compensation. Wallace, the aging lion, roared his disapproval. Wallace had "no hesitation in telling people how to do things."[22] Because of Wallace's objections, the personnel manager changed the compensation plan to make it fairer for all employees. Whereas before Wallace complained, the base salary contemplated by the company was $20,000, after Wallace pointed out the deleterious consequences of this low base on pensions and life insurance entitlements, the company raised the base to $40,000.[23]

But Wallace continued to do battle with the new managers. He objected to another provision in the new compensation plan that read:

> The sales representative will be expected to meet the standards of the business plan and the budgets as agreed to by the company and the sales representative. Should the sales representative fail to meet budget, then they will leave themselves subject to disciplinary action which may or may not include termination of employment.

Wallace told Domerecki that he was concerned that even if he tripled the output of other salesmen, he might still be dismissed for failing to reach targets. He refused to sign a contract that would authorize the company to dismiss him. Even so, the general manager praised him on his sales record, and Domerecki complimented him on how well he was going to do in the next year.

Secure in his belief that his sales performance made him invulnerable, Wallace discounted warning signs that the new managers found his style insubordinate. Two days later, Domerecki and Wallace fought about a $300 storage charge incurred by a client, Busy Bee. Against company policy, Wallace had removed the charge from Busy Bee's quote. After Wallace offered to pay, Domerecki authorized the company to deduct $300 from Wallace's draw.

General Manager Kirch ordered Domerecki to "fire Wallace on the spot." Domerecki objected, saying "We don't have any reason to. If you are talking about this one instance [$300 Busy Bee charge] then that to me is not a reason to fire someone." Still in the morning of that same day, Wallace was asked to go to the company boardroom and there Domerecki fired him while a witness watched. In the anguished words of Wallace in court:

> And I then said to [Domerecki] "for what reason"? And his answer was, "I am not prepared at this time to give you a reason." I responded saying, "You have to — why — how could you do — say something like this and not be prepared to give me a reason?" And he said, "I am not prepared to give a reason. I'm asking you to leave the building" . . . . And I said, "But I can't comprehend that." He reiterated the same statement and, and I, I was just bewildered; I was devastated. I didn't know what was happening. I couldn't — just couldn't comprehend it. [Note that the judge asks him to speak up because he cannot be heard clearly.] I still can't.[24]

After the firing, Kirch instructed Domerecki to audit Wallace's files and to locate anything negative.[25] Subsequent investigation revealed evidence of

Wallace's allegedly sloppy use of a company credit card, his unauthorized hiring of two salesmen in Toronto, and his occasional carelessness with confidential information.

Wallace was devastated by his termination, and hid it from his family. But he was not paralyzed; within a few days he retained Sylvia Guertin to pursue action for wrongful dismissal. She initially was working in the same law firm as William Riley and George Orle, and when she established her own firm, Wallace moved with her. In due course so too did Riley and Orle, and the law firm was then called Riley, Orle, Guertin, Born.[26] Wallace's extraordinary luck in his choice of lawyer and law firm is a key element in explaining the advancement of his case.[27] One week after his termination, Wallace received a letter from Domerecki advising him that he was "terminated for failure to operate and carry out responsibilities of his position." Guertin replied with a typical lawyer's letter, asking for severance in lieu of notice. The company responded that Wallace was dismissed with cause. Guertin knew that UGG only needed to offer a severance package in exchange for a release and the case would be over, so she and Wallace crafted a settlement of the wrongful dismissal suit for $75,000 — an amount based on Wallace's age, years of service, and record of success.[28] The company refused to settle and reasserted its claim that it had cause to dismiss Wallace without notice. Guertin's simple letter generated a team of opposing counsel from the UGG's law firm Pitblado, which she found shocking for a fairly routine matter, and deeply offensive.[29] Her fee-for-services was to be the lesser of one-third of the final severance, or her direct hours, plus disbursements. After seeing the obstacles that were erected against Wallace, she was prepared to wait years for settlement of even a fraction of costs, and even to provide Wallace with forceful representation from the firm irrespective of cost.

The employer's key mistake was in trying to avoid paying severance. Instead, UGG attempted to elevate a series of annoying but not normally fatal employee errors into just cause. When Wallace fought back, they dug in their heels because there actually was a pattern of aggravating behaviour that they tried to force across the just cause threshold. For a middle-aged and long-service employee earning over $76,000 a year, the normal *Bardal*-factors analysis would make for a costly severance package. Perhaps Kirch and others took an aggressive stance because they wouldn't accept that Wallace might be entitled to a "windfall" of, say, over $100,000 simply for refusing to accept the legitimacy of managerial authority and questioning policies and procedures. Moreover, discrediting Wallace in the job market would have the additional benefit of preventing him from gathering his many loyal clients and delivering them to a competitor press.

Three Pitblado lawyers, Peters, Sokalski and Watchman — all with first name, Robert — were assigned to defend UGG. The case escalated and began consuming extraordinary amounts of legal attention from two law firms. Guertin was married to her firm's partner, William Riley. She was outraged by what she perceived as bullying tactics from Pitblado, and she enlisted Riley and George Orle, to create a unified show of counterforce against Pitblado. The two sides became evenly matched, three against three. As Riley felt that the whole situation was becoming unfair to Wallace, he and Orle began appearing *pro bono*. Initially Wallace covered disbursements, and then, when he could no longer afford even those costs, the firm subsidized the fight. They hoped to recoup a portion of their real costs later on by winning their case, but were willing to take a risk of having to write off the expenses and time. The more resources Pitblado produced for the case, the more fiercely determined Riley became to provide a match, which explains how Wallace obtained the resources to continue his legal battle.

Pitblado's "lawyering up" is an oddity. The explanation for the excessively vigorous defense is startling in both its simplicity and its implications for employment litigation. UGG was renowned for its risk management practices, and was even featured as a Harvard Business School case. In the 1970s and 1980s, the company performed a risk exposure analysis. Many companies limit their thinking to traditional business risks, but UGG extended their enterprise risk planning to all operations, including human resources.[30] UGG's general liability insurance policy was truly comprehensive, and it provided compensation for legal defence costs. Insurance would not indemnify the company for the actual amount of severance in lieu of notice because salary is a foreseeable cost of doing business.[31] With UGG's litigation costs covered by insurance, however, there was no incentive to contain legal expenses. Early settlement of Wallace's claim would put a stop to Pitblado's billing, but continuing to fight the case with three lawyers could rack up billable hours without costing the client company much except the possibility of increased insurance premiums on the next policy renewal.

The lengthy discovery phase of litigation triggered Wallace's descent into rage and depression. Discoveries went from spring of 1987 through to the summer of 1988. Wallace faced his previous employers and a panel of lawyers and tried to defend against a barrage of accusations. He became irritable, erratic, and too angry even to have people visit the house. His wife

William Riley and Sylvia Guertin-Riley in the 1980s.
Photo courtesy of Justice Guertin-Riley.

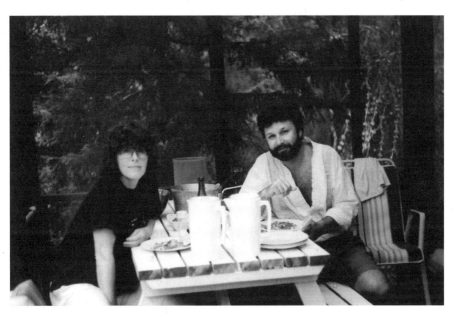

Sylvia Guertin-Riley and George Orle in the 1980s.
Photo courtesy of Justice Guertin-Riley.

urged him to see a doctor. He refused, and his relationship with his wife deteriorated. His wife was a successful executive at the Manitoba Wheat Pool, and she was losing her patience.[32] Mrs. Wallace testified that he was particularly devastated

> because he got all of his, his being from his job. That was his pride and that's what he excelled at and that's what he did. So when they took that away from him they took away everything because his life revolved around that.[33]

A man of considerable pride, he initially refused psychiatric help and also tried to hide his unemployment from two of his three adult children, so great was his shame. The eldest son, who worked in the printing business in Vancouver, was told because he was likely to hear rumours of the firing.

Patricia Wallace reported that her husband became obsessed with his case. "He — his every waking moment, that's all he thought about. He couldn't think about anything else other than what he felt that were the injustices done to him. So in my view, he should have been able to put it behind him and get on. So I started having concerns."[34] The confident man she married was vanishing, and she sought reassurance from Riley, her husband's lawyer, that there were sufficient legal grounds to justify the personal toll on Wallace. While she was a successful executive manager, her husband had deteriorated. She and Riley developed a close friendship, especially after Guertin withdrew from the case after being called to the bench. Riley gladly provided the counsel and support that Mrs. Wallace needed to sustain the many years of litigation.[35]

Wallace's attempts at mitigation were unsuccessful. He applied for jobs, but was never re-employed. Among his nine letters of application to printing jobs, he even reapplied to his first employer, Lawson Graphics, and later for his own former job at United Grain Growers.[36] Wallace was convinced that his reputation was destroyed by rumours of wrongdoing circulating in the close-knit printing trade. Although the company never alleged that Wallace was involved, he was embittered that the timing of his dismissal coincided with the unrelated dismissal for fraud of two co-workers. He worried that the unfounded negative association would render him unemployable in his trade.[37]

His wife believed that he was a step away from suicide.[38] His only activity was "walking around the malls."[39] As he put it, "[T]here was just no other place to go. What do you do when you've worked for 43 years and, and all of a sudden you're in my situation?"[40] Without the affirmation of his job, he thought life had lost all significance. He visualized driving into oncoming cars, but then didn't want to harm others, so he thought instead about smashing into a pole.[41] During this long period he also tried to divert some of his former Public Press clients to the rival printer who employed his son.

The many *Wallace* court decisions do not do justice to the effects of a company's hardball tactics on the psyche of an increasingly fragile person. Not only was the company alleging cause, but the pre-trial discovery phase of the litigation was upsetting. During discoveries, Wallace was relentlessly grilled about all his mistakes, and he was psychologically battered by the aggressiveness of UGG lawyers. Later, when Wallace's counsel tried to show how the discovery hardball tactics had harmed Wallace, the employer's counsel repeatedly tried to quash any reference because the company had rescinded its allegation of cause. This left Wallace dangling in an odd place; he had been through hell during discoveries, which could not be acknowledged in court because of the legal fiction that "to re-hash" any discovery issues was irrelevant to the case before the court.[42] Wallace said,

> I, I couldn't see how somebody could do the damage they had done to me over that period of time and then just rub them out like you had eraser and it was all like it never took place. I certainly never — I couldn't rub it out; I couldn't get rid of it. I was — all the damage had been done, all the statements, so they could do whatever they wanted. And at the last moment they could rub it out and say it never happened. We have — we remove it all. I was — it was just unbelievable to believe something like that could happen.[43]

Wallace began seeing a psychiatrist *after* the company's charges of just cause were withdrawn. Counselling commenced for an hour and a half once a week for a year or two, and then an hour a week thereafter. The members of his legal team reported that by the time Wallace appeared at the Court of Queen's Bench, he was shattered. While his wife's demeanour and testimony were "magnificent," Wallace was tentative, humiliated, and he bore no resemblance to the proud man they initially represented.[44]

The Litigation

Court of Queen's Bench

THE TRIAL OPENED AT the Court of Queen's Bench on 12 December 1988. The plaintiff's first argument[45] was that he had a fixed-term contract entitling him to compensation until he turned sixty-five. His former boss, Logan, was unequivocal in testifying that he provided Wallace with the assurance of job security. Wallace's legal team advanced the position as if it were an explicit "no cut" clause given to professional athletes; that a "no cut" contract was plausible because Wallace had rare and valuable skills when he was offered job security assurances; and Wallace was owed a breach of contract package equal to what Wallace would have earned until the normal retirement age.[46] In the alternative, they sought damages for reasonable notice and mental distress as well as punitive damages. From the outset, Wallace's advocates also tried to advance employment law by advocating new legal actions. They argued that the independent cause of action that *Vorvis* appeared to require for mental distress and punitive damages could be established either via the implied contract term of good faith or in a new tort based on bad faith at termination.

On the opening day of the trial, 12 December 1988, the employer retracted its position that Wallace was fired for cause. It had become clear during the discovery phase that UGG would not meet the burden of proving it had cause to terminate Wallace, as the testimony of both Lawson and Domericki (by this point, neither employed by Public Press) supported Wallace's claims. UGG decided to have the court determine the length of reasonable notice. The employer also protested (in a losing argument) that the *Limitation of Actions Act* in Manitoba prohibited claims for mental distress.

The trial then paused for over three years, reconvening in the spring of 1992. This lengthy delay was caused by the UGG's lawyers' "bombshell" discovery of Wallace's bankruptcy. Wallace was a compulsive gambler, and he was a bankrupt from 26 September 1985 until 29 December 1988. He had incurred debts of over $200,000. UGG amended its pleadings to include Wallace's bankruptcy, and then Pitblado lawyers argued that Wallace could not have the standing necessary to advance his own case, as the monies being sought actually belonged to the trustee in bankruptcy. In fact, Guertin contacted the trustee and was told the trustee had no interest in recovery of the funds. The trustee never advanced any claim or appeared in any action related to Wallace's litigation. The Court nonetheless accepted the UGG argument and declared the case over, but the Wallace team immediately appealed. After many months, the Court of Appeal overturned the Queen's Bench decision, and instructed Queen's Bench Justice Lockwood to proceed to hear the employment portion of the case on its merits.

During this period, the lawyers jockeyed for injunctions, protested issues of access to witnesses, and generally prevented the resolution of the case.

Justice Lockwood's patience was worn thin; at times he was peevish and even aggressively irritated. For example, he began griping:[47]

> I think the problem is, if I may say so, that there are too many lawyers on this case . . . . three on each side gives rise to some of the kinds of complications, I think, that we've had throughout the case.

Faced with a one objection after another from two teams of lawyers, he complained at times that he could not keep up with the case details.

Wallace had little money to pay his legal team and could no longer cover even routine disbursements. Four months after he was fired in August 1986, he finally received $4,500 from his employer, presumably for his commissions. He did not receive information from Public Press about the disposition of his retirement plan until late October 1988.[48] On 13 December 1991, the company provided another $3,500 to square away the commission issue. During a break in the trial in December 1991, the company made its first formal offer to settle for $150,000 inclusive of costs, which Wallace rejected. Finally, in the midst of the case in 1992, the company likely provided $100,000 severance in lieu of notice, but it is not clear whether the funds reached Wallace or were held in trust.[49] During the trial itself, the acrimony ran so high that it was not possible for the parties to provide the judge with an agreed-upon statement of facts as to Wallace's actual earnings.

The legal arguments were complex. A run-of-the-mill wrongful dismissal case only takes into consideration the conventional *Bardal* factors, but Wallace's legal team was trying to create either a new obligation of good faith in dismissal or a tort of bad faith discharge. His lawyers claimed that the employer's duty of care with regard to termination was to "avoid mental anguish and suffering in loss of reputation."[50] Thus, they had to show that the employer's hardball tactics resulted in his being needlessly stressed in the discoveries. Wallace's lawyers had to argue that "the conduct of the defendant from that point forward, constituted harassment and oppression on the plaintiff, either willful or negligent."[51] The delicate task was to raise these charges without allowing any of their substance to be revealed.

The company did not want its post-termination treatment of Wallace used to illustrate hardball legal tactics, but UGG did want to reveal that there were substantive job performance problems in the pre-discharge personnel files. The company was putting forward a covert near-cause case while explicitly adopting a without-cause position. A careful reading of the company's grudging retraction of its just cause position makes this abundantly clear:

The defendant says that while the grounds for termination set out in paragraph 8 herein did exist, the defendant after pre-trial discoveries, withdrew its allegation that such grounds were cause for termination in the circumstances.[52]

On the other hand, the company feared that Wallace would use "the fact that there were examinations for discovery in the pre-trial procedures that exacerbated their client's position . . . from which he should be entitled to damages."[53] The company saw the trap — that its allegations against Wallace might form a separate head of damages.[54] However, in order to vigorously defend against the possibility of a high monetary penalty (whether in the form of reasonable notice, damage for mental distress, or punitive damages), the company had little option but to allude, whenever possible, to matters that would tarnish Wallace's character. Justice Lockwood was inclined to allow information about the discovery allegations to be revealed in court:

I think it's important for this Court to know whether those grounds had any substance to them or not. It may even go to credibility . . . . I mean, this is the first we've heard since the filing of Exhibit 38 of insubordination, incompetence and misrepresentation of authority, and — well, I think the Court is entitled to have some particulars relating to those three heads . . .[55]

Wallace was caught in the very trap that he had set for the company. By leading with a claim of compensable mental distress, he opened himself to aggressive cross-examination designed to raise credibility issues.

Wallace's lawyers were grappling with exactly how to insert the concept of good faith into the facts of the case. They succeeded in having UGG's personnel manager admit that Justice Dickson's dissent — in essence, that employment is essential to self-worth — was an implied term in the employment contract. Orle asked the UGG manager whether this familiar phrase should be read into the employment relationship: "[I]n the sense of the policy, or practice of, of United Grain Growers, would, would you agree with this statement that a person's employment is an essential component of his or her sense of identity, self worth, and emotional well-being."[56] Justice Lockwood interrupted to say that he vaguely recalled the excerpt and the company lawyers stated that they believed it was from a textbook. This was an ephemeral fragment in a lengthy transcript of the trial, but it definitely illustrates that very early on, Mr. Wallace's lawyers were grappling with exactly how to wedge good faith into the facts of the case.[57]

Justice Lockwood's 1993 Court of Queen's Bench decision held that Wallace had been wrongfully dismissed, but did not find the Wallace side's fixed-term contract theory plausible. The justice was skeptical that any employer would agree to a fixed term some twenty years prior to retirement, especially since so many other terms of the employment agreement remained vague. Justice Lockwood had to determine the appropriate entitlement to severance pay in lieu of reasonable notice. Judges had always wielded discretion over the quantum of severance, and the monetary range was broadening across the country. Applying the classic *Bardal* factors, Justice Lockwood ordered twenty-four months pay, writing into his decision that this was the "high end" of the scale. Because Wallace could demonstrate that his efforts to mitigate his unemployment were sincere and vigorous, he received a sympathetic hearing using *Bardal*. Wallace was awarded $157,718.26 for lost wages and commissions. The Court also ordered the usual 3 percent interest to be tagged onto this amount to recognize Wallace's lost opportunity to invest these monies. For mental distress, Wallace received an additional $15,000, which Justice Lockwood hinted was a generous amount.[58] Justice Lockwood linked the damages award to the defendant's behaviours: "[M]y finding of aggravated damages was an indication that the conduct of the defendant was not proper conduct. If there was any unnecessary evidence, it resulted from the defendant's position which it maintained to the end of the trial."[59] However, he denied the punitive damages claim.[60] In truth, the Wallace team had never expected punitive damages, as these were very rare, and they actually had worried that the awarding of punitive damages might open an avenue of appeal to the UGG.[61]

Given the seven years of litigation, the issue of costs was not trivial. The Court awarded Wallace his costs taxed on a party and party basis, which did not take into account his actual costs but simply referred to a fixed schedule of fees. In other words, (as is common in such litigation) he received some recompense, but not nearly all of his lawyers' costs.

The case did not end at the Queen's Bench level, with the payment by the company. Though bankrupt, dispirited, and possibly suicidal, Wallace remained obsessed and litigious. He was the appellant throughout all subsequent litigation, although there were also a number of cross-appeals by UGG. Although analysts of *Wallace* have rarely reported it, there was considerable additional legal skirmishing before the case continued to the Court of Appeal. His wife urged him to stop his strange behaviour. A normal person would have negotiated for a package and put an end to the fight. Wallace's gambling problem might well indicate an addictive personality. According to Orle, it was clear that Wallace "had an easy eye on risk."[62]

At this point, senior lawyer William Riley's character also was a factor. Occasionally known to "tilt at windmills" (in the affectionate words of his partner, Orle),[63] and to develop fixations (according to his wife Guertin), he genuinely believed he was crusading both for his client and for a greater public interest in good faith. Riley shared Wallace's obsession with the litigation.

An Unsympathetic Manitoba Court of Appeal

AMONG THE ISSUES BROUGHT to the Court of Appeal by Wallace were preliminary matters asserting that he had been prejudiced by the trial judge's acceptance of the UGG's amended pleading to include matters pertaining to the bankruptcy (which the Court of Appeal rejected); that UGG ambushed Wallace by not raising the bankruptcy earlier and therefore was estopped from arguing matters related to the bankruptcy (which also was rejected); that Wallace was entitled to maintain his legal action rather than the trustee in bankruptcy (which the court affirmed because the trustee chose not to intervene); and then the crux of the termination case, that the trial judge erred in concluding that there was no binding fixed-term employment contract until retirement (which the court rejected); that the trial judge erred in not accepting that there was a "unique contractual arrangement" that included a "guarantee of security" and implied good faith treatment in employment (rejected); and that there was a separate independent cause of action in tort for bad faith discharge (rejected).

At the Manitoba Court of Appeal, Wallace's bankruptcy and the wrongful dismissal became interwoven strands, much to Wallace's detriment. Justice Scott, writing for all three justices, was unsympathetic to Jack Wallace. He noted that the trial judge had found that Wallace had "concealed his bankruptcy," and he recounted facts that had not been disclosed by his colleague at Queen's Bench in the first written award, including details about how Wallace's creditors "received nothing."[64] According to Justice Scott, on 16 May 1986, Wallace applied for a discharge from bankruptcy, but it was opposed by his trustees. Twice more, Wallace was examined pursuant to the *Bankruptcy Act*, and failed to disclose that he was suing his employer for wrongful dismissal. Indeed, Wallace used different counsel for his bankruptcy proceedings and his wrongful dismissal suit.[65] It appears that some members of the Court of Appeal suspected that Wallace manipulated an end to his bankruptcy without disclosing to his creditors that considerable assets were in play.

Justice Scott also noted that Wallace concealed his bankruptcy from the very psychiatrist who had testified about his mental deterioration. While Justice Lockwood had accepted that the aggravated damages from mental distress flowed from the "subsequent harassment of the plaintiff" by the employer, Justice Scott was not so generously inclined.[66]

The Court of Appeal reviewed the tendency for severance awards, particularly those of long-serving employees, to mysteriously increase. In particular, the Manitoba Court of Appeal 1994 precursor decision *Wiebe* was cited favourably in Justice Scott's decision, surely a danger sign because that Court cut Wiebe's severance award in half.[67]

The approach adopted by the Court of Appeal in *Wallace* was to take into account the manner in which the dismissal occurred as relevant only because it adversely affected Wallace's future employment prospects. Hence, it made sense to simply assess the notice period rather than develop a separate head of damage. The previous finding of twenty-four months was reduced to fifteen months, even taking into account employability issues. The court noted that in early 1992 the employer had paid Wallace $100,000, roughly fifteen months' wages. The court commented that the trial judge had been too sympathetic, in that "an element of aggravated damages must have crept into the determination,"[68] and thecourt refused any aggravated damages.

The argument by plaintiff's counsel that there existed as a separate cause of action (a tort called "bad faith discharge") was dispensed with rather curtly. Wallace's lawyers had discovered that Toronto lawyer Stacey Ball was an articulate advocate of this theory.[69] Ball had spoken on this topic at a conference and it was reported in *Lawyers Weekly*. Riley and Ball exchanged information and Riley was delighted to read Ball's 1994 *McGill Law Journal* article, "Bad Faith Discharge." Ball was convinced that it was only a matter of time before this theory of bad faith discharge would be argued before the Supreme Court:

> I thought the *McGill Law Journal* article would be my proxy to put my arguments before the Court. I knew the issue would be argued, so when I wrote my article I was putting the theory together for someone else to argue it, thinking that within ten to fifteen years it would be presented. I was writing it for someone else to use.[70]

The first use of Ball's article came quickly, but the Court was unconvinced:

No authority is advanced for this proposition, other than an article by Professor Stacey Ball entitled Bad Faith Discharge . . . in which it is argued that such a tort should be recognized by Canadian courts. Implicit in this is the obvious point that it has not yet achieved that status.[71]

After this drubbing, Wallace was left with no aggravated damages (losing the $15,000 he had been awarded), and only an amount about equal to what the employer had already paid him in anticipation of losing the case.

The parties again went to court regarding costs. The legal system embraces what laypeople describe as a "game of chicken." If a litigant refuses an offer of settlement outside the courtroom, but the court gives an award that is less than the offer, the party who refused the offer takes on the legal costs of the offeree from the time the settlement offer is made. On 30 September 1994, the company made Wallace another settlement offer that was "substantially" more generous than what the lower court awarded. Thus, the mischief of dragging the employer for another round of court meant that Wallace might have to pay his former employers' costs. However, a technicality saved Wallace. The employer's time-limited offer was withdrawn on 7 October 1994. The litigant's entitlement to costs only applies when the offer has not been withdrawn or expires.

The bankruptcy issue, always casting a shadow in Wallace, had the additional effect of coming to the rescue on costs. Wallace always met the threshold issue with respect to arguments on the effect of his bankruptcy,[72] and therefore he was awarded some costs throughout all levels of the legal system.[73]

When UGG hired new chief legal counsel Christopher Martin mid-way through the legal battle, he examined the Wallace file, and switched from Pitblado to John Scurfield.[74] Scurfield was instructed to make efforts to settle the case. Wallace's counsel, George Orle, recalls "a real turnaround after the new counsel arrived. The United Grain Grower's subsequent actions spoke well." The record illustrates that UGG made earnest settlement attempts at about the Court of Appeal stage. A substantial offer was made after the Supreme Court granted leave to appeal.[75] However, Wallace and Riley refused offers because they hoped to take the case to the Supreme Court. They were both convinced that larger issues were at stake for all Canadian employees, and that they had a moral responsibility to proceed with the case.

At this point, Wallace was beyond the normal retirement age. Ironically, three years after firing Wallace, UGG developed an early retirement incentive program for which he likely would have been eligible and he might have quietly retired in 1987. In 1991, the printing division of Public Press was sold.[76] For almost the entire time the case was being fought, the employer was defending managerial decisions of former managers of a division that no longer existed within its corporate structure.

Supreme Court of Canada

WILLIAM RILEY DESPERATELY WANTED to carry the case forward to the Supreme Court, but his health failed while he was applying for leave to appeal. His materials were ready, and he had made extensive preparations to argue the case. Stacey Ball would fill the vacuum created by Riley's illness. Ball was officially retained by the Manitoba firm, and did not meet Wallace until the case was argued before the Supreme Court. Ball never saw the earlier trial transcripts. By the time he commenced his preparations for the case, it was sanitized. The bankruptcy and dismissal issues were now completely bifurcated. Ball eventually prepared the entire leave application in a considerable rush and based it almost entirely on the idea that Canada should develop its own modern approach to employment law, with a bad faith tort and good faith implied term. He had to structure the application to meet the Supreme Court's "national importance" criterion. The agreement was that Orle would focus on the bankruptcy issue.

In Ottawa, Wallace observed the case as it was argued before the full Court, but his wife and family stayed at home. He was cognizant that the case was important for the development of public policy on employment, and rationalized that his years of torturous litigation might provide some good to all Canadians.

The Supreme Court justices were cordial and animated. Ball recalls that "it was like a thesis defense with nine exceptionally bright professors grilling you." Orle recalls correctly that Ball "had a tough go at it. Other than the justices from Quebec (who were familiar with the *abus de droit* concept), the others were aghast at taking away the right of employers to terminate in any manner."[77]

In oral arguments,[78] Ball urged the Court to undertake this "very modest increment to common law." The Court neither accepted the modesty of the submission nor understood exactly how good faith in employment could be distinguished from the concept of cause. Justice Major repeatedly asked for a definition of good faith. Justice McLachlin pointed out that good faith was already incorporated into the concept of cause. Justice Sopinka seemed irritated at the lack of precision. Ball's explanations of good faith and fair dealing were not lucid enough to satisfy the judiciary. The lack of conceptual clarity made it impossible for the justices to determine whether it was possible to have cause for immediate dismissal but a separate head of damage for bad faith in the process of discharge, or whether good faith and fair dealing would apply only to wrongful dismissals. Chief Justice Lamer tried to muddle through the concept:

> Maybe you don't like the person because he is sleeping with your wife, but he is a bad salesman, so you terminate and feel good about it, versus a situation where you like someone and feel bad about terminating, but you have to do it out of an obligation to your shareholders.

Justice Gonthier explained: "It may be a question of the manner in which you terminate; choosing a time that is particularly damaging to an employee." Only Justice McLachlin indicated she grasped the good faith concept.

Then the grilling really began. Justice Iacobucci attacked the appellant's position that good faith is a modest step. "This is quite revolutionary," he said. "Isn't this for the legislatures to make? It is such a bold step." Justice Major threw a life preserver: "You are going against a long period of jurisprudence that says that if you have bad faith it relates to the period of notice. One option is it can go to the period of notice": here is evident the inexorable tug of the majority's obvious effort to find a way of dealing with the poor conduct of employers in an incremental, non-revolutionary way.

Ball presented a list of cases in his factum and oral argument in which lower courts, and courts in other countries such as New Zealand, did provide damages for bad faith. However, he illustrated his point with a number of Canadian cases in which the courts added months to the notice period, and the justices clearly were attentive to the idea of extending the notice period.

Scurfield[79] appeared for the employer, and forcefully argued that no wrong was done in the termination itself, and that it is "not the Court's job to enforce social niceties." Justice Cory queried in his gracious way: but what if in the "manner of dismissal, an allegation of addiction to alcohol is made when that doesn't exist, or an allegation of dishonesty when that doesn't exist, or of incompetence when there was none?" Scurfield replied that these constitute defamation, and are independently actionable. He said UGG's termination was more analogous to saying "I don't like you."

Photo of Jack Wallace and Stacey Ball, *Toronto Star* (26 May 1994) D3.
Photo reproduced with permission of David Chan, photographer, and the Toronto Star.

Scurfield then ridiculed Ball's argument that he was asking only for "mild, incremental change . . . I suspect that the employers of this world will have a heart attack." He raised the spectre of the ire of the Canadian Federation of Independent Business, and of the Reform Party, and he was rebuked by Justice Lamer for his politician-like demeanour, who said, "You are in the wrong building." He quickly replied, "I'm in the wrong building. Yes, that's exactly my point! It is for the legislature and not the court."

Justice Gonthier began crafting a compromise position. "It is not that wild a thing. The common law reacts to what is going on around it. Some measure of nicety, of good faith could be introduced." Scurfield tried to defend his position by pointing out that almost a century earlier when common law precedents first developed that allowed perfunctory termination, there was no social safety net. Today, the notion that employees are especially vulnerable neglects the developments in public policy that provide greater social welfare programs. He urged the justices to extend the notice period rather than create the "emotionally attractive" but "deliciously vague" tort of bad faith discharge.

When asked about the *Wallace* facts, Scurfield restated a near cause theory of the case:

> I will concede M'Lord, that cause was not proven. But . . . in this particular case we are not talking about *no cause*. We are talking about cause that ultimately, after discovery, was withdrawn at the eve of trial. There was *clearly* evidence to indicate cause.

He began besmirching Wallace in earnest, using credit card charges, unauthorized hiring, and gambling.[80] He tried to make Wallace's actions the moral equivalent of the employer's by decrying: "After 25 years with his former employer, he took all his clients away and gave only one-month's notice!" (This tactic was somewhat repugnant given that UGG was the beneficiary of these clients.) Scurfield also argued that Wallace only deserved twelve months' notice because he was only an uneducated salesman.

Finally, Justice Iacobucci intervened to restore more respectful treatment of Wallace: "He was clearly a valuable member of the employer's team . . . A salesman can be more important than any other employee in the business."[81] At no point did the justices stop Scurfield from making a near-cause argument, despite the fact that they were close to dismissing the near cause doctrine in *Dowling v. Halifax* (1998) with a one sentence oral decision: "We do not accept any argument relating to near cause."[82]

Ball's argument in reply was short and sharp:

Even today, we are still receiving allegations about character in connection to Mr. Wallace even though the learned trial judge decided there was absolutely no cause for dismissal and they were trumped up reasons. Even today the way this appeal is being conducted should have a bearing on punitive damages. Mr. Wallace is here hearing this; this hasn't ended.

The next step in the proceeding was for UGG counsel to present their cross-appeal stating that Wallace did not have the right to sue his employer because he was an undischarged bankrupt. Although the arguments were technically interesting, there was a nagging sense that something was off. Schwartz, the lawyer for UGG's cross-appeal, argued as if his client was the bankruptcy trustee, when it was obvious that the actual trustee declined to get involved. Tactically, this cross-appeal seemed to be the springboard only for a further character assassination of Wallace.

With regard to costs, Ball said in a 2007 interview, "From my perspective, money was completely irrelevant. I was determined to argue that we should not be shackled by contract law from my grandfather's age." He asked only for his disbursements, which were paid by Wallace's law firm,[83] and he remains unaware of how Wallace financed the case.

In their written decision, six out of the nine justices decided that the appropriate remedy was to restore the trial judge's severance award of twenty-four months, without any additional damages. Justice Iacobucci wrote, for the majority (including Lamer, Sopinka, Gonthier, Cory, and Major, JJ.) that ". . . employers ought to be held to an obligation of good faith and fair dealing in the manner of dismissal, the breach of which will be compensated for by adding to the length of the notice period."[84] The decision was conservative, and avoided making any "radical shift in the law, again a step better left to be taken by the legislatures."[85] The majority dismissed the cross appeal on bankruptcy matters, and accepted the appeal in part with costs.

The novelty in the majority's approach in *Wallace* to bad behavior by the employer during the termination process carved out an unexpected solution that dodged good faith and a new tort, but uncomfortably shoehorned employer conduct into the determination of reasonable notice. Justice Iacobucci's decision added the following factors to the *Bardal* list for determining reasonable notice: inducement; promise of job security; assurance of fair treatment (via commission-based wages); and bad faith conduct in the manner of dismissal.[86] He extended the notice period because of the devastating results on re-employment prospects when dismissal is accompanied by acts of bad faith.[87]

The defects of the majority decision and the strength of the three-person dissent authored by Justice McLachlin have been thoroughly analyzed elsewhere. The majority decision was at best a kind-hearted though deeply internally-flawed attempt to develop a small sanctuary for employees at the mercy of their employers. The *Wallace* extension tied directly to employer conduct does not rest easily on a clear and logical foundation.[88] Suffice it to say that a sharp criticism found its way into legal scholarship.[89] The Court's unexpected "bump" fell far short of creating a doctrine of good faith dealing in employment contracts, or even the creation of a tort of bad faith discharge. It took an entirely different route to acknowledging employee vulnerability by making the bad behaviour of the employer during termination another ingredient in the notice period stew by treating it as simply another *Bardal* factor.[90]

Riley was so disappointed in the Supreme Court decision that despite being weakened by terminal cancer, he came to work with a ten-page reconsideration memorandum drafted for the Supreme Court.[91] He still believed that Wallace had entered into a "no cut" employment agreement with UGG. Orle and Wallace together told Riley to stop, and that they were not prepared to invest any further energy in fighting. The interaction between Wallace's desperate plight, the munificent resources of opposing counsel, and the company's early refusal to settle all fueled Riley's determination to see the case through to the end — of the case, and of his remaining life.[92] Riley died shortly after the Supreme Court of Canada's decision was released.

Analysis and Conclusions

SINCE *WALLACE*, THE ARGUMENTS made by plaintiff counsel and court decisions allow a clearer picture to emerge about employer conduct. Perhaps bad faith treatment always propelled certain cases forward,[93] but there was no great incentive to make explicit claims in the past. According to a list prepared by Stacey Ball, between 1998 and 2006, *Wallace* arguments were made in forty-four out of 130 reasonable notice cases, and *Wallace* extensions resulted in an average of three-and-a-half months of extensions per successful claimant, equal to a parsing out of about 22 percent of the total notice period awarded.[94] However, these findings do not mean that the severance period (including *Wallace* extensions) increased since even before *Wallace*; it is possible that some recompense for employer bad conduct might have crept into the determination of reasonable notice.

The *Wallace* extension initially had the unintended consequence of privileging wealthier plaintiffs. The emphasis on months of service meant employees who are paid much more for their service will get a higher monetary award than others. While using months to determine the notice period is appropriate, because notice is tied to performance of job duties, the use of notice tied to anguish is not, strictly speaking, correct, either legally or ethically. Had the Supreme Court awarded $15,000, then that would have become the benchmark for bad faith damages. In 2008 in *Keays v. Honda,* the Supreme Court eliminated this problem by transforming the "bump" into more fixed *Wallace* "damages," writing: "The amount is to be fixed according to the same principles and in the same way as in all other cases dealing with moral damages."[95]

Not surprisingly, *Wallace* has rolled out into all sorts of venues. It seeped into the unionized sector, *Canada Labour Code* Part III adjudications, and human rights tribunal decisions.[96] It also affects out-of-court settlements, where the vast majority of disputes are settled. In the privacy of conference rooms and telephone calls, in mediation sessions and settlement talks, issues involving bad faith and hurt feelings naturally arise and shape settlement discussions. It is only in the formality of the courts that the fiction can be maintained that good and bad faith are irrelevant. In the out-of-court venue, the parties deal with both employer and employee conduct as they negotiate appropriate severance amounts.

From a strictly financial standpoint, Wallace was best off at the Manitoba Court of Queen's Bench, or shortly thereafter when the employer tried to pay him more than the court had ordered to entice him to stop litigating. The Supreme Court of Canada did less for him than Justice Lockwood did at the Court of Queen's Bench. The employer also lost. While hardball tactics may cause capitulation and settlement in most situations, it fueled the resolve of Wallace and his legal team.

Newspaper and legal newsletter coverage in the two years following *Wallace* demonstrates that in the short term, employment lawyers — both on the plaintiff's side and on the employer's side — are probably better off as a result of *Wallace.* Lawyers on the plaintiff's side are likely consulted more often by employees who are fired in nasty ways. There was an incentive for fired employees and their counsel to allege that the employer botched the dismissal.[97] The burden of proof of establishing bad faith discharge is much lower than demonstrating an independent actionable tort for mental distress.[98] Until courts began to demonstrate a growing intolerance for the practice,[99] plaintiff-side litigators made aggressive demands for *Wallace* damages.

Employment lawyers jumped on the *Wallace* holding in order to promote good faith dealing. The Canadian Employment Lawyers Network's[100] website proclaims that the majority decision in *Wallace* (from which it quotes) affirms that a duty of good faith exists "during and after" employment, which exaggerates *Wallace*. Billable hours for the employer's counsel are not endangered by *Wallace*. Indeed, they have gained another reason for their clients to consult with them prior to dismissing employees.[101] Most importantly, aggressive tactics by employers have softened, as a hardball gambit to bring the parties to an out-of-court settlement might expose employer clients to *Wallace* damages.

Management consultants and outplacement counselors also benefit from *Wallace*. For example, in a paragraph justifying the industry in which she is situated, which was also a glowing tribute to the late Jack Wallace, the president of Bowes Leadership Group wrote:

> Thankfully, most companies today employ career transition counselors to assist former employees to deal with termination. They want to treat former employees as humanely as possible and they want to mitigate any legal damages that might arise. Career transition programs assist individuals regain their self-esteem and to recognize that their self worth is built on more than their job title.[102]

Companies have received the *Wallace* message loud and clear. "The point here has to be driven home to every employer," said Ed Ryan, vice-president of financial advisory services at PricewaterhouseCoopers in Edmonton. "A $5,000 fraud can turn into a $100,000 wrongful dismissal suit if an employer doesn't go by the book."[103] All reputable human resource management texts in Canada contain admonitions to avoid *Wallace* damages.[104]

Despite the legal defects of the majority decision in *Wallace*, and the vociferous legal and academic criticisms of the *Wallace* decision, the impact of *Wallace* on employer practices was positive. Oddly, *Wallace* helped disseminate the idea of good faith exactly as though it had been enthusiastically affirmed by the courts. Whether the Supreme Court offered an implied term, a tort, a longer notice period, or separate awards for aggravated or punitive damages, it seemed to have no bearing on the way *Wallace* rolled out into managerial practice. The case was widely disseminated in newsletters and announcements to managers.[105] *Wallace* socialized a generation of managers to believe they have a legal obligation to be considerate to employees and allow them a measure of dignity. Conventional wisdom is that Wallace won his case.

Until the Supreme Court of Canada's 2008 decision in *Honda*, the practical ramification of *Wallace* for the layperson was that the quantum of severance monies might increase simply by showing that the employer's dismissal was done in a needlessly hurtful way. However, *Honda* has raised the evidentiary bar so that the employee must now establish that there was causation and foreseeability between the employer's acts and the deleterious effects on the employee.

For public policy developments, piercing the veil of *Wallace* reveals a chilling confluence of oddities — an obsessive litigant, a benevolent law firm, two sympathetic management witnesses, and a cost-cushioning bankruptcy angle. Yet these circumstances have formed the springboard to justice for Canadian workers. Why should Wallace's misfortunes cause him to shoulder the burden of a broader public policy battle over good faith in employment? In the idiosyncratic backstories of common law cases, there must be legions of employees whose temperaments or wallets cannot withstand the fight for justice. *Wallace* is instructive because of its unique aspects, not despite them. This is not a sensible way to craft employment law.

Notes

1   *Wallace v. United Grain Growers Ltd.*, [1997] 3 S.C.R. 701 [*Wallace* SCC]. I am grateful
     for the contributions of Harry Arthurs and Geoffrey England, for whom earlier
     drafts of this paper were written in an Osgoode Hall LLM program. Valuable com-
     ments from Judy Fudge and Jim Phillips greatly advanced the chapter. Research as-
     sistance from Cameron Bean is appreciated.

2   In the aftermath of *Honda Canada Inc. v. Keays*, 2008 SCC 39, 66 C.C.E.L. (3d) 159, 166
     A.C.W.S. (3d) 685, 376 N.R. 196 [*Honda*], it is technically correct to deal only with
     "*Wallace* damages" as a fixed sum of money, and only if the employee meets the
     onus of establishing that the bad faith caused the employee's emotional distress.
     In future it is likely that it will not be so much the action of the employer, but the
     impact on the employee, that will give rise to the *Honda* threshold for *Wallace* dam-
     ages. Between 1997 and 2008, however, it was possible to achieve an extension to the
     notice period. The terms "*Wallace* extension" and "*Wallace* bump" which permeated
     employment law for a decade probably are no longer accurate.

3   The term micropolitics encompasses three elements: first, a level of analysis high-
     lighting individuals and groups; second, a label for their exchanges and the content
     of their interactions; and third, a connotative flavour that captures the political na-
     ture of the interactions among the parties, involving the amassing and reallocation
     of resources such as money, time, emotional support, or influence. This chapter is
     part of a larger SSHRC-funded study on the micropolitics of justice in selected Su-
     preme Court decisions involving employment and labour law.

4   Lawyers Stacey Ball and George Orle, Justice Sylvia Guertin-Riley, and retired
     United Grain Grower manager Michael McAndless have been interviewed. Concert-
     ed attempts have been made to interview others, and to contact the Wallace family.
     This chapter establishes the story using transcripts, interviews, and secondary
     sources, but there remain significant gaps.

5   These points are directly from Bowes' posting in *Workopolis*, commemorating Wal-
     lace after his death. B. Bowes, "The Wallace Factor" *Winnipeg Free Press* (20 May
     2005), online: www.winnipegfreepress.com/careers/bowes/story/2781958p-3220204c.
     html [Bowes].

6   A tort must arise from an additional damaging act, and not from the dismissal it-
     self. If an employer reasonably foresees that her harsh action during dismissal will
     cause anguish, this will create aggravated damages for committing the tort of inten-
     tional infliction of mental distress. See Ronnie Cohen & Shannon O' Byrne, "Cry Me
     a River: Recovery of Mental Distress Damages in a Breach of Contract Action — A
     North American Perspective" (2005) 42:1–6 Am. Bus. L.J. 97.

7   Obituary, *Winnipeg Free Press* (6 May 2005): "Suddenly on May 4, 2005 Jack passed
     away. Jack will be missed by his wife and soul mate Pat; three children . . . . Jack
     worked in the printing industry for over 40 years and was active in thoroughbred
     racing. A celebration of Jack's life will be held on Monday, May 9 between 1:30 and
     3:30 p.m. in the Terrace Dining Room, at the Assiniboine Downs Race Track."

8   For discussion of the visions, see David M. Beatty, "Labour is not a Commodity" at 313, and Katherine Swinton, "Contract Law and the Employment Relationship: The Proper Forum for Reform" at 337, both in Barry J. Reiter & John Swan, eds., *Studies in Contract Law* (Toronto: Butterworths, 1980). See also Mark Freedland, *The Personal Employment Contract* (Oxford: Oxford University Press, 2003), and Douglas Brodie, "Beyond Exchange: The New Contract of Employment" (1998) 27 Indus. L.J. 79.

9   Good faith in employment dealings already extended to Canadians living under the civil law system in Quebec. There, the doctrine of *abus de droit* of the general law had made its way into the employment setting. In 1990 the Supreme Court expressly affirmed an implied contractual term of good faith and fair dealing under the civil law of Quebec in *Houle v. Canadian National Bank* [1990] 3 S.C.R. 122.

10   *Addis v. Gramophone Co.*, [1909] A.C. 488.

11   *Ibid.* at 491.

12   *Peso Silver Mines Ltd. (N.P.L.) v. Cropper*, [1966] S.C.R. 673.

13   See, for example, the cases *Cronk v. Canadian General Insurance Company*, [1995] O.J. No. 2751, 25 O.R. (3d) 505 [*Cronk*], *Linkson v. UTDC Inc.*, [1991] O.J. No. 2567; and many others. In a 1987 study by McShane and McPhillips, the weightings given to various factors are parsed out of the Canadian wrongful dismissal data. Even though there is a general pattern, there also is considerable variance among and between the cases. Steven L. McShane & David C. McPhillips, "Predicting Reasonable Notice in Canadian Wrongful Dismissal Cases" (1987) 41 Indus. & Lab. Rel. Rev. 108.

14   *Vorvis v. I.C.B.C.* (1989), 58 D.L.R. (4th) 193 (S.C.C.) [*Vorvis*]. For a scholarly treatment of *Addis*, *Peso*, and *Vorvis*, see Judy Fudge, "The Limits of Good Faith in the Contract of Employment: From *Addis* to *Vorvis* to *Wallace* and Back Again?" (2007) 32 Queen's L.J. 529 [Fudge].

15   John Swan, "Extended Damages and *Vorvis v. Insurance Company of British Columbia*" (1990) 16 Can. Bus. L.J. 213. However, David Cabrelli argues that there is not much evidence that the duty of mutual trust and confidence is becoming an "over-arching principle" in "The Implied Duty of Mutual Trust and Confidence: An Emerging Overarching Principle?" (2005) 34 Indus. L.J. 284.

16   *Vorvis*, above note 14 at 1103.

17   From *Reference Re Public Service Employee Relations Act (Alta.)*, [1987] 1 S.C.R. 313, dissent at 368. This dissent is firmly embedded within his discussion of the particular importance of freedom of association for unions, and the role of unions as a means of protecting working people. The dissent is often taken to mean that Justice Dickson was commenting on employment in general. See pages in Robert J. Sharpe & Kent Roach, *Brian Dickson: A Judge's Journey* (Toronto: University of Toronto Press, 2003) at 357–64.

18   *Bardal v. The Globe and Mail Ltd.*, [1960] C.C.S. No. 755 (Ont. H.C.J.) [*Bardal*].

19   Much of this section is based on 1,200 pages of trial transcript at the Manitoba Court of Queen's Bench. The public record is truncated because hundreds — perhaps thousands — of additional transcripts were lost or destroyed, and discovery transcripts are not available.

20 *Wallace v. United Grain Growers Ltd.*, [1993] 7 W.W.R. 525 at 547 (Man. Q.B.) [*Wallace* Man. Q.B.].

21 *Ibid.* at 547.

22 Interview of Orle (7 May 2009) [Orle interview]. Please note that three interviews took place on the same date (7 May 2009): an interview with Orle, an interview with Guertin, and a joint interview with both [Guertin and Orle interview]. The endnotes are written as such.

23 *Wallace* Man. Q.B., above note 20 (Testimony of Personnel Manager Cousineau, 4 May 1992, at 30–32).

24 *Ibid.* (Wallace, direct examination, 1 May 1992, at 19–20).

25 Domerecki's testimony is quoted in *Wallace* Man. Q.B., above note 20 at para. 25.

26 In July 1995, Guertin became Justice Guertin-Riley of the Manitoba Court of Queen's Bench (Family Division) in Winnipeg and the firm was renamed.

27 To meet her is to appreciate the strength of this assertion. She is a formidable woman and would become easily activated by perceived injustice. Interview of Sylvia Guertin (7 May 2009) [Guertin interview].

28 Orle interview, above note 22.

29 Guertin interview, above note 27.

30 Interview of McAndless, then corporate risk manager of United Grain Growers (10 October 2008).

31 One policy extension is formally known as "Employment Practices Liability Insurance," and is commonly referred to as "litigation insurance." It was developed in insurance companies in the early 1990s, largely due to the costs associated with discrimination cases in the United States. It is "analogous to an HR malpractice policy": J. McGovern, "Evolving Canadian Employment Risk" (December 2005) *Canadian Insurance* at 24.

32 Guertin interview, above note 27.

33 *Wallace v. United Grain Growers Ltd.* (7 May 1992), Winnipeg 86-01-15299 (Man. Q.B.) (Trial transcript at 69–70).

34 *Ibid.* at 67.

35 Guertin interview, above note 27.

36 *Wallace v. United Grain Growers Ltd.* (1 May 1992), Winnipeg 86-01-15299 (Man. Q.B.) (Trial transcript at 80–82) [Transcript, 1 May 1992].

37 Guertin interview, above note 27. The co-workers had been fired in December 1985, and Wallace even cancelled his winter vacation to help UGG cover the workload.

38 *Wallace* Man. Q.B., above note 20 at para. 64.

39 Transcript, 1 May 1992, above note 36 at 40.

40 *Ibid.* at 40–41.

41 *Ibid.* at 42.

42 *Ibid.* at 51.

43 *Ibid.* at 70.

44 Guertin and Orle interview, above note 22.

45 The first three partners shared his case. The firm reconfigured into Orle Davidson Giesbrecht Bargen after Ms. Guertin joined the judiciary and Riley's death in 1998.

46 Orle interview, above note 22.

47 Quotes from Man. Q.B. transcripts, 4 May 1992, 27 and 36; See also Transcript, 4 May 1992 at 51; Transcript, 4 May 1992 at 52–53 [Transcript, 4 May 1992].

48 Transcript, 1 May 1992, above note 36 at 27–28, Wallace on direct.

49 The sum and timing are listed in para. 7 of the Court of Appeal decision *Wallace v. United Grain Growers Ltd.*, [1995] M.J. No 344. Neither Orle nor Guertin can recall the specifics on this matter. They do recall that Wallace was a "gentleman" throughout, and that he provided the agreed-upon one-third of settlement without protest, which, as Guertin put it "was much the lesser" of settlement or hours (7 May 2009 interviews).

50 From page 4 of their December 1988 pleading.

51 Transcript, 1 May 1992, above note 36 at 53.

52 *Ibid.* at 57. Wallace's lawyer is quoting from Public Press's re-amended statement of claim, para. 8 (c) & (d).

53 *Wallace v. United Grain Growers Ltd.* (4 May 1992), Winnipeg 86-01-15299 (Man. Q.B.) (Transcript, 4 May 1992, above note 47 at 23).

54 Transcript, 1 May 1992, above note 36 at 59.

55 *Ibid.* at 60–62.

56 UGG manager Raymond Cousineau's testimony also was used by defendant counsel to refute Logan. Cousineau testified that there were never any employees who had been given guaranteed employment until retirement (Transcript, 4 May 1992, above note 47, p. 8, line 20). The Dickson dissent tactic was used by plaintiff counsel in cross-examination on 26 April 1993, at 71–73, and 75 (lines 10–13). Mr. Cousineau's affirmative reply is at 76 (lines 16–21).

57 Such statements are used to imply a term of "fairness" into the contract of employment in the United Kingdom line of cases.

58 And indeed it is a generous amount. The frugality of Canadian courts is a feature of the system. Perhaps this helps prevent frivolous lawsuits. Canadians frequently ask for, and rarely get, damages. Even when they get damages, higher courts tend to reverse or decrease the amounts.

59 *Wallace v. United Grain Growers Ltd.* (27 October 1993) Winnipeg 86-01-15299 (Man. Q.B.) (Trial transcript).

60 *Wallace* Man. Q.B., above note 20. Wallace's lawyers had asked for "punitive damages or aggravated damages." Just in case the litigants were uncertain about the punitive damage issue because of a linguistic construction within the pleading, Justice Lockwood pronounced that the conduct of the employer was not sufficiently reprehensible to warrant punitive damages.

61 Orle interview, above note 22.

62 *Ibid.*

63 Riley's wife gave him a sculpture of Don Quixote, but George Orle's 1998 eulogy for the late William Riley noted that, "[i]t is often forgotten that Don Quixote did not deliberately go out to fight a windmill. Don Quixote saw a giant and where others would have retreated to safety he chose to do battle. Bill was like that." January 1998 eulogy notes. Other notes provided by Guertin contain descriptions of his personal

attributes as a lawyer, noting his bravery, determination, fighting spirit, tenacity, passion, courage, and fierce loyalty to clients.

64 *Wallace v. United Grain Growers Ltd.*, [1993] 7 W.W.R. 525, 49 C.C.E.L. 71, 87 Man. R. (2d) 161 at para 7 (Man. C.A.) [*Wallace* CA].

65 *Ibid.* at para. 26, Scott J.

66 For example, he makes negative comments about Wallace's concealment of his bankruptcy. *Ibid.* at paras. 15, 28, & 29.

67 *Wiebe v. Central Transport Refrigeration (Man.) Ltd.*, [1994] M.J. No. 279 (Man. C.A.). At para. 62, Justice Twattle commented that, "I mean to demonstrate my concern about the excessive length of the notice period for which employers, acting wrongfully but not in bad faith, have been found liable in recent years. This trend cannot be explained by inflation and only to a limited degree by other economic factors . . . . I do not understand why, when the principles to be applied in determining reasonable notice remains constant, the amount of time determined should be significantly larger now than it was in the past." Note that the Manitoba Court of Appeal seems to have tried to crack down on lengthening notice periods.

68 *Wallace* CA, above note 64 at para. 79.

69 He had also rehearsed many similar arguments, acting as plaintiff's counsel in *Ruggeiro v. Emco Ltd.* (1993), 6 C.C.E.L. (2d) 57 (Ontario Ct. Gen. Div). See Stacey Ball's important contribution: "Bad Faith Discharge" (1994) 39 McGill L.J 568.

70 Interview of Ball (29 January 2007).

71 *Wallace* CA, above note 64 at para. 104.

72 Analysis of the bankruptcy issue is beyond the scope of this study.

73 Wallace used this opportunity to argue that the interest rate ought to have been 8.5 percent (and not the Q.B.'s 3 percent). The Court admitted that the matter had been "overlooked" and that Wallace would get his award of interest to trial at the higher rate.

74 From 1982 to 1994, he practiced law as an associate and subsequently as a partner with Wolch, Pinx, Tapper and Scurfield in Winnipeg.

75 Orle interview, above note 22.

76 The Printing Division and Public Press Printing sale came into effect on 8 July 1991. Company information can be found in the University of Manitoba Archives and Special Collections, Agricultural Experience, United Grain Growers.

77 This section is based on an analysis of the two hours and twelve minutes of videotaped trial proceedings. Verbatim quotes are taken from the videotapes rather than from the trial transcripts. *Wallace v. United Grain Growers Ltd.*, [1997] 3 S.C.R. 701 (videotape of trial proceedings). For information about *abus de droit*, see note 9.

78 All the quotes in this section are from the oral arguments. The videotape of oral arguments was acquired from the Supreme Court of Canada and transcribed.

79 Now a Justice in the Manitoba Court of Appeals.

80 See *Wallace* SCC, above note 1 (Appeal book of the United Grain Growers at paras. 165–74).

81 In *Cronk*, above note 13 at para. 8, Justice MacPherson accepted arguments that despite Edna Cronk being only "a small cog" in a large enterprise, an employee's

position in the hierarchy of a company ought not to be a major factor in determining the notice period. The Ontario Court of Appeal overturned this approach and restated — in a split decision — that the character of employment remained a deeply embedded principle in the common law of employment.

82 That employee misbehaviour can shorten the notice period was rejected in *Dowling v. Halifax City* (1995), 147 N.S.R. (2d) 43 (N.S.S.C.); (1996), 152 N.S.R. (2d) 18 (N.S.C.A.); (1998), 1 S.C.R. 22. The near cause doctrine was declared "dead" in a decision characterized by Geoffrey England, "*Dowling v. Halifax (City)*: The Shortest Case Ever?" (1998) 6 C.L.E.L.J. 455. I am indebted to Rosalie Armstrong for her analysis of *Dowling*. However, near cause seems to be re-entering employment law through such cases as *Mulvihill v. Ottawa (City)*, 2008 ONCA 201, [2008] O.J. No 1070 and *Sommerard v. I.B.M. Canada Ltd.* (2006), 265 D.L.R. (4th) 484 (Ont. C.A). In both cases, justices held that failed just-causes defenses ought not to be punished with *Wallace* damages if the allegations of the employer were made in good faith.

83 Orle interview, above note 22.

84 *Wallace* SCC, above note 1 at para. 95.

85 *Ibid.* at para. 77.

86 *Ibid.* at paras. 81–83.

87 *Ibid.* at para. 95.

88 The decision contained two messages that contradict the main holding: (1) at *ibid.* at para. 104 ("However, in my view the intangible injuries are sufficient to merit compensation in and of themselves.") and at para. 107 ("I fail to see how it can be onerous [to employers] to treat people fairly, reasonably, and decently at a time of trauma and despair. In my view, the reasonable person would expect such treatment. So should the law.").

89 See, for example, Fudge, above note 14 at 549 and 553, and her description of Justice Iacobucci's decision as an "improbable and remarkable feat" that "undermined any pretence of rationality and logic in the determination of reasonable notice." I was unable to locate a single academic review in employment law that supported the majority decision. See, for example, Shannon O' Byrne, "Bad Faith — Contexts of Employment — *Wallace v. United Grain Growers Ltd.*" (1998) 77 Can. Bar Rev. 492; Lee Stuesser, "Wrongful Dismissal — Paying Hardball: *Wallace v. United Grain Growers*" (1997–98) 25 Man. L.J. 547; John Swan, "Damages for Wrongful Dismissal: Lessons from *Wallace v. United Grain Growers Ltd.*" (1998) 6 C.L.E.L.J. 313; Geoffrey England, "Recent Developments in the Law of the Employment Contract: Continuing Tension Between the Rights Paradigm and the Efficiency Paradigm" (1995) 20 Queen's L.J. 557; Simon Heath, *Good Faith in Wrongful Dismissal: Canadian Employment Law after Wallace v. United Grain Growers Ltd.* (Kingston: Queen's University-IRC Press, 2000); Kelly Van Buskirk, "Damages for Improvident Employer Behaviour: Two Judicial Approaches" (2004) 83 Can. Bar Rev. 755 [Van Buskirk]: Van Buskirk claimed that the approach "defies established contract law principles." She posed the perplexing question at the heart of the various critiques: "If the 'good faith' requirement (the breach of which leads to application of the *Wallace* Factor) is neither contractual nor tort based, how does a dismissed employee become entitled to additional damages

by virtue of its breach?" (at 782); David J. Doorey, "Employer 'Bullying': Implied
Duties of Fair Dealing in Canadian Employment Contracts" (2005) 30 Queen's L.J.
500. I. McKenna, "The Aftermath of United Grain Growers — Time to Revive the Employer's Contractual Duty to Provide a Safe Workplace?" (2000) 27 Man. L.J. 415.

90 See *Bardal,* above note 18 at para. 145.

91 Orle's eulogy notes for Riley confirm that "He intended to tell them how they can
make the *Wallace* decision better and where they went wrong. I doubt that there is
even one 'with all due respect' in the whole letter" (January 1998).

92 Orle and Guertin interview, above note 22.

93 In 1995, I interviewed twenty Calgarian workers and lawyers involved in wrongful dismissal lawsuits. Consultation of a lawyer upon dismissal was mainly
determined by the manner in which the employee was treated at the point of employment rupture. If employees were offended by their treatment — even if the employment relationship had otherwise been excellent over many years — they sought
legal assistance.

94 From a list of cases in Stacey Ball, *Employment Law* (Aurora, ON: Canada Law Book,
1995–2006) at ss. 9:50.1–9:50.6. *Wallace* extension cases are listed in 9:50.8. Care should
be taken in interpreting these figures, as there was one double-counted case, and
these may not be the universe of applicable cases.

95 *Honda,* above note 2. Quote from para. 59.

96 See, for example, *Sunset Lodge v. British Columbia Nurses' Union,* [2003] L.V.I. 3404-
1, B.C.C.A.A.A. No. 299 (British Columbia Arbitration Board), Arbitrator Hope
[Tataryn grievance]; eight other cases were located through using *Wallace* as a
search term in Quicklaw's labour arbitration cases. For human rights tribunals,
see *Bradley v. Fire-Trol Canada Co.,* 2005 BCHRT 212, [2006] B.C.W.L.D. 5169, [2006]
B.C.W.L.D. 5174, [2006] B.C.W.L.D. 5173. It is worth noting that for the 30 percent of
Canadians who are unionized, labour arbitrators comfortably deal with matters of
bad faith because of their ability to order reinstatement. They routinely make near-
cause calculations when assessing back pay amounts as a measure of bad faith by
the employer or near-cause by the employee.

97 Howard Levitt wrote that "[l]awyers and even employers could predict with reasonable certainty how much severance an employee was entitled to. Such predictability
is now virtually eliminated. What can now be predicted with confidence, however,
is that employees' lawyers will scrutinize the conduct of employers in order to assert that it was unfair or in bad faith, and thereby obtain additional severance."
Levitt, "Firms Must be Humane in Firing or Pay . . . Supreme Court Awarded Higher Severance for Bad Faith Behaviour" *Toronto Star* (2 March 1998) D3 [Levitt].

98 This point is made by Janice Payne & Mark Chodos, "The Evolution of the *Wallace*
Duty of Good Faith and Fair Dealing" (1 June 2006), online www.nelligan.ca/e/pdf/
Ninth_Annual_Sic_Minute_Employment_Lawyer.pdf, at 20–24. However, in *Yanez
v. Canac Kitchens et al.,* [2004] O.J. No. 5238 (Ont. Sup. Ct.), Justice Echlin signals a
coming "crackdown" on dubious *Wallace* extension arguments. Employer sloppiness
in the *Yanez* case is not, declared Justice Echlin, in any way equivalent to the type of
"hardball" that won Wallace his extended notice. See also Justice Kelleher's decision

in *Jalan v. Institute of Indigenous Government*, [2005] B.C.J. No. 929 (B.C.S.C.). In an interesting twist, in *Sun-Da v. APS Architectural Structures Ltd.*, [2004] B.C.J. (B.C. Prov. Ct.) at paras. 96–97, $500 was deducted from a wrongful dismissal award due to the *plaintiff's* post-termination conduct. The Ontario Court of Appeal reversed the payment of *Wallace* damages because the employer had made allegations of just cause in good faith, and although the employer rescinded the charges later in order to effect settlement, this was not found to be a hardball tactic. *Mulvihill v. Ottawa (City)*, 2008 ONCA 201, [2008] O.J. No 1070. See also *Sommerard v. I.B.M. Canada Ltd.* (2006), 265 D.L.R. (94th) 484 (Ont. C.A). Justices are no longer punishing employers with *Wallace* extensions for failed just cause defenses when they are made in good faith.

99 In *Yanez, ibid.*, Justice Echlin suggested that plaintiffs making frivolous *Wallace* claims could face cost sanctions.

100 *Canadian Law*, Canadian Employment Law Network, online: www.celn.org/index. php?rollid=canadian_law. CELN is devoted exclusively to the individual employee's side of the employment equation. The Canadian Association of Counsel to Employers (CACE) is the employer side organization.

101 Levitt, above note 97. See also Howard Levitt, "Courts Recognize Value of Reputations: Handsome Awards in Cases of Employer Misconduct" *National Post* [national edition] (14 June 1999) D9.

102 Bowes, above note 5.

103 Quoted in R. Ziegler, "Use Golden Rule with Employees: Even with Cause, Dismissals Can Backfire" *Edmonton Journal* (10 March 1999) F7.

104 Ten textbooks in human resource management, personnel management, and organizational behaviour were consulted before making this claim.

105 The rollout of *Wallace* through practitioner newsletters would make a fascinating subject in its own right. As Edelman, Abraham, and Erlanger noted in their comprehensive study of this phenomenon in the US: "Personnel journals make the threat of wrongful discharge lawsuits more vivid by giving employers advice on what actions they must take to minimize the likelihood of being sued and of liability should lawsuits occur." Employers were offered worst-case scenarios, with ominous warnings that reinforced the need for both vigilance and professional advice from employment lawyers. See Lauren B. Edelman, Steven E. Abraham, & Howard S. Erlanger, "Professional Construction of Law: The Inflated Threat of Wrongful Discharge" (1992) 26:1 Law and Soc'y Rev. 47 at 67. My scan of Canadian practitioner literature reveals the same tendency to inflate the dangers post-*Wallace*.

Afterword: Looking Back

Harry Glasbeek

CONVENTIONALLY, THE TALE OF the movement toward our contemporary collective bargaining scheme is seen as a progressive one. There is a widely shared belief that, as liberal capitalism matured, it became imperative to engineer statutory interventions with the preceding reign of the common law regulation of capital and labour relations. The old regime was insensitive to the inevitably harsh outcomes of its workings, an institutional indifference that did not sit well with the emerging spirit of inclusive citizenship and Keynesian welfarism. In this telling of the tale, the guardians of the common law, the courts, tend to be cast as the villains of the piece, with legislators and their administrators as the rescuers of the imperilled. One of the benefits of this volume is that, taken together, the chapters suggest that the picture is far more complicated. The road toward modernity was not a straight one; there were many bends and occasional U-turns. The narratives, by situating legal struggles in their social and political contexts, invite closer scrutiny of the interplay between the old regime and the newer one, between the judiciary and the legislature, between individualism and collectivism. A nuanced portrait emerges from the collection, one that suggests that there is a continuum, that, as well as conflict between the courts and statutory engineers, between individual contract law and collective bargaining law, there is symbiosis, even congruence.

The offering from Brown and Llewellyn is typical of the way in which this collection invites analysis of this more perplexing kind. The usual lawyers' riff on the Privy Council decision in the *Snider* case is that it went against the grain of Canadian needs and public policy and that it demonstrates the rigidity, the formalism, and the outdated, to-be-rejected colonial cast of the English judiciary. The chapter provides some support for this perspective, but it does more than that. The authors point out that the employer took the view that a Conciliation Board was likely to impose wage increases that, in the prevailing labour market, it would not have to grant to its workers. Opportunistically, the employer sought to take advantage of a perceived reluctance by the federal government to enforce its own compulsory conciliation scheme. It refused to participate in the convening of a Board. The famed constitutional litigation was, thus, the consequence of the usual pursuit of a narrow self-interest combined with a (nicely highlighted) far less common political ambivalence within a government about the utility of its own policy. While the arguments before the courts were, as is the norm when the judiciary deals with constitutional issues, reduced to a pretend logic as to how lines could and should be drawn between obviously overlapping heads of jurisdiction, it is plain from the case study that the judges had their own "take" on what motivated the parties and the politicians. The piece gives us more than an inkling of what non-constitutional facts might have informed the various judges who dealt with the dispute. This opens up new avenues when reading the case.

The chapter proffers evidence that the local judges thought that stability required some regulatory scheme. Also noted is the fact that reliance on direct repression — albeit readily enough available by reference to judicially established law — was explicitly sought to be avoided by the federal government. Brown and Llewellyn also show that Canadian judges did not want the federal government to have to resort to legally sanctioned coercion. The judges had every reason to believe that their ideological/structural framework was not being questioned in any serious way by the *Industrial Disputes Investigation Act* (*IDIA*) and the practices under it —collective activities were still to be exceptional and the *IDIA* mechanism was to be a mere gloss on private property, freedom of contract, and individualism. The Canadian judges in favour of this regime were joined at the hip with progressive forces for labour.[1] These progressives also did not question the fundamentals of employment relationships crafted by the courts. Their support for the *IDIA*, and subsequent disappointment with the Privy Council, reflected both their desire to escape the restrictions of the judicially-created labour regulatory regime and their hope that this unmuscular, but nationally based, regime might be a springboard for a more union-friendly scheme in due course. However, the material provided in this valuable account of the *Snider* case suggests that there was a general consensus that the common law rubrics were to continue to furnish the fundamental criteria for the regulation of the relations between labour and capital.

A similar suggestion may arise from Bilson's presentation of the intriguing *John East Iron Works* litigation. It picks up the story after the *Wagner Act* concept of industrial relations had come to Canada. After World War II there was a new understanding: long-term relationships between employers and unions were to be promoted as a matter of public policy, and unionization was not just tolerated because it was inevitable. Inherent in the legislative schema was the notion that regulators, mediators, and administrators were to settle individual disputes as part of an evolving and continuing dynamic relationship between an employer and the union representing its workers.

Bilson's chapter sketches out how the recent popularity of social engineering in Saskatchewan boosted the belief of the government and its allies that the courts were mired in processes designed to deal with disputes arising out of past events and were unsuited to the polycentric decision making that was demanded by a regime that asked decision makers to weigh the impact of a particular resolution on ongoing and future bargaining and power structures. Specially designed administrative agencies had to be, and were, entrusted with these tasks. Courts needed to understand that they could not assert their original position as if it were untrammelled. Those who thought they might be able to profit from the pre-collective bargaining regime contested this curb on the judiciary in this early litigation on the Saskatchewan statutory regime.

The statutory intentions of the government were found to be so clear, however, that, when the case reached the Privy Council, it had little difficulty in upholding the jurisdictional scope the Labour Relations Board needed to attain the policy goals evident in the legislation. The case study shows how the Privy Council supported its holding by emphasizing that the judiciary would never have carved out the remedial powers and decision-making sphere now given to boards and that, therefore, nothing precious was being taken away from the courts. This was something of an acknowledgment that the common law's objectives and, therefore, the judiciary's roles, were to some extent distinct from those of the new regulatory regime. But the chapter also makes it clear that the Privy Council ruled that the courts were not to be ousted where they had carved out a role for themselves in capital/labour relations. It was decided that a court was still entitled to assess the amount of damages to be awarded for a breach of an individual's contract of employment. This residual jurisdiction was to be respected, even though the basis for upholding the Board's jurisdiction was that the issue as to whether there had been a breach of contract that violated the *legislative* regime should be left for the Labour Relations Board's sole determination. There was also a bow, then, to the continuing applicability of judicial power over individual contracts inasmuch as these invoked questions about judicially established remedial orders. Something of a shared set of responsibilities was embedded in this Privy Council decision that is usually — and in the Bilson chapter — rightly seen as an endorsement of the emergence of administrative autonomy over collective bargaining schemes. Negatively put, the decision recognized that the judiciary did not have to be the sole regulator of capital-labour relations; positively put, and more significantly, it was understood that the judiciary could be relegated to a secondary role in respect of some contractual issues, provided another *compatible* and legitimate regime was available to take up the slack. This is why, in the absence of specific limitations on the judges' powers to tailor remedies or an acceptable statutory substitution for them, they were to remain free to interfere with *Wagner Act*-type collectivism.

These chapters furnish evidence that there was a residual understanding that there was to be some continuing role for the common law, providing it respected some pro-collectivist measures. The courts responded positively to this unarticulated understanding. It can now be seen that the judiciary acted as a brake, but not as a total nay-saying institution. In any one case, of course, the need to honour this unarticulated understanding would not have been all that obvious to a judge. Thus, while there was an overall recognition by the judges of the need to transcend the original "sin of collectivism" position in order to provide political and economic stability, at times they leaned toward privileging the old thinking over the new. That is, repression had to give way to tolerance, but it did not do so in any linear form. Inevitably, this schizophrenia led to haphazard decision making in the courts.

The nature of judicial decision making is illustrated in Davidson's chapter on the Royal York Hotel case. The holding that the contract of employment could not be ended during a lawful strike made *functional* sense once the *Wagner Act*-type policy of limited tolerance for union activities had been established: the constrained entitlement to strike at a particular point of time, over a limited number of subject-matters, would have no political resonance if workers could be dismissed if they used this power properly. But, that said, the rhetoric employed in the case, and later by Laskin, the father figure of the movement that sought to deny that the common law of contract of employment had any role to play in the collective bargaining regime,[2] was just that: overblown rhetoric, a kind of cracking hardy to assert, rather than to prove, that the advent of statutory collective bargaining has done away with the outmoded and inapposite common law contract of employment doctrines and ideology. In fact, as is clear from Davidson's lucidly presented account, the decision was pragmatism at work, a decision aimed at giving the statute scope without declaring, once and for all, that older rules, ideals, and ideas, were dead and buried.

The legal reasoning in the Royal York Hotel case was technically unpersuasive. The fact that it was even thought legally plausible that a court might hold that a striking employee lost her job was testament to the respect accorded to the contract doctrine that a cessation of work amounted to a fundamental breach of contract by an employee. After all, as Davidson notes, the governing statute explicitly stated that "no one shall deemed to have ceased to be an employee by reason only of . . . a strike or lockout." Yet, the case that the contract might cease was hotly pressed and the courts felt it necessary to resort to peculiar reasoning to counter what they manifestly were convinced were, potentially, respectable common law arguments. They held that there were individual contracts of employment but that an employee's security could not be governed by contract law as the rules incidental to the contract of employment's enforcement had been displaced. The contract's viability in creating an enforceable relationship thus was validated, while its other attributes were not. The judges were not saying that the common law principles had been abrogated; rather they had been put on hold whenever a collective bargaining statute could be invoked. This clever side-stepping, however, left questions dangling. The courts' reasoning logically should have meant that a striking employee would never lose her status as an employee, no matter how long the strike were to last. This was not only absurd on its face, but it challenged prevailing practices.

Until that holding, no one had doubted the right of a struck employer to hire replacement workers, or his right not to give work to a returning striker if there was no work available. These underlying verities forced one of the members of the Supreme Court of Canada, Locke, J., to issue a strong dissent in the Royal York Hotel case. Moreover, in some of today's legislation, there are provisions that safeguard the strikers' right to return to their old jobs for a specified time only and/or to protect their entitlements to retain their seniority and/or their right to vote on collective bargaining issues. These protections for workers on strike make it obvious that, in their absence, the employment relationship and its incidents, may be terminated. There is no consensus, then, that the principles that govern the status of employment at common law had ever been totally abrogated.[3]

What is clear is that the guardians of the common law were willing to manipulate, indeed, mangle, their own rules to enable them to endorse the prevailing practices in capital/labour regulation. These judges, like their predecessors in *Snider* and *John East Iron Works*, in a quest for their own legitimacy and in deference to legislators and policy makers, showed they were ready to acquiesce to the polity's movement toward the promotion of unions and their collective activities. There was an implicit entente, however, that made it easier for the courts to allow some of the common law doctrines to be pushed aside to enhance collective bargaining purposes: the legislators and policy makers were not, and were not to be seen, to overturn the fundamentals of capitalist relations of production engineered by those judges. And this understanding was built into the collective bargaining models. Most significantly, they retained those features that enable employers to deal more efficaciously with their enduring problem: how to translate the commodity they purchase, labour capacity, into actual labour. This remains true today. Incidents of the common law contract of employment, such as the workers' duty to obey, to be of good faith and fidelity, and to exercise reasonable skill and diligence, are built into grievance and arbitration and employment standards' jurisprudence.

This organic, unarticulated alliance between the norms of the contract of employment and collective bargaining emerges from another aspect of Malcolm Davidson's chapter. He notes that one of the issues that agitated the union was the fact that the employer had tried to deal directly with the workers when seeking to dissuade them from taking action. Under the new regime of industrial relations, union security and legitimacy were to be promoted by the statutory understanding that workers would not be direct parties to the collective agreements that were to govern their lives. When the courts in the Royal York Hotel case held that the employment contract was not ended by a strike, they were endorsing this notion. From a strictly judicial vantage point this should have been a troubling issue for the judges: common law of contract logic does not sit well with a scheme in which people, whom both the courts and legislators classify as contractual employees, are bound by the terms of an agreement, but not parties to it. From the legislative perspective, one interested in a labour policy rather than contract law, it is a convenient position to take. This is not true for the judicial arm of the State. The pliability the decision revealed goes to the judiciary's willingness to tolerate incoherence to get the "right" policy outcome. It was a manifestation of the interest the judiciary shared with the other branches of the capitalist State in the maintenance of labour peace and productivity and of the courts' understanding that the *Wagner Act*-type scheme presented a better means than the pure common law of contract did in the emerging political economic circumstances.

Kaplan's story of the 1945 Ford strike draws attention to the extent of the shared concern with industrial peace. The elites who managed the famed dispute identified the problem of the closed shop to be the pivotal policy issue to be resolved. In one respect the case study is illustrative of the significance of the character of the players in any particular situation. The story makes it clear how important the intelligence and worldview of Rand, the judge appointed to cut the Gordian Knot created by intransigent parties, was to the eventual resolution. But, it is that judge's resolution that commands most attention. The innovative solution devised by Rand (and his advisors) was to bestow exclusive bargaining agent status on unions provided, and it was a crucial proviso, that they accepted the responsibility for the maintenance of discipline over the workers they represented and that they would do everything in their power to avert impermissible collective actions.

This resolution, because it was explicitly aimed at containing the dangerous-looking political and economic power of unions if they were accorded a positive right to use collective power by law, did much to sell the new collective bargaining model. On the one hand, it appealed to working class protagonists because it loosened the serious restraints imposed by the common law; on the other, it reassured liberal market capitalists by indicating that the regime was to be far from radical: unionism, by all means, but not all means for unions. Unions were to be representative and managers of discontent, not agents for real change.

Kaplan spends a good deal of time on the attributes of Rand and how they contributed to his design of a scheme of union security. However, it is also pertinent to note that Laskin, the intellectual leader of the arbitration bar, in his day and beyond, and of the academics who hold the view that the common law doctrines were unenlightened, did his level best to ensure that the conservative Rand's principles were cemented into collective bargaining law as early as possible. In *Re Polymer*,[4] Laskin laid down the proposition that unions and their officials could be held responsible and sanctioned for strike activities by workers in the bargaining unit they were certified to represent. Staunch protagonist of collectivism over individualism that he was, he nonetheless shared the view that the countervailing power of workers should not get out of hand; it was to be a limited form of collectivism. Just as the originator of the union dues check-off scheme had envisaged, the new regime was not to give workers any more assistance than political realities required. Rand's resolution to meet this problem was ingenious; Laskin's holding (which, as it turned out, gave directions to future arbitrators and courts) gave sharp fangs to this clever tool.

Unions had hoped that the new bargaining model would give them much more clout. From the beginning, they fought for industry-wide bargaining but, on the whole, employers found allies in the various labour relations boards which favoured plant-by-plant certification and bargaining.[5] At the risk of overstating the case, the overall tendency was for multi-employer or sector-wide bargaining to get an approving nod when it favoured employers, rather than workers. This trend showed up early on and has continued to be a dominant one.

Cadigan's chapter provides a contemporary example. The fascinating story told about the only instance of unionization of an oil rig in North America is remarkable for the evidence it furnishes about the limited commitment to true industrial pluralism. Cadigan notes how a government, driven by its desire to attract private investment, but under pressure to legitimate its decision to allow dangerous drilling to continue after the dreadful *Ocean Ranger* disaster, had to promote unionization to demonstrate its concern for workers. It is a well-told tale of extremely complex machinations to get to a satisfactory result — the government insisted on a form of representation that best suited the peculiarity of the industry and the legitimacy problems arising out of the apparent dangers of the operations and the aspirations of fractious union protagonists, while retaining the potential to maintain long-lasting industrial peace. Cadigan describes the result as a distorted form of corporatism, rather than an effectuation of established industrial pluralist principles. One of the emphases is that this apparent tolerance for unionization was evinced during a period when the government was imposing restraints on union activities in all other sectors. The chapter demonstrates that manipulation as to who is an appropriate agent and what is the scope of appropriate bargaining, while paying lip service to the voluntary nature of favoured collectivism always has been part and parcel of the scheme's working. Profitable productivity has been a central criterion.

As the scheme matured, there were many signals that collective bargaining was a public policy that courts should honour and, importantly to this comment, not worry about too much: inasmuch as the common law-crafted fundamentals had held worker economic and political power in check, there was no intention that that would change greatly. Of course, these signals were not plain to all and sundry, certainly not in the early days of the industrial pluralist regime, which explains the heat generated by the debates over whether or not the judiciary should just butt out. This debate was at its most pitched during the 1960s and early 1970s when there was a great deal of political turbulence. Workers and social movements were asserting claims in vigorous and extra-legal ways. There was a generalized apprehension that radicalism was in the air and that unions could not, despite Rand's and Laskin's urgings, be relied upon to still workers' militancy. Undoubtedly, this inclined the judiciary to impose restraints when called upon by discomfited employers. They turned back to re-establish the fundamental private property/contract institutions structures and the accompanying ideology they believed the new regulatory regime ought to preserve. On the face of it, the courts were looking backwards. It is this which made progressive academics, and the injured unions, portray the judiciary as a reactionary institution, as a forum that was not methodologically equipped to deal with multifaceted disputes. The discussions in the chapters by Tucker and Girard and Phillips are instructive.

As Tucker demonstrates in *Hersees*, the judicial methodology was impoverished, which made it easy for academics to raise the argument that the judiciary was heedless of its own methodology, just so that it could reach the anti-worker results it favoured. The overt class privileging language used by the Ontario Court of Appeal was a bonus and further explains the fascination this case had for academics. In discussing the storm of criticism, Tucker notes that scholars tried to identify a universalizing principle that could explain the courts' repeated anti-statutory decision making. They came up with one — the right to trade was to be defended by the judges, at the expense of apparent democratically designed policies, if need be. To the academics, this (usually unstated) old-fashioned objective made sense of the rigidities and formalism in the courts and made them feel justified in calling the courts a force of reaction that ought to be pilloried and marginalized.

With the benefit of hindsight, this academic criticism may have had a perverse effect on the jurisprudence. The criticisms were not to the effect that property and contract were no longer fundamental values, just that the courts' protection of them lacked elegance and manifested an unwarranted disrespect for novel statutory policies. This approach may have reinforced the courts in the belief that, if only they used technical law better, they would be justified in their restraint of collectivist strategies whenever these infringed the undisputed sphere of private property and contract. This would not have been hard. All that was needed was a finding that the impugned conduct infringed one of the almost countless, judicially created, protective shields around private property and contract, for example, inducement of a breach of contract, interference with contractual relations, trespass, or nuisance.

The point here may be that *Hersees* is important precisely because it was technically flawed and got the result that made sense to the court: a stout defence of the basic private property/private contract regime inasmuch as it had not been overtly affected by statute. Here the question asked, in this nicely documented paper, as to why it might be that the unions did not take alarm over *Hersees* and merely sought some alleviation by getting *procedural* relief from common law-based restrictions, takes on an edge. It may be that it was instinctively understood (and thoroughly internalized) by labour that the *Wagner Act* machinery was not intended to move all that far away from the original pre-*Wagner Act* model, that private property and contract were not only relevant, but still fundamental. Procedural inhibitions could lessen the impact of the otherwise legally and historically justifiable issue of judicial orders.

The chapter by Girard and Phillips gives weight to these observations. In a penetratingly analytical manner, the point is made that, when it came to assess the validity of union picketing, the courts treated it as just another variant of the exercise of freedom of speech that had to be exercised in a geographic space. Necessarily it had to be weighed against the right of the owners of any private property of that space to exclude all others from its use. With a tinge of chagrin, they record how even the chief apostle of collective bargaining law and marginalizer of the reign of individual contract making, Laskin, was unable to rise above this notion. Despite the legislation's support for collectivism, he held that workers had to prove on a case-by-case basis that their exercise of free speech rights incidental to collective action did not impinge unduly on private property rights. They sagely and sadly conclude that union activity, even though statutorily promoted, had been seen and, with very few exceptions, continues to be seen, through the lens of private property.

In sum, the judiciary undoubtedly had (and has) a large number of visceral anti-working class members amongst its functionaries. But, the stories in this collection also suggest that, in a general sense, the judiciary was responding in an understandable way to the push toward industrial pluralism. While the courts shared (and share) an interest in stability, they are also charged with the protection of certain basic principles that underpin liberal market capitalism. In the judicial mindset, it never has been authoritatively stated that the courts' role as primary guardians of fundamental values has been abrogated. It recognizes that this role has had to be adjusted somewhat. Thus it is that, unless they are explicitly forbidden from interfering with any statutory regime that may threaten the original position, courts reflexively will attempt to return to it. While some judges have been all too eager to search for ways to find that the legislature has not explicitly excluded the common law principles and rules, on the whole, the courts have acknowledged that there is a sphere of collective action that has to be left to other institutions to regulate. They sometimes show a sense that it is time to let modernism have its way, especially if it is perceived that to do so will advance the goal they share with the legislative scheme, namely that of long-term stability with limited union power. Much depends on the time, place, consciousness of a court about the need to accept a modicum of change, and on the way in which the dispute before the judges has arisen.

Mark Leier's engrossing story of the larger-than-life political dissentient, Myron Kuzych, provides a marvellous illustration of this phenomenon. The courts were confronted by a conflict between a trade union they had to accept as legitimate, given its procedurally correct certification as a bargaining agent under the statutory provisions, and an individual who claimed to have been disciplined in a discriminatory, capricious, and arbitrary manner by that union. Two valid policy purposes in tension had to be reconciled. The Privy Council finessed the intractable issue as only lawyers would even think of doing. It defended the individual's right to express and think for herself as a general principle. Undoubtedly this proclamation of its love of free speech gave the Privy Council a warm glow. Leier paints a portrait of Kuzych as an independent leftist, one whose views were anathema to many of his union comrades, let alone to judges. From this vantage point, the Privy Council's wholehearted support for the rights of an individual, whose behaviour and politics were unappetizing, reinforced the image judges have of themselves as fearless defenders of sovereign individuality. The court also held that, despite the fact that a union was given special standing by modern labour laws, it was, to the common law, just a body formed by a series of individual contracting parties and, that, therefore, the rules of contract applied to the parties, here the union and Kuzych. Accordingly, Kuzych had come to court for a remedy too early. He may as a free-thinking, unfairly disciplined member, be entitled to a remedy from the court, but not before he had exhausted the processes stipulated by the contract by which he, as an individual, was bound. The Privy Council had provided itself with further reasons for congratulating itself on its cleverness. Its findings implicitly upheld one of the tenets of industrial pluralism that, as noted above, the judiciary had favoured, namely that a certified union should have disciplinary powers over its members in order to make collective bargaining work in an unthreatening manner.

The contention has been that these chapters reveal, sometimes explicitly, sometimes implicitly, that the judiciary has been left with reasonable ground to believe that it retains a significant role in the regulation of employment relationships, even if a statutory collective bargaining regime has intervened with its immediate jurisdiction. Its role has, however, no precise boundaries. In the main, it can be confident that the contribution it made in laying down the structures and ideology on which all employment relationships are to be based, whether governed by statutory reform or not, remains intact. Further, if these basic precepts are endangered by social engineers, the judiciary is deemed to be entitled to defend the basic precepts it has done so much to establish, although it will lay itself open to criticism if it fails to adhere to its own methodology. Today, there is a novel and intriguing problem for the judges: if the industrial pluralism that the courts have been asked to respect comes under attack from the executive or legislative branches, should the judiciary accept the burden of defending the regime?

Courts have become increasingly eager to show that they too respect workers and acknowledge the dignity of work and the need for workers to be treated with dignity. Daphne Taras' story about the indefatigable Wallace and his assiduous lawyer, provides a neat illustration of this judicial sentiment. The narrative is proof, if any were required, that litigation has human costs. It is costly and prolix, often not allowing the principals involved in the drama to bring out the issues that trouble them most as individuals. Legal battles tend toward the abstract. This, of course, is part and parcel of the case made against the judicial forum: it is peculiarly ill-suited to deal with disputes that concern dynamic, ongoing relationships and in which time is a crucial element.[6] The judges in *Wallace* were no doubt aware of the fact that the case before them provided something of a litmus test. The employer had behaved harshly and to allow it to rely on a creaky procedural system to cow the badly treated employee into submission aided, as the employer was, by the established authority of the decision by the House of Lords in *Addis v. Gramophone Co. Ltd.*,[7] would be bad optics. In *Addis*, the employment contract had been characterized as one that allowed an employer to dismiss an employee for cause summarily, that is, on the basis that the employee had breached his obligations to the employer, or by giving notice without giving any reason whatsoever. This characterization meant that the brusqueness, rudeness, and capriciousness of the employer, along with the embarrassing nature of the dismissal, had no legal impact: the employee could not get damages for unfair, harsh treatment in the manner of dismissal, provided there was proper cause or appropriate notice had been given. One of the issues in *Wallace* was whether the employer owed a duty to treat an employee decently when terminating that employee.

By the time the case got to the Supreme Court of Canada, the need to look compassionate and understanding had come to weigh heavily on the judges' minds. A judiciary under siege is eager to prove that, as a relatively autonomous institution, it will not allow oppression of the vulnerable in its name. Despite its pedigree, *Addis* had the potential to become an embarrassment. Taras nicely brings out the fact that, by the 1980s and 1990s, courts had been falling over themselves to trumpet their adherence to the notion that respect was owed to the dignity of labour and the individuals who provide it. She has dug out evidence that this kind of mantra has become so routine that lawyers and judges use it even if they are not too sure what, if any, authority there is to give this sentiment legal force. The Supreme Court of Canada in *Wallace* declared its devotion to it. It was thus forced to prove its ability to treat workers as respected industrial citizens.

Taras finds the ensuing analysis disappointing and she argues, correctly in my view, that Justice Iacobucci's was, methodologically, an incoherent approach and one that did not match his rhetoric. Why did the Court not provide a good faith cause of action? Here the subtext, namely the complexities of the contest between and collaboration by the courts and legislatures in respect of the regulation of employment relationships, struggles to surface.

The Iacobucci decision might be seen as a compromise, rather than another methodologically flawed judgment. While it affirms the long-term judicial view of the contract of employment, it pays attention to the need to mould it to new understandings about the employer/employee nexus, in particular to the politically promoted notion that, in advanced liberal capitalism, it is no longer appropriate for judges to be perceived as approving the characterization of a work-for-wages contract as if it were a mere variant of a contract for the purchase of a tractor. The holding that extra damages could be awarded because of aspects of the behaviour of the employer goes some way toward an endorsement of the idea that employees should be treated as equal citizens. At the same time, the holding also stays in line with the conceptual framework of *Addis* and its vast progeny. In its details, it makes the award of extra damages contingent on the dismissed employee demonstrating that she will find it more difficult than she otherwise would have to find comparable alternative employment because of the employer's conduct. The decision, then, does more than pay mere lip service to the dignity of labour and labourers *and*, while the chapter does not emphasize this, it also adheres to market/contract principles. Painted in this way, it is part of the portrayal of the courts as being both an institution determining and guarding basic precepts and a component of the overall industrial pluralist machinery.

In sum, this chapter, like the others discussed, reflects the sub-theme that the post-World War II mechanism of adjustment was only one step up from the individual contract of employment regime in terms of its protection of workers — there remained severe limitations on the right to strike and to picket, those limitations being referable to the dogmas of the common law. The indications to the judiciary were that, while there were now other remedial processes, their overall conceptual framework was to be internalized by policy makers and workers. The courts could, therefore, still supervise and exercise some controls, albeit there was pressure on them to acknowledge the tendency toward a more evenhanded approach both to the viability of increased countervailing power for workers and to the emerging vision of the social sovereignty of workers (as tremulously evidenced in *Wallace*). From this perspective, the judges' role as an integral component of a scheme that had, and has, to maintain a balance of ideas and ideals in tension was, and is, a delicate one. Signals that encourage the courts to believe that they have a mandate to participate in this balancing act are discernable in the last two papers to be discussed.

As contended, the *Wagner Act*-type models as they evolved in Canada constitute only the smallest step up on the ladder of possibilities once legislated collective bargaining is to be permitted. It moves the game from a contract between one employer and one employee to one between one employer's plant and its unionized workers. This is not to belittle the real material advances this wrought, but there are many other rungs on this ladder of possibilities, all of them further removed from the one-on-one model. In conceptual terms, the advance was to move from an individual contract model available to all to an opt-in, representational scheme of unionization for those practically placed to benefit from this potential collectivization. This was most suited to large extraction and manufacturing settings and spread only gradually and unevenly to other sectors. It has been a model that led to the exclusion of many workers. Women were not intended to be, and were not made, an integral part of this deal. The labour market was, from the beginning based on the sexual division of labour, a division that was taken as a norm by policy makers, administrative labour boards defining bargaining units, and trade unions who sought certification.[8] Systemic discrimination was not, and largely is not, confronted directly by the advances in collective bargaining. Inevitably, unions and their progressive allies tend to reach out for other institutional tools, in particular to human rights mechanisms and the *Charter of Rights and Freedoms*. These tactics give the courts more of a role than does the industrial pluralist collective bargaining regime. The paradox of working class activists having to turn for help to what many saw as a primary source of oppression is manifest. This tinges the powerful concluding chapters by Sangster and by Fudge and Lessard, with a sense of apprehension.

The systemic gender and race issues these chapters discuss all too often come to light because crass xenophobia and sexism is presented as a permissible exercise of the prerogative of management. The fact that employers actually were able to make legally plausible cases to the effect that their conduct was justifiable as a reasonable exercise of their managerial tasks is rightly decried in both papers. The conduct of the employer in the *PWA* case was transparently sexist and the arguments about the employer's concern for health and safety risible. The Sangster account is scathing about the pretences. The extraordinary lengths to devise a "test" that, in the end, bore no relation to the requirements of the job in the *Meiorin* saga spoke loudly to the employer's belief in unjustifiable stereotypes. Fudge and Lessard expose not only the shamelessness of the employer arguments, but also the errors that should have been plain to the judiciary, but apparently were not. The fact that the employers had legal legs to stand on says a good deal about the legal mountains left to climb. Unsurprisingly, both essays raise the question of the utility and manipulability of the human rights and bills of rights' processes. Sangster makes a point of noting that it is the dearth of other remedial routes that pushed her claimants to adopt the litigation strategies they did. Both essays note the paradox of having to rely on judicially-inspired individualism for help to solve systemically created problems. These chapters, by inference, illuminate the speed-up of the ongoing fight by the judiciary to reposition itself as a central institution. As deregulation, privatization, and the phenomenon crudely labelled as globalization all contribute to the demise of the *Wagner Act* model, the notion that transcendent human rights can be called on to safeguard workers' interests becomes more salient. The courts may well be eager to establish themselves as protectors of individual rights. In this way, these two essays nicely complement a theme that underlies the other stories told.

The *Wagner Act* model has left deep institutional holes that need to be filled before the industrial citizenship goals aspired to by that model can be attained. The failures of a system that is male dominated and is otherwise non-inclusive, has left a gap that the judiciary is beckoned to fill. Its internal methodological constraints do not make it an ideal complementary institution, but its prestige, derived in some measure from those very constraints, adds to its attraction for those who find it difficult to exert direct economic or political influence. It is able to position itself as a respected institution in which arguments of principle, arguments based on reasoning underpinned by the liberal ideals of equality and respect for the individual, and arguments not available in the more overtly political capital/labour settings may be made. That is, the lacunae in the *Wagner Act* model are visible and the courts are there to complete the unfulfilled agenda of that model that supposedly militates toward a fairer and less sexist and racist society.

In sum, courts are perceived to have, and increasingly feel comfortable about playing, a role that not only preserves fundamental principles of private property and contract, but also furthers the industrial citizenry aspirations of the post-war settlement. This becomes ever more important as the legislative/executive branches of government are resiling from their support for industrial pluralism. In this sense, the contributors to this volume have not only provided rich materials and contexts in which to reconsider some of the more significant cases and events in labour history, but they also will enable us to understand current developments, especially in the always-shifting relationships between various legal institutions.

Notes

1   As recorded by Francis R. Scott, "Federal Jurisdiction over Labour Relations: A New Look" (1960) 6 McGill L.J. 153. See also Harry Glasbeek, "The Impact of Federalism on Canadian Labour Law" in Martin Vranken & Othmar Vanachter, eds., *Federalism and Labour Law* (Antwerp/New York: Intersentia, 2004).

2   In *McGavin Toastmaster Ltd. v. Ainscough* (1975), 54 D.L.R. (3d) 1, Laskin, C.J., argued that the contract of employment had no place "but for the act of hiring" once a collective agreement concluded under a labour law code of the contemporary variety had been reached. He relied on the arguments he had made much earlier, as an arbitrator in *U.A.W., Local 458 v. Cockshutt Farm Equipment* (1959), L.A.C. 324, and as an academic in "Collective Bargaining and Individual Rights" (1963) 6 Can. Bar J. 278.

3   Inevitably, this has led to further incoherence. There have been a series of disputes about whether replacement workers hired during the strike are members of the bargaining unit for the purposes of voting, whether junior members who returned to work before more senior members of the bargaining unit had to give way on a seniority basis if the available work warranted a layoff, and the like. *Canadian Airline Pilots' Association v. Eastern Provincial Airways Ltd.* (1983), 5 Can. L.R.B.R. (N.S. S.C. (T.D.)) 368; *Shaw-Amex Industries Ltd.* (1986), 15 Can. L.R.B.R. (N.S.) 23; *Canadian Association of Smelter and Allied Workers, Local No.4 v. Royal Oak Mines Inc.* (1993), 93 C.L.L.C. 16,063. This is not the place to elaborate the cycle of decisions dealing with the contested continuation of the individual contract of employment status and the reforming legislation they spawn. It suffices to make the point that the contest is alive and well, despite the grandiose language about the irrelevance of the common law doctrines.

4   (1958), 10 L.A.C. 31; aff'd [1962] S.C.R. 338 (*sub nom. Imbleau v. Laskin)*; see also Laskin's earlier arbitral decision in *Re C.G.E.* (1951), 21 L.A.C. 608.

5   Harry Clare Pentland, *A Study of the Changing Social, Economic and Political Background of the Canadian System of Industrial Relations* (Draft Study prepared for Task Force on Labour Relations, Chair: Woods, Ottawa: Privy Council, 1968). For the early fights around the scope of bargaining agencies, see Judy Fudge & Harry Glasbeek, "The Legacy of PC 1003" (1995) 3 C.L.E.L.J. 357.

6   The usual slow pace of the courts is an element in the anger felt by those who see their participation in collective bargaining relations as anathema. It has not escaped anyone's notice that the same courts that take years to deal with a dispute like *Wallace*, can issue anti-worker injunctions even before an applicant has finished speaking.

7   [1909] A.C. 488.

8   Ellen Scheinberg, "The Tale of Tessie the Textile Worker: Female Textile Workers in Cornwall During World War II" (1994) 33 Labour/Le Travail 153; Anne Forrest, "Securing the Male Breadwinner: A Feminist Interpretation of PC 1003" in Cy Gonick, *et al.*, eds., *Labour Gains, Labour Pains: Fifty Years of PC 1003* (Halifax: Society for Socialist Studies/Fernwood, 1995) at 139–62.

Contributors

Harry Arthurs is a professor emeritus, former dean of Osgoode Hall Law School (1972–77), and former president of York University (1985–92). He has also been an academic visitor at Oxford, Cambridge, and University College, London. He has served as Commissioner reviewing Canada's labour standards legislation (2004–06) and as Commissioner reviewing Ontario's pension legislation (2006–08). His academic contributions have been recognized by his election as an Associate of the Canadian Institute for Advanced Research, a Fellow of the Royal Society of Canada, and a Corresponding Fellow of the British Academy. In 2002, he was awarded the Canada Council's Killam Prize for his lifetime contributions to the social sciences as well as the Bora Laskin Prize for his contributions to labour law.

Beth Bilson has been a member of the faculty of the College of Law at the University of Saskatchewan since 1979, teaching and writing in the areas of torts, administrative and labour law, and legal history. She chaired the Saskatchewan Labour Relations Board from 1992 to 1997, and is currently an arbitrator and part-time member of the Public Service Labour Relations Board. She has served as dean of the College of Law.

R. Blake Brown is an associate professor in the Department of History at Saint Mary's University. His first book, *A Trying Question: The Jury in Nineteenth-Century Canada*, was published by the University of Toronto Press and the Osgoode Society for Canadian Legal History in 2009.

Sean T. Cadigan is a professor and head of the Department of History at Memorial University. From 2006 to 2009, he was the director of the Master of Employment Relations program at Memorial. His research interests include the social and ecological history of fishers and fishing communities, and management and development policies in cold-ocean coastal areas. He is working on the history of labour relations in the Newfoundland and Labrador offshore oil and gas industry.

Malcolm E. Davidson is a lawyer member of the Law Society of Upper Canada. He practices criminal law in Toronto. He recalls with pleasure his work as a research assistant for Professors Judy Fudge and Eric Tucker on their book *Labour Before the Law: The Regulation of Workers' Collective Action in Canada, 1900–1948*. He has published or co-published articles in Canadian Historical Review, Urban History Review/Revue d'histoire urbaine, Canadian Journal of Native Studies, Journal of Mithraic Studies, and in the proceedings of the International Symposium on Slavic Archeology, at Rila Monastery, Bulgaria, in 1977. He is currently continuing his research in labour history and labour law history.

Judy Fudge is the Lansdowne Chair in Law at the University of Victoria. She has co-authored and co-edited several books, including *Labour Before the Law: The Legal Regulation of Workers' Collective Action* (Toronto: University of Toronto Press and the Osgoode Society for Canadian Legal History, 2001, with Eric Tucker), *Privatization, Law and the Challenge to Feminism* (Toronto: University of Toronto Press, 2002, with Brenda Cossman), *Precarious Work, Women and the New Economy: The Challenge to Legal Norms* (Oxford: Hart Publishing, 2006, with Rosemary Owens). She is a member of the Inter-University Research Centre on Globalization and Work, and in 2009 she received the Bora Laskin National Fellowship in Human Rights.

Philip Girard is professor of law, history, and Canadian studies, as well as a research professor at Dalhousie University. His published works include *The Supreme Court of Nova Scotia, 1754–2004: From Imperial Bastion to Provincial Oracle* (Osgoode Society for Canadian Legal History and the University of Toronto Press, 2004, with Jim Phillips and Barry Cahill) and *Bora Laskin: Bringing Law to Life* (Toronto: University of Toronto Press, 2005).

Harry Glasbeek is a professor emeritus and senior scholar from Osgoode Hall Law School where he taught for twenty-two years and currently is a Visiting Professorial Fellow at Victoria University, Australia. He is the author of eleven books. He has written books and articles on Australian and Canadian labour relations law, as well as books and articles on corporate law. His latest book is *Wealth by Stealth: Corporate Crime, Corporate Law and the Perversion of Democracy* (Toronto: Between the Lines, 2002).

Jim Phillips is professor of law, history, and criminology at the University of Toronto, and editor-in-chief of the Osgoode Society for Canadian Legal History. He has published on British imperial history and eighteenth-century India, on property and charities law, US legal history, and, principally, Canadian legal history. He has co-edited four volumes of the Osgoode Society for Canadian Legal History's *Essays in the History of Canadian Law* and a volume on the history of Canada's oldest surviving superior common law court — *The Supreme Court of Nova Scotia, 1754–2004: From Imperial Bastion to Provincial Oracle* (Osgoode Society for Canadian Legal History and the University of Toronto Press, 2004, with Philip Girard and Barry Cahill). He is also the co-author of *Murdering Holiness: The Trials of Franz Creffield and George Mitchell* (UBC Press, 2003, with Rosemary Gartner).

William Kaplan is a Toronto lawyer. Educated at the University of Toronto, Osgoode Hall Law School, and Stanford University, William Kaplan has published numerous books on Canadian legal history including, most recently, *Canadian Maverick: The Life and Times of Ivan C. Rand* (Osgoode Society and University of Toronto Press, 2009).

Mark Leier worked for several years at a number of jobs, including bridge tender, short-order cook, dishwasher, construction labourer, printer, folk singer, and first-aid attendant before going to university. He teaches history and labour studies at Simon Fraser University and is the author of three books about BC labour history. His most recent book is *Bakunin: The Creative Passion* (New York: St. Martin's Press, 2006).

Hester Lessard is a professor of law at the University of Victoria. Her areas of research include feminist legal theory, human rights law, social movements and law, and Canadian constitutional rights jurisprudence. She is a co-editor of *Reaction and Resistance: Feminism, Law, and Social Change* (Vancouver, BC: University of British Columbia Press, 2007).

Jennifer Llewellyn is an associate professor at the Schulich School of Law, Dalhousie University. Her teaching and research is focused in the areas of public law, human rights law, constitutional law, and restorative justice. Professor Llewellyn is currently the director of the Nova Scotia Restorative Justice Community University Research Alliance (NSRJ-CURA).

Joan Sangster teaches labour and women's history at Trent University, Peterborough, where she is also affiliated with the Frost Centre for Canadian Studies and Indigenous Studies. She has written on the history of the Left, labour, law and social policy, and sexual regulation, including *Regulating Girls and Women: Sexuality, Family, and the Law in Ontario 1920–1960* (Don Mills, ON: Oxford University Press, 2001) and *Girl Trouble: Female Delinquency in English Canada* (Toronto, ON: Between the Lines Press, 2002). Her most recent book is *Transforming Labour: Women and Work in Postwar Canada* (Toronto, ON: University of Toronto Press, 2010).

Daphne G. Taras is dean of the Edward School of Business, University of Saskatchewan. Until 2010, Dr. Taras was a professor of industrial relations and an associate dean at the Haskayne School of Business, University of Calgary.

Eric Tucker is a professor at Osgoode Hall Law School, York University. He has published extensively on the history and current state of labour and employment law. He is the author of *Administering Danger in the Workplace* (Toronto: University of Toronto Press, 1990) and co-author of *Labour Before the Law: The Legal Regulation of Workers' Collective Action* (Toronto: University of Toronto Press, 2001, with Judy Fudge) and *Self-Employed Workers Organize* (Montreal: McGill-Queen's University Press, 2005, with Cynthia Cranford, Judy Fudge, and Leah Vosko). He is also the editor of *Working Disasters: The Politics of Recognition and Response* (Amityville, NY: Baywood Publishing Company, 2006).

Index

PUBLICATIONS OF THE
OSGOODE SOCIETY FOR CANADIAN LEGAL HISTORY

2010   Judy Fudge & Eric Tucker, eds., *Work on Trial: Canadian Labour Law Struggles*
Christopher Moore, *The British Columbia Court of Appeal: The First Hundred Years*
Frederick Vaughan, *Viscount Haldane: The Wicked Step-father of the Canadian Constitution*
Barrington Walker, *Race on Trial: Black Defendants in Ontario's Criminal Courts, 1858–1958.*

2009   William Kaplan, *Canadian Maverick: The Life and Times of Ivan C. Rand*
R. Blake Brown, *A Trying Question: The Jury in Nineteenth-Century Canada*
Barry Wright & Susan Binnie, eds., *Canadian State Trials, Volume III: Political Trials and Security Measures, 1840–1914*
Robert J. Sharpe, *The Last Day, the Last Hour: The Currie Libel Trial*

2008   Constance Backhouse, *Carnal Crimes: Sexual Assault Law in Canada, 1900–1975*
Jim Phillips, R. Roy McMurtry & John Saywell, eds., *Essays in the History of Canadian Law, Vol. X: A Tribute to Peter N. Oliver*
Gregory Taylor, *The Law of the Land: Canada's Receptions of the Torrens System*
Hamar Foster, Benjamin Berger & A.R. Buck, eds., *The Grand Experiment: Law and Legal Culture in British Settler Societies*

2007   Robert Sharpe & Patricia McMahon, *The Persons Case: The Origins and Legacy of the Fight for Legal Personhood*
Lori Chambers, *Misconceptions: Unmarried Motherhood and the Ontario Children of Unmarried Parents Act, 1921–1969*
Jonathan Swainger, ed., *The Alberta Supreme Court at 100: History & Authority*
Martin Friedland, *My Life in Crime and Other Academic Adventures*

2006   Donald Fyson, *Magistrates, Police and People: Everyday Criminal Justice in Quebec and Lower Canada, 1764-1837*
Dale Brawn, *The Court of Queen's Bench of Manitoba 1870–1950: A Biographical History*
R.C.B. Risk, *A History of Canadian Legal Thought: Collected Essays*, edited and introduced by G.Blaine Baker & Jim Phillips

2005   Philip Girard, *Bora Laskin: Bringing Law to Life*
Christopher English, ed., *Essays in the History of Canadian Law, Vol. IX: Two Islands, Newfoundland and Prince Edward Island*
Fred Kaufman, *Searching for Justice: An Autobiography*

2004   John D. Honsberger, *Osgoode Hall: An Illustrated History*
Frederick Vaughan, *Aggressive in Pursuit: The Life of Justice Emmett Hall*

Constance Backhouse & Nancy Backhouse, *The Heiress versus the Establishment: Mrs. Campbell's Campaign for Legal Justice*

Philip Girard, Jim Phillips & Barry Cahill, es., *The Supreme Court of Nova Scotia,1754–2004: From Imperial Bastion to Provincial Oracle*

2003   Robert Sharpe & Kent Roach, *Brian Dickson: A Judge's Journey*

George Finlayson, *John J. Robinette: Peerless Mentor*

Peter Oliver, *The Conventional Man: The Diaries of Ontario Chief Justice Robert A. Harrison, 1856-1878*

Jerry Bannister, *The Rule of the Admirals: Law, Custom and Naval Government in Newfoundland, 1699-1832*

2002   John T. Saywell, *The Law Makers: Judicial Power and the Shaping of Canadian Federalism*

David Murray, *Colonial Justice: Justice, Morality and Crime in the Niagara District, 1791–1849*

F. Murray Greenwood & Barry Wright, eds., *Canadian State Trials, Volume Two: Rebellion and Invasion in the Canadas, 1837–8*

Patrick Brode, *Courted and Abandoned: Seduction in Canadian Law*

2001   Ellen Anderson, *Judging Bertha Wilson: Law as Large as Life*

Judy Fudge & Eric Tucker, *Labour Before the Law: Collective Action in Canada, 1900–1948*

Laurel Sefton MacDowell, *Renegade Lawyer: The Life of J.L. Cohen*

2000   Barry Cahill, "*The Thousandth Man": A Biography of James McGregor Stewart*

A.B. McKillop, *The Spinster and the Prophet: Florence Deeks, H.G. Wells, and the Mystery of the Purloined Past*

Beverley Boissery & F. Murray Greenwood, *Uncertain Justice: Canadian Women and Capital Punishment*

Bruce Ziff, *Unforeseen Legacies: Reuben Wells Leonard and the Leonard Foundation Trust*

1999   Constance Backhouse, *Colour-Coded: A Legal History of Racism in Canada, 1900–1950*

G. Blaine Baker & Jim Phillips, eds., *Essays in the History of Canadian Law, Vol. VIII: In Honour of R.C.B. Risk*

Richard W. Pound, *Chief Justice W.R. Jackett: By the Law of the Land*

David Vanek, *Fulfilment: Memoirs of a Criminal Court Judge*

1998   Sidney Harring, *White Man's Law: Native People in Nineteenth-Century Canadian Jurisprudence*

Peter Oliver, "*Terror to Evil-Doers": Prisons and Punishments in Nineteenth-Century Ontario*

1997   James W. St.G. Walker, "*Race," Rights and the Law in the Supreme Court of Canada: Historical Case Studies*

Lori Chambers, *Married Women and Property Law in Victorian Ontario*

Patrick Brode, *Casual Slaughters and Accidental Judgments: Canadian War Crimes and Prosecutions, 1944–1948*

Ian Bushnell, *The Federal Court of Canada: A History, 1875–1992*

1996   Carol Wilton, ed., *Essays in the History of Canadian Law, Vol. VII: Inside the Law — Canadian Law Firms in Historical Perspective*
William Kaplan, *Bad Judgment: The Case of Mr. Justice Leo A. Landreville*
Murray Greenwood & Barry Wright, eds., *Canadian State Trials, Volume I: Law, Politics and Security Measures, 1608–1837*

1995   David Williams, *Just Lawyers: Seven Portraits*
Hamar Foster & John McLaren, eds., *Essays in the History of Canadian Law, Vol. VI: British Columbia and the Yukon*
W.H. Morrow, ed., *Northern Justice: The Memoirs of Mr. Justice William G. Morrow*
Beverley Boissery, *A Deep Sense of Wrong: The Treason, Trials and Transportation to New South Wales of Lower Canadian Rebels after the 1838 Rebellion*

1994   Patrick Boyer, *A Passion for Justice: The Legacy of James Chalmers McRuer*
Charles Pullen, *The Life and Times of Arthur Maloney: The Last of the Tribunes*
Jim Phillips, Tina Loo, & Susan Lewthwaite, eds., *Essays in the History of Canadian Law, Vol. V: Crime and Criminal Justice*
Brian Young, *The Politics of Codification: The Lower Canadian Civil Code of 1866*

1993   Greg Marquis, *Policing Canada's Century: A History of the Canadian Association of Chiefs of Police*
Murray Greenwood, *Legacies of Fear: Law and Politics in Quebec in the Era of the French Revolution*

1992   Brendan O'Brien, *Speedy Justice: The Tragic Last Voyage of His Majesty's Vessel Speedy*
Robert Fraser, ed., *Provincial Justice: Upper Canadian Legal Portraits from the Dictionary of Canadian Biography*

1991   Constance Backhouse, *Petticoats and Prejudice: Women and Law in Nineteenth-Century Canada*

1990   Philip Girard & Jim Phillips, eds., *Essays in the History of Canadian Law, Vol. III: Nova Scotia*
Carol Wilton, ed., *Essays in the History of Canadian Law, Vol. IV: Beyond the Law — Lawyers and Business in Canada 1830–1930*

1989   Desmond Brown, *The Genesis of the Canadian Criminal Code of 1892*
Patrick Brode, *The Odyssey of John Anderson*

1988   Robert Sharpe, *The Last Day, the Last Hour: The Currie Libel Trial*
John D. Arnup, *Middleton: The Beloved Judge*

1987   C. Ian Kyer & Jerome Bickenbach, *The Fiercest Debate: Cecil A. Wright, the Benchers and Legal Education in Ontario, 1923-1957*

1986   Paul Romney, *Mr. Attorney: The Attorney General for Ontario in Court, Cabinet and Legislature, 1791–1899*
Martin Friedland, *The Case of Valentine Shortis: A True Story of Crime and Politics in Canada*

1985   James Snell and Frederick Vaughan, *The Supreme Court of Canada: History of the Institution*

1984   Patrick Brode, *Sir John Beverley Robinson: Bone and Sinew of the Compact*
David Williams, *Duff: A Life in the Law*

1983   David H. Flaherty, ed., *Essays in the History of Canadian Law, Vol. II*
1982   Marion MacRae & Anthony Adamson, *Cornerstones of Order: Courthouses and Town Halls of Ontario, 1784–1914*
1981   David H. Flaherty, ed., *Essays in the History of Canadian Law, Vol. I*

Thank you again for your interest in the Osgoode Society.

Jim Phillips
Editor-in-Chief
Professor, University of Toronto Law School

The Osgoode Society
For Canadian Legal History

Osgoode Hall, 130 Queen Street West
Toronto, Ontario, M5H 2N6 (416) 947-3321

November 5, 2010

Dear New Member:

Many thanks for responding to our offer of a membership in the Osgoode Society for Canadian Legal History.

Established in 1979, the Society is a unique venture in the common law world, and we are keen to interest more law students in our operations. For more information on the Society visit our website at www.osgoodesociety.ca.